Communication and Cooperation in Early Imperial China

SUNY series in Chinese Philosophy and Culture

Roger T. Ames, editor

Communication and Cooperation in Early Imperial China

Publicizing the Qin Dynasty

Charles Sanft

Published by State University of New York Press, Albany

© 2014 State University of New York

All rights reserved

Printed in the United States of America

No part of this book may be used or reproduced in any manner whatsoever without written permission. No part of this book may be stored in a retrieval system or transmitted in any form or by any means including electronic, electrostatic, magnetic tape, mechanical, photocopying, recording, or otherwise without the prior permission in writing of the publisher.

For information, contact State University of New York Press, Albany, NY
www.sunypress.edu

Production by Diane Ganeles
Marketing by Kate McDonnell

Library of Congress Cataloging-in-Publication Data

Sanft, Charles.
  Communication and cooperation in early imperial China : publicizing the Qin dynasty / Charles Sanft.
      pages cm — (SUNY series in Chinese philosophy and culture)
  Includes bibliographical references and index.
  ISBN 978-1-4384-5037-7 (hardcover : alk. paper)
  ISBN 978-1-4384-5036-0 (pbk.: alk. paper)
    1. China—History—Qin dynasty, 221–207 B.C. 2. China—Politics and government—221 B.C.–220 A.D. 3. Communication—Political aspects—China—History—To 1500. I. Title.

DS747.6.S26 2014
302.20931'09014—dc23   2013015890

10 9 8 7 6 5 4 3 2 1

To Hsiu-yi

Contents

Acknowledgments	ix
1. Introduction	1
2. Communication and Cooperation: A Framework	17
3. Communication and Cooperation in Early Chinese Thought	33
4. Mass Communication and Standardization	57
5. Progress and Publicity: Qin Shihuang, Ritual, and Common Knowledge	77
6. Roads to Rule: Construction as Communication	101
7. Law, Administration, and Communication	123
8. Conclusion	147
Notes	159
Bibliography	205
Index	237

Acknowledgments

Many colleagues and friends assisted me in writing and revising this book. In order to avoid giving too long a list here, I name a limited number and hope that those not mentioned will understand and know that my gratitude extends to them as well.

Reinhard Emmerich gave me much advice and support over the course of this project, as so often before. Tomiya Itaru provided vital assistance and textual resources. Yuri Pines, with characteristic generosity and acuity, read the entire manuscript more than once and offered many suggestions for its improvement. I am greatly indebted to Mark Edward Lewis and Robin D. S. Yates for their comments on earlier drafts. Finally, I thank Maxim Korolkov, Cameron Moore, and Gideon Shelach, who also read and commented upon the text.

The Institute for Advanced Study (Princeton), the Starr Foundation East Asian Studies Endowment Fund, and the Japan Society for the Promotion of Science provided financial support for this project. The University of Tennessee Exhibit, Performance, and Publication Expense Fund contributed to publication expenses.

I submitted a version of this project as *Habilitationsschrift* at the University of Münster in 2011. The *Journal of Ritual Studies* 22.1 (2008) published an early version of chapter 5, and I thank the editors, Dr. Pamela J. Stewart and Professor Andrew Strathern, for permission to include the revised and expanded version. Part of chapter 7 appeared in the *Journal of the Economic and Social History of the Orient* 53.5 (2010), and I thank Koninklijke Brill NV for allowing me to incorporate it.

1

Introduction

This book treats communication and cooperation in the function of political power in early imperial China, particularly under the short-lived Qin dynasty (221–207 BCE). In essence I am interested in the collective decision of a group to obey a government and respect its dominion. I argue creating common knowledge among the population through communication in multiple media was a necessary part of ruling processes in early imperial China and helped solve the coordination problem presented by the unified empire. Through their active and innovative communication, the Qin dynasty resolved these problems so well that the echoes of their success are still ringing today.

The Qin dynasty was the first imperial dynasty in China. The famous First Emperor of Qin (Qin Shihuang 秦始皇, r. 221–210 BCE) established the empire by uniting formerly separate polities to create a new state, a process that lasted years and ended in 221 BCE. He governed a territory much larger than any preceding sovereign of the area we now call China.[1] The rulers of Qin confronted a new situation, and they adapted existing practices and technologies to meet its exigencies.

The Qin were obsessed—already before unification—with making things as big as possible.[2] And during the reign of the First Emperor, the Qin were constantly *doing*. Their deeds were noticeable, and deliberately so. Mark Edward Lewis has written that the Qin were a model for later dynasties: "While the First Emperor's actions became a topic for later censure, they also provided an unacknowledged pattern for imperial power, an ideal type at the origin that later rulers emulated."[3] As such, I hope the Qin case will be amenable to comparison with later dynasties in future studies. If nothing else, the tireless activity of the Qin dynasty makes it an interesting case study.

Despite my primary focus on the Qin, I draw from texts dating to the time before and after that period. This is necessary and proper:

necessary because so little has been transmitted that links directly to the dynasty, and proper because the underlying ideas and forms of government inevitably grew out of what went before and reverberated in what came after.

The available sources do not directly relate the views of the common population, and as such the voices of ordinary inhabitants of the early Chinese realm are effectively lost. The study of material culture in conjunction with textual sources offers one way to counter the limitations of the textual record.[4] Yet there is no way to directly prove the degree to which the communication I propose was perceived by the population of the realm—if by proof one means a written attestation from members of the population or their representatives. In the past, scholars have often assumed little or no awareness of higher-level governance on the part of commoners, combined with a passivity that would have made such information irrelevant. The theoretical framework I lay out in chapter 2 shows that aspects of those explanations are untenable. It also provides a way to make reasonable inferences about the role of the common population in government, which required their cooperation in various forms as well as the necessity of specific kinds of communication for that cooperation.

This theoretically informed approach recognizes the necessity of cooperation, and not coercion, as the basis of human society. Each member of a cooperating group is a strategic decision-maker whose individual choices, together with the choices of others, translate into high-level effect.[5] Each individual member has power, which is limited and yet real. This was the case in early China as in other societies.

Theoretical work on communication, cooperation, and power allows me to draw new conclusions about what was going on during the years of Qin reign and explain the success, however short-lived, of Qin rule under the First Emperor. This analysis entails study of what Vivienne Shue refers to as the "*social intertexture* that forms the stuff of political life," encompassing all fields of the social sciences and requiring simultaneous attention to detail and to overarching pattern.[6] The conclusions I reach challenge current scholarly consensus on early China in significant ways.

Legacy Approaches

Previous accounts of imperial power in early China generally fall along a spectrum between two poles. At one end are those that stress the theoretically absolute authority of the ruler in imperial China. Those at the other end of the spectrum accept that proposition in the abstract, but they give greater weight to the constraints, especially practical constraints, that inhibited the exercise of the sovereign's authority. Writers all along this spectrum present power in early imperial society as flowing from one part of society outward and downward.

Most historians agree that the emperor was theoretically the ultimate power and the wellspring of state authority in dynastic China. Ray Huang describes the emperor as residing atop a pyramid, "the source of power" and "the final authority on earth."[7] Benjamin Schwartz puts politics at the center of early Chinese society and the emperor at the center of politics. He notes that not all emperors engaged in the tasks of rule to the same degree but still posits the emperor's supremacy, calling him "the universal king . . . [who] comes to embody within his person both the supreme political authority and the spiritual-ethical authority of the entire society."[8] Wang Yü-ch'üan expresses this clearly when he says the Qin emperor "was the head of the state, and so to speak, the state itself. As the Emperor possessed absolute power over state affairs and the people, the government of Ch'in [Qin] was, to use a modern term, authoritarian in form."[9] This sort of conception underlies Liu Zehua's 劉澤華 assertions that "imperial power was superior to everything; there was no force that could restrict the ruler's power, and the entire apparatus of the state was an apparatus for the sovereign to manage affairs."[10] Wan Changhua 萬昌華 and Zhao Xingbin 趙興彬 assert the First Emperor, founder of the Qin dynasty, "hijacked" power, then set up a stratified bureaucracy to surveil his officials and ensure their compliance with his will.[11] Vitaly Rubin takes a similar view of the Qin regime, presenting it, before and after unification, as a "totalitarian state" in conflict with the rest of society.[12]

Victoria Tin-bor Hui has written about state formation under the Qin dynasty. She asserts that Qin imperial rule was theoretically absolute, but that the available technology prevented full realization of this theory. She further suggests that the First Emperor actively enlisted the aid of the populace before unification, when he needed their support. Afterward, she says, "the imperial court entered into a state of war with . . . society." Hui attributes tremendous influence to the changes carried out under the Qin, crediting them both with establishing a more unified culture as well as what she calls "the authoritarian tradition" in China.[13]

Michael Loewe, eminent historian of early imperial China, has written frequently on the power of Qin and Han emperors and the corresponding powerlessness of the common population.[14] Loewe describes the emperor as the foundation of all power in the first centuries of imperial governance, saying, "From the outset, it was accepted that the emperor held supreme powers of government. . . . It was from him that all authority to govern the population and administer the land devolved."[15] Elsewhere he calls the emperor "the sole authority that could command recognition" and the "essential head from whom all power came."[16] Loewe acknowledges variations in the exercise of imperial power due to individual characteristics or other factors but insists that the person of the emperor was the foundation of the state. He emphasizes that the population of the realm was passive before the exercise of imperial power and played no active role in governance. [17]

Charles Le Blanc, like Loewe, notes that emperors differed in the ability to effect individual will; he furthermore distinguishes the limited power wielded by each emperor from the absolute power intrinsic to the position.[18] Le Blanc refers to Hans Bielenstein's work on Han bureaucracy, in which Bielenstein discusses institutional restrictions on the exercise of imperial power. Bielenstein asserts that one reason for this was the idea that "the empire belonged to the people, not the Son of Heaven." Yet when Bielenstein discusses the function of power, he portrays it as existing only at the highest echelons of society:

> Power flowed to and fro between the throne (empress or empress dowager) supported by the eunuchs, the cabinet . . . the imperial secretariat, and, when in existence, the regency. The relative balance between these institutions varied from period to period, depending on personalities, shifting alliances, and factional struggles.[19]

Bielenstein's conception attributes ownership to the common people but no power.

Historians have long stressed constraints on imperial power in China. Already in the nineteenth century, Thomas Taylor Meadows (1815–1868) wrote that the Chinese emperor was "autocratic" but not "despotic": although an absolute ruler, he was obliged to maintain broadly held standards of governance and behavior or face a rebellious populace.[20]

Similarly, Karl Bünger has asserted that the Qin "were absolute rulers" but that their version of absolutism did not accord with widely held conceptions of rule, which led to their overthrow.[21] Henri Maspero describes the emperors of Qin and Han as rulers whose power was "absolute, but not arbitrary," in that they were obliged to consult with the high officials at the top of the bureaucracy.[22] More recently, Enno Giele has written that the emperor was the theoretical head of the bureaucracy but that compulsory processes of deliberation and consultation checked the untoward exercise of his power. Giele notes that others sometimes arrogated the emperor's powers, but when they did so, they acted—or claimed to act—in his name.²³

There is also a long tradition of emphasizing practical limitations on the exercise of imperial power. Max Weber (1864–1920) argued that the lack of rapid transportation and communication prevented centralization of the early Chinese state.²⁴ Jacques Gernet says, "The emperor occupies in China a truly central position; he is the person around whom everything is organized." At the same time, Gernet points to limits on imperial power, distinguishing between the emperor, who was hemmed in by bureaucracy, and a state that was theoretically omnipotent while limited by concrete factors.²⁵

This sort of approach also appears in interdisciplinary work like that of Norman Yoffee, who attacks depictions of early states as "totalitarian regimes" that consolidated large geographical areas. Yoffee describes both curbs on central authorities' power and the persistence of local diversity. He moderates his stance slightly when he writes that there were "linkages," which "are quite often weak in the earliest states and also that centrality is mainly concerned with the creation of new symbols of social identity, ideologies of power, and representations of history."²⁶ For Yoffee, those kinds of influence were of little real importance.

Historical research on later dynasties and modern times, too, often depicts checks on central authority. Leif Littrup has these checks in mind when he argues for the notion of "The Un-Oppressive State," saying flatly that in Qing times, "[t]he emperor could give orders but he and the bureaucracy did under normal circumstances not have the means to penetrate into the subbureaucratic level of local society."²⁷ John K. Fairbank argues that these limitations enabled imperial rule: he says that Chinese emperors were theoretically absolute, but their rule was possible "precisely because it was so superficial. The emperor remained supreme as a symbol of unity because his officials did not attempt to rule directly in the villages."²⁸ For Fairbank, nominal ascendancy did not translate into a reality of control.

The hindrance of central power forms a major theme of Shue's work on modern China. She rejects the idea of Chinese society as a "totalitarian monolith" and points to the lack of total control by its leaders. She considers specifically how central powers delegated authority to local authorities to act on their behalf, but those at the local level in turn used their power to thwart the state. Shue distinguishes between "modern states" and "classical states," arguing that premodern states did not seek total penetration in the manner of modern states. Rather, she suggests, premodern states sought only to exploit existing local structures, without significantly changing them.²⁹

Although I challenge aspects of previous conceptions of power in early China, there have also been arguments made that bear similarities to my own. Herrlee Creel, for instance, noted that the Western Zhou did not rule its territory by military force alone but also through suasion. He gave credence to "the widely held conviction that the Western [Zhou] Kings could not, with the resources and the techniques available to them, organize and maintain a centralized administration. . . . But the [Zhou] rulers had one great advantage: they did not know this." In the end, Creel proposed that publicity in the form of declarations of authority was one means by which the Zhou succeeded.[30]

In his discussion of the emergence of the Chinese empire under the Qin, Robin D. S. Yates argues that the Qin dynasty sought to create "myths" across their territory, "the myth of cultural uniformity" and "the imperial myth."[31] I argue the Qin in fact created at least a degree of uniformity. In this regard, I am in agreement with Hui, who says, "The level of cultural homogeneity in present-day China is better understood as the product rather than the cause of Qin's success."[32] I show that the Qin dynasty communicated messages about their rule corresponding to Yates' imperial myth. But Yates deems these messages to have been myths and as such untrue. I do not disagree with Yates' critique of these assertions as they have featured in historiography. But I set aside the question of these claims' objective truth-value to consider how they worked to enable cooperation in the Qin case, and essentially made those claims become true.

Among the approaches I have described here, there are aspects that are conceptually similar to mine, though still different. Hui, for example, argues that the government of the state of Qin sought the support of its population, but this ended with unification. I will argue that the need for cooperation and communication only expanded with the founding of the realm. Giele talks about the movement of information, especially into the highest reaches of the bureaucracy, including the emperor; I want to reverse the flow and think about information that was sent out from the center, as well. Gernet speaks of the utility of "psychological factors, such as the consciousness of belonging to the same civilization," which is not far removed from the messages I propose the Qin broadcast. Gernet also says that the imperial state in China worked because it "took advantage of natural forms of social organization."[33] I accept this connection but reverse the chain of causation, proposing that governance was a highly developed outgrowth of natural human tendencies, not a wholly artificial and oppressive contrivance.

The Power of the Common Population

All of the aforementioned conceptions put power in the upper echelons of society. The common people of the early imperial realm are tacitly or explicitly assumed to have been, in practical terms, without any real power. They are thought to have been passive—on the receiving end of governance—and so far removed from the world of imperial power that they hardly even registered as spectators. Most scholars have accepted that a political elite controlled the ordinary populace in early China.[34] From this conception followed the idea that commoners were utterly passive in matters like law, and that the common people were not the intended audience of things like public ritual.[35]

In many ways, these notions resulted from the historiographical problems presented by the silence of the common population in records of early China.[36] Historians have naturally focused on processes of writing and reading, from which most commoners were more or less excluded.[37] There has been little consideration of communication directed at the common people, within and beyond the borders of the written word, and limited contact with theoretical work in other disciplines that could support such consideration. There are exceptions, in the form of studies that acknowledge the power of the lower classes to determine the course of events and the limited ability of central powers to exercise power in the face of local-level resistance. But these have so far focused on later periods.[38]

Although many scholars have accepted the notion of a passive populace in early China, it has shortcomings, including one that is quite basic: research I discuss in chapter 2 shows that government is impossible without significant cooperation from a large proportion of the population. Interdisciplinary research also tells us that the function of power—including political power—always entails choice. In complementary ways, these two lines of argument reinforce the role of the individual person as actor in social situations, including under apparent political domination: a sovereign whom nobody obeys has no power and cannot rule, and obedience is ultimately a decision. The lasting tyranny of a single person or a small group is impossible without convincing (not forcing) most members of the society to comply.[39] Oppression of course occurs and has occurred, but it requires a much greater degree of persuasion and cooperation than has often been recognized. My analysis suggests the Qin rulers were aware of this and used communication to resolve the coordination problem that the unified realm presented.

In many ways, previous assumptions about absolute control by a sociopolitical elite were natural. In the absence of a conceived social contract or participatory governmental system, as was the case in early China, it may be hard to imagine large groups of people working together except under compulsion. The existence of both penal systems and (of course) criminals only served to strengthen these assumptions. And such ideas were prominent in early Chinese discourse. Yet recent research in other fields offers a new perspective on these problems. My discussions furthermore show that those scholars who predicated limitations of communication on perceived technological constraints did not take all communications media into account.[40] Political authorities in the early empire did communicate across the realm and with all levels of society.

K. E. Brashier has written about the deep-seated preference in Western scholarship for what he calls "adversariality," the tendency to perceive and focus on conflict and difference.[41] Brashier's context is early Chinese religion and intellectual history, and he concentrates his arguments there. Yet his observation surely applies more broadly. I would suggest that the tendency to concentrate on particular forms of conflict and perceptions of political structure that emerged from them has helped determine the forms of historians' research on early China, leading scholars to underestimate the importance of cooperation and ideas about noncoercive governance. Recent interdisciplinary theory provides a way of approaching the questions of imperial rule that simultaneously distinguishes my work from that of my predecessors and remains faithful to the available historical sources.

I do not contend that previous work on the political systems and thought of early China has been incorrect; rather, it has focused in certain areas, on specific aspects of political theory to the exclusion of others. Researchers in early Chinese studies have left other areas relatively unexplored—and it is those areas that I want to concentrate on. I build on previous scholarship while bringing in an interdisciplinary research framework so as to approach my questions in a new way. I hope that this approach will interest not only specialists in Chinese history but also those in other fields who study communication and cooperation.

Cooperation

A major way my work differs from previous studies of early China lies in the weight I place on the role of cooperation. For, as research I discuss in chapter 2 shows, cooperation is at the core of how human societies work. Here I will just make a few general points by way of introduction.

The word "cooperation" is hard to define and a thorough discussion of its meanings would exceed the scope of my work here.[42] Cooperation in the sense I apply it goes beyond the basic, dictionary sense of "working together towards the same end, purpose, or effect."[43] In abstract terms, cooperation denotes a situation in which one person bears a cost in order to benefit another. The costs need not be in terms of resources: expenditures of time, increased risk, and forgone opportunities are all costs. Often, the advantage gained from some cooperative act will benefit not just a single other individual but also a larger group, of which the cooperator is a member. An important part of research on cooperation is examining how the interests of the member and the broader group intersect. Yet researchers who study cooperation tell us it does not necessarily require or reflect a particular mindset or intent; nor does it imply an absence of conflict. Cooperative systems need not be—and often are not—egalitarian, and not all cooperators will benefit equally or in the same way. Power and cooperation are not mutually exclusive. Nor is direct coercion necessarily excluded from cooperation; it is simply not the primary means by which it functions. Coercive power in various forms can work to establish or maintain cooperation without becoming the sole means by which a given institution or practice functions.[44]

In chapter 3 I discuss an early Chinese argument about authority, which suggests that it "uses one to get ten."[45] Coercion is not absent from this conception of power and cooperation, but its role is limited: communication magnifies each instance far beyond its original scope without requiring its repetition. An accurate understanding of how power worked in early China calls for an understanding of this point and how such non-coercive methods worked.

Cooperative social function can rely on communication with far less content, far less intensity, than historians have often imagined. Fairbank calls imperial rule in China "superficial" and says it did not penetrate to all levels of society. But as I discuss in chapter 2, the power that elicits cooperation does not require perfect distribution of detailed information: it suffices for a simple message to be broadcast widely and effectively. Later chapters, especially chapter 6, show that in early imperial China the central authorities in fact penetrated all levels of society, not with highly detailed messages but with information-poor messages transmitted in multiple modes. These include the sort of messages that Yoffee mentions as the sole effects of empire. But these are far from inconsequential, as he implies: they constitute the necessary framework for cooperation.

Clarifications

As a final step before outlining the contents of this study, I want to make some clarifications about its relationship to other work in the field. The most important of these is the fact that an analysis focusing on communication and cooperation does not eliminate other causes and effects, which are often conspicuous and in many—but not all—cases provided the apparent impetus for a given course of action. For example, asserting that the standardization of weights and measures communicated, as I do in chapter 5, does not mean the change did not have other consequences. It surely eased trade and taxation, too. But it also communicated, and that is my focus here. Analyzing communicative aspects of the changes and other acts enhances understanding of those outcomes without diminishing their importance in other realms.

The second clarification concerns the degree to which the rulers of Qin consciously set out to communicate in order to create political power. The short answer is that there is little evidence available concerning intent: we know virtually nothing about what the First Emperor was thinking and little about most of his assistants' ideas. There are indications that they were acting deliberately: the conspicuous role of these things in political thought of the Warring States period (475–221 BCE), which I discuss in chapter 3, shows the requisite understanding existed at the time. And as I point out in chapter 4, the evidence shows that at least one of the measures—the imperial progresses—was recognized as a medium of communication in early times. Ultimately, however, the point is moot. As will be shown in the next chapter, neither intent nor self-consciousness is necessary for the effects I propose in the realm of political power to exist.

Finally, I must address the question of historical materials, above all Sima Qian's 司馬遷 (ca. 145–ca. 86 BCE) *Historian's Records* (*Shiji* 史記), the most important transmitted source of Qin history. *Historian's Records*, along with its author and his motives, have long been the subject of scrutiny in and outside China. There is good reason for that. Like any historian—any author—Sima Qian had his reasons for writing; and like any ancient text, corruptions and interpolations have crept into *Historian's Records* over the centuries.[46] All of these matters are important objects of scholarly inquiry and deserve attention. But that does not mean that we should disregard *Historian's Records* as a source. Yuri Pines describes the difficulties Sima Qian faced when writing and concludes, "The result is not always satisfactory for the modern critical historian. Yet rather than ignoring Sima Qian's accounts or blindly following them, we should do our best to integrate them with the newly obtained sources to obtain a better, less biased picture of the pre-imperial age."[47] In this book I attempt just this sort of integration. I draw from *Historian's Records* and other early texts, as well as the results of archaeology, including excavations and the paleographical materials they have provided. Many writers and scholars, from the Han dynasty (206 BCE–220 CE) until today, depict the Qin dynasty and its founder as hubris-filled and obsessed with self-aggrandizement. My interpretation brings together transmitted sources, excavated materials, and interdisciplinary research to reconsider activities of the Qin dynasty and to propose what, in my view, the underlying causes were.

One specific issue concerning *Historian's Records* concerns the veracity of its accounts of the First Emperor's reign. Historians rightly question Sima Qian's descriptions of his ritual and other activities. In my discussions of early imperial examples, I strive to connect recorded history with the material remains of the Qin dynasty. Archaeologists have recovered paleographic documents, ancient buildings, and other concrete remnants from the time of the Qin and early Western Han that support conclusions about what happened. Archaeological results are, of course, far from transparent and unambiguous records, being themselves subject to interpretation. But such is the case for all aspects of intellectual inquiry. By connecting historical sources with archaeological research and interdisciplinary research, I hope to arrive at reasonable and reliable conclusions about early imperial political practices.

Preview of Chapters

Chapter 2. Communication and Cooperation: A Framework

In chapter 2 I present an interdisciplinary framework to support the analysis in later chapters. The first half of this chapter presents relevant theoretical and empirical research by anthropologists, economists, and others concerning cooperation, communication, and power in human societies. I begin with the central position of cooperation in all human groups, the evolved nature of our predilection to cooperate, and the difficulties inherent in working together. Cooperation in the form of social life is what enables humans to succeed so well; hence the drive to cooperate is an inherent part of humanity, and we have evolved capacities and abilities that support it. Cooperation offers benefits in situations where it may at first not be obvious; even enemies can cooperate for mutual benefit.[48] In a social system, leaders and followers all benefit from cooperation, not equally, but in comparison to the available alternatives. The primary means for resolving the difficulties of cooperation is communication in different forms. The broadest of these is the transmission of culture, defined technically as "socially transmitted information."[49] A culture is a body of information, and although people are often unaware of it, it provides ways to achieve the goal of coordinated action. Culture provides ways for human groups to coordinate their actions, and one way it does that is through establishing what Thomas Schelling calls "focal points."[50] Just one characteristic defines focal points: they must be obvious to the people involved. Beyond that, virtually anything could potentially be a focal point. Economist and political scientist Michael Suk-Young Chwe has applied Schelling's concepts to concrete political situations.[51] Chwe considers political situations as "coordination problems," in which the decisions of each person involved depend on their perceptions of how others act and will act. Chwe treats matters like ritual and changes to communal praxis as means for communication and how these establish new focal points for cooperation.

Chapter 3. Communication and Cooperation in Early Chinese Thought

Chapter 3 relates early Chinese concepts of government to the ideas I explore in chapter 2. I bring in received sources and texts recovered by archaeologists in recent decades to show that early Chinese thinkers analyzed successful societies as functioning by means of cooperation. In this discussion, I take seriously things that others in the past have dismissed as idealistic. By connecting these ideas to interdisciplinary research, I show that these thinkers were not proposing a hypothetical possibility; they were presenting an understanding of how human societies work. Thinkers in early China recognized the importance of communication for the function of governance. I demonstrate the degree to which their analyses and arguments put perceptions, which depended on communication to the whole population, at the center of social function. The most salient aspect of this, for those writers and for me, was simple unity: communicating the presence of the single ruler, the ultimate focal point, and the unified realm was a key step toward realizing rule. The thinkers proposed the active promulgation—creating common knowledge—of the ruler's political self as stand-in for his dynasty, an image intended for reception across all levels of society. It is this sort of communication that the First Emperor of Qin and his cohort engaged in with such assiduity.

Chapter 4. Mass Communication and Standardization

Chapter 4 begins the study of the Qin case by examining the standardization of weights and measures, which the Qin dynasty carried out immediately after unification. I show how the text commanding this change also advertised the First Emperor's achievement and that there is evidence indicating the Qin actively disseminated this text across the realm. Archaeologists have recovered numerous clay vessels, bronze plaques, and other implements bearing this text. The wide geographical distribution of these finds demonstrates the extent to which the Qin spread this message across their territory. The near ubiquity of these objects reinforces the mass communication aspect of their creation: the text was everywhere and on media of varying prestige, implying an audience of commensurate universality. This change must have touched the general population of the realm and created common knowledge of the instituting power, the Qin dynasty. I also discuss precedents for this sort of communication, concentrating on the potential for text, especially reproduced text on various media, to communicate among a group and create common knowledge. Evidence shows that people in pre-imperial China recognized this potential yet used it only in limited situations and to reach limited groups. The Qin rulers built upon existing ideas and processes to resolve the unparalleled problems they faced.

Chapter 5. Progress and Publicity: Qin Shihuang, Ritual, and Common Knowledge

Beginning soon after his accession to the throne, the First Emperor of Qin performed five tours around the realm. My analysis treats these progresses as public rituals that communicated the existence of the emperor—and, by extension, the empire—to the populace. These tours demonstrated the unchallenged position of the emperor in the realm before the audience of the general population and did so in a way that was sure to spread beyond the immediate audience of witnesses. In conjunction with the five tours, the First Emperor and his collaborators actively carried out a number of changes to the landscapes they passed through: they put up inscribed stone slabs, knocked down walls, constructed new ritual centers, and more. By doing these things, the First Emperor and his assistants ensured that the messages they were sending about the emperor and the empire persisted beyond the moment of the progress and into the future. Reasoning in terms of political communication permits me to show the connection between the progresses and other events of the same time and to give all these their proper importance. Seen thus, some of the most famous but frequently doubted events of the progress, like the putative punishment of a mountain, no longer seem incongruous or ludicrous but rather appear as well-designed signals that continue to capture the imagination and generate publicity today.

Chapter 6. Roads to Rule: Construction as Communication

The Qin dynasty made changes to modes of transportation that had communicative effects. In and around the imperial capital, the Qin constructed raised ways and walled roads that shielded and elevated the emperor away from contact with the common population. But even as they hid his person, they advertised his presence by changing the face of the city through permanent construction. While the emperor was concealed, his otherwise ephemeral path through the capital became a durable sign of his political self. Around the same time, the Qin created a highway system based on roads that already existed. But the Qin instituted rules to establish a lane marked off with trees and reserved for the emperor everywhere the road ran. Like roads and elevated ways in the capital, this lane turned the highway network into a constant reminder of imperial presence and power. The second part of this chapter takes up one road in particular, the Qin Direct Road (Zhidao 直道), which they created around the same time as the highway system. The Direct Road stretched from the area of the Qin capital at Xianyang 咸陽 (near modern Xi'an) to the northwest border region. This road communicated to the people living on and around its course, including the semi-nomadic tribes living to the north of the Qin realm. Both its endpoints had established political and religious significance, and the mountaintop course of the road likely built on existing conceptions of mountain spaces as well. As such, the Qin Direct Road was a case in which religious connotation worked to augment transmission and reception of the imperial message.

Chapter 7. Law, Administration, and Communication

The rulers of the Qin empire developed and expanded existing bureaucratic structures and practices in innovative ways to meet the needs of the empire. This chapter examines two examples. First is the system of universal registration of the populace, by which the Qin both amassed information about the realm and came into contact with each subject of the polity. This universal contact, I argue, turned the collection of information into a means of communication. In the second part of this chapter, I consider activities connected with the law. Qin and early Western Han statutes and ordinances were themselves the subject of much communication, as their deterrent purpose required. Records from Qin and Han times show that legal procedures and changes to the law functioned as media for communication, especially for the transmission of messages of political power. This final case shows how systems of control and compulsion—in ordinary function, in periods of interruption, and when changed—worked to create common knowledge and as a way to broadcast claims to power.

2

Communication and Cooperation

A Framework

This chapter lays out the theoretical basis for my interpretation. The first section draws upon interdisciplinary theory and analysis from fields such as anthropology, economics, and biology that tell us about the nature and function of human communication and cooperation. A consideration of power concludes the chapter.

Cooperation

The ability to cooperate so well is one of the things that set human beings apart from other forms of life on our planet. People form groups far larger than those of any other living things, with the exception of some social insects like ants and termites, and the biggest human societies outnumber even their groups. Forming societies is a key for human success: large groups are more effective than small groups across species, and humans are able to better exploit a wider variety of environments than other species because people work together better and in larger groups. The benefits of cooperation are such that they can support its emergence even in the absence of a controlling authority; even enemies can spontaneously cooperate, provided there is repeated interaction. Many researchers now believe that people have evolved a predisposition to cooperate because of the advantages cooperation brings. Our advanced brains may well have evolved to enable successful social cooperation.[1]

Cooperation, of course, has requirements and limitations, especially in big groups. Larger groups have the potential to bring greater advantage to their members, but at the same time they bring problems that require complex solutions. A group must cooperate effectively or it cannot function, and as group size expands, the difficulties of cooperation increase.[2] Yet groups that cooperate better are more successful than those that do so less effectively, and the benefits of cooperation alone can support small groups. As the size of the group and attendant complexities increase, this becomes insufficient, and in particular the need to sanction anti-cooperative behavior emerges.[3] Successful, interdependent, and cooperative human societies face increased risk of breakdown because of the many variable factors group life brings; if nothing else, more people means more exposure to the ordinary risks of existence.[4] The problems of organizing and maintaining cooperation also multiply. Societies that successfully resolve these problems achieve increasing gains that allow them, in turn, to expand further.[5] The gains from cooperation need not be equably distributed among members of the group for it to work. It is only necessary that the result be better than the available alternatives. Even highly hierarchal societies, which distribute privileges and material goods unequally, are still at core cooperative entities.[6]

Nor does cooperation preclude some role or roles for coercion in political processes. For example, under a penal system like that of early China, an instance of punishment was itself coercive. This is one way that governments work to foster cooperation: punishing anti-cooperative behavior counterbalances and outweighs the benefit a non-cooperating individual would otherwise achieve through the act. Yet that strictly retributive aspect does not define the whole scope of the punishment's effective function. The most important function does not lie in the punishment itself, but in the communication of that punishment. It reinforces that cooperation is the best option, should any member be tempted to act in a different way. It is deterrence—in other words, persuasion not to do something. Researchers have argued that a sizable proportion—it need not be all—of any human population consists of people who tend both to cooperate themselves and to punish those who do not cooperate. This group constitutes a base for successful group function, but the perception that non-cooperators are not punished will undermine their willingness to cooperate. A publicized penal system can fulfill this requirement and reinforce cooperation even among those unlikely to violate its requirements.[7]

Culture and Coordination

The decisive factor for successfully resolving the problems posed by cooperation is disseminating particular kinds of information—in other words, communication. This communication works at several different levels, the broadest of which is that of culture. "Culture" is a term that has proven difficult for social scientists to define effectively. One definition, accepted by many researchers in evolutionary anthropology and related fields, holds that culture is "socially transmitted information."[8] Culture is distinct from behavior, some of which results from culture and some from environment, evolution, and other factors. Anthropologist Lee Cronk expresses this point with a metaphor: "Culture is neither the act of baking a cake nor the cake itself, but the recipe, the *socially transmitted information* that tells a person how to bake a cake."[9] Culture depends on sharing information.

Michael Tomasello and other researchers have argued that human beings alone among living things have the faculty for "cumulative cultural adaptation," which enables us to function in such large groups. People transmit, learn, and build upon the experiences and innovations of current and past generations, which are relayed through the medium of culture. Culture provides ways for people to resolve the coordination problems presented by group action through shared understandings of how things should work. History in various forms extends this process by making available experiences outside of one's own time and so extends the reach of cumulative cultural adaptation. History's ability to make available experiences from the past is thus a highly developed facet of this broader human characteristic.[10]

One specific area in which culture functions is supporting group coordination. Michael Alvard argues that in a group action or other coordination problem, the manner in which the action is carried out can matter less than simple coordination. Just working together can achieve significant improvement in group function, even without further enhancement to the process. Culture—socially transmitted information—offers ways for a group to resolve the coordination problems it faces by establishing shared modes of action. This function applies whether or not the members of the group explain the purpose of the point in question differently. Culture can be so effective at resolving the problems of group life that people overlook it and may not realize how much it serves to facilitate cooperation. This is even—or especially—so when some particular manifestation of culture has another explanation. It may well be the case that an aspect of culture that objectively serves one or more purposes is differently explained by those to whom it belongs.[11]

There is a human tendency to adapt and change information transmitted as culture, which works even when those concerned profess to follow established patterns of behavior. The perfect acquisition of any piece of information is intrinsically impossible: there is no direct transfer of data from one brain to another. The fuzziness inherent in all interpersonal communication makes close approximation the best possible outcome, including for culture. But there is also a more active aspect of this, as received culture is often changed, then later taken up and built upon again.[12] Linguistic anthropologist Webb Keane points to the mismatch between assertions of cultural conservatism and the reality of constant change when he says, "Cultures are creative projects as much as they are conservative traditions."[13] Nor does culture force a group to act a certain way. Sociologist Ann Swidler describes it as a "toolbox" from which members of a group can draw at need but which does not compel any particular course of action.[14]

Members of human groups use socially transmitted information—culture—to address the requirements of group function. Communication spreads the means for cooperation, helping to resolve the problems posed by group activity. At the same time, culture is constantly changing and developing through both innovation and inevitably imprecise transmission as people adopt, adapt, and build on what was done before.

Focal Points

When Alvard argues that coordinating group action can do more to improve the outcome than the specific way the action is carried out, he refers to "focal points," a concept developed by Thomas Schelling.[15] Schelling is concerned with situations in which effective coordination allows those involved to achieve more than they would under different conditions. Many people are used to thinking of interactions in which a gain for one side necessarily results in less for the other, but in fact these are very rare. It is far more common that all participants stand to benefit from cooperation. Even during active conflict, "[t]here is some range of alternative outcomes in which any point is better for both sides than no agreement at all."[16] People need to cooperate, and successful cooperation leaves each participant better off than she or he would be without it. Even when the interests of people cooperating are at odds (or appear to be so), the need to act creates the need for coordination. Focal points are a means for this.

Focal points can be anything around which people coordinate activity. They can be human creations, like buildings or ideas; natural features, like mountains or rivers; or past practices or events. Focal points need only be conspicuous and known to the parties involved: "[They] seem less important for their practical convenience than for their power to crystallize agreement."[17] Focal points work by concentrating the attention of those involved in a given coordination problem. They create "convergent expectations—everyone's expectations of what everyone expects of everyone."[18] This entails communicating and evaluating intent, as each person's actions depend on their expectation of what others will do, and the actions of others determine the most advantageous course of action in a situation.[19]

Political activity can work as a focal point for group coordination. Following a leader is an effective way to resolve coordination problems, and leadership itself may be considered a focal point that functions because it is able to communicate its signals effectively.[20] Naturally, there are different levels of leadership ability, and the characteristics of the specific person in authority will help determine the outcome of a leadership situation. But evident communication with the coordinating agents, causing each group member to believe that others will act in a given way, is an integral part of the process of leadership. Since the ability of one individual to compel the behavior of a group is limited, authority is a matter of persuasion, "a process of influence."[21] This remains the case even in institutionalized systems of rule. As Robert Axelrod writes, "Governments cannot rule only through deterrence, but must instead achieve the voluntary compliance of the majority of the governed."[22]

The past is a source of focal points. The most common form this takes is tradition—doing something a particular way just because that is the way "we" do it.[23] When a focal point is taken up by a group, used and reused over time, the potency of its influence will increase. A group's history affects how it coordinates its actions and decisions: a decision made in one situation, in all its particularity and under the influences of precedent on that decision, constitutes a focal point that may be used in yet another, different case. For any group, the fact that *we* once did something a certain way, and everyone knows we did it that way, can become a way to coordinate future group action. History and other forms of recording expand this. These practices coordinate group activities, even if they, like all other manifestations of culture, are constantly changing.[24]

The existence and function of focal points is a process closely linked to a shared body of socially transmitted information—in other words, to culture. More than one person must perceive the focal point for it to exist, and in practice, a group must know it for it to work. A focal point relies on obviousness for effectiveness, but what is obvious will depend on context. It could depend on the natural environment: for people living on a plain, a single large hill could be a focal point; while for those living among mountains, a flat area would be. Most of all, history—the collective memory of relevant, empirical events—works to determine what will become a viable focal point, and how these can change over time. A focal point is both product and part of culture and history.[25]

Coordination Problems and Common Knowledge

Michael Suk-Young Chwe has explored the role of coordination problems in political contexts, expanding Schelling's ideas and connecting them to concrete examples.[26] Chwe considers situations in which the actions of an individual as part of a group depend on his or her expectations about how the other people involved will act. This sort of coordination problem has important implications for the study of governance, as "coordination problems include . . . overarching matters such as political and social authority."[27] According to Chwe, a person will only accept authority when she or he perceives that others will, too: "Submitting to a social or political authority is a coordination problem."[28]

Chwe's analysis particularly concerns the ways "common knowledge" works to resolve coordination problems. Common knowledge in this sense denotes a state of shared knowledge within a group. It exists when individuals have knowledge of some matter combined with the knowledge that other people also know about it and know that others know as well. Focal points, which exist only insofar as they are known and known to be known, are thus objects of a specific kind of metaknowledge.[29] Common knowledge shapes expectations about what others are likely to do. It thus influences the behavior of individuals and translates readily into political power. Common knowledge can be a determining factor in the creation of a new political entity or destruction of an old one: believing that others will obey tends to produce obedience, and the converse is also true. Chwe says that simply making strong claims to authority matters of common knowledge will tend to create obedience.

Chwe treats public rituals as means to create common knowledge. Such rituals not only communicate to their observers but also generate knowledge that everyone else who sees or learns of the ritual has received the same message(s). This applies to many sorts of cultural practice, which work to create shared knowledge among those involved. This kind of analysis often requires thinking about practices in a new ways, stepping back from the details of the message to consider other effects. "Most interpretations of cultural practices focus on the 'content' or 'meaning' of what is communicated. . . . Cultural practices must also be understood in terms of 'publicity' or, more precisely, common knowledge generation."[30] Communication works together with and beyond the content transmission that often forms what we think of as the goal of communication.

Thinking in terms of common knowledge creation does not negate the importance of content, but it adds an additional level to those messages. This works even when details are not successfully transmitted, are not meant for transmission, or just do not exist. A person could fail to grasp the ostensible primary message of a given signal and still learn enough to have metaknowledge of the authority involved. The most significant piece of information in terms of common knowledge creation could well be simple and vague. A message could be false and nevertheless succeed in establishing common knowledge, enabling coordination and perhaps making itself true.[31] However, as I will show, successful communication depends on reliability, and completely empty claims are unlikely to be effective. I will return to this point later.

Chwe's main focus is ritual, but he also points out that establishing new, shared practices creates common knowledge of the authority that instituted them. Such changes are themselves a coordination problem: shared practices are effective only because and to the degree that a group uses them, and changes require group-level change. Language is one example of this sort of problem: introducing or adopting new vocabulary requires a large number of people to do something differently.[32] Chwe refers specifically to systems of measures and weights, which are meaningful only to the extent that a group uses them. Once they are in common use, any change to the system will be a coordination problem. Any alteration to such a system requires people to change what they do, to coordinate with others. Change will also create common knowledge among those who use the system: changing standard practices creates publicity both of the change and its cause, whether or not overtly political content is part of the message. Altering the ways people do things creates common knowledge.[33] Common knowledge can also exist in the absence of deliberate publicity. Schelling argued that past actions, for example, constitute focal points; or, as Chwe puts it, "In terms of common knowledge, history is just like publicity."[34]

Chwe notes that common knowledge can come to be even when there is disagreement or difference in motive, or when the result is not beneficial for everyone. This differentiates common knowledge from propaganda—although propaganda can work to create common knowledge. The dictionary definition of propaganda is: "The systematic dissemination of information, esp. in a biased or misleading way, in order to promote a political cause or point of view."[35] Propaganda is concerned with advancing a particular political opinion; if that opinion is rejected, the propaganda is a failure. But the propaganda could still create common knowledge: neither agreement nor endorsement is required. At the same time, if some particular piece of propaganda should gain popular acceptance, opinion can later change quickly. Common knowledge would continue to exist, although it could well change its implications. Along the same lines, understanding of a particular event can change while common knowledge of it remains.[36] This mutability is rooted in the semiotic nature of the messages. Keane has written about the materiality of signs, including linguistic signs. He argues that signs of all sorts are unstable. Once created, they are part of a public discourse and no longer under the control of their creators, and their meaning can shift. Once an authority creates common knowledge, there will always be the chance that it may turn to be used against the creators.[37]

I noted earlier that researchers have postulated a large proportion of people are innately predisposed to cooperate (according to the models, it need not be all) because of cooperation's benefits. I also discussed the necessary conditions of this cooperation, including the perception of the readiness on the part of others to cooperate. Axelrod and Chwe make the same point: the best strategy for an individual in a given situation depends on what that person thinks others will do; decisions thus depend on perceived intent to cooperate and in what manner. The importance of perceptions links this back to the role of common knowledge in determining obedience to government.[38]

The predilection for cooperation helps explain why common knowledge works: it gives shape to tendencies that already exist. Common knowledge of a law or standard practice could fulfill the condition of perceived readiness on the part of other group members to cooperate, just as the content of the messages has the potential to communicate the requisite intent to cooperate.[39] The necessity of both cooperation and common knowledge means that both leaders and followers are (and were) using information to make decisions. This underscores the point that political power ultimately works by persuasion, not compulsion. It follows that no part of a society can be treated as exclusively passive; making decisions about cooperation, consciously or not, expressed or not, means an active part in determining and ultimately guiding group function (even without voting).

Reliable Communication

A central problem of communication, especially crucial communication, is the reliability of the information communicated. Messages need not be complicated or information-dense to be important. But communication of any sort is most effective when it is believable. (Untrue communication can be effective but in more restricted settings.) Despite the fact that common knowledge can work even if false, false claims will usually be less effective than true claims. And even true claims must also be successfully transmitted for them to work. Reliable communication is a central issue of cooperation.

Amotz Zahavi has articulated a theory of communication that explains it as fundamentally concerning the transmission of reliable information by means of indexes.[40] Zahavi is a biologist and gives most of his attention to animal communication, but he also brings in and explains human behavior by the same means. And in fact his approach, although representing an advance in understanding and the incorporation of empirical evidence, is similar to some longstanding ideas about human social behavior (see next section).[41] The core of Zahavi's theory concerns ostensibly wasteful behavior or traits and holds that these actually serve to communicate about characteristics that cannot be directly observed. These behaviors include things like apparent altruism, which seems wasteful in evolutionary terms, as it brings no direct advantage to the actor. It also includes behaviors that may seem to serve no purpose but are actually indexical signals. In Charles Peirce's semiology, indexes are those signs that are intrinsically linked to their referents. Indexes contrast with other signs, which relate to what they stand for because of some kind of resemblance or because of convention. This makes indexes impossible or impractical to falsify and thus the key to a functional semiotics.[42]

Human beings frequently use indexical signs and not just to communicate physical qualities. Zahavi cites the example of lace used for clothing in Europe. Historically, making lace took a great deal of time and labor, rendering it expensive to produce and buy. Wearing lace was then simultaneously—and not coincidentally—fashionable and a sign of wealth. When mechanical production made it cheap, lace no longer communicated wealth. It lost its cachet and went out of style. Clothing can function to communicate different qualities or traits, sometimes but not always self-consciously. These can be quite general, including things like adherence to—or rejection of—broad social norms. Indexical signs may also serve practical purposes. An example from the human realm is the longbow: a longer bow requires more strength to wield effectively than a shorter bow and also has a greater range. A longbow of greater length is both an index of physical power and a correspondingly more effective weapon. In the social realm, people convey information about power by many means, including signals in the form of granting rewards or enacting punishments, both of which are indexes.[43]

The costs involved with this sort of communication take various forms. Costs can take the form of risk: to the degree an act or state brings increased chance of harm, it is functionally a cost. And indeed this is one mechanism by which advertised signals remain credible. Zahavi says this sort of cost is part of how markings of rank and/or status work. They show off particular traits, allowing comparison, which brings with it the chance that another will be superior and open the bearer to criticism. Dress and/or its constituents often call attention to some attribute precisely in order to facilitate this kind of comparison. Such systems communicate information that is trustworthy because of its cost. It may be possible for a signaler to bear a particular cost temporarily—that is, to deceive. But over time the demands of the charade will become insupportable, leading to exposure of the deception. Zahavi tells us that communication is an—or *the*—important element of competition, even when conflict seems like the main thing. In competitive display or fighting, the adversary is not the only recipient or even the real focus of the communication: the observers that make decisions according to the information they derive from the display or battle are ultimately more important. Thus, when humans compete, the opponent is not necessarily the primary audience: rather, it is those who watch or learn about the results in other ways that matter, for it is they who will make decisions based on the information the competition conveys.[44]

Signaling Theory

Many researchers have worked to develop Zahavi's ideas in the field of what is most commonly referred to as signaling theory. Rebecca Bliege Bird and Eric Alden Smith have summarized this research and elucidated its application in the human realm. They call special attention to its affinity with the social theories of Thorstein Veblen, Marcel Mauss, and Pierre Bourdieu. Signaling theory improves upon these by integrating analysis of symbolic communication with evolutionary theories that treat individuals as making strategic decisions with finite information.[45]

According to signaling theory, signs often communicate things that are not directly observable: leadership ability and political power, for example, are themselves invisible. In such a situation, costs in one form or another can endow a signal with an indexical character that guarantees its reliability by making it impossible or impractical to fake. These costs can render the act in question inefficient and might be perceived as wasteful, but in fact that is what makes them work, because bearing those costs reflects a particular quality. Alternately, the costs may link the sign directly to the quality it represents, making faking impossible or impractical.[46] Signaling theory works when accurate communication benefits communicators whose interests may not otherwise coincide.[47]

Bliege Bird and Smith gather examples from ethnographic research on human social groups showing how this plays out in the real world. They argue that ceremonial feasts, inefficient methods of growing or obtaining food, and even creative expression can work to communicate things like wealth, skill, and dexterity. Group performance requires coordination and practice and so indexes the success of the group's function and invites comparison between groups.[48]

Two specific types of signal are especially important to my discussion here: ritual and monumental architecture. Bliege Bird and Smith cite work that uses signaling theory and related approaches to analyze ritual behavior, for ritual often brings with it significant costs. They speak specifically of time spent, assets consumed or otherwise disposed of, and even exposure to danger during ritual, all of which are often without any direct benefit to the actor. But these things can reasonably be explained as part of communicative processes: they are costs that turn rituals into indexes.[49]

Numerous definitions of ritual exist. One that has found relatively wide acceptance is that of Roy A. Rappaport. Rappaport says that ritual is characterized by having a source outside the one performing the ritual. A particular sense of formality or propriety also characterizes ritual. There can still be elements of humor, sensuality, or unregulated action, but in a ritual even those will come as part of a structure. Rituals are by nature repeated and repeatable yet also evolve and change with the passage of time and the requirements of a given situation. Finally, someone must carry out a ritual for it to match Rappaport's conception; descriptions or instructions alone do not suffice.[50]

Rappaport gives considerable attention to how ritual conveys information. He divides its messages broadly into two types. The first are those that make known the state of the performer of a given ritual at the time of performance. The second is the "canonical," forms that performers receive and do not create, which create symbolic links to events and contexts larger than the individual. Together, these two represent both the mutability and the stability of ritual. People who perform a ritual take up something received from elsewhere and use it, inevitably changing it in the process, to communicate about themselves. Rappaport asserts that ritual has special abilities as communication, in that it can turn a complex situation of innumerable gradations into a clear and intelligible statement, thus enabling the transfer of the information between different systems.[51]

The recipients of this information include not only those who observe the performance or learn about it secondhand but also the performer him- or herself. The message has at least two aspects. The first is what the ritual says about the performer. But there is also a larger message: performing a ritual is an indexical sign that the performer recognizes the social order of which the ritual is part, with all its obligations. This is not a description of or assertion about an internal state; instead, it is an external sign of acquiescence and acceptance, which, like other aspects of ritual, is directed at both others and the self.[52]

Joel Robbins has expanded and clarified several aspects of Rappaport's conception of ritual as communication. Robbins specifically connects distrust of language to reliance on ritual, as ritual has particular communicative ability. Despite the importance Rappaport gives to performing rituals, Robbins makes the important point that rituals are often not performative in the sense made famous by J. L. Austin, according to whom performative utterances effect changes in conventional states. Rather, rituals often seek to persuade others—what Austin calls "perlocution." When persuasion is the goal, communication assumes paramount importance, for without it, no suasion can occur.[53]

Anthropological research shows that ritual helps groups work better because of its unique capacity for communication. Although much of this work concerns religious ritual, the researchers specify that nonreligious ritual can achieve many of the same effects, especially when it incorporates religious or quasi-religious elements. This approach has been used to study historical records of utopian communities, both supporting the conclusions based on anthropological investigation and demonstrating the application of these concepts to the study of history.[54]

Oversized construction projects are another kind of costly signal, one that is particularly effective at sending political messages. As Bruce Trigger put it, "Monumental architecture expresses in a public and enduring manner the ability of an authority to control the materials, specialized skills, and labour required to create and maintain such structures." Extravagant and seemingly wasteful construction works as an index of power, a sign that cannot be faked, because of the costs involved. And since such constructions are giant, they are seen by all; everyone perceives the message and knows that others do, too, which makes it common knowledge. This sort of strong message is a highly effective political signal.[55]

Of course many factors affect the success of communication and help to determine its forms. For instance, research shows that signals sent simultaneously in multiple media are more effective than those sent in just one. Important messages come in multiple media. And as messages that create common knowledge can be both low in detail and separate from the perceived content of the signal, we should also expect to find messages that create common knowledge in multiple media, bundled with other messages in order to draw attention.[56] The later chapters of this book show how the rulers of early imperial China did just that.

Foucault and Power

Michel Foucault's analysis of power clarifies a few final points about power and its function in political systems.[57] Although Foucault's ideas are not commonly used in studying the history of early China, Karen Turner has pointed out how much ancient Chinese thought and practice presaged Foucault's political concepts.[58]

Foucault explained his primary understanding of power this way: "Power means relations, a more-or-less organized, hierarchical, co-ordinated cluster of relations," which exist "between individuals (or between groups)."[59] Power relations are not simply present; they are "an ensemble of actions which induce others and follow from one another."[60] Foucault describes and rejects several understandings of power. He dismisses "[t]he idea that there is either located at—or emanating from—a given point something which is a 'power.'"[61] He sees power in all social relationships, not power that derives from that of a ruler, but instead that constitutes the medium in which the latter functions.[62] Foucault does not deny the existence of top-down power so much as insist that other forms exist as well.[63] But he rejects the idea of power as something possessed and/or given away, or which only restrains. In Foucault's analysis, power creates and influences as well.He conceives of power in terms of relations and relationships, not as something with a separate and static existence. It is not a substance to be grasped and held—or stolen or traded away.[64]

One perhaps counterintuitive aspect of Foucault's analysis is the integral role freedom has in power relationships. For he tells us that power does not exist without some degree of choice on the part of the subject. When a person acts under duress, that is not a function of power in Foucault's sense. Through power, one person can control another's actions to a degree, but it is impossible to do so completely. Foucault draws a distinction between "force," in the form of physical compulsion, and power. For, as he says, "There is no power without potential refusal or revolt."[65] This extends to the whole of the populace, which Foucault tells us cannot be truly controlled and is at best only directed. The existence of choice is an inalienable part of the problem of governance.[66]

Foucault acknowledges the close relationship of power and communication, as "communicating is always a certain way of acting upon another person or persons." He allows that communication and power can be separate from each other, but they also rely upon each other. He acknowledges that communication in and of itself can, "by virtue of modifying the field of information between partners, produce effects of power." At the same time, the components of communication are both a medium and a product of power.[67]

Previous research on political structures in imperial China has often taken approaches that Foucault explicitly rejects. Scholars have understood power to have flowed from the emperor out and down through the bureaucratic hierarchy. Constraints—ethical, personal, or practical—could block this flow, but the central image was power radiating from the center. Foucault's analysis indicates this conception requires revision. Nor is the idea of an exclusively passive populace tenable. For as Foucault tells us, the existence and function of power entails the possibility of choosing another course of action: even the ordinary people in early imperial China were making decisions. Even they wielded a degree of power. This is a point that I will come to again, from a perspective within the Chinese tradition, in the next chapter.

My study of communication's role within imperial society as a means to create cooperation and thus power has drawn much inspiration from Foucault's analyses. Its goal is to examine one aspect of how power functioned in one historical case. I do not attempt to examine power in all the forms in which it existed at the time; instead I focus on specific examples.

Despite Foucault's influence on this work and my incorporation of his ideas, I acknowledge a major point of difference, which has broad repercussions for my methodology and conclusions. This concerns the question of *why*. When people decide—and as Foucault and the researchers I draw from believe, it is a decision—to obey, to turn themselves into subjects, why do they do it? Why does Foucault himself do it? Why do I do it? Why do we ignore the freedom that Foucault says we have?

Foucault never treated this question at length. But he referred more than once to an internal fascism: "The fascism in us all, in our heads and in our everyday behavior, the fascism that causes us to love power, to desire the very thing that dominates and exploits us."[68] This seems to me an unsatisfactory answer, not least because Foucault himself elsewhere called fascism a "disease of power."[69] Essentially, his answer to the question of why people decide to submit to power when they could decline to do so is a universal affliction that drives us to wish for our own oppression. And in the end, by attributing this to a supposed universal human predilection, Foucault ends up describing rather than explaining.

The research on cooperation I use offers an understanding of human social behavior that is at once better grounded and more optimistic than Foucault's. It suggests that the benefits of cooperation have brought about types of group formation based on hierarchy, in which the benefits that accrue from this function for all group members can explain the willingness to obey power. At the very least, this approach allows us to consider human social life without postulating a universal disease. Because of its basis in interdisciplinary theory and empirical research, a framework that focuses on cooperation is robust. It also has something to offer the present. Studying cooperation and power under the Qin will help us better understand early Chinese history and society specifically. More broadly, studying cooperation and power in the past will help us to better understand these things, which will help us to see how we, as humans, are and understand how we can become better. This is an area in which early Chinese thinkers had insights that still offer benefit today.

3

Communication and Cooperation in Early Chinese Thought

This chapter presents early Chinese political thought that relates to the ideas and analysis I presented in chapter 2. My examination shows that thinkers in early imperial China shared the interest in cooperation and communication as means for governance. This discussion supports my analysis in the later chapters and works to connect early Chinese thought and history to broader concerns. For although certain aspects of political thought relating to cooperation in early China were presented in idealized terms and have often been considered as ideals alone, modern research in other fields suggests these ideas were practical and practicable.

In the previous chapter I sketched a theoretical basis for focusing on communication and cooperation in political contexts. In this chapter, I show that these ideas are compatible with the intellectual context of Qin unification. There are two primary aspects to this. First is the central place and necessity of cooperation. As I mentioned in chapter 1, many studies of Chinese politics treat the common people in early imperial China as politically passive. Those conceptions certainly represent aspects of political thought in early China. But I have argued that government in general is essentially a matter of cooperation, which requires communication and participation to function well. The participation of the common population was at least as important for the success of the imperial project as that of any other group in early China—even the group of one at the top of society, the emperor.

Political philosophers and others around the time of unification recognized the importance of information and communication in the processes of organizing and carrying out cooperation in the form of governance. I argue that their idealized and theoretical projections were practicable. These political thinkers were not dreaming, they were conveying hard-won knowledge about how human societies work most effectively, articulated in the discursive context of early China. Constructions of an exclusively passive population in early China belong to the realm of early political theory and, while important, do not tell the whole story of social function.

Cooperation in Early Chinese Thought

People in early China recognized the importance of cooperation for the successful functioning of the state and the core place particular types of communication played in that. There was no single term referring to cooperation in this context, but it is readily apparent in various accounts of rule. The *Book of Odes* (*Shijing* 詩經) poem "Numinous Tower," for instance, gives a picture of governance based on the populace's willing completion of the ruler's plans:

[King Wen of Zhou 周文王] began the Numinous Tower,	經始靈臺
Measured it and marked it out.	經之營之
The common people built it;	庶民攻之
He set no deadline, but they finished it.	不日成之
"It is just begun, don't rush!" he said,	經始勿亟
And the common people came like children.[1]	庶民子來

Philosophers from different lines of thinking in early China embraced the ideal of cooperation as the best way to rule. Mencius, for example, elaborated on "Numinous Tower" in arguing for humane governance that would bring joy to both ruler and ruled, even when construction projects required the people's labor.[2]

Recovered texts from the Warring States period demonstrate the conspicuous position non-coercive political theory occupied at the time, as Scott Cook has shown. These thinkers' descriptions show that the alternative to governance through cooperation was no rule: in short, the choice they presented was cooperation around the focal point of the sovereign or the dissolution of the state. The thinkers knew that government must function through cooperation or it would not work. At the same time, they argued that the right leader would inevitably win the allegiance of the common people and achieve cooperation.[3]

The text *Master Guan* (*Guanzi* 管子) was assembled during Western Han times from materials dating from the fifth to the first centuries BCE and associated with the early political thinker Guan Zhong 管仲 (d. 645

BCE).⁴ While it does not provide reliable information about the historical Guan Zhong, its contents fit the time frame of this study. *Master Guan* describes the willing allegiance won by King Wen of Zhou, the subject of "Numinous Tower." It contrasts with the cruel governance of the last Shang ruler, a common trope in early texts.⁵ According to *Master Guan*, King Wen's virtue was such that when he seized power, the populace wanted to obey him: "The Yin (i.e., Shang) people lifted their heads and gazed toward King Wen [from afar], wishing to become his subjects" 殷民舉首而望文王, 願為文王臣.⁶ Of course the historicity of such assertions is dubious at best. But various texts return repeatedly to the importance of cooperation, and the research discussed in chapter 2 shows we should take these conceptions of government seriously. For cooperation is not just a reasonable goal, it is part of human nature.

Master Guan speaks of the same elsewhere, with reference to ancient monarchs: "In the past, when the sage kings ruled . . . they desired that people be harmonious and united in obeying their edicts" 昔者聖王之治人也 . . . 欲其人之和同以聽令也.⁷ This may seem too idealistic to be earnest, yet *Master Guan* also expresses without ambiguity that the reason for this was practical: trying to employ an unwilling populace can only lead to failure, while its willing support brings success.⁸ The reverse was equally true: "It is rare that one whom the populace resents and curses is not destroyed" 眾所怨詛, 希不滅亡.⁹ I contend that we should take these statements as serious assertions of political theory: the pictures they present may be idealized, but it was an attainable ideal.

The "Great Learning" ("Da xue" 大學) chapter of the canonical *Record of Ritual* (*Liji* 禮記) says that a would-be ruler must gain the support of the commoners in order to become "father and mother of the people" 民之父母. Their backing would decide his success: "If one gains the support of the populace, he will gain the state, but if he loses the populace, he will lose the state" 得眾則得國, 失眾則失國.¹⁰ Military strategist Sun Bin 孫臏 (4th c. BCE) made the same point in the context of war, arguing, "The one who gets [the support of] the many will be victor of victors" 取眾者, 勝之勝者也, while a leader who failed in this respect was doomed.¹¹ Although he was speaking of armies, Sun Bin's phrasing is general. And since the armies of his day were always conscripted from the populace, not only was the problem the same for both ruler and general, but the target was, too.¹²

The Annals of Mr. Lü (*Lüshi chunqiu* 呂氏春秋), a philosophical compendium assembled in the third century BCE, puts this idea into straightforward, positive terms: "The means by which any ruler is established comes from the masses" 凡君之所以立, 出乎眾也.¹³ A Western Han commentary on the *Book of Odes* expresses something similar, saying that "the one who gets [the support of] the people will be stable" 取民者安. It recommends that the ruler should "make governance evenhanded in order to unite those below" 平政以齊下. The predicted result is respect combined with concern: "If like this, the common people will care for [the ruler] like father and mother, and be in awe of him like a divinity" 如是百姓愛之如父母, 畏之如神明.[14]

Such was the potency of willing cooperation that it could be perceived as equal to the influence of divine entities. According to the Warring States text "Three Virtues ("San de" 三德), known only from an archaeologically recovered manuscript, the ruler who aligned his governance with the wishes of the populace would receive heavenly support. It promises, "The Supreme Thearch blesses the one in which the people delight" 民之所喜, 上帝是祐, and, "The ghosts and spirits bless that which the people desire" 民之所欲, 鬼神是祐.[15] These may well have been intended as factual characterizations. But since the support of the populace was objectively a matter of human agency, they also reflect the effects of cooperation.

Thinkers in early China recognized that the successful function of social groups as social groups required more than just compliance in order to achieve political success. In different ways, these texts speak of successful rule as not just obedience but *willing* obedience, in conjunction with concord and social stability. These texts speak of cooperation.

The same conception persisted into later centuries. Emperor Zhao 昭 (r. 94–74 BCE) convened official discussions at court in 81 BCE, which are recorded as a debate between government representatives and those who criticized then-current policy in *Discussions on Salt and Iron* (*Yantie lun* 鹽鐵論). One exchange between the two sides concerns popular resistance to imperial demands for labor service and taxes. The two sides are predictably different in their analyses of this issue, yet they agree in presenting the best situation as one of cooperation. The defender of government policy phrases this in terms of an ideal past when the people labored in the fields and "did not turn away from their work" 不違其職. The critic countered with suggestions about how to achieve that state again, so that "the common people would strive at their tasks and be happy about state taxes" 百姓勸業而樂公賦 and not find corvée service onerous. He closes with reference to the poem "Numinous Tower."[16] Willing cooperation was a broadly shared ideal that remained a part of policy discussions well into imperial times.

Governance and the Common People

Yuri Pines has recently examined the intellectual aspects of emerging imperial rule in early China.[17] The core of Pines' study concerns notions of the ruler as the unique and ultimate political actor in the universal realm and the role played by the intellectual class (*shi* 士) in those developments. Pines also gives significant attention to the common population and its political roles—both active and passive. He demonstrates that from earliest historical times, political thinkers acknowledged the political importance of the common people. Pines links this to lineage-centered government that emerged during the Western Zhou period.[18] In the language of the "mandate of Heaven" (*tianming* 天命), the people reflected Heaven's stance on a given government, while "the people's sentiments [were] the decisive factor that ensure[d] divine support for the ruler."[19]

Pines argues that in the Warring States period, the common population's direct political involvement decreased at the same time polities expanded in size. Nevertheless, the people and the fulfillment of their material needs were still recognized as the route to political power; the sovereign had to bring benefit to those he ruled. Although commoners were not held worthy of respect, Pines shows all major thinkers of the time gave significant attention to the common people and their power, which could be decisive if brought to bear in extreme situations. In Pines' analysis, this usually took the form of limited institutional means for expressing political opinion.[20]

My arguments here build on Pines' work. Matters that he analyzes in the abstract, I make specific and concrete, while extending these forward in time. I focus on what the Qin did in practice to make the ideal of a unified state real, and how the Qin confronted related issues in practice. The political thinkers of Warring States times of course did not create their notions out of nothing. Pines calls their project the "creative reinterpretation of . . . centuries-old ideas."[21] My discussions in later chapters will show that the techniques the Qin used for communication were not new, either. Like the ideas behind them, they represented the active adaptation and repurposing of existing technology and techniques for purposes also informed by a creative reinterpretation of the past. The Qin dynasty is an excellent example of cumulative cultural adaptation in a historical context.

Despite our significant points of agreement, my conception differs from Pines' in two important respects. First, as discussed in the preceding chapters, modern research has shown that human beings have an inherent tendency to cooperate: the tendency is always there, however variously expressed. Pines argues that the Warring States thinkers came to believe the people were the ultimate power in the polity and I agree. However, I go one step further. I would not just call this a change in political thinking or simply another development in the conception of governance. Nor was this simply a portrayal of an abstract, ideal mode of rule. Rather, the early Chinese thinkers had made an advance in understanding about how human groups function. This new and better understanding led to techniques that were effective because they made use of insights into human behavior, enabling governance at the level of the unified state. These techniques and ideas were ideal because they were effective.

Pines concentrates on institutional means for the public to express its opinion on government matters and says rightly that the common people were excluded from these under imperial governance.[22] But as I have argued, all group organization depends in great part on cooperation, which in turn relies on communication and persuasion. The central position of cooperation in group function means that, whatever institutional structures were or were not in place, the cooperation of the common population was required for the function of the state. The common people's participation was by definition active and the people had to be persuaded to give it. This remained the case under the imperial governance of the Qin and Han dynasties. Institutions are of course important, but they form only one part of the picture.

Group Formation and Existence

Pines calls Xun Kuang 荀況 (ca. 340–245 BCE), better known as Master Xun (Xunzi 荀子), "the single most important architect of . . . imperial political culture" in China.[23] Like the thinkers and texts I mentioned earlier, Xunzi argued that the best rule would exist when all in the realm were not just obedient subjects but willing cooperators.[24] The text *Master Xun* (*Xunzi* 荀子) discusses at length the way that humanity's ability to form functioning groups sets it apart from other animals: "[People] are not as strong as oxen and they run slower than horses, yet oxen and horses work for people. Why? Because people can form groups and those others cannot" 力不若牛, 走不若馬, 而牛馬為用, 何也? 曰, 人能群, 彼不能群也.[25]

Master Xun is not the only early text in which one sees the realization that humans form groups because they bring advantages. *Mr. Lü's Annals* expresses this unambiguously, too: "Groups can be formed because [the members] benefit mutually from them. When benefit comes from a group, the way of leadership has been established" 群之可聚也, 相與利之也. 利之出於群也, 君道立也.[26] *Master Xun* says a leader could lead because of the ability to gather people together, and it goes on to explain this facility as the combination of caring for and properly employing others.[27]

Master Xun affirms that the populace benefits from having a leader and names this as the reason for rulership. At the most general level, "Heaven does not give birth to the people for the lord; heaven establishes the lord for the people" 天之生民, 非為君也; 天之立君, 以為民也.[28] Texts like *Mr. Lü's Annals* also assert that the ruler's power comes from the population he rules.[29]

The most crucial benefit that the ruler could bring was simply the establishment of government, that is, creating the conditions needed for cooperation: "There is no greater benefit than order and no greater harm than disorder" 夫利莫大於治, 害莫大於亂, according to *Master Guan*.[30] Yet early Chinese thinkers described failure in governance not as anarchy but rather as the emergence of groups that would not provide the greatest good for the larger population. There are two levels of significance to this. First is that the thinkers of early China recognized the inherently social nature of human beings and intrinsic advantages of cooperation and saw negative results in competition between groups. The second is the fact that, after an intellectual consensus had emerged concerning the unified realm, as Pines describes, the perceived threat to order was not total social breakdown. It was reversion to disunion.

The authors of *Master Mo* (*Mozi*墨子) argue for the ideal of "universal caring" 兼愛, which is their most famous philosophical notion. The reality of Warring States China was opposite of what they proposed. Yet the picture they painted of their time was not one of pure disorder or of each person for him- or herself. *Master Mo* describes powerful *groups* that attacked and exploited the less powerful, damaging the intrinsic unity of the realm. Universal caring as they described it called for disinterested concern at the individual level; but in political terms it was an argument for creating larger groups—and ultimately a single group—out of many, competing bodies.[31] *Master Guan*, too, describes the opposite of successful governance not as a total breakdown or a return to atavistic pandemonium but as the formation of other, smaller groups. It says specifically that in the absence of proper rule, local-level cliques would displace central government as people banded together to pursue narrow and selfish interests.[32]

Master Han Fei (*Han Feizi* 韓非子) argues the ideal government of the sage would bring positive change to the penal system, which would influence all of society. The first of these effects would be "to rescue the many living things from disorder, and do away with the harms of the realm; and to make it so the strong do not bully the weak, nor the many do violence to the few" 救群生之亂, 去天下之禍, 使強不陵弱, 眾不暴寡. *Master Han Fei* calls success in this respect "the greatest of merits" 功之至厚. Although harsh penalties are a part of his plan, he denounces as ignorant those who would describe such means as violent: achieving the higher goal of peace would more than outweigh them.[33] In other words, the benefits derived from successful cooperation would make up for the costs of sanctioning anti-cooperative behavior.

The First Emperor of Qin and his rhetoricians presented imperial unification as the creation of a single, orderly group of people out of a disorderly set of polities, bringing peace to the common population and thereby winning their support. An inscription proclaimed of him, "Martial, he has annihilated the violent and fractious; cultured, he has restored the innocent; and the hearts of the common people have all submitted" 武殄暴逆, 文復無罪, 庶心咸服.[34] This was also a major part of the message he transmitted across the realm as part of his change to the system of weights and measures after unification in 221 BCE (see chapter 4).

The early Han political thinker Jia Yi 賈誼 (200–168 BCE), who strongly criticized the Qin rulers, echoed this. Jia Yi knew the power of establishing peace in place of war's tumult and the loyalty that achievement could bring. He described the context of Qin's final rise and the reaction of the populace to their final success in terms similar to those found in *Master Han Fei* and elsewhere:

> The strong had bullied the weak and the many done violence to the few. There had been war without cease, and the clerisy and people were exhausted. Now Qin faced south and ruled the realm as king.[35] This meant there was a Son of Heaven above. Among the multitudes of people who wished for stability in their lives, there was not one who did not wholeheartedly look up in hope to him. 強凌弱, 眾暴寡. 兵革不休, 士民罷弊. 今秦南面而王天下, 是上有天子也. 即元元之民, 冀得安其性命, 莫不虛心而仰上.[36]

Master Xun and other texts present the result of proper rule as a state that functioned with coordination and cooperation. They employ the body as a metaphor for the best sovereign, who rules the realm with the same effortless and perfect control the mind exerts over the physical form: "The realm follows him as a united body, as the four limbs follow the heart" 天下從之如一體, 如四胑之從心.[37] For *Master Xun* and others, the sovereign's goal was to foster the sort of cooperation that the poem "Numinous Tower" attributed to King Wen, in which the populace worked together of its own accord to carry out his plans.

These early thinkers were not so naïve or disingenuous as to suggest that everyone in society would benefit equally from rule. Those of high station would have duties in high places and commensurate emoluments.

But the common people below would be better off than otherwise, and this would bring their allegiance to the ruler. That accords with the conceptions of leadership and cooperation as being mutually but differentially beneficial.[38]

The Role of Information in Unification

The main way different political writers in early China developed their concept of group coordination was in terms of singleness or unity (*yi* 一/壹). Pines has shown that the single ruler, governing the entire population of the realm, was accepted as an ideal before political unification under the Qin.[39] Unity was both a goal and a means. This is implicit in many texts but was perhaps most clearly articulated in the early Han: "The sage wields unified governance in order to align the common folk, and holds a single standard with which to classify the myriad people. This is the means to bring together unified rule and show unified control" 聖人執一政以繩百姓, 持一槩以等萬民, 所以同一治而明一統也.[40] Early Chinese thinkers knew it was necessary for the populace to perceive its sole ruler as such. This was ultimately a matter of creating and maintaining common knowledge of the ruler among the populace. The task was one of communication, and the goal was functional coordination.

Simple political unification did not suffice to create a new polity; the goal was not just confederation but coordination and cooperation. *Master Xun*, for example, presents the task of unification as easy, even if the target is enemy territory. It names consolidating a society and enabling cooperative governance as more difficult and complex problems. *Master Xun* recommends using different means for different groups: ritual to bring together the educated population and governance for the common people, both working toward the same goal of integration.[41]

The most important step toward integration—more important than the actual establishment of the ruler—was generating the perception of unity among the common population: the commoners had to know that they were a single polity under a single monarch, a group coordinating around the ultimate focal point. *Master Xun* expresses this by saying, "If the sovereign is one, then those below are one" 上一則下一矣.[42] *Mr. Lü's Annals* describes leaders as means for unification, then concludes in blunt terms: "If there is one, there is order; if there is two, there is chaos" 一則治, 兩則亂.[43] Another text expresses the same idea by depicting the result of failure in this respect: "If the person [i.e., identity] of the sovereign is doubted, then the common people will be confused" 上人疑則百姓惑 and disorder will ensue.⁴⁴ *Master Guan* paints a dire picture of failure in this respect, equating the inability to create the perception of unity with the inability to achieve stability—the first task of governance.⁴⁵

Since the danger that threatened the ruler was division and doubt about him in the hearts of the people, it follows that the most important means for unification was communication that would make doubt concerning him impossible. The decisive message was the simplest: the existence of the sole ruler and his unified governance, the one intrinsic to the other. This was often expressed metaphorically, with reference to "brightness."

The Book of Lord Shang (*Shangjun shu* 商君書) asserts in direct terms that unification equals this sort of brightness: "If rule is bright, then it will be unified; if rule is dark, there will be differences" 治明則同, 治闇則異.⁴⁶ *Master Xun* hortatively describes an imagined past, saying, "The first kings made ritual and duty bright in order to unify [the people]" 先王明禮義以壹之.⁴⁷ *Master Guan* extends the same idea by arguing that failure in this will bring disobedience: "If the way of the lord is not bright, then those who receive commands will be doubtful" 君道不明, 則受令者疑.⁴⁸ This recalls Chwe's assertion about the position of common knowledge in realization of political power: making governance widely known will lead to obedience and allegiance. Governance left uncommunicated—"dark"—will result in heterogeneity and disorder.

Common Knowledge and Sovereign Power

Master Xun underscores the importance of common knowledge of the ruler when it refutes approaches to governance that propounded secrecy as a means to rule. Many texts link political power and secrecy. *Master Lao* (*Laozi* 老子) is probably the best known of these, and it says, "The state has sharp tools, which cannot be shown to others" 國有利器, 不可示人. This is surely related to its well-known recommendation to keep the populace ignorant. Other texts advocate secrecy, too, and refer with approval to *Master Lao* in this context.⁴⁹ *Master Xun* flatly rejects such arguments:

> The vulgar persuaders of our age say the way of rulership benefits from secrecy. That is not so. The ruler is the song-leader of the people and the gnomon of those below. The others hear him sing and respond; they watch the gnomon and move. But if the singer is quiet then the people will not respond, and if

the gnomon is hidden then those below will not move. 世俗之為說者曰, 主道利周. 是不然. 主者, 民之唱也; 上者, 下之儀也. 彼將聽唱而應, 視儀而動. 唱默則民無應也, 儀隱則下無動也.⁵⁰

Master Xun calls confusion about the identity of the monarch one of the dangers of secrecy: keeping the ruler secret would result in the chaos that it warns against.⁵¹

Thus, no later than the third century BCE, political thinkers recognized that the people had to know about their ruler in order for him to rule. Such conceptions treated the leader as a focal point for coordinating cooperation, and to be effective in this way, a leader must be a matter of common knowledge among the led. Only this would lead to what *Master Xun* calls a close relationship between ruler and ruled, which in turn was the sole route to real stability.⁵² The First Emperor of Qin certainly seems to have taken recommendations like this to heart. Nevertheless, the doctrine of stealth leadership did not die out with the establishment of the empire but lasted into the Han and beyond.⁵³

Projecting the Ruler's Political Self

Conceptions of rule that focused on public knowledge of the ruler did not advocate publicizing his actual person across the whole realm: the sovereign's physical image was not important. What these texts propose is the universal projection—creating common knowledge—of the ruler's political self and, by extension, the united polity he ruled. The "Ritual's Changes" ("Li yun" 禮運) chapter of *Record of Ritual* indicates how this would function when it says, "Governance is the means by which the lord hides himself" 政者, 君之所以藏身也. The second-century commentator Zheng Xuan 鄭玄 (127–200) clarifies, "'Hiding' means that while he shines brilliantly beyond the court, his form is not shown—like the spirits of the sun, moon, and stars" 藏謂輝光於外而形體不見, 若日月星辰之神.⁵⁴

This hiding was not secrecy but rather the eclipsing of the individual person by the projection of a political identity. The monarch's body was not seen, but his quality would make itself known at a distance, like the light of celestial spirits, and so be widely perceived. *Mr. Lü's Annals* expresses the same combination of obscurity and eminence through prescriptive description of antiquity: "Among the ancients, [the ruler's] person was hidden but his achievements were evident; his form was at rest but his reputation resplendent. . . . He benefited the entire realm, but the people did not recognize him" 古之人, 身隱而功著, 形息而名彰, 說通而化奮, 利行乎天下而民不識.⁵⁵ It was not the physical form of the good ruler that would achieve fame: his face would remain unknown. Fame would attach instead to a political being constituted by his achievements and reputation.

As noted earlier, *Master Lao* recommends keeping aspects of the means for rule secret. Nevertheless, *Master Lao* also advocates common knowledge of the ruler: in its counterintuitive style, it predicts that keeping the ruler dark and clandestine would make him manifest below, while overt self-promotion would work counter to its desired effect.⁵⁶ *Master Lao* names common knowledge among the populace of the ruler's existence as a characteristic of the best governance—indeed, this is the *only* characteristic it specifies: "Under supreme rule, those below know [the ruler] exists. Next best to that is that they are close to him, or praise him. Next best to that is that they fear him, or scorn him" 太上, 下知有之; 其次, 親之豫之; 其次, 畏之侮之.⁵⁷ Better than closeness to or acclaim for the ruler is simple universal awareness that he is there. *Master Lao* argues against propaganda, not common knowledge, which has premier place. Another text attributes a comparable conception to Confucius himself: "I have heard that the Great Way cannot be hidden. I say, when the lord expresses it in the court and practices it in the state, there will be none among the people of the entire state who does not know of it" 丘聞大道不隱. 丘言之, 君發之于朝, 行之于國, 一國之人莫不知.⁵⁸ The ruler's governance was the projection of his political self and ideally would be known everywhere in a state of perfect common knowledge.

Projecting Authority

This projection of the political self was to occur through communications media, though naturally not media in the modern sense. Rather than modern technological networks, early texts propose turning existing systems to this purpose.

Many texts endorse the general proposition that communication was necessary for creating and maintaining political power. *The Book of Lord Shang*, for example, describes publicity's potential for effecting political power, saying, "Authority uses one to get ten, and uses reputation to attain reality" 威以一取十, 以聲取實.⁵⁹ This recalls Chwe's argument that making a strong claim to power known will tend to make that power real, and a reputation for rule will lead to rulership. Authority does not work without coercion in Lord Shang's formulation, but coercion is only a part of a process that ultimately relies on communication to achieve its effect.

The "Employing the People" ("Yong min" 用民) chapter of *Mr. Lü's Annals* says that an effective ruler will be able to project his leadership beyond the scope of his formal authority, and will be "able to employ those he does not possess" 能用非其有, even to the point of attracting the subjects of another ruler. An exclusive reliance on authority, on command, though, is impossible: The ruler "must have authority, but it is insufficient to rely on that alone" 威不可無有, 而不足專恃. More important—and preceding authority—was communication of the ruler's proper desire to benefit the common people.[60]

The primary concern of *Master Han Fei* was preserving and extending the power of the sovereign relative to officialdom, especially the high ministers of state.[61] The text speaks often of the "two handles" (*erbing* 二柄) of rule: reward and punishment. And it says that if the ruler were to leave control of the "two handles" in his ministers' hands, the people would give their respect and loyalty to those ministers, weakening the ruler's power. This reflects that these two things functioned as points of contact between the commoners and the central government and at the same time as means for communicating about the ruler's power. *Master Han Fei* argues that since the common people were subject to manipulation through punishment and reward, it was necessary to ensure the populace *knew* the two handles were in the ruler's hands alone. The sovereign's ability to derive power from the system of rewards and punishments depended on the population's perception that he was responsible for both positive and negative sanctions.[62] The monarch had to communicate this social power, not as an end in itself but as part of the persuasive apparatus that worked to convince and keep convincing the common population that he was in charge.[63]

Master Han Fei proposes systematizing this so that, "if the important subjects act properly [and are rewarded], they respect the ruler; if the commoners achieve merit [and are rewarded], they attribute the benefit to the sovereign" 大臣有行則尊君, 百姓有功則利上.[64] *Master Guan* makes a similar point concerning common knowledge of the fact that the power to reward and punish originated with the ruler.[65]

The Book of Lord Shang predicts that these perceptions of the ruler would penetrate all of society, even becoming part of popular culture through incorporation into songs.[66] The processes of reward and punishment did not function as ends in themselves; they were part of the ruler's publicity apparatus, a way for him to project his political self. This connects these interests with the broader emphasis on communication and creating common knowledge among the population as a condition for rule.

Ritual Communication

Another of the most important means for communication with the broader public in early China was ritual. Chwe, Rappaport, and others' ideas about ritual as communication tally well with conceptions of ritual current in early China. The text "Black Robe" ("Zi yi" 緇衣), for instance, treats the leader's clothing and ceremonial deportment as ways to communicate with the populace in order to ensure that they would know to whom they owed their gratitude and obedience. "Black Robe" emphasizes the visual function of these media. An excavated version of the text dating to the Warring States period reads, "If the sovereign can be seen from a distance and recognized, and underlings can be sorted and ranked, then the ruler will not be doubted by his subjects, nor will the subjects be confused about their ruler" 為上可望而知也, 為下可類而等也, 則君不疑於其臣, 臣不惑於其君矣.[67] The canonical commentary is that of Kong Yingda 孔穎達 (574–648), who explains these lines as referring to the external expression of interior states.[68] But the text itself does not seem to support this reading. Rather, it conveys that recognition of the ruler and others holding high rank and means for classifying those in subordinate positions are of great importance.

Writing in the first decades of Han rule, Jia Yi quoted the same two passages. He attributes them to Confucius, and his discussion makes it clear he takes them to refer to the easy visual differentiation of status.[69] Elsewhere, Jia Yi argues for the differentiation of rank in every aspect of life, insisting on the utility of standard status markers and sumptuary privileges to set those in high rank above their inferiors in all respects. These markers and privileges were to be enforced by laws punishing any deviance from the norms—above or below each person's station. Jia Yi furthermore says that the way to realize this hierarchy is to institute laws to make them known through repetition. The common people, then, would comprehend the signs and perquisites of hierarchical position.[70]

Jia Yi understands perception and recognition of rank as predicated on two things. First, he assumes that people of lower status would directly observe their superiors and that the ability to know the status of those superiors was necessary. He also assumes that subordinates would be able to interpret garb and insignia, which in turn would require these things to be common knowledge. Jia Yi proposes creating laws and establishing officials that would not only enforce norms but also propagate information about the hierarchies of dress and insignia. He promises this system could itself bring social and governmental stability. This is in keeping with his conception of systems of governance generally, which he believed would run more or less automatically, if properly instituted—itself a conception carried over from Warring States times.[71]

Writers in pre-imperial China recognized ritual as a highly effective medium for communication. *Zuo's Commentary* (*Zuozhuan* 左傳) puts forth ritual as a means for enacting governance, which would serve as a defense for the ruler. It links this back to secrecy and publicity, asserting that ritual extends the political self but guards the person, something I will return to in chapter 5.[72] *Master Xun*, too, treats ritual as a tool by which to effect governance: "Ritual is the cart-puller of governance; if one does not rule by means of ritual, proper government cannot be put into practice" 禮者, 政之輓; 為政不以禮, 政不行矣.[73] "Ritual's Changes" gives an idea of how ritual worked to project the ruler's political being in the form of a description of the past: "[The sage rulers] were all punctilious concerning rituals. They used them to demonstrate dutifulness and perfect trustworthiness, to demonstrate when someone had made an error, model humaneness, enjoin proper yielding, and display constancy to the people" 未有不謹於禮者也, 以著其義, 以考其信, 著有過, 刑(:形)仁, 講讓, 示民有常.[74]

The prevalence of sight-oriented expressions reflects that in many ways rituals were a visual medium. Similar ideas were also expressed in terms of sound.[75] But however it occurred, the goal was the same: creating a situation in which all inhabitants of the realm knew about the ruler. Each person was not only to know about the single sovereign but would also know that others knew. There would be common knowledge of the ruler, and ritual was a means to create this. Hence the second-century BCE compendium of political philosophy *The Master of Huainan* (*Huainanzi* 淮南子) asserts, "The ancients . . . structured ritual to suffice for supporting reality and conveying meaning" 古者 . . . 故制禮足以佐實喻意而已矣.[76]

One common but difficult concept in early Chinese thought is relevant here, and that is *de* 德, often translated "virtue." David Nivison has suggested *de* is better understood as "gratitude credit," the feeling that one owes something to another, typically a superior; in a political context this is usually willing obedience to a ruler or other superior. What is seen and later portrayed as virtue was in fact the capacity for evoking this sort of willing obedience.[77]

Although *de* was intangible, it was transmitted through action and influence rather than speech, communicating without words with the goal of persuading the people.[78] "Black Robe" links *de* together with clothing as a means to effect political unification: "If the one who leads the people does not vary in dress, has constancy in his actions, and thereby brings his people together, then the people will owe him alone gratitude credit" 長民者, 衣服不貳, 從容有常, 以齊其民, 則民德壹.[79] Ritually prescribed and legally enforced clothing was central to the function of the political system. It communicated the being of ruler as ruler and enabled him to act as a focal point. According to *Master Xun*, if the ruler were able to make his quality widely known, then "the realm would go to him, like a cicada goes to the bright flame" 天下歸之, 若蟬之歸明火也.[80] *Master Xun* counts the ruler's reputation as one of the principle means for winning the support and willing compliance of the populace and says that a ruler's reputation, if properly established, could spread into neighboring lands to expand his territory without bloodshed.[81]

Change and Constancy

Systemic change and constancy had complex roles in early Chinese concepts of governance. Many have argued that the mainstream of early Chinese thought was generally opposed to change, an understanding based on readings that did not sufficiently consider historical context. Michael Puett has shown that attitudes varied and were linked to broader philosophical debates, not an all-encompassing conservatism.[82]

As noted in chapter 2, change is an important way to create common knowledge. It is one of my core contentions that the Qin dynasty succeeded in creating a united polity because their changes to common practice created common knowledge of the dynasty. Texts that came to be associated with Ru 儒 (commonly translated "Confucian") thought proposed that some constants could be changed without affecting the underlying moral values. One such text is "The Great Tradition" ("Da zhuan" 大傳), now part of *Record of Ritual*. It indicates without ambiguity that a sage ruler's governance will begin with numerous changes:

> Establishing weights and measures, revising the ritual systems, altering the calendar, changing the colors [of imperial draught and sacrificial animals], distinguishing the types of pennants, distinguishing ritual utensils and military equipment, and differentiating official clothing. These are things that one may change with the people. 立權度量, 考文章, 改正朔, 易服色, 殊徽號, 異器械, 別衣服, 此其所得與民變革者也.[83]

Context makes it clear that these changes are to come with the establishment of a new regime—especially that of the ideal monarch. Of immediate relevance to the discussion here is the great degree to which the Qin dynastic founder's actions at the start of their reigns accorded with the things on this list.

Important thinkers in the fourth and third centuries BCE insisted change was necessary. Without a doubt, the best-known arguments in this respect are found in *The Book of Lord Shang*, the first chapter of which is a discussion of "Changing the Law" ("Bian fa" 變法). It asserts that the only requirement necessary for altering established practice is that it would strengthen the state or benefit the people. The arguments are based on differences among the rituals of the prehistorical dynasties.[84] Other thinkers also made this sort of assertion, too. *Master Guan* tells us that the paradigmatic rulers of antiquity differed from each other and had good reason to do so: "Their paths were not necessarily the same, not because they purposely contradicted each other, but because each followed his time and changed, acting on the basis of common practice" 迹行不必同, 非故相反也, 皆隨時而變, 因俗而動.[85] *Master Han Fei* asserts the advisability of change and expands on the link between it and successful rule:

> There are no constants in ruling the people: proper rule alone is the law. If law and the times turn together, there will be rule; if rule is appropriate to the generation, there will be success. ... But if the times shift and governance does not, there will be chaos. ... Thus, when the sage rules the people, law shifts with the times. 治民無常, 唯治為法. 法與時轉則治, 治與世宜則有功 ... 時移而(治)[法]不易者亂, 能(治)眾而禁不變者削. 故聖人之治民也, 法與時移.[86]

In its discussion of *Master Lao*, *Master Han Fei* links changing to follow the times with the teachings of non-active governance, which argue the ruler should be simultaneously unseen and renowned.[87]

There was tension between the importance of change and the risks of too much change; a successful ruler had to ensure alterations were not excessive. *Master Guan* calls attention to this danger:

> If, once weights and measures have been systematized, you shift them again; or, when penal law has been put in place, you alter it; then even if rewards are weighty, the people will not

be motivated, and even if capital crimes are many, the people will not be afraid. 度量已制，又遷之，刑法已錯，又移之，如是，則慶賞雖重，民不勸也. 殺戮雖繁，民不畏也.⁸⁸

There are two sides to this. First is that repeated changes to weights and measures or legal systems will have negative consequences. Yet *Master Guan* does not reject the establishment of new institutions under a new king, as proposed in "The Great Tradition"; it rejects repeated changes.

Another text, *Master Shen* (*Shenzi* 申子) describes an idealized past in a similar way: "When the Yellow Emperor ruled the realm, he established laws and did not change them, which made the people delight in his laws" 黃帝之治天下，置法而不變，使民安樂其法也.⁸⁹ But these acts should be performed just once. As *Master Guan* puts it, "Do not make repeated changes; this will destroy your success" 毋數變易，是為敗成.⁹⁰ *Master Han Fei* also acknowledges that too frequently altering the laws will not benefit the population, citing the famous dictum from *Master Lao*, "Ruling a large state is like cooking a small fish" 治大國者若烹小鮮, which can be spoiled by too frequent turning.⁹¹

Arguments opposing change to shared practices often reflect the communicative powers of those changes. For example, "The King's System" ("Wang zhi" 王制), which was incorporated into *Record of Ritual*, lists a variety of innovations that could "make the masses doubtful" and "disorder governance." This includes things like changing names, introducing new technology, and asserting supernatural agency. It specifies that the ruler uses these things for the benefit of his rule, as a means to unify the people. Their alteration or promulgation by anyone except the ruler (or his delegate) represented an attempt to undermine that authority. Since this was the case, "The King's System" says that laws enforcing these standards required strict enforcement without exception.⁹²

The list of activities "The King's System" forbids in this context does not stop with those I have mentioned. It also encompasses a variety of actions in the context of commercial transaction: it forbids the sale of ritual vessels from imperial lineage temples, military arms, and utensils and cloth that did not adhere to official, standard dimensions. The last would ensure that such standards would be a matter of common knowledge. Recovered legal documents confirm this sort of regulation was in place under Qin and Western Han law.⁹³

The arguments in favor of controlled change in certain contexts did not lose their relevance with the establishment of empire; according to Puett, they carried over into the Han times.⁹⁴ And as I discuss in chapter

6, Western Han rulers made changes to the legal system in order to communicate with the broader population, demonstrating that people in early times indeed recognized the power of altering systems to create common knowledge with political effects. Change remained a highly effective way to create common knowledge among the general population.

Different Levels of Understanding in Different Social Groups

Communication concerning the ruler and his governance was supposed to reach the whole realm, but this does not mean that every member of the public would have the same level of understanding. As one would expect in a situation of mass communication, the majority was expected to comprehend only uncomplicated and unambiguous information.

Generally speaking, even as they advocated the creation of common knowledge for political purposes, early thinkers knew that the degree of knowledge possessed by various social classes and groups would differ. The "Essay on Ritual" ("Li lun" 禮論) in *Master Xun* makes this point with regard to ritual:

> As for the offerings: . . . The sage fully understands them, the scholar-gentleman serenely carries them out, the official takes them as his responsibility, and the commoners have them as their set customs. Gentlemen take them as the Way of man, while commoners take them as serving the spirits of the dead. 祭者. . . . 聖人明知之, 士君子安行之, 官人以為守, 百姓以成俗. 其在君子以為人道也, 其在百姓以為鬼事也.[95]

This argues that ritual, of which the offerings were a subset, was a human creation: vital, and the work of sages, but artificial.[96] By saying here that the gentleman understood offerings as a human matter, *Master Xun* advocates that point of view. Yet it does not dismiss the understandings of the common population, who understood them as care of the dead. *Master Xun* acknowledged and accepted that wholly divergent understandings of a particular matter could exist among different groups, without undermining its value.[97]

A similar conception existed in the realm of law. Many thinkers acknowledged that ordinary people would not be in a position to grasp legal subtleties. But the conclusion was not to exclude them from legal knowledge; instead, it was necessary that the law be designed so that they could understand it. Only then would law serve its deterrent purpose. *The Book of Lord Shang* says, for example, "If the legal system is clear, then the people will fear punishment" 法制明則民畏刑 and goes on to describe the problems that would result if it was not clear.[98] *The Book of Lord Shang* advocates a legal system that actively communicates the law, including answering questions about it posed by commoners, all with the goal of creating common knowledge: "Thus, among the officers and people of the realm, there will be no one who does not know the law—the officers clearly understanding it, the people knowing the laws and edicts" 故天下之吏民, 無不知法者, 吏明知, 民知法令也.[99] *Master Han Fei* also argued for readily comprehensible law, which it proposed incorporating into a system of governance centered on ease of communication: "The enlightened ruler's signs are easy to see, so they are seldom set up; his instructions are easy to understand, so his words are put to use; his laws are easy to follow, so his commands are carried out" 明主之表易見, 故約立; 其教易知, 故言用; 其法易為, 故令行.[100] *Master Han Fei* goes on to explain that, combined with a lack of self-interest on the part of the ruler, easily understood governmental directives will lead to social order that comes from the population itself, without requiring coercion; in other words, they will bring cooperation.

Elsewhere *Master Han Fei* addresses the need to balance intelligibility with completeness, taking account of the needs of ordinary intellectual capabilities, while reining in those whose superior abilities might make them a danger to rule.[101] A like notion appears in recovered Qin legal materials, and the early history *Historian's Records* even quotes the almost-universally decried Second Emperor of Qin as saying, "If the ruler gives importance to making the law clear, then those below will not dare do wrong" 主重明法, 下不敢為非.[102] Later texts show the same idea carried over into Western Han times.[103]

The interest in simple and comprehensible communication from the ruler and government may have resulted from the practical difficulties inherent in getting complex messages across. "Black Robe" uses silk as a metaphor to portray the diminishing levels of detail possible when a message from the ruler was disseminated: "If the words of the king are as fine as silk thread, when promulgated they become like string. If the words of the king are like string, when promulgated they become like rope" 王言如絲, 其出如綸. 王言如綸, 其出如綍.[104] The fact that a message is—or becomes in the course of transmission—simple, very clear, and/or lacking detail does not mean it is insignificant. Complexity does not equal significance, nor simplicity unimportance. Common knowledge generation does not require detail.

In the context of the unified realm, whether at the theoretical level or when the ideal was realized, the most important message to communicate was the simplest: the existence of the single ruler. As *Master Lao* put it, the common population should simply know the supreme monarch was there, with all the political unity and duty that would entail.

Consulting with the People

Despite their interest in winning the people's cooperation, early thinkers never proposed bringing the common population directly into government.[105] As mentioned at the beginning of this chapter, it has been argued that the common people were excluded from political decision-making beginning in early imperial times. I suggest that although the thinkers deprecate public opinion in certain respects, they in fact argue only for excluding specific aspects of it from policy decisions. They did not propose ignoring the common people's opinions, but insisted the ruler had to look further than an ordinary person, to see eventual good that would counteract negative possibilities in the interim.

The most famous rejection of including common people in policy decisions comes in *The Book of Lord Shang*, which says, "One cannot consider beginnings with the common people, but one can delight in success with them" 民不可與慮始, 而可與樂成. The context of this assertion is a putative court discussion: Lord Xiao of Qin 秦孝公 (d. 338 BCE) wants to change the laws and rituals of his state but fears that the population would "discuss him" 議我, implying such discussion could be only negative. Shang Yang urges Lord Xiao to act with decision and to work for change. His well-known pronouncement comes here, and he urges Lord Xiao to plan for the future, not only the present.

Although the discussion quickly moves on to other things, it is clear that the commoners are excluded because some matters Shang Yang believes necessary for rule will be, at least in the short term, unwelcome. Nevertheless, over time, he argues, these will bring stability and order. Tellingly, Shang Yang never rejects the importance of the people's opinions; he just insists they are not a suitable basis for planning. In the end he acknowledges that the ruler's reputation is one of the ways that authority translates into real power.[106]

Master Xun goes so far as to say that the people can *easily* be unified, provided the ruler works with the Way. But the people cannot be permitted to join in deliberations, nor should the ruler allow himself to be swayed by the people's criticisms. Nevertheless, the good estimation of the populace remains the ultimate mark of a ruler's success: "[The ruler] who wins the praise of the common people is truly glorious" 得百姓之譽者榮.[107]

Mr. Lü's Annals contains a chapter entitled "Delighting in Success ("Le cheng" 樂成), the title of which derives from the above *Book of Lord Shang* quotation. Both the title and content of "Delighting in Success" show it to be a commentary on *The Book of Lord Shang*'s arguments against bringing commoners into policy planning. It records narratives about men in positions of political leadership whose actions were initially criticized by the common population for being harsh or making onerous demands but who were later vindicated because of the good they achieved. The manner of vindication is significant, for it is the praise of the people that proves success.[108]

This shows that the populace's opinion remained the ultimately decisive factor, but the ruler needed the discernment to see what would benefit the population in the future. This long view would sometimes lead the ruler to temporarily ignore the voice of the common population. One ground for this was the mismatch between what people want in the short term and what in fact serves the commonweal, a point that texts like *Master Han Fei* make. From this perspective, the ruler cannot become caught up in common opinion. He must make decisions like a parent caring for a child who opposes its wishes for its own good: he must be "father and mother of the people."[109]

The most evident example of this is the penal system. *Master Han Fei* deems harsh penalties necessary for successful governance, even if the populace dislikes them. A sage sovereign must be ready to go against the common mood. In the same way, *Master Han Fei* presents getting caught up in the praises of contemporaries as a danger to proper rule: The ruler's goal is neither to win short-term praise nor avoid criticism but to bring benefit to his people. The ultimate basis for evaluating his success or failure lies with the latter.[110]

Another perspective, perhaps cynical but certainly familiar, indicates that people were (and perhaps are) inclined to complain no matter what, so trying to heed their every wish could not lead to success. "Black Robe" cites the text "Jun Ya" 君雅 (named for a person in the text) to the effect that the populace will complain of heat and rain in the summer, just as it moans of cold in winter. Yet "Black Robe" immediately goes on to quote "Jun Chen" 君陳 (also named for a person in the text), which recommends, "Let your actions be planned by the troops and match the words of the many" 出入自爾師虞, 庶言同.[111] Both of these texts are found in chapters of the transmitted *Book of Documents* (*Shangshu* 尚書) that scholars believe to be spurious, but their presence in the excavated "Black Robe" manuscripts confirms their early provenance, if not originally as part of *Book of Documents*. These texts suggest that what appears like a potential contradiction is best understood as acknowledgment that although the common population holds great power and its views must be respected, not every grumble is equally worthy of note. A successful ruler needs discernment.

Beyond the universality of complaining, another part of this could be what *The Book of Lord Shang* refers to when it says that rulers with unusual plans—including things like changing the laws and rituals—are sure to encounter criticism. There need be no further reason for this than an innate conservatism, a reluctance to change. There is also the practical fact, alluded to in *Master Xun* and *Mr. Lü's Annals*, that many mouths lead to gossip, which can obscure ability or lack thereof; thus the ruler must sift through the mass of opinion carefully.[112]

Considered as a group, these passages indicate that, while each would limit the people's involvement in government and the weight given to their opinion in specific respects, a blanket rejection of popular influence was not intended. The valuation of the populace was important, but a leader had to be ready to look beyond the immediate. Given the weight they placed on cooperation, these thinkers clearly knew that it was necessary to communicate with and persuade the population, in order to secure their active support. These thinkers argued for rejecting only specific kinds of negative opinion that focused on short-term results.

It follows from this that despite initial appearances, these passages imply affirmation of popular opinion's place in political consideration: dismissing only one part of it confirms the value of the rest. Rather than arguing for rejection of all common opinion, these texts argue for farsighted leadership. Ultimately the successful ruler still had to win the active support of all levels of society to succeed. As *Master Guan* says of the ideal sovereign, "He is the one with whom the lords join and from whom the common folk derive benefit; for this reason the realm makes him king" 諸侯之所與也，百姓之所利也，是故天下王之.[113] In subsequent chapters I discuss the means by which the Qin created common knowledge of themselves across the realm, shaping the population's perceptions and bringing central rulership into being.

Conclusion

Thinkers in early China were aware of the necessity of cooperation for a successful society. Despite proclaiming the sole power and unique position of the emperor and the superiority of the upper classes, they also recognized the power of the people and the impossibility of coercion as the means for durable and stable governance. They realized the central position of common knowledge for social function; their rhetoric of imperial supremacy can be understood concretely in terms of focal points that worked to resolve coordination problems. Aside from shedding light on the political thought of early imperial times, these conceptions challenge analysis of early Chinese society as functioning primarily or only as a top-down, coercive hierarchy.

Problems of communication, especially establishing common knowledge of the sole ruler, were thus central problems of the Qin dynasty, and this was known to be the case before unification. The Qin rulers, especially the First Emperor and the members of his entourage, responded brilliantly—so brilliantly that their creations are still communicating today. They employed means of mass communication that penetrated throughout the realm.

Yet they did not create these means out of whole cloth. The Qin rulers actively and creatively adapted existing practices and ideas to their situation. The Qin built upon concepts and processes and applied them to the problems they faced. In the rest of this book, I examine important examples of these, treating them as case studies. The first example is that of the standardization of weights and measures under the First Emperor of Qin, the topic of the next chapter.

4

Mass Communication and Standardization

In 208 BCE, Li Si 李斯 (d. 208 BCE), the First Emperor's former advisor and chancellor, wrote from prison to the then-reigning Second Emperor. In this famous letter, Li Si lists what he sarcastically calls his seven crimes against the Qin dynasty. Each item is in fact a putative contribution to the dynasty's success, and Li Si had indeed played a major role in the unification of the realm. Number five on this list of accomplishments reads:

> I changed the engraved marks [on measuring instruments], standardized units of measure and the ritual system, promulgated these in the realm, and thereby established the name of Qin. 更剋畫，平斗斛度量文章，布之天下，以樹秦之名.[1]

"Name" here could be understood as something like fame, and certainly that sense is at work. But I think Li Si's claim is best understood more literally. For in a real sense, the changes he refers to served to "establish the name of Qin."

In this chapter I examine the change Li Si refers to, the establishment of a unified weights and measures across the realm, and the communication connected with that. Using concepts presented in chapters 2 and 3, I argue that this change is best understood in terms of communication and common knowledge creation, which facilitated cooperation at the level of the empire. Common knowledge also helps explain the variety of changes and standardizations the First Emperor commanded by arguing they helped to communicate the message that there was a new ruler and drawing the people's attention to his presence in their daily lives. By making the common people aware of his power, the First Emperor created common knowledge of himself, simultaneously compelling a new order in small matters and promoting obedience in large.

I begin with a discussion of the standardization and the text of the edict that commanded the change. Scholars and archaeologists have recovered and described a variety of relics bearing this edict, especially weights and measuring vessels, from places distributed across the whole of the Qin empire. I also consider the connections that exist between those inscriptions and others from the same time. Furthermore, there were important precedents in the centuries before unification for the Qin dynasty's publicity blitz, in the form of reproduced texts and materials that communicated at a distance. Yet the Qin dynasty made large advances over earlier techniques, and the Qin rulers won corresponding success by building on earlier media. As I show, previous scholars' explanations of these matters offer important interpretive possibilities. However, analyzing the standardization as communication with the goal of creating politically effective common knowledge represents an advance on prior conceptions, as it better explains how the change worked and links it with other changes and accomplishments around the same time.

The Standardizations

In 221 BCE, the first year he ruled the entire realm, the First Emperor standardized a number of practices that had formerly differed across geopolitical areas, including units of measure. Prior to this, each of the polities that formed Warring States–era China used a different system. That uniformity within each polity resulted from a process of replacing still earlier, local units with state-level standards. The Qin did away with the others and instituted their own nationwide. Different types of scales also existed, dividing at the very least into two general styles, northern and southern, and the standardization of units of measure brought with it the institution of a single type of scale.[2]

Shang Yang had implemented a uniform set of measures in the state of Qin in 350 BCE. One well-known artifact—a rectangular bronze scoop measure—reflects this change: it bears an inscription that dates its creation to 344 BCE and names Shang Yang as responsible for the new system. The volume of this measure accords with the system instituted in 221 BCE, and the command instituting the new system at that time was added alongside the earlier. The measure and the changes it embodies show that the First Emperor's extension of these across the realm was part of both a larger trend toward standardization and a program specific to Qin underway well over a century before. Paleographic materials confirm the Qin enforced the new system by law.[3]

When the First Emperor decreed a single system for use in the whole country, it was not something newly invented but rather that of the state of Qin, which subsequently persisted into Han times.[4] The 221 BCE command instituting the new system comes to us in the following form:

> In the twenty-sixth year of his reign, the emperor unified the lords of the realm, the common people had great peace, and he established the title of emperor. Now he commands chancellors Wei Zhuang and Wang Wan: "As for the laws and units of measure that are disparate or doubtful, in all cases clarify and unify them." 廿六年皇帝盡并兼天下諸侯, 黔首大安, 立號為皇帝. 乃詔丞相狀綰, 灋度量則不壹(歉)[嫌]疑者, 皆明壹之.[5]

This text announces the success of the First Emperor over his rivals in unifying the realm, proclaims the beneficial peace he brought to the common people, and decrees the standardization of the system of measures as the next step in his political program. The command to institute the standardization is given to the chancellors but made known to many more by publicizing the text.

The command's phrasing makes use of vocabulary the First Emperor had just previously instituted. He had, for example, formulated his own title ("emperor," *huangdi* 皇帝). This was not a completely new invention, but that and its long use afterward do not lessen the title's novelty at the time.[6] The text also uses a newly sanctioned designation for commoners (*qianshou* 黔首); although this, too, was not a new word and the shift to it was not immediate, its use was expanded and systematized at this point in time.[7] A recently recovered Qin list of terms to be avoided and their mandated substitutes attests to the vocabulary change; it specifies such things as referring to the sovereign as "emperor" and not "king."[8] The terminology used in the edict to describe the First Emperor's former rivals, the erstwhile rulers of the other polities, is also telling. They had called themselves kings for more than a century before unification, and the First Emperor elsewhere referred to them as kings and lords.[9] But here they are collectively just the "the lords." That retroactively made them subordinate to the emperor in the time before the conquest, a message that served to legitimate the unification.

The Second Emperor, in the first year of his own reign (209 BCE), supplemented the First Emperor's message with one of his own—an addition longer than the text it was appended to:

> In the first year [of his reign, the Second Emperor] commanded chancellors Li Si and Feng Quji (馮去疾): "The First Emperor

established standard measures, and there are inscriptions concerning this. Now I have taken on the title [of emperor], and the inscriptions do not refer to the First Emperor by name. In the distant future, it could seem like [the standardization] was carried out by the successor, which would not match [the First Emperor's] achieved merit and splendid virtue. Inscribe this proclamation to the left of the previous inscription to let there be no doubts." 元年制詔丞相斯去疾, 灋度量盡始皇帝為之, 皆有刻辭焉. 今襲號而刻辭不稱始皇帝, 其于久遠也, 如後嗣為之者, 不稱成功盛德. 刻此詔故刻左, 使毋.[10]

Although there are numerous objects bearing only the First Emperor's command, there is no weight or measure that appears intended to have only the second inscription. An anomalous example shows that this was deliberate. One recovered weight has an embossed (and thus necessarily cast-in) inscription of the Second Emperor's command together with an inscribed version of the First Emperor's. This indicates the 221 BCE text was added after casting and reflects that the Second Emperor's addendum was incomplete without the First Emperor's text and so only a supplement to it.[11]

Artifacts with Inscriptions Concerning the Standardization

Neither the First nor the Second Emperor's text is found in *Historian's Records* or any other dynastic history, and *Historian's Records* makes only passing mention of the standardization.[12] Both texts have been known since premodern times from a passage in a medieval work that records that a weight bearing the two inscriptions was recovered at Chang'an 長安 (Shaanxi) in 582.[13] Other premodern texts also mention inscribed Qin weights.[14] Modern archaeologists have recovered many examples of these and related objects from Shaanxi, and in Gansu, Hebei, Jiangsu, Jilin, Liaoning, Inner Mongolia, Shandong, and Shanxi.[15] This wide geographical dispersion reflects the scope of the edict's dissemination and the resources the Qin invested in spreading it across the realm.

The command exists in inscriptions on a large number of objects and in a variety of forms, from a ladle to the weights and measuring vessels that form the core of the discussion here.[16] Some of these are preunification objects, which were reinscribed with the edict. I mentioned one of these earlier: the bronze measure from 350 BCE that bore Shang Yang's name. Another famous example of this sort is a late Warring States–era weight recovered from an area near the Qin capital in May 1964.[17] The weight was cast with an inscription containing the name Gaonu 高奴 (Shaanxi), a place located more than 300 km from where the weight was found. Both the First and the Second Emperors' edicts were added to the weight. Apparently it had been recalled from Gaonu to be inspected and marked with the Second Emperor's edict, but the breakdown of Qin government prevented its return.[18]

Archaeologists have recovered far more examples of objects dating to after the Qin unification and bearing one or both of the Qin inscriptions. One catalog of bronze measuring vessels lists two rectangular and nine oval examples with only the 221 BCE proclamation and two oval measures bearing both. Weights with the text of one or both edicts are numerous. One study names some fifty-eight examples bearing the First Emperor's edict of 221 BCE, two examples that first had the 221 BCE edict alone and the Second Emperor's edict of 209 BCE added later, and seven examples where both texts were inscribed at the same time.[19] All these weights are for steelyard-type scales, and all have or had built-in loops of various sorts for suspension, including half-rings and recesses. There are also cast iron weights, some of which are inscribed with the 221 BCE edict and others with mounted bronze plaques containing the command. The text is identical in nearly all cases, although the division of the characters into lines and sections varies.[20]

These plaques are a subset of a larger type called "proclamation plaques" (*zhaoban* 詔版), which have been found in different forms. In addition to those examples that were found still mounted on weights, a number have been recovered separate from other objects; others are loose but were clearly made to be attached to other items.[21] This medium is especially noteworthy because the plaques, in themselves, serve no concrete utility and can only have been created to communicate. The fact that they were mounted onto other objects shows the importance the Qin put on adding this content.

Zhao Ruiyun 趙瑞雲 and Zhao Xiaorong 趙曉榮 divide the proclamation plaques into three types and argue that all such objects served to communicate their contents to a broad audience. The most commonly recovered proclamation plaques are small rectangles of durable material, usually bronze, though some are of pottery and a few of iron, about 5–8 cm wide by 6–11 cm high and about 0.2–0.3 cm thick. A recovered artifact reflects another type: It consists of a piece of bronze, roughly square and with rounded edges, inscribed with the whole of the 209 BCE proclamation text on one side and with a ring for a lanyard on the other. This was clearly intended to be a portable version of the inscription, and its similarity to a carved seal may be more than chance, as researchers believe it served to replicate the text by means of impression.[22]

The third type is the "signboard-style" proclamation plaque, which is known only from two examples.[23] The original, oversized bronze tablets were cut up for reuse, and what had been the back was inscribed with the text of the 221 BCE proclamation.[24] The two examples consist of brief sections of text preserved on the repurposed pieces' reverse sides. Because only these fragments remain, the exact dimensions of the signboard-style proclamation plaques are unknown. However, based on the size of the text on one example, researchers estimate it must have originally been some 30 cm by 65 cm. The researchers also believe the larger plaques suggest processes of mechanical reproduction of the text in oversized characters.[25] While this conjecture is appealing, there are no examples of reproductions that could have been made with them.

Nevertheless, we do have numerous examples of objects with inscriptions demonstrably created through processes of mechanical reproduction. Archaeologists have found many pottery vessels, both partial and complete, bearing the text of the First Emperor's edict formed by a series of seal impressions. Only five of the sixty-three known examples of pottery fragments bearing the text of the First Emperor's edict recovered before 1949 have carved inscriptions. All others were formed from seal impressions, ten seals with four graphs on each, and the outlines of the seals themselves are clearly visible on the recovered pieces. Many more such fragments have been found since 1949.[26] There seems to have been a high incidence of errors in the edict texts inscribed on pottery, and I believe that mechanical reproduction served, at least in part, to prevent copying mistakes under conditions of mass production.[27]

Making impressions in wet clay for various purposes was the oldest use of seals. The Qin put seal impressions to work in manufacture, using them, for example, to track the products of particular workshops in order to assure quality. But the promulgation of the edict of 221 BCE is the earliest known use of sequenced seal impressions to reproduce a longer text. As such, it has been suggested that the origins of printing lie here.[28]

While most examples of pottery vessels bearing the text of the 221 BCE edict are fragments, there are at least four mostly complete vessels containing the entire text. Two of these four texts have empty spaces where the characters for the word "emperor" would be. This is definitely deliberate, as it occurs in both instances that word appears in those texts. It seems this resulted from a taboo on the emperor's title. Leaving an empty space was one way to avoid breaking a taboo, and the Qin system of avoidances was still relatively loose, which explains why the word is not elided in all examples.[29] Retaining the spaces for the emperor's title while leaving it out had a double effect, in that it simultaneously evoked and effaced him. (I will present a similar dual effect in chapter 6, where I discuss walled roads and raised ways that hid the emperor and at the same time made his presence permanent.) The versions of the edict on bronze and other materials do not show the avoidance phenomenon, which perhaps reflects the relative prestige of those materials and/or their audiences.

Connections to Other Qin Inscriptions

Both the First and the Second Emperor's inscriptions have connections to other texts created around the same time. The most important of these are the famous stele inscriptions the First Emperor put up during his progresses through the realm, which I discuss again in the next chapter.[30] The steles did not use the same text, but they communicated similar core messages and thus reflect the purposeful dissemination of comparable content.

The First Emperor's edict of 221 BCE conveys (at least) four pieces of information: 1) the successful unification of the realm; 2) the peace he had won for the populace; 3) the new title he had created for himself and the newly sanctioned official terminology for the commoners; and 4) the command enacting the standardizations.[31] All four are also present in the stele texts. The emperor's success in overcoming his rivals and unifying the realm under Qin imperial rule is a repeated theme in those texts.[32] The stele inscriptions also boast of the peace won by the First Emperor for the common people and the attendant benefits of the same.[33] The same new vocabulary that appears in the edict ordering standardization features in the steles as well: the title "emperor" occurs many times in those inscriptions, as does the fact that he created his own title.[34] The newly approved term for commoners appears less frequently but still repeatedly.[35] The standardization itself finds mention in the stele texts, although depicted as a completed task and not a command to be carried out.[36] All this reflects that the Qin rulers communicated the same messages to the realm in these different ways.

The Second Emperor's inscription, which he added to many weights and measures, also has a parallel in the case of the steles, as the Second Emperor added his own inscription to each of them.[37] In that inscription, as in the addition to the inscription on weights and measures, the Second Emperor declares his desire to avoid taking credit for the First Emperor's achievements. The core messages of the Second Emperor's two additions are the same, and some of the phrases match exactly. But the text added to the steles has the three-part form of a legal act, in which the ruler expresses a desire, the officials recommend the corresponding action, and the ruler finally enacts the recommendation by decreeing it accepted.[38] This could imply a different legal status of the two versions. However, the overall congruence of content shows these to be two versions of essentially one text, with that on the weights reflecting the concision required of material for mass distribution.

There is one more example of a related text worth noting. The First Emperor commemorated the 221 BCE appearance of "giants" in Linzhao 臨洮 by casting twelve huge bronze statues representing them.[39] Each statue is said to have had the following inscription on its chest:

> In the twenty-sixth year [of his reign], the emperor first united the realm and made it into commanderies and prefectures. He corrected the laws and unified units of measure.[40] Giants came and appeared in Linzhao: they were 11.6 m tall and their feet were 1.4 m long. 皇帝二十六年初兼天下以為郡縣, 正法律同度量. 大人來見臨洮, 身長五丈足六尺.[41]

This inscription puts the standardization of laws and measures alongside the unification of the realm, treating all them as accomplished tasks.

Historian Ban Gu 班固 (32–92) says the giants appeared as a supernatural warning against Qin gigantism, a portent that the First Emperor misunderstood as an endorsement of his rule. I suggest the creation of this text and its inscription on the statues was an attempt to capitalize on the giants' notoriety and piggyback its messages on rumors about them.[42] Yet in its timing, its conspicuous use of the new title, its proclamation of the new realm, and its self-congratulatory tone, this inscription presents another form of the text inscribed on the weights. It presents the same basic messages found in the First Emperor's 221 BCE command regarding the standardization of measures and so constitutes another part of the same publicity campaign.

Martin Kern has argued that "[t]he stele inscriptions are not seven individual . . . texts, but rather a series of variations of what might be considered one basic text."[43] And insofar as it preceded the steles and conveyed the same core messages of Qin imperial success, the edict commanding standardization of measures was an essentialized and unadorned version of the text at the root of the stele inscriptions. The stele inscriptions are today much more famous than the edict standardizing the system of measures and receive much more attention. This has long been the case. *Historian's Records*, for example, incorporates most of the stele inscriptions and leaves out the command decreeing standardizations completely. We know about that command only because of recovered artifacts—although some of these artifacts were recovered in premodern times.

Modern archaeologists have found literally dozens and dozens of examples of the 221 BCE inscription in various forms across the whole of Qin imperial territory. It seems to have been almost everywhere now and must have been even more so during the Qin period, and probably was in Han times as well.[44] Despite—or perhaps because of—this, Sima Qian left it out of *Historian's Records*, the most important transmitted history of Qin.

The relative fame of the stele texts and the inscriptions of the 221 BCE edict in the present does not match their contemporary presence. Transmitted history was produced by a small segment of society and reflects its tastes and views, influencing and to some extent determining our knowledge of early history. In this case, we have a set of texts (the steles) that came to dominate another, larger set (copies of the 221 BCE edict), primarily through the influence of a single author, Sima Qian. Perhaps Sima Qian made his decision because of the superior literary qualities of the stele inscriptions and the elevated audience that implied, in contrast to the plain style and plebian audience of the command effecting the standardizations. Or maybe the very ubiquity of the First Emperor's ukase enacting those changes made its inclusion unnecessary or just uninteresting.

Finally, bronze weapons in the hands of common soldiers bore inscriptions that served to identify government property or track quality control. They were short and focused on specifying sources and keeping inventory and were without messages of an explicitly political nature.[45] Nevertheless, insofar as they declared that the Qin government owned and monitored those items—in short, that the Qin government was there—these, too, created and reinforced common knowledge of the dynasty.

Precedents

Scholars researching inscriptions of the First Emperor's 221 BCE edict and the Second Emperor's 209 BCE addition have noted that transmitted texts mention what seem to be earlier forms of related practices.[46] The general idea of unifying weights and measures as a way to enact or improve governance did not originate with the Qin. Both Confucius and Guan Zhong are said to have recommended this as a way to promote rule.[47] *Master Xun* names the official rectification of weights and measures as one of the advantages of Ru-style governance.[48] Canonical texts speak of this, including the "Great

Tradition" chapter of *Record of Ritual*, which says that sage rule would entail unifying systems of weights and measure.⁴⁹ The text *Zhou Rituals* (*Zhouli* 周禮) probably dates to the Warring States period, and David Schaberg has argued it had a particularly close relationship to the administrative structure of the Qin, reflecting and/or having inspired it.⁵⁰ *Zhou Rituals* lists the standardization of weights and measures among the tasks of an official called the "unifier of places."⁵¹ Ritual monthly ordinances prescribed that such checks be carried out biannually.⁵² And as noted earlier, standardization within states had also occurred before the Qin unification.

The Qin rulers were not the first to create and preserve multiple copies of texts to disseminate information among groups, creating common knowledge of their contents, and when they did so, they relied upon earlier practices. At the same time, there are significant differences between these examples and the Qin cases. This was inevitable because although the Qin worked with media and methods that already existed, there was no exact precedent for their rule or its exigencies. In what follows, I examine specific ways the First Emperor and his entourage built on and adapted precedents. I treat forerunners of the communications media used by the Qin rulers, with particular attention to archaeologically recovered materials. I do not consider all cases of reproduced text in early China. Instead I concentrate on examples that are especially relevant to common knowledge creation under the Qin and show how the Qin took up and adapted existing practices for political purposes.

Textual Accounts

Zhou Rituals describes a number of officials whose duties included reproducing and/or preserving texts. For example, the "manager of covenants" (*simeng* 司盟) made and kept copies of agreements—both state covenants and contracts made by the common people—for distribution in case of bad faith. The "grand scribe" (*taishi* 大史) copied the canons and laws and made duplicates of various agreements, also for future reference. The "manager of contracts" (*siyue* 司約) "was in charge of the contract documents of the state and the myriad people" 掌邦國及萬民之約劑; the description of that office specifies, "All major contract documents would be written on lineage [temple] vessels, and minor contract documents would be written on red-[inked] tablets" 凡大約劑書於宗彝, 小約劑書於丹圖.⁵³ Another text, *The Lost Documents of Zhou* (*Yi Zhou shu* 逸周書), says that after King Wu 武 received guidelines for seasonal governance from the Duke of

Zhou 周公, "He then commanded the founder to cast [bronze], inscribe it [with the laws, and make] a bronze plaque, to be stored in the treasury and examined monthly" 乃召昆吾冶而銘之金版藏府而朔之.[54] The story is surely apocryphal, but it reflects a conception of rules that existed in the form of a durable text for verification and yet also circulated, in some form, broadly, in that its provisions applied to the populace.[55]

Covenant Texts

Covenant texts recovered from sites at Houma 侯馬, Shanxi and Wenxian 溫縣, Henan, dating to around the early fifth century BCE and studied by Susan Weld and Crispin Williams, illustrate one way that repeated text worked to advance group formation and function before the time of the Qin. These short, formulaic pledges of loyalty to specific leaders were copied with ink onto stone tablets and buried as part of a ritual. The texts name each individual oath-taker personally, and an animal sacrifice sealed the covenant. The covenants oblige allegiance to the leader and enmity to his antagonists, threaten the destruction of the pledge-taker's lineage if he should break his oath, and enjoin the spirits of dead rulers to observe any infraction. A number of different formulas occur, but they always come in groups, with as many as more than a hundred examples of a particular version. The texts come to us on tablets of differing shapes, using stone of different types, perhaps intimating that participants' social status varied. The timing of these texts is important, as they come from a time when political structure in the state of Jin, where the covenants were found, was shifting away from organization according to lineage relationship. A distinctly political form of organization was emerging, which incorporated members of different lineages into a single political entity by means of repeated text.[56]

Reproduced Texts, Limited Audiences, and Communication at a Distance

The utility of making multiple copies of texts for spreading and cross-checking information—for creating and confirming common knowledge among small groups—was acknowledged and put to work before the Qin but only in limited contexts. Considering examples of replication and audience limitation will highlight how the Qin used existing ideas and technology in a new way in order to disseminate the 221 BCE edict and the supplement to it from 209 BCE.

Although inscriptions of the command standardizing measures are unique in their plenitude, many other kinds of texts existed in multiple instantiations. I have already mentioned some examples from Qin times, like the inscription on the statues of giants and the Second Emperor's postscript to the seven steles. And of course the single most famous example of Qin art, the terra cotta army, was produced under conditions that combined the mass production of elements by cross-applied pipe manufacture techniques with handcrafted, variable elements to efficiently create a large and diverse set of figures. The products were marked with brief inscriptions such as seal impresses specifying the manufacturer.[57] Longer texts existed in multiple copies, too, on clay and bronze.

Inscribed Tablets

Archaeologists have recovered a bronze tablet engraved with a command that represents a precedent for and alternative to the proclamation plaques. In 1977, excavations at a Hebei site identified as the tomb of a king of Zhongshan 中山 and dating to the late Warring States period produced a bronze tablet 94 by 48 cm and 1 cm thick. The tablet's most prominent feature is a diagram of the gravesite. But it also contains the text of a command from the king that orders recipients to follow the diagram in construction of the tomb and sets execution to three generations as the punishment for failure to do so. The closing line of the command specifies that one copy should be interred on site, presumably the recovered example. Another was to have been preserved in the treasury, where it would have been available for later consultation and confirmation.[58]

A conceptually related object was recovered in Shaanxi in 1948. It is a rectangular clay tablet from the state of Qin, 24 by 6.5 cm, varying between 0.5 and 1 cm thick. The tablet is inscribed on both sides, and the text refers to itself as a "clay document" (*washu* 瓦書), a previously unknown term.[59] The creators of this document inscribed the text on clay before putting it into the kiln, six lines on the front and three on the back, and after firing colored the graphs of the inscription red. The text has two sections, which are not obviously related to one another. The first refers to the 334 BCE ceremonial gift of meat from temple offerings to the semi-legendary sage kings Wen 文 and Wu 武, which the Zhou overlord presented to the Qin ruler. This event is also recorded in *Historian's Records* and provides the basis for dating the tablet.[60] While the 334 BCE gift did not bring with it a formal change in status, Li Xueqin 李學勤 says such gifts were originally limited to lineage members of the Zhou ruling house or descendants of sage-kings Wen and Wu. Thus, this was an indication of respect that reflected the Qin state's emerging power. And it may have signified more than that. Yang Bojun 楊伯峻 (1909–1992) interprets the gift as a sign that Qin—like Lord Huan of Qi 齊桓公 before—was in a position to assume overlordship.[61]

The second part of the inscription on the clay document conveys the occasion of the document: the grant of land to an individual as his "lineage settlement" (*zongyi* 宗邑). It also specifies that the grant was to continue to be held by his descendants in perpetuity. The tablet was then buried at the border of the grant. As such, it can only have been a copy of a text that existed in at least one—and in all likelihood more—copies elsewhere.

Guo Zizhi 郭子直 points out that inscriptions of this sort one are common on Zhou bronzes. He also notes the relative scarcity of Qin inscribed bronzes. Although much Qin pottery bearing some sort of text exists, those inscriptions are typically quite short, often just the imprint of a single seal with the name of the manufacturer. That makes the clay document and its inscription especially significant, perhaps even unique, although the text itself cannot have been unique at the time. It has long been known that pottery influenced the shape and style of bronze vessels.[62] This tablet suggests that bronze and its uses could also help shape pottery and hints that economics could have been a factor in this: the advantages of pottery were its lower value and ease of creation. A text on bronze would be kept secure in a temple or archive, but a pottery copy would not attract thieves and so could be buried out in the open at a boundary. The existence of multiple copies of the text meant that the grant was common knowledge among a group broader than just those directly party to it. The incorporation of apparently unrelated political content into the text resembles the way the Qin rulers piggybacked their messages on other texts, as in the case of the edict commanding standardization, which also proclaimed the unification of the realm and the emperor's position over it.

Texts on Bronze

Reproduction was an important part of bronze manufacture long before the Qin dynasty. Li Feng has written about virtually identical texts on groups of Western Zhou bronze vessels, including both multiple examples created simultaneously and later copies of earlier inscriptions on either a single type or different kinds of bronze vessels. No later than the fifth century BCE, "highly organized workshops" used mass production techniques to put a single decorative design created by one skilled craftsman onto multiple bronze vessels of various shapes. And insofar as Zhou-era bronze ritual vessels bore inscriptions that were copies of documents kept elsewhere, those inscriptions always existed in multiple copies.[63] The covenant texts used repeated formulae to form oath-takers into groups owing loyalty to a given ruler, and according to Crispin Williams, those rituals may well have included persons of commoner status.[64]

Limited Audience

Pre–Qin dynasty bronzes share another characteristic that is important for my discussion here: a very limited audience. This was typical of bronzes generally. Even things like bronze bells, which served important functions in providing standards for music (standards that themselves may have related to those for measures), were exclusively the province of the aristocracy and unseen by commoners. Sets of bells also carried inscriptions, and there are examples from Qin marked with reproduced text making an overt claim to political ascendancy. There are indications that bronzes, especially bronze vessels, served communicative purposes that went beyond those provided by a single vessel that required close-up examination. But the audience was still very small compared to the entire populace.[65]

  Zuo's Commentary records the famous "Document on Penal Law" ("Xingshu" 刑書), which was cast—probably as a tripod (*ding* 鼎)—in the state of Zheng in 536 BCE.[66] Glum remarks attributed to Confucius in *Zuo's Commentary* and dated to 513 BCE concern a tripod inscribed with penal law in the state of Jin and predict that the people would put their stock in the tripod text instead of following the unwritten dictates of respect.[67] But it seems unlikely the common people would have inspected such objects, which would have had a limited audience.

  The same goes for the First Emperor's terra cotta army, which was buried. Even the statues of the giant barbarians and their inscriptions were limited in audience: they may have been open to public view because they were placed outside palace gates, though it is also possible they were behind still other walls. Yet even if in public view, the potential audience—like that of the steles—was limited to those who actually went to that place.

  The limitation of audience also applied for the other documents as well. Bureaucratic structures portrayed in *Zhou Rituals* provide for agreements that would be both known to the parties involved and duplicated but also stipulate that those documents and copies would remain away from the public. In some cases, officials were to maintain original documents and/or reliable copies for later consultation. Those with access were to be few in number. And although the inscribed plate recovered from the king of

Zhongshan's tomb bore a command that applied to a large group of people, it likewise could have been seen by only a small group. The clay document tablet was buried—and being made of pottery, it would not attract thieves to dig it up. The copies of these documents retained in the archives would also have been available only to a small number.

Communication at a Distance

The capabilities of bronze and bronze vessel inscriptions for effective communication at a distance were recognized in early times. Bronze was known as a medium for transmitting information across periods of time to later generations. Bronze vessels often mentioned this, specifying the transmittal of the vessel and by extension the information contained in its inscription down to the descendants of those involved.[68] In Han times, Ban Gu wrote about the usefulness of bronze's durability for promulgating standardized measures and unifying custom across the geographical expanse of the realm.[69]

Bronze could function as a medium for communicating with spirits. For example, *Zhou Rituals* describes the "director of bronze," who was responsible for all important matters regarding precious metals and stone, including providing the bronze plates used for requests made during prayer.[70] Inscriptions on ritual bronze vessels may also have been conceived of as having a similar ability to communicate with the supernatural, perhaps through the secondary medium of the offerings.[71] Stone, too, had such capabilities, and Susan Weld has suggested that covenant texts were, among other things, "[a] form of communication with the spirit world."[72]

Mass Communication

The situation around the time of unification in the third century BCE, then, was that the capability for mass production of bronze—and simpler wares as well—and even for mechanical reproduction of text existed and had existed for a long time. People knew these things could enable communication over distances of time or space. Yet this potential of bronze and other durable materials for communication had been exploited only in limited contexts, with limited audiences and limited results. Bronze and other media were underutilized. The Qin, particularly the First Emperor and advisors like Li Si, exploited this previously unused potential to disseminate the imperial command of 221 BCE unifying weights and measures, along with the accompanying, broader claims to legitimacy. The Second Emperor subsequently continued the same with his edict of 209 BCE.

In recent decades, at a distance of more than two thousand years, the edict of 221 BCE has been found dispersed over a broad area. There is no single text of that time or earlier with comparable presence. Although the Qin were following precedents that had long existed, the First Emperor's edict of 221 BCE marks an attempt at something new: true mass communication, spreading a single, brief text as widely as possible. This is part of the long-term process through which bureaucratic communication under the Qin and later the Han grew out of earlier religious and ritual practice. I argue the Qin used and adapted these techniques in this specific case in order to create common knowledge.

Previous Explanations

Many scholars have offered explanations for the Qin dynasty establishment of unified standard measures, and most have presented it as a necessary and/or inevitable part of economic and political unification.[73] Ma Chengyuan 馬承源 wrote about the necessity and direct utility of instituting unified systems, first in the state of Qin, then under the dynasty.[74] Yu Weichao 俞偉超 and Gao Ming 高明 considered it as part of economic development and integration, which together with the other standardizations served to strengthen the unification of the state.[75] Shi Shuqing 史樹青 and Xu Qingsong 許青松 assert that the standardization was intended to facilitate taxation and had other positive effects, such as promoting trade.[76] Zhu Xiaoxin 朱筱新 focuses on economic integration and also brings in cultural unification.[77]

There is doubtless no little truth to the idea that standardization furthered integration of the new state; my analysis is compatible with this understanding. But I approach the issue from a different standpoint, which enables me to postulate broader and deeper effects and how those effects were achieved.

The argument that standardization, once accomplished, brought with it convenience and efficiency surely has some truth to it, too. But considered objectively, there was no absolute necessity for instituting a single system of measure. One need only look at the People's Republic of China (where the metric system is the official standard, but vegetables are still sold using traditional units in traditional markets) or the United States (where both metric and customary units are widespread) to find examples of countries that function with multiple systems in use. Qin government bureaucrats regularly performed mathematical calculations to compare the volume of unhusked grain to that of husked as well as to legumes.[78] So at the very least we can be sure converting between different units of measure would have presented no new mathematical problem.

Inscribing texts on items intended for dispersal is a related but distinct issue. A common explanation for the inscriptions is that this showed the marked implements had been inspected and approved or otherwise endorsed for use.[79] There is evidence that a system of centralized inspection of measures functioned during Qin times, so this is a possible factor.[80] However, many Qin objects exist that bear just a few graphs or a single seal, and according to Qin law things too hard for carving could be marked with paint for identification.[81] That sort of marking would have been an equally effective and far more efficient method to show official approval of weights and other objects involved in measurement. There was no need for a long text, to say nothing of mounting a plaque with that text on the items. Something more important must have been going on in the case of measures.

Hou Xueshu 侯學書 points to measuring utensils with variances outside legally established tolerances, as well as the existence of unmarked examples, to argue that the explanation of engraving as endorsement falls short. Hou asserts political purposes were the main motivation behind the inscription of the 221 and 209 BCE edicts, with any economic effects being secondary. Hou specifically argues the edicts worked by "proclaiming authority" and so strengthening central control and emphasizing that the central government must be obeyed.[82] Zhu Xiaoxin makes a related argument, saying that putting the text of the First Emperor's edict on approved vessels invested those vessels with authority as well as indicating official approval. Zhu further asserts that the vessels so marked were not for actual use but were instead to function as standard examples available locally for reference. However, the existence of heavily worn examples of inscribed measures and weights, which thus are certain to have been used, contradicts this aspect of his hypothesis.[83]

The proclamation plaques deserve special mention. As I have discussed, scholars studying them have suggested the oversized plaques were for public display in different contexts. I think that is a reasonable hypothesis, especially since their size would have left little other possible use. Speaking generally, however, the existence of all sorts of plaques underscores that the edict of 221 BCE got special treatment, as demonstrated by the resources invested in publicizing its contents. The plaques served no other purpose than to do just this, and no other edict received this treatment.

Wu Hung argues that the dissemination of both the First Emperor and the Second Emperor's commands fulfilled legal requirements.[84] Dispersing information about the new system was surely part of what was going on. Although in earlier times the law was kept from general knowledge, the Qin attitude toward law was different: beginning at least from the time of Shang Yang, it seems the Qin were consciously engaged in disseminating knowledge of the law to all levels of society (see chapter 7). So communicating this was important. The institution of the new system was the first step of common knowledge creation, making the people know of the new polity and its ruler.

But the 221 BCE text reflects a larger purpose than fulfilling a legal requirement. From a strictly practical perspective, the fact that there are no details about the newly unified system in the inscription means that those must have been communicated and/or instituted by other means. The proclamation plaques, either mounted on those implements or circulated separately from them, imply that other methods of communication bore the details of the change. At the same time, such a long text and resource-intensive distribution would have been unnecessary if the sole purpose was to indicate that the utensils had been approved.

Common Knowledge through Change and Communication

In this section, I argue that the establishment of a single, countrywide set of weights and measures created common knowledge of the Qin dynasty. The inscriptions attached to the new weights gave a particular form to that common knowledge they generated. By means of bronze, iron, and pottery, long-existing methods of mass production, and new developments in mechanical reproduction of text, the Qin made the new state known to its populace. The Qin rulers also made themselves known to the people they ruled—not just the former ruling classes, who, if they still lived, had presumably noticed that they had been deposed, but to the commoners as well. The need for common knowledge drove the interest in mass communication.

The inscriptions indicate that the First Emperor, and later the Second Emperor, paid attention to image management, in that they sought to give a specific form to the common knowledge they were creating. The First Emperor's inscriptions not only communicated the command and so worked to create knowledge of Qin authority, they also told the people they were enjoying a new peace because of what the emperor had done. The Second Emperor's inscription made it clear that the First Emperor had been responsible for the unification of the realm and the subsequent standardization of measures. At the same time, that text made it common knowledge that the Second Emperor had taken the throne and positioned him as the filial, dutiful, and legitimate successor to a remarkable monarch. In terms of creating common knowledge, what at first look like secondary matters may have been more important than the apparent main point. The accompanying political messages may well have been more important than communicating the new standards.

In chapter 3 I mentioned Yuri Pines' demonstration of the fact that the idea of a unified realm existed long before unification.[85] Yet it was, by all appearances, restricted in its circulation to the ruling and intellectual classes. Gideon Shelach and Pines have shown that Qin high culture incorporated elements from the culture of the lower classes, and the ruling classes also used their own culture and ideas to influence the behavior of the lower classes.[86] All of these points factor in my analysis. For in the end the Qin communicated to the commoners the culmination of a notion that had been limited in its audience, and they did so by means that had previously been mostly limited in audience. The First Emperor made use of the opportunity presented by the changes to the system of weights and measures, which itself created common knowledge, and pushed it further to his advantage. The Qin dynasty rulers turned high culture into common knowledge, and they did it by mass communication.

How exactly the content of the inscriptions was communicated to the common people must remain for the present a matter of inference. The available sources do not give much consideration to this sort of question. But it is reasonable to think the content of the edict was a matter of common knowledge. As I discuss in chapter 7, there were systems used in Han times with the explicit purpose of communicating between the imperial government and commoners at the local level. These functioned through a combination of distributed documents, publicly posted official texts, and public reading of those texts by government representatives.[87] Although those processes postdate the edicts I focus on here, they indicate how a slightly later bureaucratic system successfully transmitted similar sorts of information to its population and thus suggest how the Qin probably approached the same problem.

Nor should we think that the contents of the texts were unavailable through simple reading. In the past, the common assumption has been that literacy in early China was restricted to officials and other holders of elevated social status. Recent research suggests literacy, in various degrees, was widespread in Qin and Han society, including among commoners. Robin D. S. Yates and Miyake Kiyoshi 宮宅潔 have argued that the requirements of military service, including record-keeping, probably required a degree of facility with reading and writing among soldiers. Yates goes one step further to argue that the requirements of living under a government based on document bureaucracy obliged many others to acquire familiarity with the written word as well.[88] Since the Qin rulers went through so much trouble to transmit these messages, we can reasonably assume that they were received.[89] The broader the distribution was, the broader the receiving audience must have been.

There is good reason to believe common knowledge of the new weights existed. The fact that taxes paid in grain would be measured according to the new system meant that essentially every legal household of the realm would encounter them.[90] The marketplace was another site where common people would necessarily have encountered the new measures.[91] Common knowledge of the new measures, and thus concomitant common knowledge of the instituting authority of the Qin dynasty, is sure.

Constancy, Change, and Communication

I have argued here that the First and Second Emperors of Qin made use of existing culture in creating common knowledge that the longstanding ideal of the unified realm had been realized. I have also shown there was precedent for nearly every aspect of this process. But that does not preclude creativity. The Qin dynasty's achievement was based in large part on the ability of the First Emperor and his confederates—as well as their intellectual antecedents, men like Shang Yang—to note the underutilization of different media, to exploit affordances inherent in old systems and methods, and to put them to novel uses for communication.

Li Si claimed responsibility for "establishing the name of Qin" and said he did it by reforming the system of weights and measures. I doubt he did this by himself, or that it happened through one process alone. But there can be no doubt the Qin rulers created common knowledge of themselves. Changing the system of weights and measures was indeed one way they established their name.

5

Progress and Publicity

Qin Shihuang, Ritual, and Common Knowledge

This chapter considers the First Emperor of Qin's five imperial progresses from the perspective of common knowledge generation. I argue that they were part of what was in effect a mass communication campaign, in which the First Emperor used a public ritual to communicate with the population of the empire. He and his collaborators maximized the communicative potential of the progresses by making use of other acts in the same context to spread and make durable the otherwise transitory and localized moment of each progress. As argued elsewhere in this book, the purpose of this communication was to create common knowledge of the new empire, the Qin dynasty, and the emperor who ruled it. The effect of this common knowledge was the ongoing creation and reinforcement of the Qin empire in a dynamic process of expanding rule.

The chapter begins with the historical background of the progress in pre-Qin times. Then I briefly outline the First Emperor's five progresses and the single tour his son and successor, the Second Emperor, made. Next I outline a number of explanations scholars have offered for the progresses and the points of agreement of that research with my own, along with the insufficiencies of those explanations. My interpretation of the First Emperor's progresses follows, along with consideration of the additional acts that worked to strengthen the progresses' communicative effects. Finally I bring in information from early sources to show that my arguments are compatible with understandings of the sovereign's progress that existed in early China.

The Progress before the Qin Dynasty

Many sources record that rulers in pre-imperial China toured their territories and those of their subordinates. While these tours are widely recorded, their existence is sometimes doubted because of the great distances they are said to have covered. And in all likelihood they did not encompass the areas reported in the canons. However, there are many indications that progresses occurred in early times.[1]

Some scholars believe the progress grew out of visits between equals, the heads of different polities, which changed in character as rulership developed and an overlord emerged. Others also point to hunting and military expeditions and inspections. Whatever their origin, perhaps already in predynastic times and no later than the Shang period, these travels became inspection tours by the ruler. David Keightley has suggested that the movements of the almost constantly traveling Shang sovereign defined the scope of the late Shang state. Progresses during the Shang and Zhou periods included making sacrifices to mountains and rivers and visiting local lords and elderly people in each state. Keightley analyzes the tours in terms of a shifting power center rather than a communicative process, but structurally his description of the situation already in Shang times is compatible with my conceptualization. A variety of early sources report their occurrence, including bronze inscriptions dating to Zhou times.[2]

Received sources indicate that progresses occurred at intervals of once every five years up through the Shang dynasty and once every twelve years in the Western Zhou. Thus, *Zhou Rituals* says, "[Every] twelve years, the king makes a progress through the subordinate states" 十有二歲, 王巡守殷國.[3] Such specificity must of course be taken with a grain of salt. But evidence from Zhou bronze inscriptions and canonical records confirms that the progress, in some form, occurred in pre-imperial China. After the end of the Western Zhou and the effective rule of the Zhou house, there was no sole monarch to undertake the sovereign progress, although some local rulers took shorter journeys by that name.[4]

The single most important aspect of progresses for this discussion is their total ritual character. The Shang and Zhou tours were characterized by ceremonial meetings of all sorts, and the First Emperor's journeys included not just stops for ritual observances at significant sites but were filled with rite from beginning to end. This is so much the case that Chen Shuguo 陳戍國 has argued the progress was not *a* ritual but was rather the "convergence of every kind of ritual."[5] My discussion here will show how accurate that observation is.

The ruler's progress had died out as an actual practice long before the Qin achieved hegemony. So when the First Emperor of Qin performed it, he was the first to have done so in living memory. Indeed, he may well have been the first to actually perform a progress that covered distances like those reported in classical sources. There were important immediate precedents, however. At the general level, the rulers of the preunification state of Qin appear to have been partial to long-distance journeys, and a number of them traveled widely for various purposes. Furthermore, the First Emperor visited some of the territories he had conquered or was in the process of pacifying in the time leading up to final unification. So when the first imperial progress occurred in 220 BCE, it was neither a total innovation nor the First Emperor of Qin's first such tour.[6]

Outline of the Progresses

The "Annals of the First Emperor of Qin" ("Qin Shihuang benji" 秦始皇本紀) chapter of *Historian's Records* describes the First Emperor's five imperial progresses, and many other sources mention these events. I will briefly outline them, noting aspects and events relevant for my discussion, before examining specific elements at greater length later.[7]

220 BCE: First Progress

The new Qin emperor conducted his first imperial progress in 220 BCE, soon after unification in 221 BCE. Traveling west from the capital, the First Emperor went to Longxi 隴西 and Beidi 北地 and visited Mt. Jitou 雞頭山 (all in Gansu). *Historian's Records* says that the legendary Yellow Emperor 黃帝 had ascended Jitou while on his version of a progress.[8] Although assertions about the Yellow Emperor are doubtful as history, this one reflects that this mountain was associated with both ruler archetypes and ancient progresses. After Jitou, the First Emperor returned to the capital via Huizhong 回中, Gansu, without having left the borders of the pre-imperial state of Qin.

219 BCE: Second Progress

In 219 BCE, the emperor made a second progress, this time traveling east to pass through the areas of former states Han 韓, Wei 魏, Qi 齊, and Chu 楚.[9] According to *Historian's Records*, he stopped at a number of mountains to make sacrifices. The first of these was Mt. Zouyi 鄒嶧, to which he made a ceremonial offering.[10] The First Emperor also had the first of his well-known engraved stone steles erected at Mt. Zouyi. He then summoned scholars from the former states of Lu and Qi and proceeded to the famous Mt. Tai 泰.¹¹ At the foot of Mt. Tai they discussed the details of the sacrifices to be carried out. When the scholars began to bicker, the First Emperor grew impatient and, deciding their opinions were useless, sent them away. He ascended the mountain and carried out one sacrifice, then descended and carried out another at nearby Mt. Liangfu 梁父, establishing ceremonies that did not then exist. The rites employed were derived from those formerly used for ceremonies held at Yong 雍, but the details are unknown.¹²

The First Emperor and his entourage then traveled east to reach the Bohai 渤海 seacoast. They followed it north and ascended Mt. Cheng 成 and Mt. Zhifu 之罘, where, according to *Historian's Records*, they erected a stone memorial to Qin virtue.¹³ Mt. Zhifu was the location of one of the stele inscriptions, but since *Historian's Records* incorporates that text later, it was probably put up during a different progress.

Historian's Records tells us that during this progress the emperor stopped to offer sacrifices to important mountains and rivers, as well as to the Eight Spirits associated particularly with the former state of Qi.¹⁴ Some of these spirits were honored with sacrifices carried out at specific places: Mt. Tai and Mt. Liangfu were both locations for sacrifices to the Lord of Earth (Dizhu 地主), while Mt. Cheng and Mt. Zhifu were locations for sacrifices to the Lord of the Sun (Rizhu 日主) and the Lord of Yang (Yangzhu 陽主), respectively. Other mountains with specific associations were located along the Bohai coast, and the First Emperor presumably made offerings at a number of them. *Historian's Records* says other kinds of sacrifices were performed next to large mountains, atop hills, and at altar mounds in swamps.¹⁵

On his way back to the capital, the First Emperor visited Langye 琅邪 (Shandong), a place associated with sacrifices to the Lord of the Four Seasons (Sishizhu 四時主).¹⁶ The First Emperor spent three months at Langye, built a terrace, and transferred many commoner households there, essentially founding a city. He also erected a stele on the mountain. The cycle of seasons was of primary importance to early Chinese political thought.¹⁷ So although *Historian's Records* says only that the First Emperor stayed at Langye because he liked the place, its religious significance surely also played a part.

The First Emperor then continued his journey back, and further along on the way, passed through Pengcheng 彭城 (Jiangsu) then headed southwest to reach Mt. Heng 衡 (Anhui), the Southern Marchmount. According to *Historian's Records*, the legendary sage ruler Shun 舜 had visited this mountain, and the "King's System" chapter of *Record of Ritual* links it to the progress as performed in high antiquity. No later than the fourth century

BCE, the marchmounts were revered, particularly, in connection with the welfare of the realm.[18] Thus, although the stories connected to Shun deserve little credence, Mt. Heng was a place associated with sage rule, the ruler's progress, and politically themed religious practice.

A local official's personal chronicle recovered at Shuihudi 睡虎地 (Hubei) mentions the First Emperor's passage through Anlu 安陸 (Hubei) in Nanjun 南郡 commandery, which *Historian's Records* says he visited during this tour.[19] Nanjun's location suggests that the First Emperor probably visited on his way to Mt. Xiang 湘 (Hunan), where he performed a sacrifice.[20] When that sacrifice was completed, heavy winds ensued, which prevented the party from crossing a river. The emperor blamed the spirits in the mountain and decided to punish them. According to *Historian's Records*, he ordered convict laborers to cut down the trees on Mt. Xiang, essentially subjecting the mountain to punitive shaving, a standard penalty for human criminals; he also commanded the workers to turn the mountain the reddish-brown color of a convict laborer's uniform by exposing its soil.[21] That done, the emperor and his entourage headed back to the capital.

218 BCE: Third Progress

On his third progress, in 218 BCE, the First Emperor traveled east from the capital Xianyang to pass through the former states of Han, Wei, Qi, Zhao 趙, and Yan 燕. He went as far as Bolangsha 博狼沙 (Henan), where Zhang Liang 張良 (d. 189 BCE), from the former state of Han, led an attempt to assassinate him. The emperor instituted a nationwide search for the perpetrators that lasted ten days. The emperor then visited Mt. Zhifu again, this time leaving behind a stele bearing a long text and another on the eastern face of the same. (Mt. Zhifu is surrounded on three sides by the Bohai Sea, and its eastern side faces out to sea.) After those rituals, the progress continued on to revisit Langye, after which the First Emperor and his companions returned to the capital by way of Shangdang 上黨 commandery (Shanxi).[22]

215 BCE: Fourth Progress

The First Emperor carried out his fourth progress in 215 BCE, when he and his companions traveled to the seacoast and turned to follow it far to the north, leaving an inscription at Jieshi 碣石 (Liaoning).[23] Although received history makes no mention of it, the Qin constructed a large complex of buildings at Jieshi. The complex includes an encircling wall, rooms of various sizes, and a number of packed-earth platforms—the largest of which was some 8 m high and located on the seaside facing an unusual three-rock formation in the sea, along with other, smaller platforms associated with this one. Archaeologists believe that the buildings were connected with the First Emperor's visits to the area. They have suggested specifically that the largest of the three rocks was the eponymous Jieshi and that the other two formed the "Jieshi Gate" 碣石門, which the First Emperor had inscribed.[24]

One point of particular interest about the Jieshi archaeological site is the elaborate baths discovered among the remains of a Qin palace built there. Bathing was required as preparation for many important rituals. There is limited historical information available about Western Han imperial baths and none concerning those of the Qin.[25] So we cannot be sure to what degree such bathing facilities were part of the ordinary outfitting of the emperor's accommodations, as opposed to special facilities for a ritual site, if these two can be distinguished: Given the ritual responsibilities of the emperor, he must have had frequent recourse to bathing for purification, if not for other purposes as well, no matter where he was. But given the attested connection between Jieshi and ceremonial observances, and the mention of such practices as part of the second progress, these baths strongly suggest ritual ablution.

A second important aspect of Jieshi is the presence of pre-Qin remains at the site and in the area. Although the majority of archaeological finds at Jieshi have been dated to the Qin and Western Han periods, archaeologists also report the presence of apparent preunification pottery and tiles, which they tentatively date to Warring States times. Even more significant may be a site located some 2 km to the west near a prominent rock hill called Heishantou 黑山頭. Although this is predominantly a Western Han site, beneath those later remains archaeologists have discovered objects dating to Shang and Zhou times, including pottery, tripods, and stone objects, reflecting the importance of the place in multiple periods.[26]

Other remains in the Jieshi region further underscore that the Qin were busy leaving their mark on the area. Archaeological excavation at a site called Jinshanju 金山咀, located further northwest along the coast, has shown this. The archaeologists describe a three-part complex of Qin buildings located on a promontory, the construction materials and size of which indicate it was an imperial project. The report authors call its structure, scope, and location very like that of the Jieshi site and unlike sites associated with official buildings or common peoples' dwellings. This, combined with the imperial nature of the buildings and the site's location in an area the First Emperor visited, suggest that the construction must have been associated with one or more of the progresses.[27]

According to *Historian's Records* and *Book of Documents*, the legendary sage ruler Yu 禹 visited Jieshi while on his own travels through the realm.[28] As in the cases of the Yellow Emperor and Shun, such accounts cannot be taken as evidence of a visit by an actual Yu (supposing he ever existed). But they attest to an association between this site and legendary personages and their journeys. Reports of pre-Qin construction at and around this spot suggest that the association was not to some imagined, invented, or long-forgotten place, but rather one that was in use and had been in times preceding the Qin as well. The combination of this ongoing use and mystical association indicates this was a place for ritual observances. By coming here, the First Emperor made use of existing ideas in order to communicate about himself and his rule. The construction of a palace and mounds used for sacrifices reflect that this was not a one-time occurrence but rather the continuation or resumption of longstanding ritual practices.

When he was done in the Jieshi area, the First Emperor traveled westward along the northern border of the empire then turned south to return to Xianyang. Although the records of this trip are brief, they mention that while on his travels the emperor commanded the destruction of dikes and fortifying walls in places he passed through.[29]

211–210 BCE: Fifth Progress

The First Emperor of Qin died in 210 BCE during his fifth and final progress. The *Historian's Records* account of this trip describes more than in other cases the variety of rituals the emperor carried out before and during the progress. These included selecting the retinue, sacrifices to mountains and rivers, and ceremonial activities extolling the quality of Qin rule, like the steles.[30] The emperor set out on November 1, 211 BCE.[31] He traveled south into Yunmeng 雲夢 commandery, not far from Anlu. He again visited Mt. Xiang and performed an offering there. He continued further south to the nine peaks of the Jiuyi 九疑 Mountains. One of these was supposed to be the location of legendary sage ruler Shun's burial place, and the First Emperor performed a sacrifice to Shun there.[32] He then traveled by inland waterways to the area of Mt. Kuaiji 會稽, famous for being visited by the legendary sage ruler Yu and the location of his tomb. Many texts mention this, and the First Emperor must have known about it.[33] He set up an inscribed stele praising Qin there before beginning his circuitous return to the capital.

The entourage traveled north to Langye, where *Historian's Records* says the First Emperor wanted to kill a whale but did not see one. The party continued north along the coast to Mt. Cheng, which was the location for offerings to the Lord of the Sun. No whale appeared at Mt. Cheng, either, and it was only when they got to Mt. Zhifu—where sacrifices to the Lord of Yang occurred—that they succeeded in killing a whale.[34] The progress then followed the coast and soon afterward the emperor fell ill with the unknown disease that killed him in 210 BCE. His death was kept secret until the entourage returned to the capital.

209 BCE: The Second Emperor's Progress

The First Emperor's successor, the Second Emperor of Qin, carried out an imperial progress in 209 BCE, traveling through the empire to perform sacrifices and visit his father's steles and add his own inscription. His expressed purpose was to avoid looking weak before the people of the realm in comparison to his father, who had so sedulously communicated with the population. The Second Emperor traveled east from the capital, reaching Jieshi. The Second Emperor then headed south along the seacoast, passing Mt. Tai and visiting Mt. Kuaiji.[35] He commanded that a text be appended to each stele inscription, which said in part,

> The inscriptions on bronze and stone were all made by the First Emperor. Now I have taken on the title [of emperor], and the texts inscribed on bronze and stone do not name the First Emperor. In the distant future, it could seem like they were made by his successor (i.e., me), and that would not correspond to [the First Emperor's] perfect merit and splendid virtue. 金石刻盡始皇帝所為也. 今襲號而金石刻辭不稱始皇帝, 其於久遠 也如後嗣為之者, 不稱成功盛德.[36]

The Second Emperor and his entourage went all the way to Liaodong before returning to the capital. Many emperors of later dynasties also performed the progress as inaugurated by the First Emperor, though these were of a substantially different character and fall outside the scope of this discussion.[37]

Explanations

As acts, the First Emperor's progresses have been variously explained. In *Historian's Records*, Sima Qian quotes the Second Emperor, who said the Qin founder "made progresses through the commanderies and prefectures in order to show his strength and overawe the realm" 巡行郡縣, 以示彊, 威服海內.[38] Some modern historians have concentrated on the ritual and religious character of many of the progresses' components. Others have pointed to more directly practical functions such as demonstrating military power and promoting trade.[39]

The most commonly named reason for the progresses is politics, in different formulations. Martin Kern focuses on the steles, which he connects to the ritual-political nature of the progresses. Lao Gan 勞榦 (1907–2003) said the First Emperor's progresses served to suppress dissent. And Lei Ge 雷戈 has called the progresses huge political ceremonies, which worked to create a new relationship between the ruler and the ruled and to simultaneously invest the emperor with mystical potency and bring him close to the common population.[40]

These various understandings and interpretations all have merit: the progresses doubtless resulted from many factors and had numerous effects. But given the context of the newly established empire, political factors are not just most commonly named, they are also the most compelling—especially since the First Emperor had toured newly conquered territory in the time before unification, as noted earlier. This is important evidence against taking other factors as primary reasons for the progresses, even if they were important aspects of the practice.

Scholars have so far not resolved the question of how or why the First Emperor's progresses worked as a political tool. Some researchers have suggested that demonstrating military strength served to cement Qin control. But it is not clear why the First Emperor would need to go to such lengths to repeatedly show off his military power before the disarmed populace of recently defeated enemies (to say nothing of the people of the former state of Qin, his stronghold and the location of the first progress). Surely his army had proved its might to any who cared to observe it. He had further reinforced its military supremacy by ordering the confiscation of privately owned weapons and instituting controls on production of the materials for making weapons.[41] It seems like simply touring a territory could have nothing more than a short-term influence, the troops being conspicuous by their absence afterward.

Furthermore, if the First Emperor wanted his soldiers to tour the territories and remind everybody that they were still around, there was no need for him to go on the progresses. The stresses of travel and the emperor's workaholic habits (even on the road) make it unlikely that the progresses were pleasant journeys. He encountered dangers that could well have cost him his life, and it is no coincidence he died on one of his tours. The First

Emperor could have delegated leading the march and the attendant hardships and risks to a subordinate. Indeed, when he was once presented with a cryptic document appearing to predict that northern nomads would end the Qin dynasty, the First Emperor sent General Meng Tian 蒙恬 (d. 220 BC) at the head of three hundred thousand troops to patrol the northern border against their incursions.[42] But the First Emperor did the progresses himself.

I suggest that through the progresses, Qin Shihuang achieved more than a military show of force, religious observance, or pageantry—though in practice the journeys incorporated aspects of these. He used the progress of bygone sage kings as one method of creating common knowledge of the newly unified empire and its sole ruler among all levels of society in the conquered areas, including the commonality. This understanding builds on lines of interpretation opened up by Kern, Lao, and others who treat the progresses as ritual with political functions, and on Lei's incorporation of the progresses and steles into a broader communicative program. I develop these by bringing in the notions of communication and cooperation I discussed in chapter 2 and showing links to other events surrounding the progresses.[43] Before turning to the question of interpretation, I want to clarify a few points about the role of religious elements in the First Emperor's communicative activities.

Religion and Communication

Asserting that the First Emperor and his advisors accepted these practices simply because they *believed* in them might be a possible objection to focusing on the progresses as creating common knowledge. However, such an approach would present a number of problems. On the one hand, faith and belief are not equally valued among all religions, and concentrating on them often leads researchers to disregard more important questions of practice. Even belief is itself a problematic criterion, not least because the cause and effect relationship between belief and action is often unclear, and belief may actually be a result, not a cause, of practice. My approach neither takes acts as either lacking all deeper significance nor sees them as signifying only at the level of abstraction. Instead, I treat them as part of the world—material, if intangible, like ideas and words. Religious practices should not be taken just as signs pointing to discarnate referents; they themselves are part of the real and substantial world. And as I noted in chapter 2, the audience of a given ritual is not limited to those participating: insofar as others are observing, they are deriving information, and the ritual is communicating to them as well. Directing an action toward a supernatural entity or entities does not preclude communication of the same to other people and in fact aids the latter. Religious practice acted as another medium, and sending a message simultaneously in multiple media makes that transmission more effective.[44]

In what follows I focus on concrete effects from Qin practices, in keeping with recent evolutionary research on religion. There are two main lines of discussion on the evolution of religion. Some researchers focus on religion in its connections to ritual, acknowledging that both are communicative and serve to facilitate and improve cooperation.[45] Others focus on how supernatural concepts confound intrinsic human expectations, which makes them especially memorable and thus more easily transmitted and retained, an interpretation supported by cross-cultural research.[46] Thus, one approach treats religion as an adaptation that benefits groups; the other considers it a by-product of evolution, which depends on traits that developed for other purposes. Despite their differences, the two perspectives do not necessarily exclude each other, and both attribute beneficial social functions to religion.[47] Rather than interpreting the First Emperor's religious activities as evidence of belief, I combine these lines of interpretation to suggest that religious activities helped the Qin communicate their claims with the goal of improved social function. The progresses and activities the First Emperor carried out in combination with them created supernatural and/or religious linkages that improved the transmission and recall of political messages.

Interpretation

I argue the First Emperor's progresses were ritual signs that indexed the position of the sole ruler as a means to create common knowledge. Rappaport says that ritual can summarize complex information, making the complex and equivocal definite and certain. The First Emperor's progresses were part of a communicative program that summarized the complexity of a new empire emerging from the chaos of war and political disunity into a clear message of Qin supremacy.

The progresses accomplished this on a number of levels. First, the rituals of the progresses were a canonical message of rulership, taken up and adapted by the First Emperor. The First Emperor adapted a form attributed to former kings of Shang, Zhou, and before to communicate the existence of a new supreme ruler. He borrowed the practices of ancient monarchs to make the new one known and built legitimacy by linking himself to those distant rulers. The whole sequence of rituals communicated his new position and communicated his sage rulership through the indexical message of the progresses, with potency and persuasiveness that went far beyond the canonical content of any specific aspect. In this way, he used the undisputed legitimacy of ancient sage rulers to augment his own political position.[48]

Since the First Emperor adopted ancient rites of rulers, the travels and sacrifices of his progresses were in obedience to an older order (Rappaport's canonical), which he accepted as a way to increase his own power. The First Emperor of Qin did much more than offer sacrifices to spirits while on the progresses. But insofar as religious and other observances were an integral part of the rituals constituting the progresses, those ceremonies helped give them shape. The canon of ritual—not just the texts but the body of transmitted practice—provided the First Emperor with a ceremonial language in which to make his claim to rule. The religious and cosmological significance of the sites he visited made his acts more noticeable and memorable than they otherwise might have been.[49]

Trying to assign a single impetus to the progresses is probably futile. In the end, it is sure that many factors were involved, as reflected by the variety of scholarly opinion on the topic. But the function of the progresses goes beyond the content of the steles or any other text or act. Whatever else he accomplished while underway, the progresses were indexical proof that the First Emperor ruled. He traveled throughout the realm, performed the rituals suitable to a sovereign, and no one stopped him. To carry out the ritual of the ruler's progress was to be the ruler and made everybody who saw or heard about the ritual aware of the same.

These indexes of authority were particularly important after five centuries of titular rule by Zhou kings who had long possessed little actual power. The Qin dynasty established real central control. And by moving through the territories of his former rivals, the First Emperor communicated and proved that fact. The First Emperor left his capital and stronghold and made himself potentially vulnerable to possible enemies. This was an indexical sign that made his power and position known.[50]

If the canonical aspect of the progresses was the ancient ritual of the progress, the indexical aspect lay in *doing* it. These rituals marked the end of the old circumstances of war, disunity, and chaos and the start of the new state of peace, unity, and stability.[51] Through repetition of the progress, the First Emperor emphasized that the new situation was continuous, that this was not just another respite from war but a new order. Repeated transmission of the message served to strengthen its effects. Also important was the audience of these public rituals: the people of all the places the emperor passed through. By means of his travels, the First Emperor made himself known to the populace, creating common knowledge that a new sovereign existed and ruled the entire realm as a unified whole.

From a broader perspective, the progresses showed the people that their former lords had been replaced. In the days when distance communication was slow and difficult, this was an effective way to communicate the existence of a new ruler. Since the common people did not leave behind their own written records, it is impossible to prove the extent of this audience, but there are indications that the progresses were understood this way in early China, as I will show later.

My analysis indicates that through the repeated performance of the ritual progress, the First Emperor created common knowledge of himself and the existence of the new empire and ruler, common knowledge that could be expected to spread through interpersonal networks into places not visited. The ritual creation of this common knowledge then served to establish the political power of the Qin. As Chwe notes, just making authority commonly known is a big step in actualizing it—an effect no doubt strengthened when this communication came about through an uncontested show of authority in the territories of former enemies. The sovereign's progress was a ritually modulated statement of rulership, an index of status. To do the Son of Heaven's ritual was to be him and to make the people know it.

Furthermore, the rituals the First Emperor used were historical, which functioned like additional publicity: they gave a canonical name to his acts, a name that was familiar, at least to the educated. As Kern argues, the First Emperor borrowed the practice of "the tour of inspection[,] which was already well-established as a most noble demonstration of sovereignty," while creating a new tradition for its use.[52] The reinstituted progress was both old and new, which gave strength and immediacy to this ritual index of the emperor's position.

The First Emperor helped resolve the coordination problem of rulership and the associated problem of obedience to a new political authority by creating common knowledge of himself and his dynasty, and the progress was one medium for this communication. Through the progresses and the rituals he performed, he proved that there was a new state and a new ruler with power beyond that of language.

Additional Acts

With my framework for analysis in mind, I would also connect other acts of the First Emperor to this same process. For as noted in my outline of the progresses, beginning with the second journey, the First Emperor performed a variety of other remarkable actions in conjunction with each one. Zhang Zhongli 張仲立 argues the progresses and related matters were parts of a deliberate campaign of the part of Qin Shihuang to increase his authority.[53] I agree, and suggest that the following were part of the same process as the progresses and also worked to generate common knowledge of the new ruler and realm: erecting steles, the punishment of the Mt. Xiang spirits, the manhunt for Zhang Liang, the destruction of walls and dikes, and the killing of the whale all worked to create publicity.

Steles

First and foremost are the steles. They are unique among the noteworthy events in that they themselves have a distinct ritual character. However, in this analysis they are subsumed within the convergence of rituals that formed the progress. Although the steles helped to make known the new Qin supremacy, they did so as a part of the progresses and not alone.[54]

The stele inscriptions refer to the Qin dynasty, but they were based on Zhou-era material from across the main trends of thought in early China.[55] Furthermore, the First Emperor did not invent the general idea of such inscriptions, various types of which had long existed, though he should perhaps be credited with refining this specific form. Engraved texts had an important role in the creation and function of bronze vessels as memorials of events and agreements, and the First Emperor's steles may ultimately derive from them.[56] The goal in all cases may have been the creation of a permanent mark, of what Wu Hung has termed "monumentality."[57] Other rulers before the First Emperor of Qin are said to have left engraved messages on mountains to record visits, prayers, and remarkable occurrences. King Zhao of the state of Qin, for example, is recorded to have commanded workmen to build an oversized game board on Mt. Hua to commemorate that he played against a celestial being there.[58] In the case of the steles, too, the First Emperor borrowed and adapted existing practices.

As both the form and content of the stele inscriptions was derived from earlier models, they meet the definition of what Rappaport calls a canonical message, a received form. The implication of this is important: insofar as it was formalized and formulaic, the content of the steles did not transmit specifically self-referential information and so does not directly reflect Qin ideology.[59] The self-referential message was the occurrence of the progress, memorialized by the steles. This is not to say the stele texts are not worth study; as ritual literature, they surely are. But rather than reflections of Qin political ideology, the inscriptions used canonical signs to communicate what the First Emperor and his advisors wanted to project as the political self of the Qin ruler.

At the same time, there was the fact of the steles' materiality: they were left in prominent locations on mountains, at the seashore, and other places, where they were seen and read. Local populations may well have had little or no direct access to the written content of the inscriptions, although the degree of limited literacy present among the common people of early China has been underestimated in the past. As I noted earlier, Yates and others have argued that the existence of universal military conscription meant that male members of the population had come into contact with writing and in all likelihood needed to develop some literacy. The existence of officials whose task it was to read official documents aloud to the common people means that we should not assume that all those unable to read themselves were cut off from imperial texts.[60]

The location of the steles on top of mountains with religious significance does not mean local residents did not see them. The mountains in question are not especially high: for example, despite its relative prominence as the highest mountain in eastern China, the altitude of Mt. Tai's peak is about 1,545 m above sea level.[61] There is no reason that ordinary people would have been unable to visit the site. Han sources record that predynastic rulers did not apportion control of prominent mountains to local rulers for two reasons: to prevent those rulers from accumulating the resources found in such places and to allow the local population to share in the produce of mountains.[62] Laws recovered at Shuihudi reflect that in Qin times these included firewood, although goatherds and others surely also made use of mountains generally. Qin laws forbid gathering firewood on mountains in specific seasons and do so without reference to general bans from the area, indicating that the common people were permitted to ascend mountains and indeed did so.[63]

Since the steles were thus open to view and left in areas that people visited, regardless of whether or not the content was read, the huge inscribed slabs would surely have attracted their attention and kept the memory of the progress alive. Han skeptic Wang Chong 王充 (27–97) wrote that the steles had the power to persuade "those who see and read them" 觀讀之者 to believe in the greatness of the Qin, reflecting that the effects of the steles in this regard were not limited to the literate but also included those who merely "saw" them.[64]

The First Emperor put up the steles not only to commemorate the progresses but also to expand the audience to include posterity, extending the scope of the common knowledge created through the rituals into the future.[65] Indeed, steles were only one part—albeit the most famous part—of a whole set of traces the First Emperor left of his progresses, which also included other inscriptions and various construction projects at many places, as well as the deeds I discuss here.[66] Whether or not these were convincing propaganda is unknown, but they surely worked to create common knowledge of the new dynasty and its achievements.

The First Emperor of Qin did not travel in order to erect steles; he and his entourage erected steles to mark his travels. In context, the content of the steles was less important than ensuring ongoing transmission of the message that the progresses had occurred. Again we see the ritual employment of canonical messages to send the self-referential message that the First Emperor was the new ruler of the realm, a message sent in multiple media, including stone.

Punishing a Mountain

Another act that served to create common knowledge was punishing the Mt. Xiang spirits, which publicized and commemorated the second progress. This is not to say that the First Emperor did not have the motivation reported: revenge for meteorological lèse-majesté. That is impossible to know. But whatever the proximate cause, in his choice of action Qin Shihuang chose what had to be a most noticeable way to go about it, namely, by obviously and evidently changing the scenery of the place, clothing the spirits' mountain home in convict's colors. This was an index of his command over resources and the very land itself. It was another way to generate publicity and create common knowledge among the local people, who would most certainly have marked and remarked on the change—all the more so if it were perceived as punishment of spirits.[67] This is to say nothing of the large numbers of people involved directly and indirectly with the project, who could be counted on to remember and speak of it.[68]

The communicative value of this act was magnified by Mt. Xiang's location. It was in an area relatively cut off from regular communication with the central government. At the same time, it was near Dongting Lake, which connected to four rivers, including the Yangtze, and early on developed as a center for the regional waterborne economy.[69] The change to the mountain was a public message of the emperor's power, left in a location where it was sure to spread through the population—a population that could ordinarily be reached only with difficulty.

Broadcasting Leviathan

During the final progress, the First Emperor's entourage killed a whale from shore, an act of great publicity value. The whale was known in early times as something beyond the reach of ordinary hunting methods; slaying one was by definition extraordinary.[70] The First Emperor's putative purpose was to drive away a bad spirit by destroying its avatar, the whale. As in the case of Mt. Xiang, a supernaturally charged motivation would only add to the power of this act to grab attention and memory and so generate more discussion and better function as a message of the emperor's power. It is also reported that the First Emperor had commanded the creation of a large statue of a whale in the capital area at the beginning of his reign. Killing an actual whale may well have been an attempt to build on this to extend common knowledge.[71]

The three locations named in connection with the hunt for the whale are also significant. The plan was conceived of at Langye, where the First Emperor had constructed a terrace, which was also the site for observances in honor of the Lord of the Four Seasons (see earlier in this chapter). *Historian's Records* next reports that the party traveled to Mt. Cheng but that no whale appeared there. That indicates the second locus of the hunt was at the mountain where one sacrificed to the Lord of the Sun. Finally the First Emperor successfully killed a whale at Mt. Zhifu, site of observances in honor of the Lord of Yang.

The fact that only these three names occur in the context of the whale hunt suggests that the First Emperor limited it to places with religious significance. The whale is described as something like the avatar of an evil spirit, which Sima Qian says the First Emperor believed to have been obstructing his hunt for longevity drugs. But I suggest that this reflects how the integration of the two aspects served to magnify the publicity effect of both: on the one hand leveraging the fame and import of the place to make the fact of the killing more memorable and a better signal, while also using the noteworthy event of taking a whale to make the fact of the visit more worthy of discussion and thus a more effective bearer of information. Ultimately the important message was the existence of the First Emperor and the unified realm he ruled. Although a whale is not a supernatural entity per se, it is fantastic. By linking their whaling success to spirits, the emperor and his collaborators further strengthened the broadcast power of the imperial message.

Manhunt as Medium

The unsuccessful search for the would-be assassin Zhang Liang throughout the realm is another example of an event that was linked with the progresses and possessed a definite communicative character. Lin Jianming 林劍鳴 cites this attempted assassination as an example of ongoing resistance in the eastern part of the new empire, where the states that had withstood the Qin longest were located and anti-Qin sentiment persisted.[72] But in terms of communication, the Qin response is more important than Zhang Liang's motive. For despite Sima Qian's apparently straightforward reportage on this event in *Historian's Records*, the reaction seems strange; there are several reasons that a search for Zhang Liang throughout the empire and lasting ten days does not add up. First, given the large size of the new empire and the slowness of transportation at the time, ten days was hardly enough time to complete a serious search. This is clear from records of other cases. For example, the First Emperor was attacked near the capital in 216 BCE, while traveling in disguise at night with only a party of four warriors to protect him. The search for those assailants remained entirely within modern Shaanxi Province yet lasted twenty days.[73] And a 148 BCE search for two specific men who had plotted an assassination lasted over a month.[74]

By the same token, Zhang Liang's possibilities for flight were limited. A focused search would have been more effective—if the goal was catching the criminal. If we accept that political disquiet was concentrated, as Lin Jianming argues, then it seems impractical to search the whole country for a would-be assassin. The Qin had laws about household registration and shared responsibility for crime.[75] Any new residents in an area unable to give a proper account of themselves would attract the attention of both neighbors and authorities, and someone like Zhang Liang would be unable to hide easily without aid. The Qin also gave considerable attention to capturing escaped prisoners, the interest in and techniques of which would surely transfer to catching a criminal.[76] Zhang Liang should have been expected to take shelter among sympathizers. Indeed, his hiding place at Xiapi 下邳 (Jiangsu) was located to the east, in an area Lin argues harbored much anti-Qin feeling. The search could have been focused on these areas and need not have covered the whole empire.

However, considered in light of common knowledge creation, the empire-wide manhunt makes better sense than a focused one would have. As in other cases, those who were looking were also seen: a broad search could generate knowledge of the new monarch and make his universal reach known. An explicitly national search means that metaknowledge also existed: each person who received this message of government action and power knew that many others did, too. Casting a net wider than needed turned the necessity of pursuit into an opportunity for indexical communication, and in a sense recreated the sort of ancient hunt that the progress sprang from originally.

Additional Communication

In the foregoing I have concentrated on specific events that seem to have been designed to garner attention, but many other actions taken in conjunction with the progresses surely worked the same way. The construction at Langye is a good example. The entourage not only installed a stele praising the emperor's deeds, but they also built an enormous terrace and other buildings in the area. Such changes, like baring the soil of Mt. Xiang, were indexical signals showing the ability of the Qin dynasty to affect the world and permanent reminders of Qin Shihuang's visit. Nor was this the only more or less permanent change effected in conjunction with the progresses.

During the fourth progress, the First Emperor commanded the destruction of fortifications and dikes in areas he visited. In the *Historian's Records* account, these acts seem out of place, so much so that some readers have proposed changing the text to move or remove them. Thinking in terms of common knowledge creation suggests that Sima Qian may have grouped these actions with the progresses because they were part of a single undertaking. By altering the landscape in a way bound to be noticed, the First Emperor indexed his power and communicated it to the people. Lin Jianming says these changes benefited the economy, which may well have been the case, but that just underscores how broad the effect would have been.[77] This changed the land and brought positive change to the lives of the people as well, showing them the breadth of the emperor's reach and communicating his power.

The shift of thousands of households to Langye meant that none of these events could escape notice: like the thousands of convict laborers who worked to denude Mt. Xiang, each member of the affected population would relay the message, speaking of the move for years to come. They would of course also know that their former neighbors also knew. The result was the creation of core groups to spread common knowledge of the First Emperor's progress and sojourn at Langye out into broader society. The connection of Langye with religion lent this message additional potency.

Common knowledge creation offers a way to think about events reported in *Historian's Records* that are often doubted by scholars. Two examples from the second tour illustrate this well. After his observances at Langye, the First Emperor, acting on the advice of esoteric practitioners, sent thousands of the area's sons and daughters to search for immortals believed to be living on mystical islands in the ocean.[78] Such a tale immediately evokes suspicion, but sending children to sea in search of immortals would have had the effect of sending a potent and supernaturally charged message to thousands of common families. In another example, *Historian's Records* says that while at Pengcheng during his second tour, the First Emperor ritually purified himself and prayed before dispatching a large number of men to dive into the river in an unsuccessful attempt to recover one or more Zhou dynasty bronze tripods supposedly lost in the River Si 泗水. It is doubtful that Zhou bronzes had sunk in the Si. Yet the story was famous in ancient times. The tripods' connection—imagined or not—with the Zhou lent them what Wang Chong, writing in the first century CE, called a "mystical reputation" (*shenming* 神名). That repute was so potent he suggested the whole story of them having fallen into the Si was invented because of it.[79] Perhaps the story of unsuccessful recovery reflects the First Emperor's attempt to exploit that fame.

Throughout the progresses the First Emperor and his advisors went to great pains to ensure that the messages of Qin imperial rule were broadcast in multiple media across a wide geographical area, often framed in mystical terms. These records should not be dismissed, and understanding them in the framework I offer here can explain why these acts took place and why they have loomed so large in historical and popular imagination ever since.[80]

Early Evidence for the Progress as Public Communication

Since we have virtually no written materials directly from the common people of early China, their perceptions of the progresses are lost to us. There is also little direct indication from the First Emperor about the motives for carrying out the progresses. Religious ritual clearly played a part. Yet beginning already in *Historian's Records*, many have argued that power and politics were involved, and I agree. The lack of information concerning what the people and the First Emperor thought about the progresses makes my interpretation of them as a communicative process necessarily tentative. However, the framework I outlined in chapters 2 and 3 shows this to be a viable interpretation. Evidence in sources from both before and after the Qin dynasty supports the assertion that the progresses were also so understood in early times.

Early thinkers like Xunzi, Shang Yang, Han Feizi, and others recognized the necessity of getting broad support for the ruler and the absolutely vital role of communication in this process. Early texts show that the progress specifically was a means to achieve this sort of goal. This comes in pre-Qin writings like *Zuo's Commentary*, which says, "If not to expand [knowledge of] his rectitude, the Son of Heaven does not make a progress" 非展義不巡守.[81] The progress was also portrayed as a way the ruler could exercise authority, as when the *Book of Changes* (*Yijing* 易經) asserts, "The first kings, by inspecting places, observed the people and established influence" 先王以省方觀民設教.[82] Similar ideas can be found in Han materials. *Huainanzi* contains the normative assertion that the sage ruler Yao "made a progress and exerted influence" 巡狩行教.[83] And Han Emperor Zhang 章 (Liu Da 劉炟, r. 76–88) explained, "The system of the progresses serves to promulgate my renown and influence" 巡狩之制, 以宣聲教.[84]

Thorough Discussions at White Tiger Pavilion (*Bohu tong* 白虎通) records a scholarly meeting from 79 CE, and its chapter on progresses provides early support for my analysis in two respects. It calls the personal performance of the progress by the ruler "the acme of conscientiously respecting and giving importance to the people" 謹敬重民之至也. *Thorough Discussions* also makes certain practical matters part of the progress, including "correcting standards and measures" 正法度 and "unifying musical scales and calendars" 同律曆. And it says that these things and the progresses were "all done for the people" 皆為民也.[85] This confirms the notion that a progress was directed at the people, and supports my contention that acts like the First Emperor's standardizations, which I talked about in chapter 4, can be understood as part of the same process.

We know that commoners observed the progresses.[86] And it is impossible that the presence of the emperor and his entourage could fail to make an impression on the locals during a visit—not least because common people from all levels of society could be called upon to provide logistical support for his visits.[87] The personal chronicle of the low-level Qin official found at Shuihudi mentions the First Emperor's passage near where he lived, showing he was cognizant of it.[88] Because of limitations in available source materials, the communicative effects of the progresses among the broader population must remain an inference but certainly a reasonable one.

Conclusion

In this chapter, I have demonstrated that we can best understand the First Emperor's progresses as communicative practices that worked to create common knowledge of the new sovereign. The staccato historical record might seem like a scattershot barrage of disconnected acts around and including the progresses. But it is better to interpret them as a tremendous publicity campaign carried out in multiple media.

It is impossible to prove that the First Emperor and his advisors acted deliberately in this respect. However, their aggressive borrowing from and adaptation of practices connected with the former rulers of the state of Qin and of the realm, and the repeated and exaggerated nature of many of the acts, suggest they did. The inclusion of unforeseeable events among these (e.g., killing the whale) mean that even if the First Emperor acted deliberately, there was no way the whole sequence could have been planned. But if the First Emperor realized the importance of common knowledge, and the power of ritual and other acts to create it and strengthen its effects, as I suggest, then he may have been alert for and ready to take advantage of such opportunities when they presented themselves—as they were sure to do.

This early version of a publicity campaign was a success. It was part of a set of policies that stabilized the state and connected the First Emperor personally to his position. The realm was generally quiet during the years between unification and the First Emperor's death, free from large-scale disturbances both internal and external. The quick fall of the Qin after the First Emperor's death and the political turmoil characterizing the early decades of Han rule emphasize how extraordinary this situation was.

But the success of this campaign may also have contributed to the end of the Qin dynasty soon after the First Emperor's death. For by creating so much common knowledge of himself, the First Emperor made his legitimacy highly personal. We know the First Emperor resisted making arrangements for his death, including transferring power to a successor.[89] Furthermore, the Second Emperor was not the heir selected by the First Emperor to succeed him and lacked the personal characteristics and perceived legitimacy required to rule effectively. These factors combined to leave the dynasty vulnerable after the First Emperor's death, especially in the absence of a clear and authorized succession, and may have left the Second Emperor unable to effectively assume his father's position. The Second Emperor and his supporters seem to have realized this, and the Second Emperor's recapitulation of his father's progresses, including adding inscriptions to the steles, may be best understood as a failed attempt to appropriate the gains of the First Emperor's publicity campaigns for himself.

The success of the progresses in generating publicity may also have contributed to the negative historical portrayal of the Qin by later scholars. Rappaport argues that performing a ritual demonstrates submission to the moral order sanctioning that ritual. It follows that by using the ritual progress associated with the sage kings, the First Emperor was obligating himself to adhere to their standards. Even if we set aside as inconclusively proven the commonplace portrayal of Qin rule as harsh, clearly the problems of a unified empire were not amenable to the idealized methods attributed to former rulers of much smaller territories. By publicly accepting those standards in front of an audience comprising the whole realm, the First Emperor obliged himself to follow that system. When he acted otherwise, he helped ensure a negative historical portrayal for himself and his dynasty. The mantle of sage rule he had claimed became the means to criticize him. Through his publicity campaign, the First Emperor determined the same signs that were later redeployed against his dynasty's memory.

6

Roads to Rule

Construction as Communication

Roads and ways featured prominently among the First Emperor of Qin's projects. He is not the first successful conqueror recorded to have expanded roads. Confucius supposedly said that one of the first acts of King Wu—exemplary ruler and founder of the Zhou dynasty—when he won power was to make roads to the territories of neighboring groups.[1] Nor is this limited to China. Ray Laurence has written about the role roads played in effecting and expanding political power under the Roman empire.[2] Yet historical materials and archaeological research indicate that the First Emperor's system of imperial roads was in many ways unprecedented and had effects far broader than have been acknowledged. For among their many activities in the years after unification, the Qin rulers' road projects must have been among the most conspicuous at the time.

Due to the evident utility of roads, the possibility of another or an additional impetus or effect for these developments has received little consideration: the consensus has been that the roads were built to travel on. Disagreements, when they arise, concern routes and periodization, or the type(s) and significance of various kinds of movement. And of course, roads *were* built for travel. Yet I will show reasons to doubt the sufficiency of the commonsense appraisal exist, not least because there is evidence that the changes involved in establishing these roads were less than often assumed: while there was surely change at this time, there had been no lack of roads connecting the areas of the empire before then. Something more was going on.

As elsewhere in this work, I will argue that a primary effect of the changes that did occur was communication and the creation of common knowledge of the new state among the entire population of the empire—and even among some of those outside its borders. I begin this chapter with consideration of a set of roads in and around the Qin capital, the walled roads (*yongdao* 甬道) and raised ways (*fudao* 復道). I then discuss the national network of highways, which is commonly understood to have been built at the order of the First Emperor. I will argue that roads designated as highways were, as far as can be determined, mostly not new. As such, the changes to the road system did not link together places that had not been connected before, and the significance of the changes lay elsewhere—specifically, in communication. In the second part of this chapter, I will examine one particularly famous road from this perspective: the Direct Road, which stretched from Ganquan Mountain in the vicinity of the capital to the northwestern border region.

Walled Roads and Raised Ways in the Capital

The historical sources that describe Qin road projects in the years after unification are limited. *Historian's Records* lists a series of events from 220 BCE, which includes the construction of walled roads in the area of the Qin capital Xianyang and construction of a highway network throughout the realm, among other things.[3] A few years later, in 212 BCE, the First Emperor constructed a number of additional walled roads and raised walkways connecting the hundreds of palaces and towers within 110 km of the capital. Raised ways would become common in the Han period and later, but during the Qin there were few.[4]

The first reference to walled roads in *Historian's Records* names them as part of a burst of building activity after unification, without attributing further, specific cause. The second reference portrays them together with raised ways as an expression of deluded paranoia, which made hiding the First Emperor a way to avoid demons.[5] I suggest that we may accept the account of this occurrence without necessarily accepting that the supernatural purpose Sima Qian names was the sole or even the primary function. For it was not unreasonable for the First Emperor to wish to keep his whereabouts secret in the interests of personal security. As would be expected, there were multiple attempts on his life.[6] And at the same time the walled roads and skyways concealed and protected him, they also announced his presence. The use of walled roads in warfare is an analogue that helps illustrate this point.

Walled roads featured in military action around the fall of Qin and in the subsequent civil war that lasted until 202 BCE, when Liu Bang defeated his rival to become emperor. According to the Eastern Han writer Ying Shao 應邵 (fl. 189–194), the primary purpose of walled roads in a military context was to prevent observation of wagons transporting stores, which would enable the enemy to calculate troop strength. Other times, the walls enabled transports to move safely by blocking their presence from view.[7]

Early Chinese generals made use of walled roads for only a relatively short time. Historian Wang Zijin 王子今 suggests this resulted from developments that increased mobility and transportation speed, which made walled roads unnecessary.[8] Yet even if such developments played a part, the intrinsic strategic weakness of using permanent or semi-permanent walled roads was surely a greater factor—although, obviously, in certain cases they could still be useful. Walled roads may have blocked one's enemies from gathering certain information from a distance. But at the same time they communicated the simpler yet more important message that the roads with walls were those that mattered, that they were the ones worth protecting. An enemy's success in cutting off transport lines marked and guarded by walls could force a general to ask for terms, or it could lead to the defeat of those who had depended on those supplies. Wang Zijin says this is because cutting off or blocking walled roads was the key to success or failure.[9] This is true but not because of the walled roads themselves. Rather, it was because the walls invariably sought to protect the most vital routes. Walling in key roads thus comprised a signal, which communicated information about the importance of transport routes.

Walled roads would be much more useful for protecting a single individual in the capital from direct attack than for guarding a military supply line. A train of wagons bearing matériel requires time to pass, and alerting the adversary to its probable route would enable opposing forces to monitor the road and prepare an attack. The passage of a single man, even with an entourage, is relatively quick, and simply concealing it from view would do much to prevent attack. But walled roads in and around the capital also signaled which roads were the emperor's. Those walls communicated.

At the same time they were making walled roads, the Qin were building raised ways for the emperor through and around the capital. These elevated roads lifted the First Emperor above the level of the street, protecting him and keeping his person from public view. Yet the common people knew whose roads those were. This is clear from an event that occurred slightly later. In early times, imperial travel required the common population to clear the road; records show these laws were widely known and the period of each interruption was long. Emptying the way eased the emperor's travels and protected his safety, but frequent imperial travel meant equally frequent inconvenience to those whose lives were interrupted. A historical incident from the early Han period shows this. In 191 BCE, Han Emperor

Hui's trips back and forth from the Changle Palace 長樂宮 disturbed local residents.¹⁰ As a result, an elevated road was built from the south of the imperial armory to the palace, permitting the emperor to move about without having to clear the roads. But there was a problem: the new skyway overlooked a road upon which the monthly ceremonial display of the cap and clothing of the Han founder took place. The ritual expert Shusun Tong 叔孫通 objected on the grounds that this constituted disrespect. Nevertheless, he rejected the frightened emperor's initial reaction to this observation, which was to destroy the raised road. The reason is telling: "The lord of men makes no mistakes. Now you have already built [the raised way], and the common people all know it" 人主無過舉, 今已作, 百姓皆知之.¹¹

The ordinary inhabitants knew the emperor was responsible for building the elevated way, and dismantling it would have indicated to the people that its construction had been wrong. It was unacceptable for the people to perceive that their ruler had erred, and it was a serious matter if they believed he had. Such reasoning confirms that the common people were observing and drawing conclusions about their rulers based on constructions like the raised ways—and surely walled ways, too—and these conclusions mattered.

Mark Edward Lewis has written about the connection between secrecy and political power in early China. He makes specific reference to the early emperors' measures, including raised ways, walled roads, and similar constructions that concealed the ruler from view. Lewis notes that hiding the emperor's movements was also a security measure that hid him from would-be assassins.¹² Wang Zijin and Ma Zhenzhi 馬振智 have connected raised ways to defensive constructions described in *Mozi* that enabled a defender to see without being seen.¹³ This would be an obvious security benefit to any ruler—to say nothing of someone like the First Emperor, who had won his position by conquering a number of rivals within a short time and lived under the real threat of assassination. But more resulted than this.

Just as walling in roads and building elevated walkways erased the person of the emperor from the view of the public, they also made his presence and his ways permanent and known. What would have been transitory was fixed in place, and what would have been a brief occurrence became permanent. As a walled road in a battle zone told an enemy *this is the important road*, walled roads in the capital area said *the emperor walks here*. At the same time these walls obscured the emperor's movements, they made his paths permanent and communicated his presence in an enduring manner, communicating his political self.

The ritual clearing of the people from the roads and streets before the emperor passed forced everyone out of the imperial presence but also made everyone aware that he was passing. It simultaneously created common knowledge of the same: for each person knew of the emperor's passing, and knew that everyone else along his route did, too.

Walled roads and skyways obviously functioned in a different manner. Clearing the road for the emperor's passage was a publicly announced and legally enforced injunction that temporarily converted public space into an area reserved for the emperor and his entourage. The walled roads and raised ways were permanent structures and permanent changes to the lives of the people. Walled roads and raised ways would certainly have attracted the notice of those who passed through streets that were suddenly blocked, indeed of everyone who was forced to detour around the walls. This would have changed the lives of local residents and most certainly would have gotten their attention. Raised ways were less disruptive, in that they permitted people to pass beneath them. Yet this sort of permanent change to the cityscape could not but have attracted the notice of those living there. And ritual experts like Shusun Tong cannot have been the only ones who interpreted the position of the skyways above as one of superiority.

All in all, few living in the area of the Qin capital could fail to see and/or be affected by the existence of the emperor, in the streets, if nowhere else. Walled roads and skyways for imperial use shielded the emperor's person from view, and at the same time they formed a permanent sign of imperial presence in the capital area. In the next section, I argue that the Qin imperial highway system served a similar function across a broader area.

The Qin Highways

Naturally, many roads existed before unification under the Qin, and early texts record that there were also highways in pre-imperial China. But there is no clear indication of a unified system of highways before the one described in *Historian's Records*, which existed first under the Qin.[14] And while there is passing mention of the Qin highways at a number of places in *Historian's Records*, accounts of their construction are terse and give no details.[15]

In the early second century BCE, Jia Shan 賈山 (fl. ca. 179 BCE) wrote an essay in which he criticizes the Qin dynasty at length, linking their perceived mistakes to the fall of their dynasty. The biggest of these purported mistakes, and something that became a trope among Han writers on the Qin, was the Qin mania for gigantic public works. Archaeological research shows the Qin were in fact building oversized structures well before

221 BCE. Jia Shan deems the Qin highway system an example of this predilection. He describes a network of roads that connected the whole of the Qin realm to its capital, Xianyang. At least five such highways existed during the Qin dynasty, leading to the east, southeast, northeast, west, and southwest. This network formed the basis and inspiration for the roads of future dynasties, and its creation made the Qin the most influential road builders in Chinese history.[16]

Jia Shan describes broad roads on packed-earth beds with rows of trees marking off a lane in the middle. Legal materials confirm that travel in the center lane was forbidden to all except the emperor. Officials with authorization and certain others were permitted to use the side lanes. Additional, outside lanes alongside these probably existed for the use of ordinary officials and people. Illegal use of the reserved sections was punishable with banishment and confiscation of any livestock and/or conveyance involved. According to Qin statutes, if the officials responsible for enforcement should fail to punish offenders, they were fined. Similar laws existed under the Han and historical records show the laws were enforced.[17]

Under ordinary circumstances it may have been illegal to even cross the restricted center section of the highway. An event from Han times suggests this. While the future Emperor Cheng was still crown prince, he was once tardy in responding to an imperial summons; his excuse was that he had detoured to avoid crossing the imperial road. This respect pleased the emperor, who granted the crown prince special permission to cross the imperial way.[18]

During the Han, groups and sometimes individuals were given the privilege to use the reserved lanes of the highways. From the first years of the Han, if not earlier, commoners who held a "king's staff" (*wangzhang* 王杖) were allowed to travel in the lane reserved for authorized officials. This staff was about 2 m long, with a bird-shaped head, and was granted to men of advanced age—the precise number of years depending on the individual's rank.[19] No later than the early first century BCE, the common people widely disobeyed the laws concerning the roads.[20] This seems inevitable. Given that the network covered thousands of kilometers, it would have been difficult to police effectively, even if only to keep ordinary people out of the reserved lane(s). But that dates to long after the Qin.

In terms of creating common knowledge, the Qin highway system had characteristics that made it a very effective means of communication. Because of the limited information available to us, it is difficult to know exactly what the systemization of highways entailed. But the available evidence indicates an expansion and improvement of existing roads, linking those together into a national network, and dedicating part of those roads to imperial use. At least a part of each Qin highway was set aside like this, while another was open for use. Whether the latter part was officially considered "in" the highway or alongside it, this must have changed the lives of the people whose communities it passed through in different ways. Some studies on the topic argue that an economic effect resulted from the highways and this seems likely. Indeed, any expansion of transportation would have had such effects, which would have depended on the use of the highways by the broader population.[21] But I would take this line of interpretation one step further. Like the unification of weights and measures I talked about in chapter 4, the Qin creation of the highway system represented the expansion of a specifically Qin type of government across the realm. It created common knowledge among the populace not only of a new governance but of Qin governance. The common people required knowledge of the system to avoid transgressing its strictures, even as they benefited from its presence.

By setting aside a section of each highway for exclusive imperial use, the Qin essentially made the emperor always present and declared his existence to all. The highway system made the emperor's path permanent and marked it off with trees. This turned the road into a communication, an indexical sign of imperial presence and power. Like the walled roads and skyways in the capital area, the center lane marked and communicated imperial presence, even—or especially—in the absence of the emperor. The fact that officials and certain others were permitted to use part but not all of this reserved road could only have strengthened this effect, in that these stressed the emperor's power to make exceptions to these rules: the ultimate index of a particular power lies not in enforcement but in allowing exceptions.[22] These exceptions were sure to have been obvious to the observing public, who could see that the emperor had granted this privilege and to whom. The new road system worked to communicate to the population about the new Qin government, establishing it as the new and most important focal point for cooperation. One specific road has received special attention since ancient times, and it is there that I turn next.

The Direct Road

In the first part of this chapter, I argued that raised ways, walled roads, and the Qin systematization of highways worked to communicate, to create common knowledge of Qin rule within Xianyang and across the realm.

Here I will concentrate on one particularly famous road, the Direct Road (Zhidao 直道), which ran from the area of the capital to the northwestern corner of the empire. Because of its fame this road has been the subject of much scholarly discussion. As in the case of other Qin roads, I suggest that the Direct Road served to create common knowledge among the populations it passed through, which was also sure to spread more widely. I will furthermore discuss its endpoints and argue that the construction of this road built on the ritual and religious significance of its termini to make a more potent signal. This signal, by design, reached not only those within the empire but also the semi-nomadic people living in and near its border regions, especially the Xiongnu, a confederation of semi-nomadic herders that was an emergent power at the time of unification.[23]

The Meaning of the Name

In 212 BCE, the First Emperor commanded the construction of the Direct Road between Ganquan 甘泉 (Shaanxi) and Jiuyuan 九原 (Inner Mongolia). The name in Chinese, Zhidao, consists of the word *dao* 道, meaning "road, way," and *zhi* 直, which often means "straight." In consequence, some readers have understood the term as "straight road," believing that it was supposed to run with only minimal deviation between its endpoints. But it is more likely that *zhi* here is better understood as "direct," because one of the *Historian's Records* passages relating the Direct Road's creation says it formed an uninterrupted connection between its endpoints.[24] In the subsequent discussion I will refer to this road as the Direct Road, but I want to briefly consider the meaning of the original name. For I would suggest there was another layer of meaning to the name Zhidao.

The word *zhi* denotes straightness and directness and also had the metaphorical sense of rectitude. Lines from the *Book of Odes* poem "Mighty East" reflect this:

The way of Zhou is [flat] as a whetstone,	周道如砥
And straight (*zhi*) as an arrow.	其直如矢
It is what the superior man walks	君子所履
And the petty man watches.[25]	小人所視

The "way" referred to in the poem is at once abstract and concrete. It designates a road that is flat and straight, which, according to the canonical commentary, is a metaphor for proper methods of governance, a good Way (Dao) of rule. The canonical commentary further explains that "flat" alludes to fair taxation, and "straight" describes an unbiased legal system. Occurrences of the phrase *zhidao* 直道 elsewhere in the classical canon refer to the correct and/or undeviating fulfillment of duty.[26]

The Qin placed great value on the virtues of fairness and uprightness in their bureaucratic system of governance. A recovered Qin text on bureaucratic praxis begins by asserting the necessity of rectitude, and Qin statutes name failure to uphold it the criminal offense of being "not straight" (*buzhi* 不直).[27] The term they used for upright(ness) was the same word *zhi* that occurs in the name Zhidao, and I would suggest that the Zhidao was named as much or more for the virtue *zhi* as it was to describe the route: the Direct Road instantiated and so communicated the Upright Way of Qin.

Construction of the Direct Road

The construction of the Direct Road was exceptional among the road projects carried out during the First Emperor's reign, in that it is the only road *Historian's Records* singles out for specific mention. I suggest it received special consideration because it had a distinct purpose. *Historian's Records* speaks of the Direct Road's construction in a number of passages and a bit less laconically than it does the construction of the highway network yet still gives little detail. It records that the Qin general Meng Tian did the major work on the project as part of his campaign against the Xiongnu. The road connected Jiuyuan and Ganquan Mountain, in Yunyang 雲陽, some 160 km northwest from the Qin capital, traveling a reported distance of almost 1,000 km or even longer. There is nothing in *Historian's Records* about the specific route. We now know it lay in part at least on top of older roads, like the rest of the highway system.[28]

Historian's Records also tells us the Direct Road was not completed. This recalls another Qin mega-project, the Epang Palace (Epanggong 阿房宮). This palace, too, was known to have been left incomplete, but under the potent influence of Du Mu's 杜牧 (803–ca. 853) famous poem about it, most readers assumed the palace had been finished in all significant respects and lacked only the final flourishes. In fact these assumptions have no basis in early history, and archaeological fieldwork in recent years has shown that Epang Palace never got beyond the initial stages of construction.[29]

During his brief reign, the Second Emperor of Qin restarted construction of the Direct Road (as he did the work on Epang Palace). So perhaps the road was extended or improved under his rule. We know it was at least passable while the First Emperor was on the throne. This is clear from the first of two instances in *Historian's Records* in which people traveled the Direct Road: the Direct Road formed part of the route by which the First Emperor's entourage clandestinely bore his corpse back to Xianyang while pretending he still lived after his death while on his final imperial progress. The second important reference to the Direct Road comes in Sima Qian's first-person comments in *Historian's Records*, where he reports that he traveled the Direct Road from north to south. But even though he says he traveled the Direct Road, Sima Qian makes only a few general observations about it.[30]

In fact all references to the Direct Road in *Historian's Records* lack detail concerning its characteristics and route. The only certain facts are the endpoints. Nor does Sima Qian give explicit reasons for constructing the Direct Road, simply putting it into the context of struggle with non-Chinese nomads without further explanation. In the next section I argue the Direct Road served to communicate with the people within the empire, including those living in the areas it passed through and also with non-Chinese peoples living beyond the Qin borders. Its planning made use of existing focal points, particularly mountains and mountain ranges, which had political and religious connotations for both groups. I begin by looking at previous explanations of the reason or reasons for building the Qin Direct Road, and discuss why these do not explain its full impact.

Previous Explanations for the Direct Road and Its Route

Most explanations for the construction of the Direct Road link it to military necessity, often in the form of a general defensive purpose.[31] That the Qin built the Direct Road in the context of a struggle with semi-nomadic groups along their borders—groups like the Xiongnu—is clear from accounts in *Historian's Records*. Although researchers have offered a number of explanations for how the Direct Road worked in that struggle, I think that shortcomings in these explanations have so far left the question unresolved.

The eminent historical geographer Shi Nianhai 史念海 postulated a number of reasons that the Qin made the Direct Road. The broadest of these reasons was that it aided a counter-Xiongnu strategy of "positive defense," which combined elements of defense with elements of attack. Elsewhere, Shi asserts its purpose was a general military one, connecting this to his suggested route of the road (see later discussion). Shi argues that because the Direct Road ran on top of the Ziwuling 子午岭 mountain range, it was flatter and thus preferable to other possibilities. He also suggests that while a road following the mountain range would not be straight, a road below the mountains would have been too circuitous. He furthermore believes the high road gave a tactical advantage over the Xiongnu and others on horseback, who tended to travel along river courses. Other scholars name similar reasons, often saying the Direct Road facilitated military movement and transport to the northwestern border regions. Some point to the economic effects of the road, which they also believe helped integrate the northwest with the rest of the empire politically and culturally.[32]

A few researchers have proposed more abstract effects. Li Zhongli 李 仲立, for example, says that along with improving transportation of matériel to the border zone, the Direct Road strengthened the ideology of unification, although he does not explain exactly how the latter occurred. And although Wang Zijin believes the Direct Road to have been primarily a military project, he also says it served to commemorate Qin rule.[33]

As in the case of the imperial progresses in chapter 6, the variety of explanations for the Direct Road surely reflects the broad range of causal factors involved and effects that resulted. But many of the commonly asserted reasons are predicated on the notion that there was no transportation route between the capital area and Jiuyuan, or that the Direct Road was superior to any roads that previously existed. The first of these premises is false, the second dubious.

Shi Nianhai and others have suggested that the Qin Zhidao was constructed where no road previously existed.[34] Yet historical records indicate that travel and thus roads existed between Jiuyuan and Xianyang before unification in 221 BCE and after unification but before the Zhidao existed. For example, one of the First Emperor's predecessors in the state of Qin traveled to the area near the border of Gansu Province and Inner Mongolia in the late third century BCE. The First Emperor himself traveled through the area while visiting the northern border region in 215 BCE. Other historical records indicate, directly or indirectly, the possibility of travel to and from Jiuyuan.[35] Furthermore, the requirements of the Qin bureaucratic system of governance depended on the regular exchange of documents between the central government and local officials, in addition to periodic inspections and other contact. This movement of documents and men required transportation no later than the early fourth century BCE, when the state of Qin established administrative structures in the northwestern commandery Shangjun 上郡.[36] There can be no doubt that an established route between the Qin capital Xianyang and the northwest existed prior to unification.

There is moreover archaeological evidence that the Ziwuling mountain range was populated no later than Neolithic times and remained so during the centuries before the emergence of the Qin empire. An area with such a long history of settlement would necessarily have roads. Archaeologists have reported earlier remains along the route of the Direct Road, which show at least parts of its route were in use then, and their fieldwork has confirmed that at least some sections of it were built on previously existing roadbeds. And as they point out, this just makes sense: given the brevity of the Qin reign and the technology available at the time, the Direct Road could only have been put through on the basis of previous roads.[37]

Arguments based on the supposed uniqueness of the Direct Road generally fail to take into account that there were other roads in the area. There were in fact several. Two ran alongside the Ziwuling range, one to the east, following the Yan River 延川, the other to the west, next to the Malian River 馬蓮河. A third road, the Xiao Pass Road 肖關道, lay still further west on a flat area surrounded by grass fodder for horses, making it an especially attractive alternative for military travel. Some explanations for the Direct Road are based on a perceived superiority of its route. For example, one researcher explains that the Direct Road's elevation gave it a controlling position over the network of roads in the area. But a simple track connecting watchtowers would have enabled observation. The amount of territory involved and the difficulties inherent in traveling a mountain region in comparison to the natural roads formed by rivers makes this unsatisfying.[38]

Scholars have suggested that the route through the mountains was superior to one that stayed on the flatlands, as the latter would have to contend with topographical difficulties not present on the mountains.[39] But it is hard to imagine a road along the top of a mountain range—and all routes of the Direct Road agree it ran along the top of the Ziwuling range for much of its length—presenting a road superior enough to a flatland route to offset the increased difficulties of constructing or improving and then using an elevated route. Since the Direct Road must have still been quite uneven over its long course, and following the Ziwuling range took the road far off from the north-south line, these benefits would have to have been great indeed. The existence of other roads, including those along rivers and next to the range, indicates the advantages of those routes. The fact that the Xiongnu habitually followed rivers underscores the fact that the easiest routes in the area were most likely found in riparian zones. All in all, the arguments that assert the superiority of a mountain route as the reason for creating the Direct Road and for its route seem suspect.

A further, specific argument against thinking that the Direct Road served exclusively military purposes comes from its relationship to the Ziwuling range and the role of the Ganquan Mountain area as a buffer to outside incursion. Early writers stressed that the natural geography of the Qin state fortified it against invasion and helped its rise to power. The mountainous Ganquan region in particular was a natural barrier to attack on the Qin capital Xianyang from the west and northwest.[40] It is highly unlikely that someone of military acuity—which the First Emperor of Qin most certainly was—would fail to recognize that any road is potentially a two-way street. Building or improving roads through an important natural defense, connecting the territories either under the control or situated very close to active, able enemies, would weaken those natural defenses. Doing so when the endpoint of the road was close to the capital and connected to it by highway, as in the case of the Direct Road, would exacerbate the effect. Although roads existed in the area previous to this, improving those roads and linking them to form a Direct Road to Ganquan from outside does not make sense from a strictly military perspective, especially since alternate routes existed for the use of Qin armies. Something more must have been going on, something that more than compensated for any weakening of the natural defenses.

My contention is that construction of the Direct Road, like so many of the First Emperor's undertakings around the time of unification, served the purposes of communication and creating common knowledge. Wang Zijin makes an argument conceptually similar to mine when he says the Direct Road commemorated Qin governance.[41] But I expand this significantly. Commemoration concerns perceptions of the past, while I argue the Direct Road communicated the present existence of Qin governance and did so as part of a project of creating common knowledge. I believe the nature of this communication and the scope of the audience helped determine the road's termini and route.

The Route and Endpoints of the Direct Road

There is little dispute about where the Direct Road began and ended. *Historian's Records*, after all, tells us that the Direct Road ran between Jiuyuan in the north and Ganquan, in Yunyang, northwest of the capital. There is some slight variation in this regard, and some have suggested that the road actually connected Xianyang proper with Jiuyuan. However, none of the earliest texts describes the Direct Road as leading to Xianyang, which I think is no accident: it ran from Ganquan in Yunyang, not from the capital.[42] But because there is no early description of the Direct Road's route, historians and archaeologists have debated it for years. The most probable route has the Direct Road ascending the Ziwuling mountain range near Ganquan and remaining atop these mountains, following the range west into Gansu before descending and veering back east across the Ordos Plains.[43]

I propose that the Direct Road's endpoints indicate its significance and ultimate function. In the following I will show that the termini were sites of ritual and religious significance: for the Chinese, this applied for Ganquan; for the Xiongnu, it was the case for both places. This significance was, at least sometimes, coincident with political authority. By connecting these two, the Direct Road formed a message of Qin supremacy couched in religious and ritual terms that strengthened the transmission of its message.

Ganquan in Yunyang

Records of the Direct Road's creation put its southern end either at Yunyang or Ganquan. Yunyang was the name of a prefecture during Qin times and before. It was located northwest of modern Xi'an. Ganquan Mountain, named for the sweet springs supposedly found there, is within the former borders of Yunyang, and the two names were sometimes used interchangeably in Han times and later.[44]

The Qin administrative apparatus was present in Yunyang before unification, and the philosopher Han Feizi was imprisoned there. In that specific context, Yunyang referred to a walled town northwest of the Yunyang prefectural center, also the location of the First Emperor's Ganquan palace.[45]

Yunyang generally and Ganquan specifically had religious and mystical associations. Some texts connect the Yunyang area with one of the legendary Five Emperors, revered as the spirit of the west and an object of Qin worship, who was said to have been buried there. A number of sources report that Yunyang contained the ruins of antiquity. Ganquan was said to be the place where the mythical Yellow Emperor (Huangdi 黃帝) constructed the Bright Hall (Mingtang 明堂) ceremonial center and the location of other ancient sacrifices.[46]

The area also had connections with the Xiongnu and related groups. The term Xiongnu must be treated with special care in this context. There are references to the Xiongnu in sources from or describing the time before the late third century BCE, but these must be understood to denote one or more of the groups that eventually made up the Xiongnu or their forerunners. One such group, the Yiqu 義渠, held Ganquan until they were driven out by Chinese expansion in pre-imperial times. Medieval and later sources report that Ganquan was a locus of proto-Xiongnu religious observance in the time before Qin. Xiongnu worship was later (re)instituted in the same area because of its longstanding identification of the place as a location for religious ritual.⁴⁷

The early and medieval writings that place the Yiqu, Xiongnu, and similar groups in Yunyang and at Ganquan deserve skepticism, and I do not think they enable us to derive a specific, reliable history of those places. But whatever their shortcomings as historical sources, these texts convey the unmistakable impression, existing from early imperial times if not before, that Ganquan and Yunyang were holy and mystical, connected with legends and spirits, and that this association was shared by people within and beyond the Chinese empire—including people who, if not Xiongnu, belonged to a related culture. Yunyang and Ganquan represent the broader tendency for places of religious and ritual significance to maintain that significance over the passage of time and to acquire religious and ritual significance for other groups.⁴⁸

Historical records of construction at Ganquan Mountain also show it was associated with political power from an early time. Watanabe Shin'ichirō 渡辺信一郎 has written about how political and religious power became closely entwined at Ganquan, a tendency that continued into Western Han times and reached a peak under Emperor Wu 武 (Liu Che 劉徹, r. 141–87 BCE). Li Ling argues that in 112 BCE Emperor Wu chose Ganquan to be the location for his altars for worshipping the Grand One 泰一 because it had long been consecrated to religion and ritual.⁴⁹ I will show in the following section that the northern endpoint at Jiuyuan had comparable, if different, associations.

Jiuyuan

Jiuyuan and its surrounding area have a very long and complex history. Jiuyuan was a large commandery in early imperial times and comprised an area reaching from around the modern city of Baotou in the east to the foot of the Yinshan 陰山 mountain range in the north and ending in the west at the base of the Langshan 狼山 mountains. The commandery administrative center was located a bit to the west of Baotou. Notably, Jiuyuan encompassed the Hetao 河套 region, which contained the fertile and well-watered lands north of the Yellow River and south of the Yinshan range and included a sizeable section of the Ordos Plains in Inner Mongolia.⁵⁰

The Chinese toponym Jiuyuan dates at least to the Warring States period, when it was a commandery of the state of Zhao.⁵¹ But when Zhao's power waned, Jiuyuan—being both large and removed from the center of power—became impossible for it to control. Thus, at the end of the Warring States period, parts or all of the Jiuyuan area were in contention and may even have been under Xiongnu control. Shi Nianhai has argued that the establishment of commanderies, along with building walls and other activity in this area, should all to be understood as anti-Xiongnu actions. Qin attention to the area, including Meng Tian's campaigns, was part of a long-term struggle over this valuable piece of territory.[52]

Ecological change over the centuries has left much of the Hetao region barren. Around the third century BCE, however, it was valuable land, which is why it was a point of conflict between Chinese settlers and the Xiongnu and their forerunners. This conflict led the Chinese to construct walls and other fortifications in the Hetao area. Nicola Di Cosmo argues that rather than defending lands already in possession, the construction of these walls in the border region was actually part of Chinese territorial expansion. The state of Zhao built its walls south of the Yinshan range, yet the Xiongnu pushed south into this region as Zhao's power decreased. The Qin later built other walls, and eventually a combination of some Xiongnu leaders joining the Han and an aggressive push under the rule of Emperor Wu forced the remaining Xiongnu to move north. Before that, the Yinshan and Hetao regions were in contention, and the Yinshan area was not under the firm control of the Qin or Han governments.[53]

Because there is little historical material concerning Jiuyuan in early times, much of our understanding of it depends on archaeology. Combined archaeological and historical research show that Jiuyuan and its surroundings were of longstanding political and religious significance. In particular, the Yinshan mountain range, which lay to the north of Jiuyuan, played a prominent role in the cultural and political life of the Xiongnu.

The Yinshan Region

The Yinshan mountains have been famous since ancient times. Received history tells us the region was of religious, cultural, and political importance to the Xiongnu and other steppes-dwellers. This significance was founded on the region's history, which already went back thousands of years in Qin times, and made the place a focal point in the region.

The Yinshan area contains numerous stone carvings—images that give considerable information about the people who lived in and visited the area.[54] These peoples left little record unless, like the Xiongnu, they happened to come into contact with literate groups like the Chinese, in which case we have secondhand reports about them. Even then, the amount of information available is limited. Through the medium of the stone carvings, we can get some understanding of the denizens of the region and their cultures. They show that the Yinshan area was a center of religious and ceremonial activity for the peoples of the northern plains, including, but not limited to, the Xiongnu. The petroglyphs were created on hard rock faces of all sorts, especially cliffs, by means of drilling and/or chipping, abrasion with tools, scratching, or a combination of these techniques. Although any periodization is necessarily tentative, the earliest carved images in the Yinshan area have been dated to the Paleolithic period. Creation of the carvings continued through the Warring States, Qin-Han, and later periods, all the way down to Ming and Qing times.[55]

The fame of the images had spread already in early times, and the medieval geographer Li Daoyuan 酈道元 (d. 527) described them as a remarkable natural phenomenon:

> The mountain rocks there have natural patterns resembling the forms of tigers and horses, which are as clear and complete as drawings. Thus people call them the Painted Rock Mountains. 山石之上自然有文畫, 若虎馬之狀, 粲然成著, 類似圖焉, 故謂之畫石山也.[56]

Gai Shanlin 蓋山林 has done the most work cataloging and analyzing the Yinshan carvings, which he believes reflect the daily lives and religion of their creators. He divides their content into a number of types, including representations of domestic animals and wildlife, hunting, dancing, and war. Many images found among the Yinshan carvings depict sun worship, including stylized images of the sun, sometimes with the features of a human face or skull. According to Gai, the art reflects other supernatural practices and beliefs as well, particularly the veneration of spirits and ancestors. He identifies Xiongnu-style carvings in an area about 100 km from the former Qin administrative center of Jiuyuan, based on similarity to themes and motifs found in other Xiongnu artwork. Broader cultural traits, like sun worship and the general traits of hunter-pastoralist life were also shared by the Xiongnu. It is natural that the Xiongnu people left behind traces in this area, for as I will discuss later, evidence of various kinds indicates that the Yinshan region was a center for Xiongnu politics and religion. The Yinshan cliff images are not the only evidence that religious ceremonies occurred in the area of the Yinshan mountains in prehistoric times. Neolithic sites just 15 to 20 km east of Baotou include stone structures that archaeologists believe were used for religious rituals. The region thus had associations with religion and rite that go back to its Stone Age inhabitants, including the predecessors of the Xiongnu.[57]

Historical sources record that the Xiongnu had a particular attachment to the Yinshan area. *History of Han* quotes an official familiar with the affairs of border regions, who named the Yinshan region as both the edge of Xiongnu territory and the original headquarters of the Xiongnu leader, the place where they made their bows and arrows, and the base for their raids on Han subjects. In early times, the name "Yinshan" denoted the area to the north and slightly to the east of Jiuyuan, which is only a section of the larger Yinshan range as depicted on modern maps. This mountainous region was an important division between peoples, and Di Cosmo has called it one of the "cultural watersheds" of Northern Asia.[58]

Ma Liqing 馬利清 has surveyed archaeological research with the goal of depicting the shifts in Xiongnu territory over time. Her research indicates that the fertile lands of the Yinshan and Hetao regions enabled them to emerge as a center for proto-Xiongnu culture already in the late Chunqiu or early Warring States period. Ma's results show that when the Xiongnu confederation arose in the third century BCE, its political structures were centered on Yinshan. She also notes that the area of Jiuyuan was the location of an important pass through the Yinshan range, by which the Xiongnu traveled to and from northern Asia.[59]

According to the account in *History of Han*, the Xiongnu gathered three times a year, when they performed seasonal offerings; made sacrifices to their ancestors, spirits, and heaven and earth; and counted themselves.[60] Researchers believe that the Xiongnu leader's court did not have a set location, but—in keeping with the other aspects of Xiongnu life—moved around within a particular region. Religious activity in all likelihood occurred in areas not far removed from this court. The center of this political and religious group activity was Yinshan. The archaeological research that Ma Liqing outlines shows that the Yinshan region, along with the adjacent Hetao area, had long been a cultural and political center for the Xiongnu. Such was the Yinshan region's specific significance that it remained a part of Xiongnu cultural memory even after its loss. As *History of Han* records, "The old border hands said that after the Xiongnu lost Yinshan, they would never pass it without crying" 邊長老言匈奴失陰山 之後, 過之未嘗不哭也.[61]

Ma Liqing points out that the early Great Walls were ineffective defenses. Despite their fame during Warring States and Qin-Han times and later, the walls repeatedly proved that they could not prevent attack. But they did serve to reinforce and strengthen the natural focal point of the Yinshan range as what Di Cosmo called a "cultural watershed" dividing

China from the north.⁶² The walls were part of a concerted effort to turn that barrier into a border accepted by those living beyond it and by those within. Cai Yong 蔡邕 (133–192), looking back several centuries later, described the process this way:

> Heaven established mountains and rivers; the Qin built the Great Walls; and the Han raised border fortifications. These were the means by which to distinguish "within" and "outside," to differentiate those of dissimilar customs. 天設山河, 秦築長城, 漢起塞垣. 所以別內外, 異殊俗也.⁶³

Walls that did not prevent attack still helped form perceptions and communicated a claim to control of a territory. By placing the Direct Road's terminus at Jiuyuan, the First Emperor made that road part of the same process.

Locating the northern end of the Direct Road in a place of ritual, religious, cultural, and military significance for the Xiongnu made the road a message framed in their cultural language, and one that was sure to spread. That the road crossed the Ordos Plains, which had been the location of so much cultural development, surely also strengthened the effect. Like Jiuyuan in the north, Ganquan in the south was a place where realms overlapped: Chinese and non-Chinese, political, religious, and ritual. As I argue in the next section, this parallel helps explain why the First Emperor chose these two places for the termini of the Direct Road and why they worked to broadcast his messages of power.

Ganquan, Jiuyuan, and the Direct Road

Ganquan and Jiuyuan shared a number of characteristics. From a geological perspective, both were adjacent to mountain ranges: from Ganquan the Zhidao ascended into the Ziwuling mountains, while Jiuyuan lay next to the Yinshan range and at the location of an important pass through it. Both were in politically liminal spaces, which belonged to both non-Chinese and Chinese people within recorded history. Yinshan in particular would remain important for the Xiongnu people—in terms of cultural memory, if not otherwise.

At the same time, both Ganquan and Jiuyuan had longstanding religious and mystical associations. Ganquan appears to have been the site of Xiongnu or proto-Xiongnu sacrifices, and it also had supernatural and quasi-supernatural associations for the Chinese. Material evidence for the ritual link between the two locations exists in the form of two sets of ceremonial mounds, one at each end: at Ganquan and at Machi 麻池, near Baotou.[64] Although these mounds could date to the Han period and thus slightly later than the Qin Direct Road, their location at the Direct Road's endpoints is no coincidence. This was another aspect of the ongoing link between the two sites.

Mountains and mountain ranges are and were natural borders—focal points constituting dividing lines between polities. In K. E. Brashier's words, "Mountains marked a boundary between 'us' and 'other'" in early China.[65] Both Ganquan and Jiuyuan were located next to important border and barrier mountains. By traveling atop the Ziwuling range, the Direct Road marked and strengthened that range's role in this respect, constituting a message of the Qin claim to the territory within. Perhaps there was even a religious significance to the mountain route itself. It is believed that the Xiongnu worshipped mountains by constructing sacrificial cairns on mountains and at borders.[66] Early Chinese writers also considered mountains a space between the human and supernatural realms.[67] By following the mountains, the Direct Road effectively turned its route into a message that could be understood in those terms as well.

The section of the Direct Road that ran across the Ordos Plains made a claim to that land, too. The Qin road was not only a sign to those living in the areas it traveled through that were part of the Qin empire. The Qin road, built on the basis of existing roads, turned them into an indexical sign of Qin sovereignty over that area. The whole effect was a message of rulership, framed in ritual, religious, and geopolitical signs, with an audience both inside and outside the Qin realm.

The roads constructed during the First Emperor of Qin's reign effected something more than improved transportation—although that may well have been one of the results. More than that, the changes to the road systems communicated and thus helped toward generating common knowledge of the new political order at all levels of society. This helped foster knowledge and acceptance of Qin rule across the realm and among its neighbors. The First Emperor communicated, in large part, by making changes that directly affected the lives of the population and by changing their common practices or environment in ways that could not be missed. Roads were an important part of that.

Within and around the capital, walled roads and raised ways lifted, protected, and hid the First Emperor from public view. At the same time they turned his paths into enduring marks of his presence. The highway system did something similar across the realm: it changed and improved transportation and official communication, which surely altered the lives of those in the areas of the road. By reserving a middle lane for the emperor's use, the highway made his transitory—or even entirely theoretical—presence permanent. The Direct Road may have expanded and improved transportation in the northwestern part of the Qin realm, but more importantly, it used areas of combined ritual, cultural, and political significance to communicate Qin supremacy beyond the borders of the realm. All of these thus helped create common knowledge of the new Qin state through indexical signs of power the population could perceive.

7

Law, Administration, and Communication

In this chapter, I consider bureaucratic and legal systems, institutions, and practices through which the central government of Qin and Western Han China came into contact with the populace. These worked between the central government authorities and the population of the entire realm toward the goal of effective governance. Although scholars have considered these as mechanisms of control and surveillance—and indeed these processes had such functions—they also worked as communications media to create the common knowledge necessary for imperial rule. These institutions were one way through which the government of the early Chinese empire touched the common people. By establishing new systems and using those already in place, the Qin and Han rulers made themselves known to their people and effected political power.

I begin this chapter with a discussion of household and related registries in pre-imperial and early imperial China. I argue that the Qin and Western Han rulers used registration processes in the establishment and administration of their empires as a way to come in contact with every resident of their territory. I then examine law and related practices in the Qin and Western Han periods. Qin-Han legal practice plays an important part in my argument, as it shows unambiguously that communicating with the general population was necessary and expected. Finally, I look at forms of bureaucratic communication explicitly aimed at broadcast communication with the population, particularly the systematic display of official documents, which was one way information was transmitted to common people.

There were major interruptions in legal and other bureaucratic systems at the end of the Qin dynasty and the subsequent beginning of the Han. Exigencies similar to those that drove the Qin ruler to communicate so actively and effectively in the first years of that short dynasty also existed for the Han. But while the Qin were adapting existing practices into means for something that had not existed before—the unified realm—the Western Han dynasty, especially in its early years, had both the benefit and the burden of inheritance. The Qin dynasty bureaucracy was very effective at penetrating Qin society.[1] In establishing their own dynasty, the Han had available to them the tools and structures of government put in place by the Qin, and Han manipulation of these reflects their far-reaching purposes.

Household and Individual Registration

I begin this chapter by looking at a system that in its function sought to touch every inhabitant of the realm: household registration. I argue here, as throughout this book, that practices that served other purposes also had communicative function. The same processes that gathered basic information about every person under Qin or Han dominion simultaneously created common knowledge of the empire among those it surveyed with effects in the realm of power.

Demography was not a Qin invention. Early Chinese texts of all sorts, including paleographic materials and received historical sources, mention counting groups of people in various contexts. Over the centuries leading up and into the early imperial period, the information gathered about the population developed from just quantifying groups to recording households, which later came to include the names and eventually the ages of all household members. This information helped Qin authorities monitor and control the population, and it is there that previous studies have concentrated. But the same developments that sought out and recorded details required contact between representatives of the imperial government and the inhabitants of the realm, contact I suggest worked as a medium for communication to the people. The tasks connected with creating and maintaining records were also a form of this communication. The result was the regular dispersal of simple messages about the state among the populace. My arguments find important support in *Zhou Rituals*, provided that text is properly understood not as a record of Zhou praxis but rather as depicting Warring States–period ideas about government.

Precursors of Household Registration

Dating back some three thousand years, oracle bone inscriptions—the remnants of prognostication rituals—are the earliest known written texts in China. Some of these texts mention specific numbers of people in context of war, and scholars have suggested these constitute the earliest antecedents of Chinese document-based bureaucracy generally and population registries specifically. Western Zhou bronzes also refer to groups by size, again in military contexts, and especially with reference to prisoners. Scholars have also pointed to this practice as indicating the existence of name registries that recorded who had been captured.[2] While conceptually similar to population registration, these references do something different: they detail armies sent and prisoners taken or give the general sizes of settlements lost or won. Nevertheless, they indicate that the interest in enumerating and recording people dates to earliest times in China.

The first explicit reference to counting a population comes from the early eighth century BCE, when King Xuan 宣 of Zhou (r. 827–781 BCE), seeking to reconstitute his defeated army, reportedly wanted to "count the people" (*liaomin* 料民) and clarify the human resources available to him. One of the king's high officials argued forcefully but unsuccessfully against the plan. He reasoned that a distinct census should have been unnecessary, because the various officials and the king's own observations as he moved through his kingdom ought to have provided sufficient information about the populace.[3] This suggests that although statistics of some sort existed, they were generated indirectly, through the cumulative activities of officials.

Zuo's Commentary provides some additional relevant examples. It records a review of households in 589 BCE, which historians commonly name as an early example of population registration. The context of this case is especially suggestive: the explicit impetus was the perceived need for the king to expand his influence. Measures designed to benefit the population immediately followed this survey, presumably based on its results, including forgiveness of taxes and an amnesty for prisoners. *Zuo's Commentary* also mentions a search for escaped criminals in 621 BCE that entailed checking a populace and the submission of a document recording the inhabitants of one small area in 480 BCE. Other canonical texts refer to documents thought to have been governmental records of things like population.[4]

Although the historicity of such accounts, especially in their details, is uncertain, they appear to reflect certain general realities of early times. And it is not surprising that population records of some sort existed. But as the sporadic and scattered references suggest, there is no evidence that thorough surveys and checks were regular events. At the same time, the utility of a census as it did exist was not limited to simply counting the population: there were already hints connecting it to the noncoercive exercise of influence.

Many scholars believe that the origins of household registries in China lie in the Western Zhou, or even earlier, and they cite this sort of piecemeal evidence in support. They also refer to philosophical texts such as *Master Guan* that purport to describe earlier periods. Such texts are not reliable historical records of events: *Master Guan* was assembled only in Han times (see chapter 3), and other such texts have similarly problematic backgrounds. The primary source these scholars use to support their assertions is *Zhou Rituals*, a text that postdates the Zhou government it appears to record by centuries. But while *Zhou Rituals* is not a record of Zhou bureaucracy, it is still important. For although it does not help us to directly understand Zhou practice, as David Schaberg's analysis shows, it tells us a great deal about Warring States' political ideas and probably influenced the Qin state.[5]

Zhou Rituals describes hundreds of officials. It divides them into six primary groups, and there are officials in all six whose duties include gathering and submitting data about the population. The "manager of the people" (*simin* 司民) is said to have been in charge of recording the population, including births and deaths, verifying those records and presenting them to the king every three years. Other officials combined a responsibility for population data with communication—both explicit communication and the sort of incidental creation of common knowledge that comes from changing people's lives. The "submanager of land and population" (*xiao situ* 小司徒), for example, was in charge of disseminating information about legal systems. He was also to have the officials under him record information about the local population, its livestock and property, and submit those figures regularly to support the function of government. Each of the "heads of outer demesnes" (*suiren* 遂人) was responsible for compiling information about the residents of his jurisdiction, organizing the households into groups for governance, enforcing regulations, and summoning conscript laborers. The "matchmaker" (*meishi* 媒氏) had an even larger impact on the lives of his charges: his supposed task was to gather information about the people in order to arrange marriages at the participants' proper ages.[6]

While *Zhou Rituals* does not describe the historical Zhou bureaucracy, its numerous references to counting and recording the population show an unmistakable interest in statistics and records was part of political organization in Warring States thought. This is only logical: ordering and extracting taxes and labor service from a territory of any size would require such information. Yet *Zhou Rituals* also calls to mind eighth-century arguments against counting the population, as it consistently portrays statistics as gathered and employed by officials as part of their ongoing tasks. Nowhere does *Zhou Rituals* recommend a distinct count of the populace, nor is there much indication of contact with the people as part of gathering data. The picture is one of officials who remained disconnected from the people while counting them, or at least the numbers of their households, from a distance. Indeed, before the fourth century, only the number of households mattered: the military service system of the time centered on the obligation of each household to provide one man to fight.[7]

Despite some scholars' assertions, there is no reliable indication of ongoing and systematic general recording of people or households before the fourth century. Even *Zhou Rituals* lacks this information, with the sole exception of the matchmakers' connubial registries. At the same time, assigning responsibility for communication and statistics to the same officials indicates there was recognition of a connection between these two matters.

The general trend in the centuries before unification was toward bureaucratization and centralization, enabled by an increasing flow of official documents—all things to which the Qin gave the greatest importance. There are indications that statistical information about local areas was compiled at the prefectural level for submission to central authorities between the eighth and fifth centuries BCE. The Qin state also had these structures in place. Indeed, document bureaucracy was an important factor in their success and something the Han later took over and built upon in their turn.[8] But universal registration of the population had special communicative properties.

The Emergence of Household Registration

Beginning in the fourth century BCE, there is clear evidence of systematic, detailed, and ongoing registration of households and population. Not coincidentally, much of this evidence is closely linked to the Qin, who continued to develop these systems during their dynasty, development that continued into the Han. In his seminal study on the topic, Ikeda On 池田温 wrote that Qin practices from the fourth century represent the beginning of true household registration in China—a system that persists today.[9]

Historians date the emergence of registration proper to 375 BCE, when Lord Xiang 襄 of Qin commanded the establishment of a household registry accompanied by the division of households into groups of five. Later, this system was further developed in Qin under Shang Yang's policies in the mid-fourth century. He ordered the establishment of mutual responsibility groups that were required to report law-breaking by other members of the group, though with strict limitations on the reporting of crimes within the household. Reporting crimes earned a reward, and failure to do so was punished. Scholars have usually viewed the formation of mutual responsibility groups as an assault on traditional culture and society of the time, although I have argued elsewhere that they must also have substantially encouraged cooperation.¹⁰

The Book of Lord Shang propounds the birth-to-death registration of everyone in the realm: "Everywhere within the borders, let all men and women be registered by name with the government: those who are born shall be entered, and those who die, expunged" 四境之內, 丈夫女子皆有名於上, 生者著, 死者削. Although *The Book of Lord Shang* includes much from later hands, the section containing this recommendation probably came from Shang Yang himself. Another chapter, compiled by exponents of Shang Yang's philosophy in the centuries after his death, repeats this injunction. It advocates compiling a comprehensive set of government statistics, of which information about the population was a crucial part.¹¹

There were limited systems of registration of persons around this time in other states. In his study of registries, Du Zhengsheng 杜正勝 emphasizes the importance of the development from name records to registration of entire households under the Qin system. Earlier enumeration focused on extracting military service and so recorded only adult males. Writing strips from the late fourth century BCE found at Baoshan 包山 show this sort of system existed outside Qin. According to Chen Wei 陳偉, those documents indicate that only adult men—commoners and slaves—were subject to registration in the preunification state of Chu. Chen suggests there may have been private records containing information about all members of a household, but these were only sporadically checked. Notably, the Baoshan documents contain no evidence of the five-household, mutual responsibility groups that marked Qin society.¹²

Third Century BCE

The earliest known examples of actual household registries and related documents date to the late third century BCE and come from archaeological finds at Shuihudi and Liye 里耶. The latter include household and population registers and record not just those subject to labor service (i.e., adult males) but all members of the household by name, rank, and relationship to the householder; even slaves are included.¹³ These lists reflect the system put in place across the realm beginning in 221 BCE.

I have already mentioned forerunners of these registries, which all evidence suggests were intermittent in earlier times and which concentrated only on extracting labor service still in the fourth century. But at Liye and Shuihudi, archaeologists recovered materials indicating the existence of a well-developed system for registering each person in the realm—men and women, children and slaves—as members of households. Qin law required every person to register and remain registered in case of moving.[14] This was an important change.

This system did not emerge within the space of a few years; it resulted from long-term developments that accelerated in the fourth and third centuries BCE. Nor was it exclusively Qin. Qin legal materials from Shuihudi contain statutes from the state of Wei 魏 dating to 252 BCE concerning the formation of households that indicate multigeneration records of householders and potential householders existed in other states as well.[15]

Under the influence of ideas like those we see in *Zhou Rituals* and *The Book of Lord Shang*, Qin rulers built upon and adapted existing practices to realize a system that recorded and tracked all of their subjects. In 231 BCE, during the process of unification, the First Emperor ordered a significant revision to the system of registration: "For the first time he commanded adult males to have their ages recorded" 初令男子書年.[16] A chronicle from Shuihudi confirms this change took place and indicates each man was responsible for registering himself. This event was of double importance. First, it marked a fundamental change in the method for determining adulthood. Prior to this, adult status had been determined by height. Physical size continued to be important in specific contexts, including apparently the legal. But the primary criterion for adult status was age, and males were subject to corvée and military service beginning at age sixteen, although they did not always serve immediately.[17] The shift furthermore necessitated communicating with and gathering new data from every adult male under Qin jurisdiction and establishing contact with new subjects as the realm expanded, culminating in unification. In this way the Qin rulers sent a small but clear message of government presence and power to the men of the realm. Third-century changes in administrative practice had broad-reaching communicative effects.

Statutes and other legal materials indicate that name, social rank, and place of residence were the core identification data for each person as a Qin subject. Scholars going back to Ikeda, who wrote just a few years after the Shuihudi discoveries, have suggested that instructions for recording the property of a convicted criminal represent the form of the registration. However, the Liye examples list the members of the household, including slaves; their relationship to the householder; and rank, which also indicates adult or minor status. Information about the specific age of any members is absent. There were numerous other sorts of registries in existence, including one devoted to age. Early second-century BCE statutes from Zhangjiashan also mention separate age records. But the course of development was toward consolidation of information, and household registries included age data no later than the third century CE.[18]

Western Han

When the Han founder Liu Bang and his forces entered the Qin capital in 206 BCE, his generals rushed to the treasuries to seize the wealth stored there. But Xiao He 蕭何 (d. 193 BCE), who would go on to become chancellor, showed a distinctly administrative sense of discernment by hurrying instead to the archives. There he rescued household registry statistics and other data that provided indispensable information about the realm for its new rulers. The Han dynasty continued the Qin bureaucratic systems, and statutes from the first decades of the dynasty show that every commoner was responsible for registering with the government, although parents, other relatives, or officials could register those too young to do it themselves. The Han also continued the system of five-household groups for mutual identification, surveillance, and assistance. Both of these extended Qin practice and might seem to indicate unbroken continuation.[19]

In fact, both received history and paleographic records indicate there was a major break in registration. Accounts of this time show there was common knowledge of the system at all levels of society, and that its function was interrupted and restarted. In an act reminiscent of his sudden abrogation of the Qin legal system a few years previously, after ascending to the throne of the empire in 202 BCE (discussed later), the new Han emperor issued an edict that said:

> Previously, some of the common people banded together, took refuge in mountains and swamps, and were not recorded in the registries. Now the realm is settled. Let all of them return to their prefectures and reassume their former ranks, fields, and houses. The officers shall instruct them and communicate the written law, but shall not beat or denigrate them. 民前或相聚保山澤, 不書名數. 今天下已定, 令各歸其縣, 復故爵田宅, 吏以文法教訓辨告, 勿笞辱.[20]

In addition to its inclusion in *History of the Han*, there is also reference to this edict in archaeologically recovered early second-century BCE legal materials.[21]

Several levels of communication are at work in this proclamation. Its creators assumed that the content would reach the target audience, even though that audience was living outside of the usual bureaucratic structures. This implies a very broad distribution. The creators also assumed that the audience would be aware of the system—that is, that its existence and function was already a matter of common knowledge. The only punishment permitted was to be communication of the system, enhancing common knowledge. Finally, the timing of this act is telling and suggests that the emperor himself was making use of the system of registration to communicate his newly won position in several respects. First was evincing his power as ruler to control the system of laws. Like all sorts of amnesties and exemptions from the law, this one indexed its issuer's power over legal systems and processes.[22] In this specific historical context, it made Liu Bang known as ruler and positioned him as the one person able to suspend the rules on registration. In this way, he turned bureaucracy into a medium for communicating the new focal point of the realm.

Early Han legal documents from Zhangjiashan give an up-close picture of this system and its interruption. A case summary from 196 BCE recounts the story of a woman who had fled from enemy territory to join the Han during the civil war that followed the Qin fall. By law, the act of joining the Han annulled her slave status. However, she did not register herself with the authorities. Her former owner later recaptured her, registered her as a slave, and sold her to another. She subsequently fled from slavery again and was arrested. Although she had become free when she gave her allegiance to the Han, the authorities confirmed her reenslavement because she had failed to register as a free person. They tattooed her as punishment and returned her to the slaveholder.[23] In a different case, an escaped slave falsely presented herself to the authorities as unregistered and was enrolled as a commoner under the 206 BCE decree. The eventual discovery of this subterfuge led not only to her conviction but also to that of her husband, who was found guilty of marrying a runaway.[24] Yet another summary tells of a former slave who fled to the Han and duly registered himself as a commoner. He was falsely reported as a runaway and when a legal officer went to take him in for questioning, he resisted and harmed the officer. Because his status as a commoner was certain, local officials were unsure whether this might not have been permissible self-defense. They submitted the case for review at a higher level, where this defense was rejected.[25] These cases show how the Han rulers communicated to their new subjects, positioning themselves as the new focal point for obedience and coordination. They demonstrate understanding of national-level politics, as shown by reference to the Han specifically, and clear knowledge about the system of registration, its interruption and reinstatement.

The Han system of household registration carried forward that of Qin, but developments continued, specifically in the addition of recording land holdings and personal property. Our picture of Han practice is clearer because substantially more documentation exists for the Han. Archaeologists working at Zhangjiashan recovered an early Han statute commanding the commoners to report their ages. These texts reflect that the eighth month of the year was the time for verification of records and figures, although changes were made as necessary throughout the year to record things like unauthorized departure. The figures were collated at the prefectural level and submitted to the central government, as under the Qin system.[26]

Standard histories contain numerous references to Han systems of registration and the gathering and submission of data about the population. Late Western Han paleographic texts from Yinwan 尹灣 (Jiangsu) include summary data on the local population that must have derived from this sort of registry.[27] Han-era military bureaucratic documents from the northwestern frontier record soldiers and their families in great detail. There are examples of registrations and descriptions of wanted criminals that include details like skin tone, and some scholars have suggested registries included the same.[28] Household registration was one of the most durable bureaucratic practices of early imperial times. Archaeological discoveries at Zoumalou 走馬樓 (Hunan) dating to the third century, after the end of the Han dynasty, included large quantities of discarded writing strips, one-third of which are household registry records.[29] This attests to the persistence of what was essentially the Qin model into the time after the Han.

The Function of Household Registration

There are a number of explanations for the existence of household registration in early imperial China. The variety of proposed functions reflects the broad and varied utility that information about a populace has for its rulers. Without rejecting these explanations, I want to add another layer of interpretation by considering the way these systems worked as means of communication that helped create cooperation and integration at the national level. I have already mentioned the specific and exceptional case of Han founder Liu Bang's proclamation suspending punishment for those who had avoided registration as a form of communication. I argue that the system in its normal functioning had similar effects. Previous studies of early

Chinese bureaucracy have focused on information flows directed upward in the hierarchy, without considering how collecting that information and related processes themselves served to communicate. The development of bureaucratic practices traced a trajectory toward closer contact with the people of the realm, and registration was one medium for this.

Modern scholars, beginning at least with Ikeda On, have also explained the system of household registration as a means to control the population.[30] Many integrate this general control function with a group of similar other demands, typically taxation, labor, and military service.[31] Some focus on different aspects of this or related matters. Tu Mingfeng 涂明鳳, for example, says the registration worked both to control and to harmonize the population, to control their movements and maintain security.[32] Beyond control and extracting taxes and labor service, Han Lianqi 韓連琪 says registration served to connect the peasantry to the land. But he also astutely notes that even as demands for labor were decreasing under the early Han government, the rulers continued to emphasize registration.[33] Similarly, the abolishment of compulsory military service in the first century CE was not accompanied by a corresponding change to the system of registration.[34] This suggests other factors were—or had become—more important.

Du Zhengsheng considers the registration system a means for controlling human resources and extracting labor and taxes. But he also notes that registration was part of a shift away from lineage-based social organization. The new system created and maintained direct links between the state and the population. The result was—at least in theory—direct control of the people by the central government, without mediating groups or structures. Du portrays this as part of a broad shift toward all members of the population being politically equal before the state, no longer as units in a lineage. Wan Changhua 萬昌華 and Zhao Xingbin 趙興彬 follow Du to link registration systems to the control of individual persons and the associated attenuation of lineage groups. They expand this idea within the context of conquest and argue the Qin used household registries as a means to take new populations under control. They also note that states other than Qin did not so strictly control their populations.[35]

At the same time, there are indications that Qin control of its population was in fact not as strict as the statutes would indicate. For example, bureaucratic documents from Liye and dated to 221 BCE record one official's formal complaint about the failure of another official to forward the age records of seventeen households that had moved into his area. Many researchers cite this case as evidence of the system's rigor. But the most telling part of this case is its resolution: the official in charge of the original residence did not have the age records, so the complaining official was instructed to simply ask the new arrivals how old they were. This casual attitude about maintaining and creating records does not seem like a bureaucracy interested in accurately recording chronological age beyond the broadest of parameters.[36]

The emergence of detailed population registries in the fourth century BCE marks the creation of the individual person as subject in China, someone in a birth-to-death relationship with the state, a change first manifest in preunification Qin. Previously, most of the populace existed—from the perspective of the ruler—anonymously, as part of a household that owed a debt of service. With the developments at this time, each person became an individual in a relationship with the state. So strong was the role of registration in constituting this group that no later than around 132 BCE, it became literally synonymous with commoner status, reflecting the profound identification between the two matters.[37]

During the process of unification, the process of registration was harnessed by the First Emperor and his coterie of advisors but with new goals. Each person was individually and directly touched by governance. Each was individually obliged to maintain the relationship with the state. Repeated changes to the system of registration ensured that each person dwelling lawfully in the realm—and even those living outside the law—were aware of the system.

Communication through Changes to the Legal System

Liu Bang, founder of the Han dynasty, secured the Qin capital Xianyang and ended that dynasty in 206 BCE. (Although his dynasty has traditionally been dated to this year, Liu Bang achieved emperorship only in 202 BCE.) Records of an event from 206 BCE show that Liu Bang, famous for his leadership skills, was also a consummate communicator. After taking the capital, Liu Bang left the city and set up camp with his army some distance away, and he made the following announcement to the heads of prominent families from the area:

> Elders, you have long endured the brutal Qin laws. The entire families of those convicted of slandering [the emperor] were killed, and those convicted of plotting were executed and left in the market. I made an agreement with the various lords that the first to enter the pass should be king within, so I should

rule the area within the passes. And I make an agreement with you that the law will have only three sections: one who kills another will die, and one who harms another or steals will pay recompense for the crime. The rest of the Qin laws are all done away with. 父老苦秦苛法久矣, 誹謗者族, 耦語者棄市. 吾與諸侯約, 先入關者王之, 吾當王關中. 與父老約, 法三章耳: 殺人者死, 傷人及盜抵罪. 餘悉除去秦法.[38]

Liu Bang sent messengers to former Qin civil servants in various places to inform them of the change, which they in turn made known to those they governed, spreading knowledge of this act.

Liu Bang may have made this change in order to tap into idealized conceptions of sage rulership, some of which included just this sort of legal apparatus. Or he may simply have been trying to appeal to the populace. Whatever the proximate cause was, the novel system predictably pleased the people, and those in the area of the camp offered provisions for Liu Bang's army—provisions he declined, further cementing his popularity among the former Qin subjects. Because of the change to the law, Liu Bang won the allegiance of the population, an achievement that many praised.[39]

Liu Bang accomplished another goal as well. In his speech, knowing full well that he had his listeners' attention, Liu Bang mentions—apparently in passing—that he was ruler of the area within the passes and states the basis for his claim to legitimacy. He had come at the head of an army and held power at the time by force of arms alone. But in this moment, Liu Bang drew the common population's notice by altering the laws that had been such a large part of their lives under the Qin, thus creating common knowledge of himself. Then, by linking this change with his own legitimacy, he turned the situation into a broadcast to create knowledge of the latter, too. He combined two messages, one of great interest to everyone and another of less compelling interest to ordinary people but vital to Liu Bang himself. The information was first sent to local officials, who then passed it along to those in their jurisdiction. After this, the messages must have been passed along by word of mouth until they reached what is reported to have been full penetration.[40]

The enactment of this three-section legal code is famous and frequently mentioned in connection with Gaozu's rule even among modern writers. Yet the fame of this change seems at odds with its limited effect. For, as could only be expected, three simple precepts were insufficient for regulating the Han empire. After the country was stabilized and Liu Bang was safely on the throne, he commanded that a complete system of laws be instituted in 195 BCE. This system was essentially a revised version of the Qin laws he had so precipitously done away with not long before.[41] But the three-part code was remembered. Perhaps the same things that made the shift to that code so effective in attracting the notice of the common people at the beginning of the Han dynasty also worked to make it memorable among those in later times.

Other Han emperors reformed the legal system and won fame. Probably the most famous example is that of Emperor Wen 文 (Liu Heng 劉恒, r. 179–157 BCE). Legal penalties in early China often took the form of corporal mutilation: facial tattooing, amputation of one or both feet, and cutting off the nose were all prescribed for particular crimes. In 167 BCE Emperor Wen commanded an end to all mutilating punishments, replacing them with caning and/or penal labor. Although many people have praised him for this, beginning already in Han times, the new system actually increased mortality rates. It thus did little to benefit those convicted of crime. But Emperor Wen benefited both during his life and after from an enhanced reputation.[42]

Changes to the legal system naturally did not always bring positive results. Sometimes it was asserted that frequent changes to the law left the populace confused and unsure about which rules they should follow.[43] At other times, new laws and their effects made the people unhappy. One example of this dates to 5 CE, when Wang Mang added fifty statutes, the violation of which was punishable by exile. This case is especially important because a proclamation containing fifty ordinances and dated to 5 CE has been recovered from the ruins of a Han post in northwestern China, where they were copied onto a wall. A number of scholars have suggested that this is the text of the change. According to *History of the Han*, vast numbers fell afoul of the new laws and were banished, and the common people became resentful.[44] Like Liu Bang, Wang Mang changed the law and evoked a broad response from the ordinary people of the realm, though to opposite effect: Wang Mang earned disaffection, while Liu Bang had won allegiance.

Sometimes considerations about the perceptions of the legal system argued against change. Karen Turner has discussed a famous case from 177 BCE, in which Zhang Shizhi 張釋之 persuaded Emperor Wen with arguments based on these effects. In chapter 6 I mentioned that in imperial times, when the emperor passed by a place, ordinary people were required by law to clear the roads. One day, a man was caught with the imperial entourage approaching and nowhere to go, so he hid beneath a bridge. He misjudged the amount of time he should wait and came out as the emperor was passing, which startled the horses pulling the emperor's chariot. The emperor commanded Zhang Shizhi, then commandant of justice, to prosecute the man, and Zhang levied a fine, the standard punishment. The emperor protested that he might have been injured and demanded a heavier penalty. Zhang resisted, saying that while the emperor could have summarily executed the man, once the matter was given over to him, he was obliged to follow the law. Zhang further argued that centrally administered law was the standard of fairness for the realm and supported the people in their daily lives. Bending it to the emperor's will in even a single case would have broad repercussions for the people, who would be left unable to rely on it. He assumed that the populace would learn of the case—for without public knowledge, it could have no effect on them at all—and that they would form their own views of it. After consideration, the emperor accepted Zhang's opinion.[45]

In 64 BCE, concerns about the perceived fairness of punishments prevented a change to the penal system. That year, there was a proposal made that would permit the payment of fines in the form of grain in lieu of other punishment for many crimes. The goal was to provide needed grain for the official storehouses. Two officials argued that this change would result in punishments that were effectively unequal and unfair, even if the fines were the same for all, as the wealthy would be able to pay them but the poor would not. They predicted that people of limited means would bring privation upon themselves in order to rescue their relatives, increasing the number of people affected by penalties. Ultimately, they asserted, it would disrupt the relationship of mutual concern between the ruler and the ruled. The people would perceive the change as negative and as coming from their ruler and embody his attitude toward them. In the end, the proposal was not put into effect.[46]

Another incident shows that people of the time recognized the great potential of changing the law to affect public perceptions of the ruler and the effects that could follow if negative perceptions took root. Liu An 劉安 (179–122 BCE) was grandson of the Han founder and ruler of a territory of his own. Liu An was dissatisfied with subordinate status and plotted a revolt against Emperor Wu. But when he discussed his chances for success with his advisor Wu Pi 伍被 (d. 122 BCE), Wu Pi advised against rebellion. Liu An countered by referring to the two conscript soldiers credited with starting the insurrection that overthrew the Qin. Liu An insisted that if those two could succeed, then he should be able to defeat the Han despite lacking resources and troops.

Wu Pi responded with an analysis of how and why the situation under Han rule was different from that under the Qin. He particularly emphasized popular sentiment, which he said had been strongly against the Qin because of what he described as the harshness of their penal system, excessive taxes, and demands for labor service. Through these things, Wu said, the Qin had turned the populace against themselves. Such sentiment was—according to Wu—a necessary precondition for overthrowing a dynasty but was lacking in the Han case.

In a subsequent discussion, Wu Pi suggested creating the required anti-Han feeling by manipulating legal and administrative processes. The first part of the scheme was to falsify documents from the central authorities. The forged command would send prominent commoners and those with wealth exceeding five hundred thousand in coins, as well as convicts sentenced to punishment of or greater than punitive shaving and those who had benefited from previous amnesties, to a place in present-day Inner Mongolia. In Han times transportation to border regions was a punishment second only to death. Sometimes groups of people were sent to the border for other reasons, but they generally received financial or material incentives from the imperial government as recompense. In the absence of such inducements, the act would surely have evoked a strong negative reaction. To compound the effect, Wu Pi proposed simultaneously calling up an urgent draft of soldiers at short notice. Finally, he also recommended forging a letter from the imperial bureaucracy ordering the arrests of heirs designate and favored subjects of local lords. Wu Pi predicted this combination of acts would cause anger among the common people and fear among the lords, thus bringing about a situation favorable to rebellion against the Han.

Liu An was captured before he could act and never got a chance to test Wu Pi's advice. So there is no way to know whether or not these changes would have had the promised effect. Yet these suggestions about how to foster anti-Han feeling in the same mold as that of previous anti-Qin sentiments, at least, show that these processes were then understood to affect public opinion, which in turn could significantly influence governmental affairs.[47]

Penal Processes and Communication

The preceding has shown that changes to legal practices could work as communication. But communication also occurred through punishments in their ordinary function. The idea that punishment serves to communicate between government and subject was part of the basic function of the law in early China: deterrence. Writings attributed to pre-imperial philosophers indicate they conceived of legal punishment as a deterrent to unwanted behavior. This effect assumes communication is a part of the penal process, because a potential criminal would have to know about a penalty—that is, it must first be communicated—in order to be deterred by it.[48] Western Han sources also reflect the interest in law as deterrence. The record of a series of discussions at the Han court in 81 BCE, for example, touches frequently on legal practices. In one case, there was a recommendation to make the legal system stricter, as its perceived laxity rendered it unable to fulfill its deterrent purpose. The counterposition does not reject this assumption but asserts—among other things—that the system of laws had grown so complicated that the common people often could not understand it and consequently could not obey.[49]

Mark Edward Lewis has written that punishment, including capital punishment, was usually public in early China, as it was typically carried out in the marketplace—often expressly in order to communicate with the population. Both canonical sources and Han histories record this conception, and a second-century lexicon explains that executions occurred in the marketplace because that was where people gathered. Records in *History of the Han* indicate that trials and verdict were also public as well. And they confirm that people attended executions in large numbers. Even relatively innocuous chastisements seem to have been chosen to attract attention and thus to communicate. People must have taken note when, for example, the king of Chu 楚 dressed two learned men who had dared to remonstrate with him in convict uniforms and set them to pounding rice in the marketplace.[50]

Notorious criminals made especially good signals, as the fates of the well-known always draw attention and discussion. One common way to publicize an execution was display of the head, and sometimes the fame of the criminal rendered any further information unnecessary, while lesser-known men or crimes might call for written explication in the form of posted documents. This sort of communication was not limited to deterrence per se. For example, when Wang Mang was killed and his short-lived dynasty overthrown in 23 CE, his head was cut off and hung up in a marketplace, where a crowd gathered to revile it.[51] Although the rebellion was not a legal proceeding, exposing the head reconstructed it after the fact as an execution. Few if any members of the marketplace mob, and others who later heard about the fate of Wang Mang, were in a position to contemplate establishing a new dynasty, as he had done. And it is unlikely that anyone actually in such a position and so inclined would have been put off by the display of Wang Mang's head. So deterrence in the strict sense does not explain this. More important was making Wang Mang's death a matter of common knowledge and communicating and legitimating the end of the man and his dynasty to the populace.

The care with which penal acts were turned into noticeable, durable, and clearly labeled signs reveals their communicative purpose. For example, Wang Mang put down an attempted revolt in 8 CE and his treatment of the mutineers shows he was alert to the possibility of communicating through punishment. He had the bodies of the defeated forces gathered up and interred in five ceremonial grave mounds, which were planted with trees. He took pains to maximize the communicative potential of the situation, ordering the mounds be built next to thoroughfares and marked with a classical allusion that condemned those interred within as rebels. Wang Mang even commanded that the mounds be maintained, in order to prevent them from falling into disrepair and disrupting the ongoing broadcast of his message.[52]

This sort of act was not always so meticulously designed. An official once sealed hundreds of young hoodlums in caves as a method of mass execution. He then had the corpses buried outside his offices and labeled with the names of the executed. Only after a hundred days of this display were the families permitted to exhume the bodies and give them proper funerals. Although less ambitious than Wang Mang, this official also turned the marked burial of executed criminals into a sign.[53]

The Common People and Legal Processes

The legal processes I have described were part of a general move toward publicizing penal systems. The Qin dynasty actively publicized the content of their laws to the common population, which was a major shift in legal practice. In earlier times there had been resistance to disseminating the law. The expressed rationale was the fear that making the law known to the public would lead to contention and disrespect for human authority. Social order was supposed to derive from adherence to ritual and other communal standards of behavior, or from broad perceptions of legality, not merely following the letter of the statutes.[54] Nor were all later dynasties open about the content of their legal codes, either. In Song (960–1279) times, for instance, the government strictly controlled access to such information. "The theory was that, if the people knew the law, they could devise means to circumvent it."[55] Jin dynasty (1115–1234) law forbade ordinary people from even possessing certain legal documents, purportedly to prevent excessive lawsuits. There was a suggestion to change this practice as a way to improve adherence to law by making its contents public, but it is unclear whether this was put into practice.[56] Legal education and knowledge of the law among the common population expanded greatly during the Yuan dynasty (1271–1368) and was an explicit goal of the Ming (1368–1644) founder Emperor Taizu 太祖 (Zhu Yuanzhang 朱元璋, r. 1368–1398), indicating the previous situation was different.[57]

The Qin approach perhaps resulted from the influence of Shang Yang, who advocated making the law known to the populace, as I discussed in chapter 3. Shang Yang is famous for changing the legal system of the state of Qin, and archaeologically recovered evidence confirms at least some of Shang Yang's proposals were put into practice. Recovered Qin legal documents also specify that the common population was to be actively informed of the law.[58] It is probably not a coincidence that *Zhou Rituals* describes bureaucratic structures for publicizing the law.[59] I will return later to the Han system of posting documents, a system to promulgate this type of information.

Common people could and indeed did directly address officials of their own accord under the Qin and Han legal systems. One specific element of the Qin and Western Han penal systems that demonstrates the existence of common knowledge of the law is the central place given to informing authorities about others' crimes. *The Book of Lord Shang* propounds denunciation as part of ordinary legal practice, and such a system was in place during Qin and Han times. The goal was deterrence, to prevent a person from committing a crime because she or he believed another would report it. This system required and assumed metaknowledge about the law, at least in its basics: it depended on a situation in which each person's own knowledge of some matter combined with awareness that others also knew, and it reflects the expectation of active cooperation with government aims. Documentary evidence from Qin and Han times confirms that common people addressed legal officials to report crimes.[60]

The Book of Lord Shang further specifies that publicizing the law among the common people would deter malfeasance by officials. The reasoning was that if an official failed to follow proper procedures, the commoners involved would notice that and report him to his superiors, who would then punish him. This, too, requires and assumes both common knowledge and resulting cooperation. There were regular bureaucratic channels for the ordinary people to bring such problems and complaints to higher officials in early imperial China. An incident in the life of the famous Han official Zhu Bo 朱博 (d. 5 BCE) records this. He was appointed a regional inspector, with responsibility for oversight of many aspects of local government, including legal processes. When he first took up his position and toured his jurisdiction, hundreds of people blocked his way and filled the offices, demanding to speak with him. Zhu commanded one of his staff to address the crowd, directing it to disperse and indicating which sorts of problems should be taken to which offices, including complaints about officials and appeals to judicial decisions. Essentially, he sketched the systems that were in place for ordinary people to seek redress for unjust treatment, the locations for which depended not on the status of the commoner but rather on that of the official involved.[61]

History of the Han contains cases in which the people complained to officials and saw a result, showing that they understood legal processes and structures. One notable incident in which common people sought and received aid from an official concerned Emperor Wu personally. In 138 BCE he went out hunting, incognito and accompanied by members of his entourage. In the course of the hunt, the emperor and his companions rode their horses through farmers' fields in the area of the capital, damaging the crops. The farmers gathered together and informed the prefect of the damage, not realizing that they were complaining about the emperor and his companions. The prefect, equally ignorant of the identity of the culprits, in turn went to the riders and threatened to report the damage to the marquis of Pingyang. The prefect had his officers detain a number of the riders and released them only after they revealed their imperial livery.[62] This case shows that the people both had direct contact with officials and that officials took action as a result, implying the people had knowledge of legal processes and learned the results of their petitions. The lack of punishment for any of those involved in this matter shows that the farmers and the prefect acted within the boundaries of the law.

In other instances, common people lodged complaints against specific members of the bureaucracy. When one first-century BCE administrator proved himself too free in executing offenders, the officers and people of his jurisdiction went en masse to complain about his harshness, and in the end he was put to death. Nor was the people's power to lodge complaints limited to bureaucrats. When the king of Lu's 魯 new chancellor arrived in 147 BCE, more than a hundred commoners went to protest that the king had unjustly seized their property. The chancellor had some twenty of the leaders beaten for their temerity. Yet when the king found out, he was angry and ordered that recompense for the beating be paid from his treasury.[63] The internal logic of the king's position may seem dubious, but his reaction shows that the populace was permitted to express their dissatisfaction.

Recovered documents confirm that members of the populace actively engaged the legal system. Qin documents from Shuihudi show that commoners directly petitioned district authorities, as do Han materials recovered at Wuwei 武威 (Gansu). The Wuwei documents include an edict concerning the "king's staff," which was granted to men of advanced age (the precise age depending on the recipient's social rank). I discussed this staff in chapter 6, because it allowed holders to use the reserved sections of imperial highways. Another of the legal privileges it afforded was immunity to prosecution by local officers; any such proceedings required recourse to a higher authority. Three summaries of relevant legal cases accompany the recovered document. One of these concerns a holder of the staff, who lodged a formal complaint against a district officer for disrespect after being arrested and punished in contravention of the edict. The man addressed his complaint directly to the emperor, and as a result, the officer was sentenced to immediate execution. It is unlikely that the emperor played any personal role in resolving the complaint. But the case shows that a man with nothing to recommend him except advanced age and the king's staff knew his legal position and privileges and petitioned the government to have them.[64]

Publicly Posted Documents

The practical means by which the early central authorities promulgated edicts, statutes, and other documents have become clearer in recent decades. The recovery of bureaucratic documents, especially from border regions, has given researchers a picture of some of the systems that existed for spreading information.

Contemporary concepts of political organization recognized the necessity of communication, and theoretical predecessors of those distribution systems can be found in *Zhou Rituals*' putative description of the Western Zhou state's ritualized bureaucracy. *Zhou Rituals* does not date to the Western Zhou period, but, as mentioned, Schaberg has argued it contains late Warring States political theory concerning governance and its tools and acted as a conceptual basis for the Qin state.[65] At a number of points, *Zhou Rituals* speaks of officials whose tasks included publicizing information from the government through a combination of reading aloud and public display. Officials all the way to the top echelons of the bureaucracy were commanded to display the laws relating to various aspects of governance on exterior towers. The "submanager of prisons" (*xiao sikou* 小司寇) was supposed to disseminate information about the law everywhere and to post the legal prohibitions in written form; the job description of the "master of prohibitions" (*shishi* 士師) specifies that he was to copy the laws and hang them on gates, while "province leaders" (*zhouzhang* 州長) were charged with reading legal statutes out loud. *Zhou Rituals* even prescribes turning information about agricultural practices into documents for posting on gates.[66]

Recently excavated documents from Han times show how this took concrete form. They refer repeatedly to distribution practices that combined public posting of laws and edicts on gates and walls, combined with reading those texts aloud, in order to disseminate the contents.[67] One example commands, "When this document arrives, the prefect, senior assistant and watch post commandant will copy it clearly and in a large size for public display at obvious places in towns, markets, lanes, on the gates of villages, and in the posts" 書到令長丞候尉明白大扁書鄉市里門亭顯見(處).[68] Other examples are even more explicit about connecting the process to the common people. One says,

> When distributed documents arrive, clearly and largely write each [for public display] in markets, villages, on the doors of offices and bureaus, and in the posts and signal units, and cause the officers, soldiers, and people all to read and know about it. 移書到各明白大扁書市、里、官所寺舍門、亭、隧堠中, 令吏卒民盡訟知之.[69]

Variations in the formula like the following show that even disaffected members of society were expected to receive the information: "When this document arrives, clearly and largely write [its content] for public display in towns, posts, markets, and villages, in high and obvious places, and cause all fugitives to know about it" 書到白大扁書鄉亭市里高顯處, 令亡人命者盡知之.[70]

Other examples repeat and vary the elements of putting up information in prominent places so it can be seen and ensuring the people understand the content.[71] This was a primary means by which the Han bureaucracy distributed information. Limitations and variations in literacy are no doubt why reading the content aloud was not only explicitly a part of distribution but also prescribed in *Zhou Rituals*. Bu Xianqun 卜憲群 has noted that verbal communication between local residents and low-level officials bridged the gap between the bureaucracy and the individual and so was vital in all areas of government activity.[72] The command to read aloud the contents of posted documents was part of a set of broader governmental practices that mixed oral and written communication.

Tomiya Itaru 冨谷至 argues that posted documents never directly communicated their substance through being read by the populace. Rather, he says, they were read out loud, and through public exposure the written texts themselves became symbols of political power.[73] So communication was assured, even in the absence of literacy. On the other hand, as I have discussed, there is reason to think that literacy among the common population was not unknown. At the very least, universal military service meant that commoner males were exposed to writing and required to memorize information also contained in written regulations; thus, they were probably required to acquire a degree of literacy.[74]

Among bureaucratic records found near the Edsen-Gol River in Inner Mongolia is Wang Mang's proclamation of his new dynasty, couched in neoclassical phrasing derived from a poem in the *Book of Odes*. A group of strips from another Inner Mongolian site records a personal visit by Wang Mang's representative, who conveyed the emperor's concern for his troops.[75] Universal conscription for commoner males was still in effect at the time, so these reflect that the most extensive communication possible occurred: Through documents publicly posted and read, messages from the ruler reached all those at the lowest strata of society who were in the service that year, informing them of both the new dynasty and its ruler's care for them. In this way, the thin threads of communication that created and supported political power in early imperial China reached from the very top of society to the bottom.

8

Conclusion

Sometime around the first century BCE, the reigning Han emperor—almost certainly Emperor Wu—addressed an edict to his heir designate. In it, the emperor bemoaned his failing health and exhorted his successor to gather a retinue of talented advisors and be kind to the common people. Amid this and other conventional advice comes mention of a single, negative example—a man whose fate was to be a warning to the prospective sovereign. The edict refers to the Second Emperor of Qin by his personal name, saying, "Huhai destroyed himself, ruined his reputation, and cut off his line" 胡俆(:亥)自汜(:圮)滅名絕紀.[1]

This edict was lost to history until its recovery in 1977 among the ruins of a Han-era observation post near modern Jiuquan 酒泉 (Gansu). The edict as it exists is undated, but another document from the same site bears the date 74 BCE, providing a general periodization. A number of aspects of this edict and its context are telling. The post where it was found was a very small military installation located in the western hinterlands of the Han imperium, far from any center of government. The edict was copied onto a wooden rod that had been shaped with seven flat faces. It appears that a soldier at the post used this rod to practice writing, repeatedly scraping its surfaces clean for reuse. Other fragments from the site bear bits of the same edict.[2]

This imperial mention of the Second Emperor of Qin was transmitted to the distant reaches of the Han empire over a century after the fall of Qin. The Second Emperor of Qin's fame made any designation beyond his name unnecessary. Nor was there need to belabor the obvious by explaining the allusion: the Second Emperor was synonymous with an imperial heir who ruled badly. The edict relates the dangers of mistakes like Huhai's to a ruler's reputation and to his lineage. The text had reached such a high level of penetration that it and its mention of the Second Emperor were familiar to soldiers in the far west, in the lowest levels of government service.

Around the same time this edict was circulating, the name of Qin remained current in even more distant quarters, as the Xiongnu still referred to the subjects of the Han as "people of Qin."[3] The memory of the Qin dynasty and its rulers persisted across a wide geographical expanse and in different cultures, among the lofty and the low, among Chinese and non-Chinese. It may even be the case that the name "Qin" is the root of the word "China," which came to denote the realm in India and beyond.[4] These things reflect in different ways the success of Qin communication activities.

Han historiography was consistently critical of the Qin dynasty. The imperial edict adducing Huhai as a negative example demonstrates that this portrayal was not limited to the world of scholars. Criticism of the Qin was part of contemporary political discourse and disseminated across the Han empire. The picture of the Qin as cruel and abusive persisted for centuries; it was a trope already during the Han dynasty and remained so in later periods. The poisonous reputation of the Qin was so potent that it permitted, for example, the first emperor of the Ming dynasty to link the office of prime minister with the Qin dynasty as a justification for eliminating that position in the fourteenth century.[5]

Writing in the early twentieth century, critical historian Gu Jiegang 顧頡剛 (1893–1980) noted that the idea of a unified realm had existed already during the Warring States period. He suggested that while this conception rested on erroneous understandings of earlier history, the unification of China would not have happened without it. Yet when Gu spoke of the actual process, he did so in terms of a military victory alone, without further crediting the importance of the notion itself.[6] Gu's interpretation overlooks the fact that war was only part of the process of creating the empire. For when the Qin completed their military conquest in 221 BCE, they faced the problem of how to integrate the territory they had won.

I have suggested that interdisciplinary research on cooperation and communication offers a way to analyze Qin activities as means to resolve the problem of consolidating their rule. This book thus began with a discussion of modern research showing that cooperation is the driving force behind human sociality, and that the most important element of establishing social relations is communication. This is communication not only in the usual forms of speech and writing but also in indirect signs and signals that transmit undetailed and still important information.

Early Chinese thinkers shared these insights, although they inevitably expressed them in quite different ways. Ideas connected with cooperative governance appear among transmitted texts and those that archaeologists have discovered in recent decades. Philosophers including Mencius, Xunzi, and others recognized the necessity of communication and cooperation for successful rule, and this understanding is reflected in transmitted and archaeologically recovered texts.

Gu Jiegang and Yuri Pines have pointed out that the concept of the realm as a single entity was widely accepted before the Qin dynasty in 221 BCE. The political thinkers and writers who informed the unification of the realm under the Qin wrote in different ways of the monarch's imperative to communicate the fact of his rulership to those he governed. His territory was to be the entire realm, unified under him, and he was to make this fact known everywhere, including to the common population. The problem of communication, of how to consolidate the realm, remained.

Existing modes of distance communication had previously been used to reach only limited groups. Rather than limiting themselves to old forms and methods, the Qin adapted other practices and turned them into communications media. They invented virtually none of these. Instead, they tapped the unexploited potential of systems and processes. The establishment of a single system of weights and measures across the realm, for instance, became a medium for political communication. The change itself was an index of the emperor's power, and the announcement connected it specifically to the Qin. The Qin included the message of imperial unity onto those weights and measures and other objects, then reproduced the text throughout their territory.

The First Emperor of Qin himself indexed his new power when he traveled through the realm on his series of five imperial progresses. The emperor and his courtiers crossed the realm, visiting places connected with sage rulers of antiquity, spirits, and rituals. No ruler in living memory had performed one of these tours. The scale of the imperial progresses meant the residents of the areas they passed through would be sure to remember and to speak of them. The Qin also changed the places the emperor passed through, constructing buildings and removing walls and making other changes to ensure that memory of his passage would persist.

The Qin dynasty rulers were innovative administrators, whose bureaucracy reached out to communicate to every member of the population. The statutes obliged each person and household to register with local officials and to maintain that registration in case of moving. The functioning of this system both generated data for the government and transmitted messages of Qin governmental power to the people it tracked. Penal practices in Qin and Han times also had unmistakable communicative elements. This was not lost upon Liu Bang, founder of the Han dynasty that succeeded the Qin.

Liu Bang manipulated the legal system so as to broadcast his own claim to legitimacy. A few decades later Liu Bang's son, Emperor Wen, would make changes to legal systems that helped create the reputation for clemency he has to this day. Likewise, in its ordinary function, the early imperial legal system served as a way for government authorities to communicate broadly.

Constructing and adapting roads was another way that the Qin communicated. Construction has worked to signal political power in a variety of contexts in different times and places. The Qin used it to communicate the presence of the emperor's political person. In and around the capital Xianyang, walled roads and raised walkways turned the emperor's paths into permanent signs. Changing the shape of the city and the flow of traffic within it ensured that everyone in the capital would recognize the places where the emperor traveled. Outside the capital, the Qin linked roads together into a network of highways. By setting aside sections for the use of the emperor and those with special authorization wherever they ran, these roads, too, conveyed messages of Qin rule and imperial power. The messages that early imperial rulers sent in these ways were not complicated, but they did not need to be: much important communication consists of simple messages. A functional government requires much less detailed information to reach the populace than historians sometimes seem to expect.

This analysis does not deny the more prosaic functions of these changes. Standardizing weights and measures doubtless eased trade and taxation. The emperor and his officials surely inspected the areas he passed through on his tours. Bureaucratic institutions like household registers expedited mundane tasks such as figuring tax and labor obligations in each locality. People and goods traveled along the roads that Qin built and improved. Rather than rejecting these things, my interpretation proposes an additional layer of significance that links them together and points to an additional type of result. This was what modern researchers call common knowledge, a state of shared knowledge and metaknowledge, about the early imperial state, particularly that of the Qin dynasty in the time of the First Emperor. The political effects of common knowledge supported the Qin in their integration of the empire.

The efficacy of the Qin dynasty's communication created difficulties for its successors. The Han dynasty emerged as the victors of the civil war that followed the collapse of the Qin. From the standpoint of political morality, this was unacceptable; the Han should have restored the ruling house of Qin. The situation presented a problem for Han legitimacy. An incident from early Han times demonstrates its place in Han discourse. Around the middle of the second century BCE, well into the dynasty, two scholars debated in front of Emperor Jing 景 (Liu Qi 劉啟, r. 157–141 BCE). Their topic was the overthrow of unjust rulers as depicted in the classics. One scholar held that the fall of those bad rulers showed they had lost the "Mandate of Heaven" signifying heaven's support, and so their overthrow was proper. The other responded that good or bad, those rulers were rulers and overthrowing them was criminal. The first retorted that the situation was analogous to the Han dynasty's replacement of the Qin. At this point the emperor interrupted to end the debate, saying, "It is not foolish for those who speak of scholarship to not speak of Tang and Wu receiving the mandate" 言學者毋言湯武受命, 不為愚.[7] Tang and Wu were two ancient rulers who had overthrown their predecessors. The implication was clear: the Han were on morally shaky ground in having taken over after the Qin, and it was wise to avoid any allusion that would draw attention to this fact.

Yet the efficacy of Qin methods for making their name known made it impossible for the Han to ignore the problem. The Qin dynasty and its activities had become symbols, and the Han had to deal with the effects of Qin communication. The result was systematic derogation of the Qin and their achievements. This began no later than 206 BCE, when the Han founder's adherents began to portray him as one who rescued the realm from the Qin dynasty rather than the military victor of a civil war.[8]

Many of the means through which the Qin had created common knowledge of their dynasty became symbols of their alleged cruelty and irrationality during Han times. The Qin legal system was equated with brutality, their roads were made a symbol for excess, and their rule became a byword for bad government.[9] The use of the Second Emperor's name as metonymic shorthand for a successor's avoidable errors in the edict that opened this chapter confirms the wide distribution of these images.

Research in recent years based on paleographic sources has already done much to undermine the notion that the transition from Qin to Han was a radical break, which has long been an important element of anti-Qin historiography.[10] The interpretation I have offered in this book invites reevaluation of received accounts in yet another way. One of the things my arguments do is offer a way of viewing Qin activities that makes them intelligible. This undermines the traditional picture of senseless Qin barbarity.

As I noted in the introduction, my analysis challenges historical narratives that portray early imperial China as a time in which absolute authority and coercion were the primary means by which society functioned. This does not, of course, mean that violence was not an important aspect of early Chinese governance.[11] Furthermore, rhetoric of authority and hierarchy dominated political discourse and theory in imperial times. This was due, no doubt, in large part to its appeal for emperors and others who benefited disproportionately from the imperial system and had extensive access to material resources.

Analyses of political discourse in early China have given limited serious consideration to political philosophy that discusses the role of noncoercive government in creating a functional society. That my approach draws from some of the same thinkers commonly cited as advocates of authoritarianism reflects the richness of those thinkers' ideas and insights.

This study has argued on the basis of cross-cultural research that communication in particular forms—forms that the Qin used—has in and of itself political potency. Considering political messages in terms of common knowledge enables a more nuanced and multifaceted understanding of those messages. One aspect of this concerns media: historians should consider how communication, especially political communication, results from activities that also serve other purposes. Even messages designed as political propaganda work differently than often considered. Focal points can emerge even when an explicit political message fails or is absent. Some of the Qin dynasty's activities could be deemed propaganda, and bad propaganda at that, because the resulting opinion appears to have been negative. But they certainly succeeded in creating common knowledge of the Qin.

Scholars should also recognize the political power of the ordinary population as something that was functioning at all times, not only in exceptional instances. Theoretical frameworks combined with new sources and reconsidered traditional historiography permit reasonable and well-founded inferences about the power of the ordinary population in contexts where available information is limited. One specific aspect of this is interpreting the actions of imperial rulers as ways of communicating to the population.

One of my goals in this book has been to bring a different understanding of Qin projects and other activities that required the mobilization of large numbers of people. Historians present these as reflections of the Qin ability to extract labor from the population, which is true. Yet the chain of causality was two-way. Creating large buildings required the exercise of considerable political power. But those projects—both in the edifices they created and the people they enlisted to do the labor—indexed Qin power and so worked to effect and extend it. They created common knowledge among those who observed the projects and their results, those who left their daily lives to go do the work, and all those who heard about these things at second hand. Such endeavors broadcast information at every stage. This applies for mobilizations in later dynasties, too. Whenever noticeable projects have occurred, historians should consider the creation, dissemination, or manipulation of information for political purposes as an element of the situation, even (or especially) when the professed motivation was different. The ordinary population was observing, drawing conclusions, and making decisions about the function of imperial power. The outsized construction projects of Qin were not (or not only) an expression of megalomania, nor were they inevitable developments. They were part of how the Qin rulers actively adapted existing processes and technology in a creative way to communicate and thus to form their realm.

The way the Qin spread their name might seem to have been abortive. After all, it later attracted opprobrium as unparalleled as the dynasty's achievements. And the Qin dynasty was far from without success. The First Emperor ruled for ten years of relative peace, without major disturbance. Jia Yi, for instance, acknowledges this in his famous "Essay Criticizing the Qin" ("Guo Qin lun" 過秦論).[12] And when the Qin dynasty collapsed, the Han reconstituted the realm along essentially the same lines in both geographical and administrative terms.[13] The ubiquity of negative references to the Qin during the Han period attests to Qin accomplishments in generating publicity. Because the dynasty was already well and widely known, its name was subject to the sort of instability of meaning that characterizes all signs.[14] Only thus could the Han dynasty reverse it to signify the opposite of how the Qin presented themselves. By successfully spreading their name and their rule, the Qin compelled their successors to struggle with them for legitimacy, even after their fall.

Many of the Qin projects and practices discussed in this book became part of the Han portrayal of their predecessors. The reason for this lay in the same communicative effects that made such efforts important for establishing successful Qin rule. Because, for example, the Qin legal system instantiated a particular view of the world, in which the innocent went free while the guilty received punishment according to an explicit scale that modulated punishment according to the seriousness of the offense. Many aspects of the system may not appeal to modern sensibilities. But for the Qin, it was a primary sphere in which to manifest the quality of fairness as they understood it.

The Han founder Liu Bang exploited this with his announcement that suspended the legal system after the Qin dynasty's disintegration. He criticized the Qin legal system as harsh, yet he went on to institute an updated but substantially similar version of the same system just a few years later. It is no wonder that he did so. The Qin were justly proud of their sophisticated system for administering the law.[15] Branding it as excessive and turning it against them was a Han public relations victory. The legal system of imperial China would continue to evolve. Yet the Qin legal system, which played so fundamental a role in that of the Han dynasty, became a particular target for later critics. This is despite the fact that the Han system was, by all indications, at least equally deadly, even after major reform in 167 BCE.[16]

Reconsiderations

The line of argument I have followed in this book presents a new way to consider large-scale projects and undertakings from throughout Chinese history. Here I will briefly discuss just a few examples to indicate the forms this could take.

In chapter 4, I mentioned the famous Qin terra-cotta warriors and suggested that they communicated about the First Emperor. The analysis in this book suggests this sort of effect must have followed from other sorts of funerary memorials as well. Tombs are an illustrative example. Many emperors were alive during the construction of their tombs, and their opulent sepulchers demonstrated their power over human and material resources. After death, these messages would continue on behalf of successors, family, and associates. Both aspects provided a powerful impetus for the creation of tombs. They memorialized the one who had died and indexed his power, connections, and quality in a manner that would benefit his survivors. The same applies for the memorial steles that families and associates commissioned after the death of more ordinary people. We should expect these various kinds of memorials to bring concrete benefit to those who created them, both decedents, while alive, and those left behind after death. Changing prominent relics of a deceased person could also communicate about the one who died and the one remaining. The Second Emperor of Qin's additions to his father's stele inscriptions are but the most obvious example of this.

Like the Qin and Han, later dynasties instituted new laws in the early years of their reigns. My analysis indicates we should understand such actions as more than just practical measures and also in terms of publicity. The Sui dynasty (581–619), for example, instituted a new legal code in its first year. It did away with or lightened punishments current under previous law, and the Sui emperor issued an edict drawing attention to this fact.[17] The first emperor of the Tang dynasty, who overthrew the Sui, imitated the Han founder Liu Bang and instituted a pared-down legal code. But, as in the Han case, this rudimentary code proved insufficient for ruling the realm, and the Tang soon put in place an expanded version of the Sui laws.[18] The founder of the Ming dynasty promulgated a new code of laws at the start of that dynasty in the fourteenth century. It was taught at local-level schools, and government functionaries read it aloud for the benefit of the populace at ritual gatherings.[19] Such changes and developments may well have addressed concrete problems of governance, but they also advertised the existence of new rulers and so helped realize the new dynasty's control of the realm.

One of the Sui dynasty's most enduring accomplishments was the Grand Canal, which was constructed during their brief reign in the late sixth and early seventh centuries. It built upon and extended earlier canals, including a long stretch to the northeast. In this way, the Sui created a waterway that connected the region of the capital with the north and south and linked the different regions of the realm with each other. The canal had an evident economic impact and led to expanding cities and trade. The canal's influence permeated society and reached even to poetry. This project had great potency as an index of the Sui dynasty's ability to mobilize its populace to undertake public works projects. But the strongest influence of the canal may have been that it encouraged specific forms of cooperation across the area of the realm. The trade it fostered permitted areas to concentrate their economic production on certain commodities and import others from elsewhere. As Mark Edward Lewis notes, "In the tenth century, after China fractured into many independent states, regional economic specialization forced these rivals to continue to cooperate in what had become an 'international' trade in essential goods."[20] Considering communication and cooperation around the Grand Canal offers a way to analyze and explain the function of these connections in the quick reestablishment of the realm under the Song dynasty later in the tenth century.

In chapter 4, I looked at how the Qin dynasty announced itself by decreeing that its weights and measures be adopted across the realm. My approach invites reconsidering changes to standard practices in later periods as well. In the seventeenth century, the Qing dynasty made its announcement in a way even more certain to attract its subjects' notice: Qing rulers required their male subjects to wear their hair in the Manchu fashion, with the front of the head shaved and the hair in the back long and braided into a queue. This sudden, forced departure from established practices created common knowledge of the new empire among its subjects. Centuries later, around the beginning of the twentieth century, the queue underwent semiotic change. Cutting one's queue became a message about escape not just from Manchu rule but from Chinese tradition as well. And some chose to retain it out of fidelity not to the Qing dynasty but to Chinese culture.[21] Thinking in terms of common knowledge creation and cooperation indicates that these responses should be viewed as more than signs of changes occurring: they were part of the processes by which the Qing dynasty established its rule over China and by which new political loyalties took shape around the end of that dynasty.

The approach I use offers a new and persuasive way of thinking about the durability of the imperial system in China. Chwe says, "In terms of common knowledge, history is just like publicity."[22] Both of these existed in imperial China. There was publicity of many sorts already at the start of the imperial period. And there was history: beginning with the Qin, the imperial system was bound with the history of China. I suggest that the effectiveness of Qin and Western Han communication activities helps to explain the resilience of China as a political entity over the millennia since 221 BCE. The empire, its traditions and usages, became at that time the fundamental focal point of the realm. Considering these factors would provide new ways of thinking about the question of how the imperial system lasted so long.

Broader Implications

This study's implications go beyond the field of Chinese history. They begin with the recognition that using modern frameworks to consider the distant past can be fruitful. This kind of research can lead to new conclusions and provide connections between history and other fields, both of which are important and worthwhile projects. Historians need not exclude conceptual frameworks from outside the historical period under consideration, provided due care is taken in applying them.

Rather than accepting an unbridgeable gulf between early thought and modern understandings, I have tried to show that bringing the two together has the potential to improve our understanding. Such a project need not hinder engagement with the details of a specific historical situation. A robust theoretical framework permits the inclusion of tremendous detail and simultaneously provides a structure that facilitates interpretation of that detail and links it to broader themes and research topics. This is particularly the case when the concepts underlying those frameworks have analogues in early Chinese thought, as is the case in this study. This approach offers a way to bring together current, empirically based research and the study of history.[23]

One specific methodological implication of this study lies in the recognition that undetailed communication has crucial historical functions. Historians like details, and gathering and interpreting detailed information is at the center of much historical research. Chwe's work reminds us that grasping the details of a system is not the only—and often is not the primary—way that many institutions work. General concepts and vague outlines have a range of influence more extensive than the finer points that often attract scholars' attention.

The approach I have adopted in this study provides a way to think about an undetailed communication in early China that recognizes its utility. Rather than a dichotomy of knowledge and ignorance, we should recognize a spectrum of understanding, at every point along which important messages were transmitted and received. A simple or vague message—a message half or less understood—can still suffice to create sufficient common knowledge to guide cooperative tendencies and thus have profound political effects.

Scholars of Chinese history sometimes suggest that a theoretical framework is not useful unless it generates conclusions one would not have reached by another route. I would offer another way to think about this. If a given theoretical model accurately represents the world—especially when it concerns humanity in the world—we should expect its results to resonate with our experiences and understandings. Those things, then, would be recognizable and amenable to analysis through other approaches. The study of history in China has existed for over two thousand years and continues today on a broad scale. It makes sense that there are places in which theoretically informed historical research would align with existing interpretation, assuming the theoretical framework is reliable. Yet in other places this approach should offer something different. In the end, the results should combine confirmation or refinement of accounts derived through other reliable means with new conclusions and new connections.

Work in early history brings difficulties for empirical research. Study of ancient times often relies on small sets of examples, and repeatability is out of the question. Measurement is difficult when the basic constituents of research are subject to highly individual interpretation—as is the case in dealing with ancient texts, especially texts written in a language as flexible and often ambiguous as classical Chinese. Some study of historical cases in research that I draw from has occurred. Chwe incorporates historical examples into his study, and Peter T. Leeson's *The Invisible Hook* examines at length how pirates in the seventeenth and eighteenth centuries used special kinds of communication to encourage their victims' cooperation. These works demonstrate the promise of a cross-disciplinary approach that brings together history and other fields. It offers the sort of real exchange that William H. Sewell Jr. has called for.[24] This kind of project would represent an endeavor in which historians of the distant past offer content expertise to collaboration with researchers from other fields. It could thus open up a substantial new field to interdisciplinary, theoretically informed research. It would also benefit historians of Chinese antiquity, whose work and position in the academy could only benefit from an expanded audience and increased contemporary relevance.

Researchers who work with concepts I incorporate into my framework have noted that while they are the subject of current inquiry, these concepts are not new. They have clear affinities with the analyses of important nineteenth- and twentieth-century social scientists.[25] The connections I have drawn to Chinese thought and practice show that related ideas existed far earlier than that. It is clear that ancient Chinese thought has much to offer the modern world in this respect, especially as empirical research continues to expand our recognition and understanding of how profoundly cooperation shapes our world. If humanity is going to advance in our ability to draw from the best of cooperation and learn to function without war, we need new ways to think about what cooperation means and how to bring it about. Such development will require us to go beyond the borders of a single culture or cultural area and to draw from a range of cultures and contexts. Early China has much to teach us.

Notes

Chapter 1. Introduction

1. For an account of the Qin dynasty, see Mark Edward Lewis, *The Early Chinese Empires: Qin and Han* (Cambridge: Harvard University Press, 2007).

2. Lothar von Falkenhausen, *Chinese Society in the Age of Confucius (1000–250 BC): The Archaeological Evidence* (Los Angeles: Cotsen Institute of Archaeology, University of California, 2006), 328–38.

3. Mark Edward Lewis, *The Construction of Space in Early China* (Albany: State University of New York Press, 2006), 175.

4. Falkenhausen, *Chinese Society*, 13.

5. See Thomas C. Schelling, *Micromotives and Macrobehavior* (New York: W. W. Norton, 2006 [1978]).

6. Vivienne Shue, *The Reach of the State: Sketches of the Chinese Body Politic* (Stanford: Stanford University Press, 1988), 27–28; quote from 27 (emphasis in original).

7. Ray Huang, *China: A Macro History* (Armonk: M. E. Sharpe, 1997), quote from 51.

8. Benjamin I. Schwartz, "The Primacy of the Political Order in East Asian Societies: Some Preliminary Generalizations," in *Foundations and Limits of State Power in China*, ed. S. R. Schram (London: School of Oriental and African Studies, 1987), 1–10; quote from 1–2.

9. Wang Yü-ch'üan, "An Outline of the Central Government of the Former Han Dynasty," *Harvard Journal of Asiatic Studies* 12 (1949): 134–87; quote from 138.

10. Liu Zehua, Wang Maohe 汪茂和, and Wang Lanzhong 王蘭仲, *Zhuanzhi quanli yu Zhongguo shehui* 專制權力與中國社會 (Tianjin: Tianjin guji chubanshe, 2005), quote from 18.

11. Wan Changhua 萬昌華 and Zhao Xingbin 趙興彬, *Qin Han yilai jiceng xingzheng yanjiu* 秦漢以來基層行政研究 (Ji'nan: Qi-Lu shushe, 2008), 11–81.

12. Vitaly A. Rubin, *Individual and State in Ancient China: Essays on Four Chinese Philosophers*, trans. Steven I. Levine (New York: Columbia University Press, 1976), 55–87.

13. Victoria Tin-bor Hui, *War and State Formation in Ancient China and Early Modern Europe* (Cambridge: Cambridge University Press, 2005), 166, 183, 190, 219–20; quotes from 190 and 220, respectively.

14. See, e.g., Michael Loewe, "The Authority of the Emperors of Ch'in and Han," in *State and Law in East Asia: Festschrift Karl Bünger*, ed. Dieter Eikemeier and Herbert Franke (Wiesbaden: Harrassowitz, 1981), 80–111; Michael Loewe, "Imperial Sovereignty: Dong Zhongshu's Contribution and His Predecessors," in *Foundations and Limits of State Power in China*, ed. S. R. Schram (London: School of Oriental and African Studies, 1987), 33–57; Michael Loewe, *The Government of the Qin and Han Empires: 221 BCE—220 CE* (Indianapolis: Hackett Publishing, 2006); Michael Loewe, *The Men Who Governed Han China: Companion to "A Biographical Dictionary of the Qin, Former Han and Xin Periods"* (Leiden: Brill, 2004).

15. Loewe, *The Government of the Qin and Han Empires*, 8; see also Loewe, *The Men Who Governed*, 578.

16. Quotes from Loewe, "Imperial Sovereignty," 34, and Loewe, *The Men Who Governed Han China*, 572, respectively.

17. Loewe, *Government of the Qin and Han*, 11, 135 and throughout; Loewe, *The Men Who Governed*, 547, 569.

18. Charles Le Blanc, "État et Société sous les premiers Han," in *La Société civile face à l'État: Dans les Traditions chinoise, japonaise, coréenne et vietnamienne*, ed. Léon Vandermeersch (Paris: École française d'Extrême-Orient, 1994), 33–37.

19. Hans Bielenstein, *The Bureaucracy of Han Times* (Cambridge: Cambridge University Press, 1980), 143–55; quotes from 143 and 155, respectively.

20. Thomas Taylor Meadows, *The Chinese and Their Rebellions, Viewed in Connection with Their National Philosophy, Ethics, Legislation, and Administration. To Which Is Added, an Essay on Civilization and Its Present State in the East and West* (London: Smith, Elder & Co., 1856), 16–29.

21. Karl Bünger, "Concluding Remarks on Two Aspects of the Chinese Unitary State as Compared with the European State System," in *Foundations and Limits of State Power in China*, ed. S. R. Schram (London: School of Oriental and African Studies, 1987), 317.

22. Henri Maspero, "L'empire des Ts'in et des Han," in Maspero and Étienne Balazs, *Histoire et institutions de la Chine ancienne des origines au XIIe siècle après J.-C.* (Paris: Presses universitaires de France, 1967), 58; see also Henri Maspero and Jean Escarra, *Les institutions de la Chine* (Paris: Presses universitaires de France, 1952), 42.

23. Enno Giele, *Imperial Decision-Making and Communication in Early China: A Study of Cai Yong's "Duduan"* (Wiesbaden: Harrassowitz, 2006), 47–48.

24. Max Weber, *Die Wirtschaftsethik der Weltreligionen Konfuzianismus und Taoismus: Schriften 1915–1920*, ed. Helwig Schmidt-Glinzer (Tübingen: J. C. B. Mohr, 1989), 201–2 and throughout.

25. Jacques Gernet, "Introduction," in *Foundations and Limits of State Power in China*, ed. S. R. Schram (London: School of Oriental and African Studies, 1987), xv–xxvii, quote from xxvii.

26. Norman Yoffee, *Myths of the Archaic State: Evolution of the Earliest Cities, States, and Civilizations* (Cambridge: Cambridge University Press, 2005), 5 and throughout; quote from 16.

27. Leif Littrup, "The Un-Oppressive State and Comparative History: Some Observations on Ming-Qing Local Society," in *La société civile face à l'État dans les traditions chinoise, japonaise, coréenne et vietnamienne*, ed. Léon Vandermeersch (Paris: École française d'Extrême-Orient, 1994), 157–72; quote from 168.

28. John K. Fairbank, "A Preliminary Framework," in *The Chinese World Order: Traditional China's Foreign Relations*, ed. John K. Fairbank (Cambridge: Harvard University Press, 1968), 5–8; quote from 7–8.

29. On the relationship between local and central power, see Shue, *The Reach of the State*, 17, 19–20, 55 and throughout; on "modern states" versus "classical states," see 43–44.

30. Herrlee G. Creel, *The Origins of Statecraft in China*, volume one: the Western Chou Empire (Chicago: University of Chicago Press, 1970), 417–18 and throughout; quote from 417.

31. Robin D. S. Yates, "Cosmos, Central Authority, and Communities in the Early Chinese Empire," in *Empires*, ed. Susan E. Alcock et al. (Cambridge: Cambridge University Press, 2001), 351–68; phrases from 351, 356, and throughout.

32. Hui, *War and State Formation*, 166.

33. Gernet, "Introduction," xix, xxiii.

34. E.g., Loewe, *The Government of the Qin and Han Empires*, 135.

35. Shiga Shūzō 滋賀秀三, *Chūgoku hōseishi ronshū: hōten to keibatsu* 中国法制史論集: 法典と刑罰 (Tokyo: Sōbunsha, 2003); Michael Nylan, "Toward an Archaeology of Writing: Text, Ritual, and the Culture of Public Display in the Classical Period (475 B.C.E.–220 C.E.)," in *Text and Ritual in Early China*, ed. Martin Kern (Seattle: University of Washington Press, 2005), 3–49.

36. Falkenhausen, *Chinese Society*.

37. Mark Edward Lewis, *Writing and Authority in Early China* (Albany: State University of New York Press, 1999).

38. E.g., Shue, *The Reach of the State*; Vivienne Shue, *Peasant China in Transition* (Berkeley: University of California Press, 1980); Martin K. Whyte, *Small Groups and Political Rituals in China* (Berkeley: University of California Press, 1974); William L. Parish and Martin K. Whyte, *Village and Family in Contemporary China* (Chicago: University of Chicago Press, 1978).

39. Michael Suk-Young Chwe, *Rational Ritual: Culture, Coordination, and Common Knowledge* (Princeton: Princeton University Press, 2001); Robert Axelrod, *The Evolution of Cooperation*, rev. ed. (New York: Basic Books, 2006).

40. E.g., Weber, *Die Wirtschaftsethik der Weltreligionen*, 201–2 and throughout; also Albert Feuerwerker, *State and Society in Eighteenth-Century China: The Ch'ing Empire in Its Glory* (Ann Arbor: The University of Michigan Center for Chinese Studies, 1976), 21.

41. K. E. Brashier, *Ancestral Memory in Early China* (Cambridge: Harvard University Asia Center, 2011), 37–40.

42. See, for example, Raimo Tuomela, *Cooperation: A Philosophical Study* (Dordrecht: Kluwer Academic Publishers, 2000).

43. *Oxford English Dictionary*, online edition, s.v. "cooperation."

44. Martin A. Nowak, "Five Rules for the Evolution of Cooperation," *Science* 314 (2006): 1560; Robert Axelrod, "On Six Advances in Cooperation Theory," *Analyse & Kritik* 22 (2000): 131; Axelrod, *Evolution of Cooperation*, 6–7, 18, 133–34, and throughout.

45. See chapter 2 and Jiang Lihong 蔣禮鴻, *Shangjun shu zhuizhi* 商君書錐指 (Beijing: Zhonghua shuju, 1986), 1.31.

46. See discussion in Esther Sunkyung Klein, "The History of a Historian: Perspectives on the Authorial Roles of Sima Qian" (Ph.D. dissertation, Princeton University, 2010); Michael Nylan, "Sima Qian: A True Historian?" *Early China* 23–24 (1998–1999): 203–46; Grant Hardy, *Worlds of Bronze and Bamboo: Sima Qian's Conquest of History* (New York: Columbia University Press, 1999); Stephen W. Durrant, *The Cloudy Mirror: Tension and Conflict in the Writings of Sima Qian* (Albany: State University of New York Press, 1995).

47. Yuri Pines, "Biases and Their Sources: Qin History in the *Shiji*," *Oriens Extremus* 45 (2005–2006): 34.

48. Thomas C. Schelling, *The Strategy of Conflict* (Cambridge: Harvard University Press, 1960; reprinted with a new preface, 1980); Axelrod, *The Evolution of Cooperation*.

49. Lee Cronk, *That Complex Whole: Culture and the Evolution of Human Behavior* (Boulder: Westview Press, 1999), 12, discussed 1–15 and throughout.

50. Schelling, *The Strategy of Conflict*.

51. Chwe, *Rational Ritual*.

Chapter 2. Communication and Cooperation: A Framework

1. On cooperation and evolution, see Michael Tomasello, *Why We Cooperate* (Cambridge: MIT Press, 2009); Michael S. Alvard, "The Adaptive Nature of Culture," *Evolutionary Anthropology* 12 (2003): 144; Tim Clutton-Brock, "Breeding Together: Kin Selection and Mutualism in Cooperative Vertebrates," *Science* 296 (2002): 69–72; Leticia Avilés, "Cooperation and Non-Linear Dynamics: An Ecological Perspective on the Evolution of Sociality," *Evolutionary Ecology Research* 1 (1999): 459–77; P. A. Stephens, W. J. Sutherland, and R. P. Freckleton, "What Is the Allee Effect?" *Oikos* 87 (1999): 185–90; Axelrod, *The Evolution of Cooperation*, 20–22 and throughout; Dorothy L. Cheney and Robert M. Seyfarth, *Baboon Metaphysics: The Evolution of a Social Mind* (Chicago: University of Chicago Press, 2007). For a study that examines the universal tendency for order to emerge from disorder as well as the complexities involved in this, especially among humans, see Douglas T. Kenrick, Jon K. Maner, Jon Butner, Norman P. Li, D. Vaugn Becker, and Mark Schaller, "Dynamical Evolutionary Psychology: Mapping the Domains of the New Interactionist Paradigm," *Personality and Social Psychology Review* 6 (2002): 347–56.

Peter T. Leeson, *The Invisible Hook: The Hidden Economics of Pirates* (Princeton: Princeton University Press, 2009) discusses the emergence of cooperation without institutional authority in a historical context; see also Peter T. Leeson, "The Laws of Lawlessness," *Journal of Legal Studies* 38 (2009): 471–503.

2. William Irons, "An Evolutionary Critique of the Created Co-Creator Concept," *Zygon* 39 (2004): 773–90; quote from 775.

3. Robert Boyd, Herbert Gintis, Samuel Bowles, and Peter J. Richerson, "The Evolution of Altruistic Punishment," *Proceedings of the National Academy of Science of the United States of America* 100 (2003): 3531–35.

4. F. Courchamp, B. Grenfell, and T. Clutton-Brock, "Population Dynamics of Obligate Cooperators," *Proceedings of the Royal Society of London B* 266 (1999): 557–63; Avilés, "Cooperation and Non-Linear Dynamics."

5. Avilés, "Cooperation and Non-Linear Dynamics," 472 and throughout.

6. Axelrod, *Evolution of Cooperation*, 17; Mark Van Vugt, "Evolutionary Origins of Leadership and Followership," *Personality and Social Psychology Review* 10.4 (2006): 357; Mark Van Vugt, Robert Hogan, and Robert B. Kaiser, "Leadership, Followership, and Evolution: Some Lessons From the Past," *American Psychologist* 63.3 (2008): 186; Clutton-Brock, "Breeding Together."

7. Herbert Gintis, Samuel Bowles, Robert Boyd, and Ernst Fehr, "Moral Sentiments and Material Interests: Origins, Evidence, and Consequences," in *Moral Sentiments and Material Interests: The Foundations of Cooperation in Economic Life*, ed. Herbert Gintis et al. (Cambridge: MIT Press, 2005), 3–39; see also Ernst Fehr and Urs Fischbacher, "The Economics of Strong Reciprocity," in Gintis et al., 151–91.

8. Cronk, *That Complex Whole*, 12, discussed 1–15; Alvard, "The Adaptive Nature of Culture," 136; see also Kevin N. Laland and William Hoppitt, "Do Animals Have Culture?" *Evolutionary Anthropology* 12 (2003): 150–51.

9. See discussion in Cronk, *That Complex Whole*, 1–15; quote from 12 (emphasis in original).

10. Michael Tomasello, Ann Cale Kruger, and Hilary Horn Ratner, "Cultural Learning," *Behavioral and Brain Sciences* 16 (1993): 495–552; Michael Tomasello, *The Cultural Origins of Human Cognition* (Cambridge: Harvard University Press, 1999); Alvard, "The Adaptive Nature of Culture."

11. Alvard, "The Adaptive Nature of Culture"; and see, e.g., Joseph Henrich and Richard McElreath, "The Evolution of Cultural Evolution," *Evolutionary Anthropology* 12 (2003): 124.

12. Tomasello, Kruger, and Ratner, "Cultural Learning"; Tomasello, *The Cultural Origins of Human Cognition*; Alvard, "The Adaptive Nature of Culture."

13. Webb Keane, "The Evidence of the Senses and the Materiality of Religion," *Journal of the Royal Anthropological Institute* 14.1 (2008): 110–27; quote from 113.

14. Ann Swidler, "Culture in Action: Symbols and Strategies," *American Sociological Review* 51 (1986): 273–86.

15. Schelling, *The Strategy of Conflict*; the following draws from 54–107 and throughout, with additional references as needed.

16. See Schelling, *Strategy*, quote from 22; see also discussion in Axelrod, *Evolution of Cooperation*, 110–13 and throughout.
17. Schelling, *Strategy*, 68; see also Alvard, "Kinship," 149.
18. Schelling, *Strategy*, 92.
19. See also Axelrod, *Evolution of Cooperation*, 15–16, 27, and throughout.
20. Schelling, *Strategy*, 74, 91, and throughout; see also Van Vugt, Hogan, and Kaiser, "Leadership, Followership, and Evolution," 183–84; Van Vugt, "Evolutionary Origins of Leadership and Followership."
21. Van Vugt, "Evolutionary Origins," 355; see also Robert Hogan and Robert B. Kaiser, "What We Know About Leadership," *Review of General Psychology* 9.2 (2005): 169–80; Robert Hogan, Gordon J. Curphy, and Joyce Hogan, "What We Know About Leadership," *American Psychologist* 49.6 (1994): 493–504.
22. Axelrod, *Evolution of Cooperation*, 146; see also 155–58.
23. Schelling, *Strategy*, 67.
24. Alvard, "The Adaptive Nature of Culture"; see also Chwe, *Rational Ritual*.
25. Alvard, "The Adaptive Nature of Culture"; see also Chwe, *Rational Ritual*, 88–89, 97–98.
26. The following draws from Chwe, *Rational Ritual*, with additional references as necessary. See also Tomasello, *Why We Cooperate*, 70–76, on common knowledge.
27. Chwe, *Rational Ritual*, 26. Cf. Schelling, *Strategy*, 86.
28. Chwe, *Rational Ritual*, 10; quote from Chwe, 19.
29. On common knowledge, see Chwe, *Rational Ritual*, 9–10 and throughout.
30. Chwe, *Rational Ritual*, 15.
31. See Chwe, *Rational Ritual*, 79–83; see also Lee Cronk, "The Application of Animal Signaling Theory to Human Phenomena: Some Thoughts and Clarifications," *Social Science Information* 44 (2005): 603–20.
32. Alvard, "The Adaptive Nature of Culture," 143–44.
33. Chwe, *Rational Ritual*, 22–23; on indexes, see Charles Peirce, "Logic as Semiotic: The Theory of Signs," in *The Philosophical Writings of Peirce*, ed. Justus Buchler (New York: Dover, 1955), 98–119.
34. Chwe, *Rational Ritual*, 90; discussed 87–91.
35. *Oxford English Dictionary*, online edition, s.v. "propaganda."
36. Chwe, *Rational Ritual*, 16; Cf. Robert E. Moore, "From Genericide to Viral Marketing: On 'Brand,'" *Language & Communication* 23 (2003): 331–57.
37. See Keane, "The Evidence of the Senses and the Materiality of Religion," 110–27, and related discussion in Webb Keane, "Market, Materiality and Moral Metalanguage," *Anthropological Theory* 8.1 (2008): 27–42. On related issues, see Michael Silverstein, "The Uses and Utility of Ideology," in *Language Ideologies: Practice and Theory*, ed. Bambi B. Schiefflin, Kathryn A. Woolard, and Paul V. Kroskrity (Oxford: Oxford University Press, 1998), 123–45. On the mutability of messages and signs, see Moore, "From Genericide to Viral Marketing"; Chwe, *Rational Ritual*, 16; see also Michel Foucault, *Discipline and Punish: The Birth of the Prison*, trans. Alan Sheridan (New York: Vintage Books, 1979).

38. Axelrod, *Evolution of Cooperation*, 15–16, 27, 120–23, and throughout; Chwe, *Rational Ritual*.

39. See Herbert Gintis, Samuel Bowles, Robert Boyd, and Ernst Fehr, "Moral Sentiments and Material Interests: Origins, Evidence, and Consequences," in *Moral Sentiments and Material Interests: The Foundations of Cooperation in Economic Life*, ed. Herbert Gintis et al. (Cambridge: MIT Press, 2005), 3–39, especially 8; and Ernst Fehr and Urs Fischbacher, "The Economics of Strong Reciprocity," in Gintis et al., 151–91.

40. The following summarizes from Amotz Zahavi and Avishag Zahavi, *The Handicap Principle: A Missing Piece of Darwin's Puzzle*, trans. Naama Zahavi-Ely and Melvin Patrick Ely (Oxford: Oxford University Press, 1997), with additional citations as necessary.

41. See also Rebecca Bliege Bird and Eric Alden Smith, "Signaling Theory, Strategic Interaction, and Symbolic Capital," *Current Anthropology* 46.2 (2005): 221–48.

42. Peirce, "Logic as Semiotic: The Theory of Signs"; Webb Keane, "The Hazards of New Clothes: What Signs Make Possible," in *The Art of Clothing: A Pacific Experience*, ed. Susanne Küchler and Graeme Were (London: ULC Press, 2005), 1–16.

43. Zahavi and Zahavi, *The Handicap Principle*, 59–60, 82; Joseph Heath and Andrew Potter, *Nation of Rebels: Why Counterculture Became Consumer Culture* (New York: Harper Paperbacks, 2004); James L. Boone, "The Evolution of Magnanimity: When Is It Better to Give Than to Receive?" *Human Nature* 9 (1998): 5–6.

44. Zahavi and Zahavi, *The Handicap Principle*, 16–22, 55–60, and throughout. See also related discussion in Bliege Bird and Smith, "Signaling Theory," 236; Rufus A. Johnstone and Ken Norris, "Badges of Status and the Cost of Aggression," *Behavioral Ecology and Sociobiology* 32 (1993): 127–34; Michael Lachmann, Szalbolcs Számadó, and Carl T. Bergstrom, "Cost and Conflict in Animal Signals and Human Language," *Proceedings of the National Academy of Sciences of the United States of America* 98 (2001): 13189–94; Carl T. Bergstrom and Michael Lachmann, "Signaling Among Relatives. III. Talk Is Cheap," *Proceedings of the National Academy of Sciences of the United States of America* 95 (1998): 5100–5; Joan B. Silk, Elizabeth Kaldor, and Robert Boyd, "Cheap Talk When Interests Conflict," *Animal Behaviour* 59 (2000): 423–32; see also Thomas Getty, "Handicap Signalling: When Fecundity and Viability Do Not Add Up," *Animal Behaviour* 56 (1998): 127–30.

45. The following summarizes from Bliege Bird and Smith, "Signaling Theory"; on Veblen et al., see Bliege Bird and Smith, "Signaling Theory," 221–23.

46. Bliege Bird and Smith, "Signaling Theory," 224.

47. Cronk, "The Application of Animal Signaling Theory."

48. Edward H. Hagen and Gregory A. Bryant, "Music and Dance as a Coalition Signaling System," *Human Nature* 14 (2003): 21–51.

49. Bliege Bird and Smith, "Signaling Theory," 225–32; Richard Sosis, "Religious Behaviors, Badges, and Bans: Signaling Theory and the Evolution of Religion," in *Where God and Science Meet: How Brain and Evolutionary Studies Alter Our*

Understanding of Religion, Volume 1: Evolution, Genes, and the Religious Brain, ed. Patrick McNamara (Westport: Praeger Publications, 2006), 61 on the costs of rituals, including resource and opportunity costs.

50. For discussion of his definition, see Roy Rappaport, *Ritual and Religion in the Making of Humanity* (Cambridge: Cambridge University Press, 1999), 24–54. Other researchers have adopted similar definitions; see, e.g., Catherine Bell, *Ritual: Perspectives and Dimensions* (Oxford: Oxford University Press, 1997), 138, discussed 138–69; Candace Alcorta and Richard Sosis, "Rituals of Humans and Animals," in *Encyclopedia of Human-Animal Relationships*, vol. 2, ed. Marc Bekoff (Westport: Greenwood Publishers, 2007), 599.

51. Rappaport, *Ritual and Religion*, 52, 69–70, 86–106; on the general agreement among researchers that ritual is a kind of communication, see Richard Sosis and Candace Alcorta, "Signaling, Solidarity, and the Sacred: The Evolution of Religious Behavior," *Evolutionary Anthropology* 12 (2003): 265.

52. Rappaport, *Ritual and Religion*, 51, 118–33.

53. Joel Robbins, "Ritual Communication and Linguistic Ideology," *Current Anthropology* 42 (2001): 591–614; see also D. G. Gardner, "Performativity in Ritual: The Mianmin Case," *Man* 18 (1983): 346–60.

54. Sosis, "Religious Behaviors, Badges, and Bans," 61–86; Richard Sosis, "Does Religion Promote Trust? The Role of Signaling, Reputation, and Punishment," *Interdisciplinary Journal of Research on Religion* 1 (2005): 1–30; Richard Sosis, "The Adaptive Value of Religious Ritual," *American Scientist* 92 (2004): 166–72; Richard Sosis, "Why Aren't We All Hutterites? Costly Signaling Theory and Religious Behavior," *Human Nature* 14 (2003): 91–127; Richard Sosis, "Costly Signaling and Torch Fishing on Ifaluk Atoll," *Evolution and Human Behavior* 21 (2000): 223–44; Richard Sosis, "Religion and Intragroup Cooperation: Preliminary Results of a Comparative Analysis of Utopian Communities," *Cross-Cultural Research* 34 (2000): 70–87; Alcorta and Sosis, "Rituals of Humans and Animals"; Candace Alcorta and Richard Sosis, "Ritual, Emotion, and Sacred Symbols," *Human Nature* 16 (2005): 323–59; Sosis and Alcorta, "Signaling, Solidarity, and the Sacred: The Evolution of Religious Behavior"; Richard Sosis and Eric R. Bressler, "Cooperation and Commune Longevity: A Test of the Costly Signaling Theory of Religion," *Cross-Cultural Research* 278 (2003): 211–239; Richard Sosis, Howard C. Kress, and James S. Boster, "Scars for War: Evaluating Alternative Signaling Explanations for Cross-Cultural Variance in Ritual Costs," *Evolution and Human Behavior* 28 (2007): 234–47; Richard Sosis and Bradley J. Ruffle, "Religious Ritual and Cooperation: Testing for a Relationship on Israeli Religious and Secular Kibbutzim," *Current Anthropology* 44 (2003): 713–22; Richard Sosis and Bradley J. Ruffle, "Ideology, Religion, and the Evolution of Cooperation: Field Experiments on Israeli Kibbutzim," *Research in Economic Anthropology* 23 (2004): 89–117. The following discussion draws from these, with additional references as needed.

55. Bruce G. Trigger, "Monumental Architecture: A Thermodynamic Explanation of Symbolic Behavior," *World Archaeology* 22.2 (1990): 119–32; quote from 127; Fraser D. Neiman, "Conspicuous Consumption as Wasteful Advertising: A

Darwinian Perspective on Spatial Patterns in Classic Maya Terminal Monument Dates," in *Rediscovering Darwin: Evolutionary Theory and Archaeological Explanation*, ed. C. M. Barton and G. A. Clark (Washington, D.C.: American Anthropological Association, 1997), 267–90; Bliege Bird and Smith, "Signaling Theory," 231–32.

56. Candy Rowe, "Receiver Psychology and the Evolution of Multicomponent Signals," *Animal Behaviour* 58 (1999): 921–31; Cronk, "The Application of Animal Signaling Theory," 609.

57. Power was one of Foucault's major themes; for selections of relevant writings, see Michel Foucault, *Power*, ed. James D. Faubion (New York: The New Press, 2000); and Michel Foucault, *Power/Knowledge: Selected Interviews and Other Writings 1972–1977*, ed. Colin Gordon (New York: Pantheon Books, 1981 [1980]).

58. Karen Turner, "Law and Punishment in the Formation of Empire," in *Rome and China: Comparative Perspectives on Ancient World Empires*, ed. Walter Scheidel (Oxford: Oxford University Press, 2009), 77–79.

59. Foucault, *Power/Knowledge*, 198; see also Foucault, "The Subject and Power," in *Power*, 337.

60. Foucault, "The Subject and Power," 337; see also 340: "In effect, what defines a relationship of power is that it is a mode of action which does not act directly and immediately on others. Instead, it acts upon their actions: an action upon an action . . ."

61. Foucault, *Power/Knowledge*, 198.
62. Foucault, *Power/Knowledge*, 187.
63. Foucault, *Power/Knowledge*, 200.
64. Foucault, *Power/Knowledge*, 88–92; see also Colin Gordon, "Introduction," *Power*, xix.

65. Foucault, "Omnes et Singulatim: Towards a Critique of 'Political Reason,'" in *The Tanner Lectures on Human Values*, vol. 2, ed. S. McMurrin (Cambridge: Cambridge University Press, 1981), 253.

66. Foucault, *Security, Territory, Population: Lectures at the College de France, 1977–78*, trans. Graham Burchell (New York: Palgrave Macmillan, 2007), 352–53.

67. See Foucault, "The Subject and Power," 337–38; quotes from 337 and 338, respectively.

68. From Foucault, "Preface to *Anti-Oedipus*," in *Power*, 108; see also Foucault, *Power/Knowledge*, 99.

69. Foucault, "The Subject and Power," 328.

Chapter 3. Communication and Cooperation in Early Chinese Thought

1. "Lingtai" 靈臺 (Mao #242); *Maoshi zhengyi* 毛詩正義, 16–5.4b–5b. This and all references to the Thirteen Classics from *Shisanjing zhushu* 十三經注疏, ed. Ruan Yuan 阮元 (1764–1849) (Taipei: Yiwen yinshuguan, 2001).

2. *Mengzi zhushu* 孟子注疏, 1A.10.

3. Scott Cook, "The Debate over Coercive Rulership and the 'Human Way' in Light of Recently Excavated Warring States Texts," *Harvard Journal of Asiatic Studies* 64.2 (2004): 399–440.

4. W. Allyn Rickett, "*Kuan tzu*," in *Early Chinese Texts: A Bibliographical Guide* (Berkeley: Society for the Study of Early China, 1993), 244–51.

5. On the last Shang ruler and his governance as trope, see discussion in Yuri Pines, "To Rebel Is Justified? The Image of Zhouxin and Legitimacy of Rebellion in Chinese Political Tradition," *Oriens Extremus* 47 (2008): 1–24.

6. Li Xiangfeng 黎翔鳳, *Guanzi jiaozhu* 管子校注 (Beijing: Zhonghua shuju, 2004), 20.1172.

7. Li Xiangfeng, *Guanzi jiaozhu*, 5.275.

8. Li Xiangfeng, *Guanzi jiaozhu*, 12.683, 24.1448.

9. Li Xiangfeng, *Guanzi jiaozhu*, 11.617.

10. *Liji zhushu* 禮記注疏, 60.9b–10a.

11. See Zhang Zhenze 張震澤, *Sun Bin bingfa jiaoli* 孫臏兵法校理 (Beijing: Zhonghua shuju, 1984), 54.

12. See Zhang Zhenze, *Sun Bin bingfa jiaoli*, 54; on conscript armies in early imperial China, see Mark Edward Lewis, "The Han Abolition of Universal Military Service," in *Warfare in Chinese History*, ed. Hans van de Ven (Leiden: Brill, 2000), 33–76.

13. Chen Qiyou 陳奇猷, *Lüshi chunqiu xin jiaoshi* 呂氏春秋新校釋 (Shanghai: Shanghai guji chubanshe, 2002), 7.388.

14. See Xu Weiyu 許維遹, *Hanshi waizhuan jishi* 韓詩外傳集釋 (Beijing: Zhonghua shuju, 1980), 3.88–89; see also *Hanshi waizhuan jishi*, 2.43, 2.52, 4.149.

15. Ma Chengyuan 馬承源, ed., *Shanghai bowuguan cang Zhanguo Chu zhushu* 上海博物館藏戰國楚竹書, vol. 5 (Shanghai: Shanghai guji chubanshe, 2005), 292, 302; note that here and further on I convert loans and other nonstandard graphs into standard, modern characters following editorial suggestions.

16. See Wang Liqi 王利器, *Yantie lun jiaozhu* 鹽鐵論校注, rev. ed. (Beijing: Zhonghua shuju, 1992), 3.191–92; on the background of that text, see Michael Loewe, "Yen t'ieh lun," in *Early Chinese Texts: A Bibliographical Guide*, ed. Michael Loewe (Berkeley: Society for the Study of Early China, 1993), 477–482.

17. Yuri Pines, *Envisioning Eternal Empire: Chinese Political Thought of the Warring States Era* (Honolulu: University of Hawai'i Press, 2009).

18. Pines, *Envisioning*, 189–91.

19. Pines, *Envisioning*, 191 and throughout.

20. Pines, *Envisioning*, 198–218 and throughout.

21. Pines, *Envisioning*, 30.

22. Pines, *Envisioning*, 209.

23. Pines, *Envisioning*, 82.

24. Wang Xianqian 王先謙 (1842–1918), *Xunzi jijie* 荀子集解 (Beijing: Zhonghua shuju, 1988), 5.173.

25. Wang Xianqian, *Xunzi jijie*, 5.164; see also *Xunzi jijie*, 12.324.

26. Chen Qiyou, *Lüshi chunqiu xin jiaoshi*, 20.1330.

27. Wang Xianqian, *Xunzi jijie*, 8.237; see also *Xunzi jijie*, 5.165.
28. Wang Xianqian, *Xunzi jijie*, 19.504; see also discussion in Pines, *Envisioning*, 83.
29. Chen Qiyou, *Lüshi chunqiu xin jiaoshi*, 4.236, 19.1290.
30. Li Xiangfeng, *Guanzi jiaozhu*, 15.922.
31. See Sun Yirang 孫詒讓 (1848–1908), *Mozi jiangu* 墨子閒詁 (Beijing: Zhonghua shuju, 2001), 4.113–14, 7.199, 7.204, 7.213, 8.253, and cf. 4.103; see also A. C. Graham, *Disputers of the Tao: Philosophical Argument in Ancient China* (La Salle: Open Court, 1989), 41–45; and Pines, *Envisioning*, 31, 35, and throughout.
32. Li Xiangfeng, *Guanzi jiaozhu*, 1.52, 10.554.
33. Chen Qiyou, *Han Feizi xin jiaozhu* 韓非子新校注 (Shanghai: Shanghai guji chubanshe, 2000), 4.287.
34. Sima Qian (ca. 145–ca. 86 BCE), *Shiji* (Beijing: Zhonghua shuju, 1959), 6.252; cf. translation in Martin Kern, *The Stele Inscriptions of Ch'in Shih-huang: Text and Ritual in Early Chinese Imperial Representation* (New Haven: American Oriental Society, 2000), 42; for more examples, see Kern, *The Stele Inscriptions*, 46–47 and throughout.
35. "Face south" (*nanmian* 南面) and similar phrases are conventional terms for ruling.
36. Qi Yuzhang 祁玉章, *Jiazi Xin shu jiaoshi* 賈子新書校釋 (Taipei: Zhongguo wenhua zazhishe, 1974), 1.38–39. Jia Yi also touched on the Qin elsewhere, e.g., *Jiazi Xin shu jiaoshi*, 3.303–22 and throughout.
37. Wang Xianqian, *Xunzi jijie*, 5.150, 8.239, and throughout; see also, e.g., "Zi yi," *Liji zhushu*, 55.13b; cf. discussion in Robin McNeal, "The Body as Metaphor for the Civil and Martial Components of Empire in *Yi Zhou shu*, Chapter 32: With an Excursion on the Composition and Structure of the *Yi Zhou shu*," *Journal of the American Oriental Society* 122.1 (2002): 46–60.
38. See, e.g., Wang Xianqian, *Xunzi jijie*, 11.295–96; see also Xu Weiyu, *Hanshi waizhuan jishi*, 5.167–70, and previous discussion.
39. Pines, *Envisioning*.
40. Wang Liqi, *Xinyu jiaozhu* 新語校注 (Beijing: Zhonghua shuju, 1986), 132. On the usability of *Xinyu*, see Michael Puett, *The Ambivalence of Creation: Debates Concerning Innovation and Artifice in Early China* (Stanford: Stanford University Press, 2001), 259 n. 49.
41. Wang Xianqian, *Xunzi jijie*, 10.290.
42. Wang Xianqian, *Xunzi jijie*, 6.191.
43. Chen Qiyou, *Lüshi chunqiu xin jiaoshi*, 17.1143.
44. *Liji zhushu*, 55.7b.
45. Li Xiangfeng, *Guanzi jiaozhu*, 5.275.
46. See Jiang Lihong, *Shangjun shu zhuizhi*, 2.40.
47. Wang Xianqian, *Xunzi jijie*, 6.191.
48. Li Xiangfeng, *Guanzi jiaozhu*, 10.545.
49. See discussion of secrecy in Lewis, *The Construction of Space*, 153–57. The quote is from *Laozi* 36; see Zhu Qianzhi 朱謙之, *Laozi jiaoshi* 老子校釋

(Beijing: Zhonghua shuju, 1984), 145; see also *Laozi* 65, *Laozi jiaoshi*, 263–66; for other examples, see Wang Bo 王博, "Guanyu 'Tang Yu zhi dao' de jige wenti" 關於"唐虞之道"的幾個問題, in *Jianbo sixiang wenxian lunji* 簡帛思想文獻論集 (Taipei: Taiwan guji chubanshe, 2001), 83; Li Xiangfeng, *Guanzi jiaozhu*, 4.223, 4.245, 18.1044; Chen Qiyou, *Han Feizi xin jiaozhu*, 7.437; and Xu Weiyu, *Hanshi waizhuan jishi*, 7.252.

50. Wang Xianqian, *Xunzi jijie*, 12.321; on *zhou* 周 in the sense of "secrecy," see Yang Liang's 楊倞 (ca. 9th c.) commentary there.

51. Wang Xianqian, *Xunzi jijie*, 12.321–22.

52. Wang Xianqian, *Xunzi jijie*, 12.322.

53. These were part of what is referred to as "Huang-Lao" theories of nonactive governance; on Huang-Lao in Han times, see Reinhard Emmerich, "Bemerkungen zu Huang und Lao in der frühen Han-Zeit: Erkentnisse aus *Shiji* und *Hanshu*," *Monumenta Serica* 43 (1995): 53–140.

54. *Liji zhushu*, 21.22b.

55. Chen Qiyou, *Lüshi chunqiu xin jiaoshi*, 19.1264–65.

56. *Laozi* nos. 14, 22, 24; Zhu Qianzhi, *Laozi jiaoshi*, 53, 92, 98.

57. *Laozi* 17; Zhu Qianzhi, *Laozi jiaoshi*, 68–69. It may be noted that some readers emend this text to say, "Under supreme [rule, the subjects] do not know [the ruler] exists" 太上不知有之. However, the three excavated versions from Guodian 郭店 and Mawangdui 馬王堆 match the text as I have it and confirm that wording is best. See Gao Ming 高明, *Boshu Laozi jiaozhu* 帛書老子校注 (Beijing: Zhonghua shuju, 1996), 305–7, and *Guodian Chu mu zhujian* 郭店楚墓竹簡, ed. Jingmenshi bowuguan 荊門市博物館 (Beijing: Wenwu chubanshe, 1998), 121. As Zhu Qianzhi notes, the referent of *taishang* 太上 is often taken as "supreme antiquity," which simultaneously implies overall supremacy. Because of parallels with the lines that follow, I take the latter sense for my translation. I read *yu* 豫 as *yu* 譽, following the text found in other transmitted editions, as well as the Mawangdui text.

58. Wang Pinzhen 王聘珍 (18th c.), *Da Dai liji jie gu* 大戴禮記解詁 (Beijing: Zhonghua shuju, 1983), 11.208.

59. Jiang Lihong, *Shangjun shu zhuizhi*, 1.31.

60. Chen Qiyou, *Lüshi chunqiu xin jiaoshi*, 19.1279–81.

61. See Graham, *Disputers*, 278–85.

62. Chen Qiyou, *Han Feizi xin jiaozhu*, 2.120–21, 2.182.

63. See Boone, "The Evolution of Magnanimity," 5–6 and throughout.

64. Chen Qiyou, *Han Feizi xin jiaozhu*, 18.1082.

65. Li Xiangfeng, *Guanzi jiaozhu*, 11.578–79, 15.905.

66. Jiang Lihong, *Shangjun shu zhuizhi*, 4.105, 5.126.

67. See *Guodian Chu mu zhujian*, 129 and 132 n. 11. Note that although the editors of that volume emend the text, the text need not be changed, as Qiu Xigui 裘錫圭 points out in his comment. The version of the text found in the Shanghai Museum strips, although different, supports this reading; see Ma Chengyuan, ed., *Shanghai bowuguan cang Zhanguo Chu zhushu* 上海博物館藏戰國楚竹書, vol. 1 (Shanghai: Shanghai guji chubanshe, 2001), 175–76. Cf. *Liji zhushu*, 55.6b–7a.

68. Wang Wenjin 王文錦, *Liji yi jie* 禮記譯解 (Beijing: Zhonghua shuju, 2001), 828; and Yang Tianyu 楊天宇, *Liji yi zhu* 禮記譯注 (Shanghai: Shanghai guji chubanshe, 2004), 736–37.
69. See Qi Yuzhang, *Jiazi Xin shu jiaoshi*, 1.146.
70. Qi Yuzhang, *Jiazi Xin shu jiaoshi*, 1.161–62.
71. Graham, *Disputers*, 289; Pines, *Envisioning*, 82–111; Charles Sanft, "Jia Yi on the Law," *Zinbun: Annals of the Institute for Research in Humanities, Kyoto University* 40 (2007): 53–70.
72. *Chunqiu Zuozhuan zhengyi* 春秋左傳正義, in *Shisanjing zhushu* 十三經注疏, ed. Ruan Yuan 阮元 (1764–1849) (Taipei: Yiwen yinshuguan, 2001), 34.19b: "Ritual is the carriage of governance, and governance defends [the ruler's] person" 禮, 政之輿也; 政, 身之守也.
73. Wang Xianqian, *Xunzi jijie*, 19.492.
74. *Liji zhushu*, 21.5; Zheng Xuan's commentary explains *kao* 考 as "to complete, perfect."
75. Wang Xianqian, *Xunzi jijie*, 6.181, 8.244.
76. He Ning 何寧, *Huainanzi jishi* 淮南子集釋 (Beijing: Zhonghua shuju, 1998), 11.785.
77. See David S. Nivison, "'Virtue' in Bone and Bronze," in David Nivison, *The Ways of Confucianism: Investigations in Chinese Philosophy*, ed. Bryan Van Norden (Chicago: Open Court, 1996), 17–30; David Nivison, "The Paradox of 'Virtue,'" in *The Ways of Confucianism*, 31–43; David Nivison, "Royal 'Virtue' in Shang Oracle Inscriptions," *Early China* 4 (1978–79): 52–55.
78. E.g., Wang Xianqian, *Xunzi jijie*, 2.46.
79. *Liji zhushu*, 55.6a. For recovered versions, see *Guodian Chu mu zhujian*, 130; and Ma Chengyuan, *Shanghai bowuguan cang Zhanguo Chu zhushu*, 1: 183–84. For discussion of intertextuality and "Zi yi," see Martin Kern, "Quotation and the Confucian Canon in Early Chinese Manuscripts: The Case of 'Zi yi' (Black Robes)," *Asiatische Studien* 59.1 (2005): 293–332.
80. Wang Xianqian, *Xunzi jijie*, 9.261–62.
81. Wang Xianqian, *Xunzi jijie*, 5.171–73, 10.289.
82. Puett, *The Ambivalence of Creation*.
83. *Liji zhushu*, 34.4a; see commentary there and in Sun Xidan 孫希旦 (1736–84), *Liji jijie* 禮記集解 (Beijing: Zhonghua shuju, 1989), 906–7.
84. Jiang Lihong, *Shangjun shu zhuizhi*, 1–6, esp. 3–4.
85. Li Xiangfeng, *Guanzi jiaozhu*, 15.920.
86. Chen Qiyou, *Han Feizi xin jiaozhu*, 20.1178–79.
87. Chen Qiyou, *Han Feizi xin jiaozhu*, 7.454; the reference is to *Laozi* 47, see Zhu Qianzhi, *Laozi jiaoshi*, 191.
88. Li Xiangfeng, *Guanzi jiaozhu*, 6.295.
89. Preserved in Li Fang 李昉 (925–996) et al., *Taiping yulan* 太平御覽 (Song woodblock ed.; rpt. Taipei: Taiwan Shangwu yinshuguan, 1968), 638.4b.
90. Li Xiangfeng, *Guanzi jiaozhu*, 12.678.
91. Chen Qiyou, *Han Feizi xin jiaozhu*, 6.400; see also *Laozi* 60, in Zhu Qianzhi, *Laozi jiaoshi*, 244.

92. *Liji zhushu*, 13.9b; Qi Yuzhang, *Jiazi Xin shu jiaoshi*, 3.383.

93. *Liji zhushu*, 13.9a–10a; and see, e.g., regarding cloth in Qin and Western Han times: *Shuihudi Qinmu zhujian* 睡虎地秦墓竹簡, ed. Shuihudi Qinmu zhujian zhengli xiaozu 睡虎地秦墓竹簡整理小組 (Beijing: Wenwu chubanshe, 1990), 36; and *Ernian lüling yu Zouyanshu: Zhangjiashan ersiqihao Han mu chutu falü wenxian shidu* 二年律令與奏讞書: 張家山二四七號漢墓出土法律文獻釋讀, ed. Peng Hao 彭浩, Chen Wei 陳偉, Kudō Mutoo 工藤元男 (Shanghai: Shanghai guji, 2007), 194.

94. Puett, *Ambivalence*, 160.

95. Wang Xianqian, *Xunzi jijie*, 13.376.

96. Wang Xianqian, *Xunzi jijie*, 13.346; and Paul R. Goldin, *Rituals of the Way: The Philosophy of Xunzi* (Chicago: Open Court, 1999).

97. Cf. Brashier, *Ancestral Memory in Early China*.

98. Jiang Lihong, *Shangjun shu zhuizhi*, 5.130.

99. Jiang Lihong, *Shangjun shu zhuizhi*, 5.144.

100. Chen Qiyou, *Han Feizi xin jiaozhu*, 8.543.

101. Chen Qiyou, *Han Feizi xin jiaozhu*, 18.1040.

102. Chen Songchang 陳松長, "Yuelu shuyuan suocang Qin jian zongshu" 岳麓書院所藏秦簡綜述, *Wenwu* 3 (2009): 87; *Shuihudi Qinmu zhujian*, 13; *Shiji*, 6.271.

103. Wang Liqi, *Yantielun jiaozhu* 鹽鐵論校注, rev. ed. (Beijing: Zhonghua shuju, 1992), 10.565–66.

104. *Liji zhushu*, 55.4b; note that I translate *fu* 綍 just as rope, although it referred specifically to the rope used to lower a coffin; see also this line and the commentary in *Guodian Chu mu zhujian*, 130.

105. See Pines, *Envisioning*, 195–96.

106. Jiang Lihong, *Shangjun shu zhuizhi*, 1.2–4, 1.31.

107. See Wang Xianqian, *Xunzi jijie*, 16.422, 16.425; the quote is from 7.224.

108. Chen Qiyou, *Lüshi chunqiu xin jiaoshi*, 16.999–1001.

109. Chen Qiyou, *Han Feizi xin jiaozhu*, 4.287, 4.289, and 19.1147.

110. Chen Qiyou, *Han Feizi xin jiaozhu*, 4.287–89, 20.1176.

111. *Liji zhushu*, 55.13b–14b; for recovered versions of "Zi yi," see *Guodian Chu mu zhujian*, 129, 131; and *Shanghai bowuguan cang Zhangguo Chu zhushu*, 1:180–81, 195. For the quotes from "Jun Ya" and "Jun Chen," with minor textual differences from the version here, see *Shangshu zhengyi* 尚書正義, 19.11b and 18.11a–b, respectively.

112. Jiang Lihong, *Shangjun shu zhuizhi*, 1.2; Chen Qiyou, *Lüshi chunqiu xin jiaoshi*, 18.1187; Wang Xianqian, *Xunzi jijie*, 9.259.

113. Li Xiangfeng, *Guanzi jiaozhu*, 9.471.

Chapter 4. Mass Communication and Standardization

1. *Shiji*, 87.2561. *Ping* 平, "flat, equal," is here used as a verb with an object, thus, "to make something equal." The object of this verb is the sequence

douhu 斗斛, *duliang* 度量, and *wenzhang* 文章. *Douhu* is a compound of two units of weight (*dou* 斗, about 2 kg; and *hu* 斛, about 20 kg), used metonymically for units of weight generally. *Duliang* are measures of length and volume. *Wenzhang* in this context is variously understood; I follow Martin Kern, "Ritual, Text, and the Formation of the Canon: Historical Transitions of *Wen* in Early China," *T'oung Pao* 87 (2001): 58–59. Cf. translations in William H. Nienhauser Jr., ed., *The Grand Scribe's Records*, volume 1: The Memoirs of Pre-Han China (Bloomington: Indiana University Press, 1994), 354; and Yang Yanqi 楊燕起, *Shiji quanyi* 史記全譯 (Guiyang: Guizhou renmin chubanshe, 2001), 3260; see also commentary in Chen Zhi 陳直 (1901–1980), *Shiji xinzheng* 史記新證 (Beijing: Zhonghua shuju, 2006), 143.

2. Li Xueqin 李學勤, *Eastern Zhou and Qin Civilizations*, trans. K. C. Chang (New Haven: Yale University Press, 1985), 240–46 discusses the changes to the system of measurements and related relics. For an overview of the changes with reference to older archaeological results, see Chen Zhi, "Qin Shihuang liu da tongyi zhengce de kaogu ziliao" 秦始皇六大統一政策的考古資料, *Lishi jiaoxue* 歷史教學 8 (1963): 26–30. On the changes to the writing system, see Imre Galambos, "The Myth of the Qin Unification of Writing in Han Sources," *Acta Orientalia* (Budapest) 57.2 (2004): 181–203. See also Yu Weichao 俞偉超 and Gao Ming 高明, "Qin Shihuang tongyi dulianghang he wenzi de lishi gongji" 秦始皇統一度量衡和文字的歷史功績, *Wenwu* 文物) 12 (1973): 7; Ma Chengyuan, "Shang Yang fangsheng he Zhanguo liangzhi" 商鞅方升和戰國量制, *Wenwu* 6 (1972): 18–19; Cheng Ying 程穎, "'Chu heng' yu 'Qin heng'—Zhongguo zaoqi quanheng qiju sheji de liangzhong fanshi" "楚衡"與"秦權"—中國早期權衡器具設計的兩種范式, *Suzhou gongyi meishu zhiye jishu xueyuan xuebao* 蘇州工藝美術職業技術學院學報 3 (2007): 39–40.

3. *Shiji*, 68.2232; dating follows Sima Guang 司馬光 (1019–1086), *Zizhi tongjian* 資治通鑑 (Beijing: Zhonghua shuju, 1956), 2.56–57. The first reliable description of the scoop was in Ma Chengyuan, "Shang Yang fangsheng"; the object is also called the Shang Yang *tongfangsheng* 商鞅銅方升, and is included in many published collections, e.g., Qiu Guangming 丘光明, *Zhongguo lidai dulianghang kao* 中國歷代度量衡考 (Beijing: Kexue chubanshe, 1992), 140–41. Guo Moruo 郭沫若, *Shi pipan shu* 十批判書, in *Guo Moruo quanji* 郭沫若全集, "Lishi bian" 歷史編 section, vol. 2 (Beijing: Renmin chubanshe, 1982), 448. See also A. F. P. Hulsewé, "Weights and Measures in Ch'in Law," in *State and Law in East Asia: Festschrift Karl Bünger*, ed. Dieter Eikemeier and Herbert Franke (Wiesbaden: Otto Harrassowitz, 1981), 25–39; Michael Loewe and Edward L. Shaughnessy, eds., *The Cambridge History of Ancient China: From the Origins of Civilization to 221 B.C.* (Cambridge: Cambridge University Press, 1999), 609–10.

4. Wang Qi 王琦 and Du Jingwei 杜靜薇, "Qin quan" 秦權, *Dang'an* 檔案 1 (1999): 42; Chen Zhi, "Qin Shihuang," 27; Hulsewé, "Weights and Measures," 26; Denis Twitchett and Michael Loewe, eds., *The Cambridge History of China*, Volume 1: The Ch'in and Han Empires, 221 B.C.–A.D. 220 (Cambridge: Cambridge University Press, 1986), 59–60.

5. The text of this inscription is found in many articles and books; I follow Yan Kejun 嚴可均 (1762–1843), "Quan Qin wen" 全秦文, in *Quan Shanggu*

Sandai Qin Han Sanguo Liuchao wen 全上古三代秦漢三國六朝文 (Beijing: Zhonghua shuju, 1958), 1.13a–b. Zhang Wenzhi 張文質, "Qin zhaoban xundu yiyi" 秦詔版訓讀異議, *Hebei shifan daxue xuebao* 河北師範大學學報 3 (1982): 25 points out that there are graphic variations across the examples. For previous translations see Li Xueqin, *Eastern Zhou Civilizations*, 240; and Teng Ssu–yü, trans., *Family Instructions for the Yen Clan* (Leiden: E. J. Brill, 1968), 167; and translation and discussion in Imre Galambos, *Orthography of Early Chinese Writing: Evidence from Newly Excavated Manuscripts* (Budapest: Department of East Asian Studies, Eötvös Loránd University, 2006), 35–39.

Punctuating the first line is somewhat difficult. Like most readers, I break after *zhuhou* 諸侯, "lords." On the other hand, Yan Kejun marks a stop after *tianxia* and Guo Moruo, 448 puts a comma there; with this punctuation, the text would read, "In the twenty-sixth year [of his reign], the emperor unified the entire realm. The lords and common people were at great peace"; for an argument against this reading specifically, see Zhang Wenzhi, "Qin zhaoban xundu yiyi," 25. There are examples of usage that seem potentially to support both understandings.

The phrase 灋度量則不壹嫌疑者 is variously understood. Zhang Wenzhi, "Qin zhaoban xundu yiyi," 24–31 lists five readings and explains his own. The discrepancy in reading comes primarily from the understanding of two words, *fa* 灋, which can plausibly be explained here as a noun, verb, or adjective; and *ze* 則, which could be either a noun or a grammatical particle.

In particular, Sun Changxu 孫常敘, "Ze, fadu liangze, zeshi sanshi shijie" 則, 灋度量則, 則誓三事試解, in *Guwenzi yanjiu* 古文字研究, no. 7 (Beijing: Zhonghua shuju, 1982), 7–24; and Wang Hui 王輝, "Qin qi mingwen congkao (xu)" 秦器銘文叢考 (續), *Kaogu yu wenwu* 考古與文物 5 (1989): 119–21 argue for understanding *ze* here as a kind of standard measure or vessel. (See later in this note for an alternate translation, following Wang Hui's interpretation.) William G. Boltz, "Orthographic Variation in Early Chinese Manuscripts," *Acta Orientalia (Budapest)* 62 (2009): 94, suggests, "法度 'rules and measures' and 量則 'gauges and models' together as noun phrases pleonastically constitute the sentence topic."

Like Zhang Wenzhi, "Qin zhaoban," 26, I think the most important factor in reading *ze* is the fact that it is missing in the 209 BCE inscription, where the Second Emperor refers to these same events. Thus I think *ze* must denote something more easily left out in a reformulation than a noun; hence I believe it is a grammatical particle. Ulrich Unger (1930–2006), "Grammatik des Klassischen Chinesisch, II. Nominalsatz" (unpublished manuscript, version dated 1987), 87–88 (no. 2.1.5.2.2.2.1) says that one of the functions of *ze* is as "Akzentpartikel," explaining, "則 hebt das Subjekt hervor." Edwin G. Pulleyblank, *Outline of Classical Chinese Grammar* (Vancouver: UBC Press, 1995), 72 says that *ze* can, among other things, "mark an exposed noun phrase as contrastive. Most commonly, but not exclusively, the exposed element is the subject." That is how I take *ze* here: marking and accenting the subject (in this case a noun phrase consisting of two nouns in coordination). If Pulleyblank is correct about a contrastive implication, the contrast could be between the ideal purpose of *fa* and *duliang* 度量—to provide standards—and the reality of a disorder and disunity.

I take *fa* and *duliang* as two nouns in coordination. *Fa* in the sense of "law" is clear enough, probably here referring specifically to laws about weights and measures. *Du* 度 and *liang* 量 are standard measures for weight and volume, respectively; together they are metonymy for all sorts of measures. I read the phrase *fa duliang* in this way particularly because of texts like the "Jin di ming" 金狄銘 (see later), which have *fa* and *duliang* in proximity but clearly separated (although the "Jin di ming" refers to *falü*). Cf. Chen Zhi, *Shiji xinzheng* 史記新證 (Beijing: Zhonghua shuju, 2006), 19–20 on a relevant passage, where *du* 度 and *heng* 衡 refer to length and weight relatively, though as Zhang Wenzhi, 29–30, says, these should be understood as metonymy for measures generally there as well. Wang Hui, 119–21, argues *fa* here is a verb. Following a reading like his in regard to *ze* and *fa* might give an alternate translation like, "Standardize units of measure; if the measuring vessels are disparate or doubtful . . ." 灋度量則不壹嫌疑者.

6. Hsing I-t'ien 邢義田, *Qin-Han shilun gao* 秦漢史論稿 (Taipei: Dongda tushu gongsi, 1987), 44–45.

7. *Shiji*, 6.235–36. Wang Hui 王輝, "Qin qi mingwen congkao (xu)" 秦器銘文叢考(考), *Kaogu yu wenwu* 考古與文物 5 (1989): 118–19 notes that the term *qianshou* existed previously, but received official sanction at this time; Kern, *Stele Inscriptions*, 14 n. 14, also mentions this fact. Wang further points out that the conversion was not instantaneous, and the term *min* 民 continued to be used by the Qin after 221 BCE. The fact that *qianshou* was not a new term had been noted long before; see, e.g., Wu Zeng 吳曾 (fl. 1127–1160), *Nenggaizhai manlu* 能改齋漫錄, *Skqs*, 1.10a–b; for an example from Qin, see Zhongguo wenwu yanjiusuo 中國文物研究所 and Hubeisheng wenwu kaogu yanjiusuo 湖北省文物考古研究所, *Longgang Qin jian* 龍崗秦簡 (Beijing: Zhonghua shuju, 2001), 73.

8. Zhang Chunlong 張春龍 and Long Jingsha 龍京沙, "Xiangxi Liye Qin jian 8–455 hao" 湘西里耶秦簡8–455號, in *Jianbo* 簡帛, no. 4, ed. Wuhan daxue jianbo yanjiu zhongxin 武漢大學簡帛研究中心 (Shanghai: Shanghai guji, 2009), 11–15; Hu Pingsheng 胡平生, "Liye Qin jian 8–455 hao mufang xingzhi chuyi" 里耶秦簡8–455號木方性質芻議, in *Jianbo*, no. 4, 17–25.

9. On the title *wang*, see Mark Edward Lewis, "Warring States Political History," in *Cambridge History of Ancient China*, 602–3. The First Emperor referred to his former rivals as "kings" in, e.g., the stele inscriptions at "Zhifu dongguan" 之罘東觀, "Quan Qin wen," 1.12a, trans. Kern, 39 line 15; and Kuaiji 會稽, "Quan Qin wen," 1.12b, trans. Kern, 46 line 19; both of which mention the "six kings" 六王. (Although he also called them *zhuhou* once in the same sequence of texts; see the stele at Zhifu 之罘 proper, in "Quan Qin wen," 1.12a, trans. Kern, *Stele Inscriptions*, 36 line 13.) *Shiji*, 6.239 records that he called them *houwang*.

10. This inscription is found in many sources; my text follows that in Yan Kejun, "Quan Qin wen," 1.13a–b; for previous translations see Li Xueqin, *Eastern Zhou and Qin Civilizations*, 241, and Teng, *Family Instructions for the Yen Clan*,

167–68. Wang Hui, "Qin qi mingwen congkao (xu)," 123–24 discusses the multiple senses of *cheng/chen* 稱 functioning in this inscription, as well as the development of those senses.

11. The weight is listed in Qiu Guangming, *Zhongguo lidai dulianghent kao*, 354; see discussion in Hou Xueshu 侯學書, "Qin zhao zhuke yu quanliang zhengzhi mudi kao" 秦詔鑄刻于權量政治目的考, *Jianghai xuekan* 江海學刊 6 (2004): 126–28.

12. *Shiji*, 6.239; Zhu Xiaoxin 朱筱新, "Dui Qin tongyi dulianghengzhi de zai renshi" 對秦統一度量衡制的再認識, *Beijing jiaoyu xueyuan xuebao* 北京教育學院學報 2 (2000): 6.

13. See Wang Liqi, *Yanshi jiaxun jijie* 顏氏家訓集解, rev. ed. (Beijing: Zhonghua shuju, 1993), 17.455–56.

14. E.g., Ouyang Xiu 歐陽修 (1007–1072), *Ji gu lu* 集古錄, *Skqs*, 1.18a–19a; Lü Dalin 呂大臨 (11th c.), *Kao gu tu* 考古圖, *Skqs*, 9.29a–30b.

15. Wu Hung 巫鴻, "Qin quan yanjiu" 秦權研究, *Gugong bowuyuan yuankan* 故宮博物院院刊 4 (1979): 34, 43; Wang Qi 王琦 and Du Jingwei 杜靜薇, "Qin quan" 秦權, *Dang'an* 檔案 1 (1999): 42–43.

16. E.g., Liu Tizhi 劉體智 (1879–1963), *Shanzhai jijin lu* 善斎吉金錄 (s.l., ca. 1935), 12:29a–b and Fu Kaisen 福開森 (John Calvin Ferguson, 1866–1945), *Lidai zhulu jijin mu* 歷代著錄吉金目 (Changsha: Shangwu yinshuguan, 1939), 1097.

17. Shaanxisheng bowuguan 陝西省博物館, "Xi'anshi xijiao Gaoyaocun chutu Qin Gaonu tongshiquan" 西安市西郊高窑村出土秦高奴銅石權, *Wenwu* 9 (1964): 42–45; Qiu Guangming 丘光明, "Gaonu heshitongquan" 高奴禾石銅權, *Zhongguo zhiliang jishu jiandu* 中國質量技術監督 12 (2001): 62; Shi Shuqing 史樹青 and Xu Qingsong 許青松, "Qin Shihuang ershiliunian zhaoshu ji qi dazi zhaoban" 秦始皇二十六年詔書及其大字詔版, *Wenwu* 12 (1973): 15.

18. See Yuan Zhongyi 袁仲一, *Qindai taowen* 秦代陶文 (Xi'an: Sanqin chubanshe, 1987), 75; Guo Moruo, "Gudai wenzi zhi bianzheng de fazhan" 古代文字之辯證的發展, *Kaogu* 考古 3 (1972): 11–12; Han Baoquan 韓保全, "Qin Epanggong yizhi" 秦阿房宮遺址, *Wenbo* 文博 2 (1996): 26; cf. Zhang Wenzhi, "Qin zhaoban xundu yiyi" 秦詔版訓讀異議, *Hebei shifan daxue xuebao* 河北師範大學學報 3 (1982): 27 n. 14.

19. Wu Hong, "Qin quan yanjiu," 33–47. Qiu Guangming lists fifty-two examples; see Qiu Guangming, *Zhongguo lidai dulianghent kao*, 348–93.

20. Qiu Guangming, *Zhongguo lidai dulianghent kao*, 188–99; Sun Changxu, "Ze, fadu liangze, zeshi sanshi shijie," 15, mentions a fragment from a clay vessel with an inscription of the edict that has a slightly different version of the text.

21. Qiu Xigui, *Chinese Writing*, trans. Gilbert L. Mattos and Jerry Norman (Berkeley: Society for the Study of Early China, 2000), 93 renders *zhaoban* "edict plates."

22. The following from Zhao Ruiyun and Zhao Xiaorong, "Qin zhaoban yanjiu" 秦詔版研究, *Wenbo* 2 (2005): 78–83; and Zhao Ruiyun 趙瑞雲 and Zhao Xiaorong 趙曉榮, "Qin zhaoban yanjiu" 秦詔版研究, *Wenbo* 3 (2005): 89–93. See also Shi and Xu, "Qin Shihuang ershiliunian zhaoshu ji qi dazi zhaoban," 14–17, 29.

23. Zhao and Zhao, "Qin zhaoban yanjiu," discuss only one example, but Shi and Xu, "Qin Shihuang ershiliunian zhaoshu ji qi dazi zhaoban," 16, have two.

24. Cf. Li Xueqin, *Eastern Zhou and Qin Civilizations*, 246, who suggests that this reflects the original form, which he says was "probably fan-shaped."

25. Shi and Xu, "Qin Shihuang ershiliunian zhaoshu ji qi dazi zhaoban," 16.

26. Yuan Zhongyi, *Qindai taowen*, 74–75; Zhao and Zhao, "Qin zhaoban yanjiu," part 2: 90–92; Qiu Guangming, *Zhongguo lidai duliangheng kao*, 198–201.

27. For example, there are two errors on four inscribed pieces discussed in Zhongguo shehui kexueyuan kaogu yanjiusuo Neimenggu gongzuodui 中國社會科學院考古研究所內蒙古工作隊), "Chifeng Zhizhushan yizhi de fajue" 赤峰蜘蛛山遺址的發掘, *Kaogu xuebao* 考古學報 2 (1979): 234; Yuan, *Qindai taowen*, 74, mentions one of these.

28. Luo Fuyi 羅福頤 and Wang Rencong 王人聰, *Yinzhang gaishu* 印章概述 (Beijing: Sanlian shudian, 1963), 14–15; Lothar Ledderose, *Ten Thousand Things: Module and Mass Production in Chinese Art* (Princeton: Princeton University Press, 2000), 60–61; Zhao and Zhao, "Qin zhaoban yanjiu," part 2, 92; Anthony J. Barbieri-Low, "Craftsman's Literacy: Uses of Writing by Male and Female Artisans in Qin and Han China," in *Writing and Literacy in Early China: Studies from the Columbia Early China Seminar*, ed. Feng Li and David Prager Branner (Seattle: University of Washington Press, 2011), 374–78. Pigment chop impresses were also used from early times; for a recent study that discusses both types of use, see Enno Giele, "Signatures of 'Scribes' in Early Imperial China," *Asiatische Studien* 1 (2005): 353–87.

29. See Qiu Guangming, *Zhongguo lidai duliangheng kao* 中國歷代度量衡考 (Beijing: Kexue chubanshe, 1992), 198–200; Qiu's nos. 100 and 102 skip *huangdi*, while nos. 101 and 103 have it; Zhao and Zhao, "Qin zhaoban yanjiu," part 2: 91; Chen Yuan 陳垣, *Shihui juli* 史諱舉例 (Shanghai: Shanghai shudian, 1997), 3, 96. Occasional lapses in observing avoidances continued into Han times; see, e.g., Zhang Zhenze's 張震澤 introduction to *Sun Bin bingfa jiaoli* 孫臏兵法校理 (Beijing: Zhonghua shuju, 1984), "Zixu" 自序, 2.

30. The steles are studied in Kern, *Stele Inscriptions*.

31. The stele texts are anthologized in Yan Kejun, ed., "Quan Qin wen," 1.10b–13a; trans. Kern, *Stele Inscriptions*, 10–49. In notes to the following brief discussion, I refer to the texts by line, as numbered by Kern.

32. See, e.g., "Yishan keshi," lines 9, 29; "Taishan keshi," line 5; "Langyetai keshi," lines 62–68; "Zhifu keshi," lines 16–27; "Zhifu dongguan keshi," lines 15–16; "Jieshimen keshi," lines 20–21; "Kuaiji keshi," lines, 2, 19, 35–37; etc.

33. E.g., "Yishan keshi," lines 30–32; "Langyetai keshi," lines 16, 29, 55, 72; "Zhifu dongguan keshi," line 17; "Jieshimen keshi," lines 27–29, 33; "Kuaiji keshi," lines 64–66; etc.

34. E.g., "Yishan keshi," line 11; an exception, in that it does not mention the emperor, is the inscription at Jieshi, which as Kern, *Stele Inscriptions*, 41, notes is probably missing its first few lines (though the title "emperor" does appear later on in the transmitted version).

35. E.g., "Yishan keshi," line 32; "Langye keshi" line 16; "Zhifu keshi," line 26; "Kuaiji keshi," line 9.

36. E.g., "Langye keshi," lines 3 and 19, see also line 60 on communicating to the whole realm; "Zhifu dongguan keshi," line 29; "Kuaiji keshi," line 16.

37. *Shiji*, 6.267; see text and translation on [[AU: provide x-ref at galleys]].

38. Wang Ming 王酩, "Qindai 'Yishan keshi' kaoxi—jian lun gudai 'zou xia zhaoshu' zhidu" 秦代 "嶧山刻石" 考析—兼論古代 "奏下詔書"制度, *Shoudu shifan daxue xuebao (shehui kexue ban)* 首都師範大學學報 (社會科學版) 2 (2008): 36–38 discusses the similarities between the stele inscriptions and the Second Emperor's addendum on the one hand and bureaucratic documents on the other. On the three-step process, see Xu Shihong 徐世虹, "Handai falü zaiti kaoshu" 漢代法律載體考述, in *Zhongguo fazhishi kaozheng* 中國法制史考證, ed. Yang Yifan 楊一凡, part 1, vol. 3, *Lidai fazhi kao, Liang Han Wei Jin Nanbeichao fazhi kao* 歷代法制考·兩漢魏晉南北朝法制考, ed. Gao Xuchen 高旭晨 (Beijing: Zhongguo shehui kexue chubanshe, 2003), 150–51.

39. Ban Gu 班固 (32–92), *Han shu* 漢書 (Beijing: Zhonghua shuju, 1962), 27C.1472. The sizes reported for the giants are obviously impossible and thus the event of the giants' appearance itself cannot have occurred as related. However, this does not preclude the First Emperor's exploitation of whatever actually did happen for communication.

40. I take *falü* 法律 here as a binome referring to "laws and statutes," thus giving my "laws." This could conceivably be two distinct things, laws or standards (*fa*) and musical pitch standards (*lü* 律).

41. Yan Kejun, "Quan Qin wen," 1.10a; from Li Daoyuan 酈道元, *Shui jing zhu* 水經注, *Skqs*, 4.25a.

42. *Han shu*, 27C.1472; cf. Lukas Nickel, "Tonkrieger auf der Seidenstrasse? Die Plastiken des Ersten Kaisers von China und die Hellenistische Skulptur Zentralasiens," *Zurich Studies in the History of Art* 13.14 (2006–2007): 125–50.

43. Kern, *Stele Inscriptions*, 119.

44. Yuan Zhongyi, *Qindai taowen*, 75.

45. Ledderose, *Ten Thousand Things*, 69–70. For discussion of the tracking marks used by the Qin—inscriptions, brands, and paint—see Wang Sanxia 王三峽, "Qin jian 'jiu ke zhiwu' xiangguan wenzi de jiedu" 秦簡 "久刻職物" 相關文字的解讀, *Changjiang daxue xuebao (shehui kexue ban)* 長江大學學報(社會科學版) 30.2 (2007): 82–85.

46. For example, Shi and Xu, "Qin Shihuang ershiliunian zhaoshu ji qi dazi zhaoban," 16–17.

47. Cheng Shude 程樹德 (1877–1944), *Lunyu jishi* 論語集釋 (Beijing: Zhonghua shuju, 1990), 39.1360–62; also quoted in *Han shu*, 21A.955. See also Li Xiangfeng, *Guanzi jiaozhu*, 10.559.

48. Wang Xianqian, *Xunzi jijie*, 8.120.

49. *Liji zhushu*, 34.4a.

50. David Schaberg, "The *Zhouli* as Constitutional Text," in *Premodern East Asian Statecraft in Comparative Context: The "Rituals of Zhou" in Chinese and East

Asian History, ed. Benjamin A. Elman and Martin Kern (Leiden: Brill, 2010), 33–63.

51. On the *hefangshi* 合方氏, see *Zhouli zhushu*, 33.20b, 28.14a.

52. See Chen Qiyou, *Lüshi chunqiu xin jiaoshi*, 2.65, 8.427; and *Liji zhushu*, 15.5a, 16.25a.

53. *Zhou li zhushu*, 26.11a–12b, 36.3b–5b; see also Zheng Xuan's commentary at *Zhouli zhushu*, 26.12a, and Sun Yirang, *Zhou li zhengyi* 周禮正義 (Beijing: Zhonghua shuju, 1987), 68.2848.

54. *Yi Zhou shu*, *Sbby*, 4.9b.

55. Cf. related regulations in Charles Sanft, "Edict of Monthly Ordinances for the Four Seasons in Fifty Articles from 5 C.E.: Introduction to the Wall Inscription Discovered at Xuanquanzhi, with Annotated Translation," *Early China* 32 (2008–2009): 125–208.

56. This summarizes from Susan Roosevelt Weld, "Covenant in Jin's Walled Cities: The Discoveries at Houma and Wenxian" (Ph.D. dissertation, Harvard University, 1990); Susan Roosevelt Weld, "The Covenant Texts from Houma and Wenxian," in *New Sources of Chinese History: An Introduction to the Reading of Inscriptions and Manuscripts*, ed. Edward L. Shaughnessy (Berkeley: The Society for the Study of Early China, 1997), 125–60; Crispin Williams, "A Methodological Procedure for the Analysis of the Wenxian Covenant Texts," *Asiatische Studien* 59.1 (2005): 61–114; Crispin Williams, "Ten Thousand Names: Rank and Lineage Affiliation in the Wenxian Covenant Texts," *Asiatische Studien* 63.4 (2009): 959–89.

57. Ledderose, *Ten Thousand Things*, 69–70.

58. Hebeisheng wenwu guanlichu 河北省文物管理處, "Hebeisheng Pingshanxian Zhanguo shiqi Zhongshanguo muzang fajue jianbao" 河北省平山縣戰國時期中山國墓葬發掘簡報, *Wenwu* 1 (1979): 5, images 23–24; Zhongguo shehui kexueyuan kaogu yanjiusuo 中國社會科學院考古研究所, ed., *Yin Zhou jinwen jicheng* 殷周金文集成, rev. and enlarged ed. (Beijing: Zhonghua shuju, 2007), 7:5632–33, 6193 (no. 10478).

59. Note that although *wa* 瓦 often refers to clay tiles, it was in ancient times also used as a general term for items made from clay; see *Hanyu dacidian* 漢語大詞典, electronic edition 2.0. It seems that the latter sense best fits the context here, as the *washu* bears little similarity to a tile. My discussion of the *washu* draws from Chen Zhi, "Kaogu luncong" 考古論叢 (a series of articles under one heading), "Qin taoquan yu Qin ling wenwu" 秦陶券與秦陵文物, *Xibei daxue xuebao (zhexue shehui kexue ban)* 西北大學學報(哲學社會科學版) 1 (1957): 68; Guo Zizhi 郭子直, "Zhanguo Qin feng zongyi washu mingwen xinshi" 戰國秦封宗邑瓦書銘文新釋, *Guwenzi yanjiu* 古文字研究, no. 14, ed. Zhongguo guwenzi yanjiuhui 中國古文字研究會 (Beijing: Zhonghua shuju, 1986), 177–96; and Yuan Zhongyi 袁仲一, *Qindai taowen*, 75–84; Li Xueqin 李學勤, "Zhanguo Qin sinian washu kaoshi" 戰國秦四年瓦書考釋, in *Lianhe shuyuan sanshi zhounian jinian lunwenji* 聯合書院三十週年紀念論文集, ed. Lianhe shuyuan sanshi zhounian lunwenji bianji weiyuanhui 聯合書院三十周年紀念論文集編輯委員會 (Hong Kong: Lianhe shuyuan, 1986), 71–77; and Shang Zhiru 尚志

儒, "Qin feng zongyi washu de jige wenti" 秦封宗邑瓦書的幾個問題, *Wenbo* 文博 6 (1986): 43–49.

60. *Shiji*, 4.160, 5.205, 15.727; Chen Zhi, *Shiji xinzheng* 史記新證 (Beijing: Zhonghua shuju, 2006), 13, discusses the *washu* in this context. That was the second time a Zhou ruler had given such a gift to a Qin lord; see *Shiji*, 4.160, 5.203. Note that although the *Shiji* passage refers to Huiwen as "king" here (and throughout), according to *Shiji*, 15.730, he actually first assumed that title in his thirteenth year of rule (325 BCE); see also Liang Yusheng 梁玉繩 (1744–1819), *Shiji zhiyi* 史記志疑 (Beijing: Zhonghua shuju, 1981), 5.141; Yang Yanqi, *Shiji quanyi*, 214 n. 12.

61. Yang Bojun, *Chunqiu Zuozhuan zhu* 春秋左傳注, rev. ed. (Beijing: Zhonghua shuju, 1990), 326; Li Xueqin, "Washu kaoshi," 72, agrees with Yang. Yang cites Xu Zongyan 許宗彥 (1768–1818), *Jianzhishuizhai ji* 鑑止水齋集, in *Huangqing jingjie* 皇清經解 (Taipei: Yiwen yinshuguan, n.d. [ca. 1960]), 1255.22a–b [13719], commenting on the same instance in the *Zuozhuan*. Xu bases his arguments on *Zhouli*, 18.17a, and Zheng Xuan's commentary there. This *Zhouli* passage speaks of meat offered in sacrifices performed at the lineage temple, which Zheng Xuan says was shared with other states ruled by members of the same clan. Du Yu's 杜預 (222–284) commentary at *Chunqiu Zuozhuan zhengyi*, 13.10b, says this gift was an act of reverence equal to that shown the descendants of Wen and Wu, which Kong Yingda explains to mean that they also could receive the meat. However, recovered records of receiving this same bestowal in the Baoshan 包山, Hebei, Chu 楚 strips show that this was probably not as limited as the foregoing would seem to indicate and may have had an ordinary political function as well; see Hubeisheng Jingsha tielu kaogu dui 湖北省荊沙鐵路考古隊, *Baoshan Chu jian* 包山楚簡 (Beijing: Wenwu chubanshe, 1991), 33 no. 205.

62. Guo Zizhi, "Zhanguo Qin feng zongyi washu." But cf. Yuri Pines, "The Question of Interpretation: Qin History in Light of New Epigraphic Sources," *Early China* 29 (2004): 1–44, which studies a long prayer inscribed on two jade tablets.

63. Li Feng, "Ancient Reproductions and Calligraphic Variations: Studies of Western Zhou Bronzes with 'Identical' Inscriptions," *Early China* 22 (1997): 1–41; see also Kern, *Stele Inscriptions*, 121–22; Robert W. Bagley, "Replication Techniques in Eastern Zhou Bronze Casting," in *History from Things: Essays on Material Culture*, ed. Steven Lubar and W. David Kingery (Washington, DC: Smithsonian Institution, 1993), 231–41; quote from 240; see also Jessica Rawson, "Ancient Chinese Bronzes," in Jessica Rawson and Emma Bunker, *Ancient Chinese and Ordos Bronzes* (Hong Kong: The Oriental Ceramic Society of Hong Kong, 1990), 37–38, 44–45; Lothar von Falkenhausen, "The Inscribed Bronzes from Yangjiacun: New Evidence on Social Structure and Historical Consciousness in Late Western Zhou China (c. 800 BC)," *Proceedings of the British Academy* 139 (2006): 254, n. 53, and throughout; on the phenomenon more generally, see Lothar von Falkenhausen, "Issues in Western Zhou Studies: A Review Article," *Early China* 18 (1993): 164 and throughout.

64. Williams, "Ten Thousand Names," 983.

65. Lothar von Falkenhausen, *Suspended Music: Chime-Bells in the Culture of Bronze Age China* (Berkeley: University of California Press, 1993), 32, 56, 314–16; *Yin Zhou jinwen jicheng*, 307–19; Rawson, "Ancient Chinese Bronzes," 37–38.

66. *Chunqiu Zuozhuan zhengyi*, 3.16a.
67. *Chunqiu Zuozhuan zhengyi*, 13.12a; Yang, *Chunqiu Zuozhuan zhu*, 1504.
68. See, e.g., Chen Qiyou, *Lüshi chunqiu xin jiaoshi*, 22.1524; and Sun Yirang, *Mozi jiangu* 墨子閒詁 (Beijing: Zhonghua shuju, 2001), 4.120, which refers to bronze as well as bamboo and silk as materials that convey the information they contain into the future; there are many examples on bronze vessels, see, e.g., the inscriptions translated in Falkenhausen, "Yangjiacun," 278–83.
69. *Han shu*, 21A.972.
70. This is the *zhijin* 職金; see *Zhouli zhushu*, 36.8b; see also commentary in Sun Yirang, *Zhouli zhengyi*, 69.2861, which explains these plates (contra Kong Yingda) as used in prayer.
71. Falkenhausen, "Issues," 147.
72. Weld, "The Covenant Texts," 158.
73. In addition to the following, see, e.g., He Han 何漢, *Qin shi shuping* 秦史述評 (Hefei: Huangshan shushe, 1986), 205–8; Jian Bozan 剪伯贊 (1898–1968), *Qin Han shi* 秦漢史 (Taipei: Yunlong chubanshe, 2003), 50.
74. Ma Chengyuan, "Shang Yang fangsheng he Zhanguo liangzhi" 商鞅方升和戰國量制, *Wenwu* 6 (1972): 18–19.
75. Yu Weichao 俞偉超 and Gao Ming 高明, "Qin Shihuang tongyi duliangheng he wenzi de lishi gongji" 秦始皇統一度量衡和文字的歷史功績, *Wenwu* 12 (1973): 6–13.
76. Shi and Xu, "Qin Shihuang ershiliunian zhaoshu ji qi dazi zhaoban," 15.
77. Zhu Xiaoxin 朱筱新, "Dui Qin tongyi dulianghengzhi de zai renshi" 對秦統一度量衡制的再認識, *Beijing jiaoyu xueyuan xuebao* 北京教育學院學報 2 (2000): 6–10.
78. Hulsewé, "Weights and Measures," 30–31 and throughout; for Han times, see Michael Loewe, "The Measurement of Grain during the Han Period," *T'oung Pao* 49 (1961): 64–95.
79. Hou, "Qin zhao zhuke yu quanliang zhengzhi mudi kao," 123; e.g., Cheng Ying, "'Chu heng' yu 'Qin heng,'" 39–40.
80. Han Baoquan, "Qin Epanggong yizhi," 26; cf. Zhang Wenzhi, "Qin zhaoban xundu yiyi," 27 n. 14.
81. See [[AU: provide x-ref at galleys]]; see Ledderose, *Ten Thousand Things*, and Wang Sanxia, "Qin jian 'jiu ke zhiwu' xiangguan wenzi de jiedu."
82. Hou Xueshu, "Qin zhao zhuke yu quanliang zhengzhi mudi kao," 123–28; see also Wu Hong, "Qin quan yanjiu," 39–40.
83. For example, there is a weight on which the suspension loop is worn; see Qiu Guangming, *Zhongguo lidai duliangheng kao*, 356, discussed in Hou Xueshu, "Qin zhao zhuke yu quanliang zhengzhi mudi kao," 126; see also Wu Chengluo 吳承洛, *Zhongguo duliangheng shi* 中國度量衡史 (Shanghai: Shanghai shudian, 1984), 153.
84. Zhu Xiaoxin, "Dui Qin tongyi dulianghengzhi de zai renshi," 7.
85. Pines, *Envisioning Empire*; Pines, "'The One that Pervades the All' in Ancient Chinese Political Thought: The Origins of 'The Great Unity' Paradigm," *T'oung Pao* 86 (2000): 280–324.

86. Gideon Shelach and Yuri Pines, "Secondary State Formation and the Development of Local Identity: Change and Continuity in the State of Qin (770–221 B.C.)," in *Archaeology of Asia*, ed. Miriam Stark (Malden: Blackwell, 2006), 207, 221–22, 225, and throughout.

87. Ma Yi, "Bianshu shi tan"; Wu Wangzong, "Han jian suojian 'bianshu' tan xi"; Bu Xianqun, "Cong jianbo kan Qin Han xiangli de wenshu wenti" makes the broader point that written documents were certainly a part of life and government at the local level, but that oral communication was also fundamental, specifically between low-level officials and the common people.

88. Robin D. S. Yates, "Soldiers, Scribes, and Women: Literacy among the Lower Orders in Early China," in *Writing and Literacy in Early China: Studies from the Columbia Early China Seminar*, ed. Feng Li and David Prager Branner (Seattle: University of Washington Press, 2011), 339–69; Miyake Kiyoshi 宮宅潔, "Shin-Kan jidai no moji to shikiji—chikukan, mokkan kara mita" 秦漢時代の文字と識字—竹簡、木簡からみた), in *Kanji no Chūgoku bunka* 漢字の中国文化), ed. Tomiya Itaru (Kyoto: Showado, 2009), 215–17; Robin D. S. Yates, "Law and the Military in Early China," in *Military Culture in Imperial China*, ed. Nicola Di Cosmo (Cambridge: Harvard University Press, 2009), 40; Yates, "Zu, shi yu nüxing"; see also Barbieri-Low, *Artisans in Early Imperial China*, 63–66, and Barbieri-Low, "Craftsman's Literacy."

89. Shelach and Pines, "Secondary State Formation and the Development of Local Identity," 216, make a similar argument.

90. Loewe, *Government*, 142; see also Song Wenhong 宋文紅, "Qin nongye falü zhidu tanwei" 秦農業法律制度探微, *Anhui nongye kexue* 安徽農業科學 34.4 (2006): 818–20.

91. See Lewis, *The Construction of Space*, 161 and throughout on the role of markets.

Chapter 5. Progress and Publicity: Qin Shihuang, Ritual, and Common Knowledge

1. On the progresses, see Chen Shuguo, *Xianqin lizhi yanjiu* 先秦禮制研究 (Changsha: Hunan jiaoyu chubanshe, 1991), 158–63, 234–43; He Pingli 何平立, *Xunshou yu fengshan—fengjian zhengzhi de wenhua guiji* 巡狩與封禪—封建政治的文化軌迹 (Ji'nan: Qi-Lu shushe, 2003), 1–7 and throughout; He Pingli, "Xianqin xunshou shiji yu zhidu jilun" 先秦巡狩史迹與制度稽論, *Junshi lishi yanjiu* 軍事歷史研究 1 (2003): 79–87, particularly his discussion of canonical and other early sources; Zhang Rongming 張榮明, "Zhongguo shanggu guojia de chansheng ji tezheng" 中國上古國家的產生及特徵, *Shixue yuekan* 史學月刊 2 (2001): 12–15; Kern, *Stele Inscriptions*, 109, 112, and throughout; Lü Simian 呂思勉, *Lü Simian dushi zhaji* 呂思勉讀史札記 (Shanghai: Shanghai guji chubanshe, 1982), 254–57; cf. Kern, *Stele Inscriptions*, 111–12, arguing that the First Emperor was the first to have done the progresses at all. Information from canonical sources

on this topic is gathered and summarized in Du You 杜佑 (735–812), *Tong dian* 通典 (Beijing: Zhonghua shuju, 1988), 53.1499–1503.

2. See David N. Keightley, "The Late Shang State: When, Where, and What?" in *The Origins of Chinese Civilization*, ed. David N. Keightley (Berkeley: University of California Press, 1983), 523–64, particularly 548–55. On the progresses in bronze records, see He Pingli, *Xunshou*, 35–36; and Wang Yongxia 王永霞, "Qin Shihuang xunyou sixiang suyuan" 秦始皇巡游思想溯源, in *Qin wenhua luncong* 秦文化論叢, no. 12, ed. Qin Shihuang bingmayong bowuguan "Luncong" bianweihui 秦始皇兵馬俑博物館《論叢》編委會 (Xi'an: Sanqin chubanshe, 2005), 408–10. For a consideration of hunting expeditions in connection with inspections and political activities in Shang times, see Magnus Fiskesjö, "Rising from Blood-Stained Fields: Royal Hunting and State Formation in Shang China," *Bulletin of the Museum of Far Eastern Antiquities* 73 (2001): 49–191.

3. *Zhouli zhushu*, 37.20b; *Shangshu zhengyi*, 3.9a.

4. Chen Shuguo, *Xianqin lizhi*, 238–39.

5. Chen Shuguo, *Xianqin lizhi*, 242–43; Chen Shuguo, *Qin Han lizhi yanjiu* 秦漢禮制研究 (Changsha: Hunan jiaoyu chubanshe, 1993), 55.

6. *Shiji*, 5.207, 5.212, 6.233, 6.234. Wang Zijin 王子今, "Qin guojun yuanxing shiji kaoshu" 秦國君遠行史迹考述, in *Qin wenhua luncong* 秦文化論叢, no. 8, ed. Qin Shihuang bingmayong bowuguan "luncong" bianweihui 秦始皇兵馬俑博物館《論叢》編委會) (Xi'an: Shaanxi renmin chubanshe, 2001), 132–51, especially 143–44; Sun Kai 孫楷 (1871–1907), *Qin hui yao* 秦會要, ed. and expanded by Yang Shanqun 楊善群 (Shanghai: Shanghai guji chubanshe, 2004), 73–74; Zhang Huasong 張華松, "Shitan Qin Shihuang dongxun de yuanyin yu dongji" 試探秦始皇東巡的原因與動機, *Dongyue luncong* 東岳論叢 23 (2002): 105; Yang Jianhong 楊建虹 and Yin Ying 殷英, "Qin Shihuang liuci xunyou chuyi" 秦始皇六次巡游芻議, *Yunnan shifan daxue xuebao* 雲南師範大學學報 30 (1998): 99.

7. I draw the following outline from *Shiji*, 6.242–68, and *Zizhi tongjian*, 7.237–50, with reference to Sun Kai, *Qin hui yao*, 74–77; Li Rui 李瑞 and Wu Hongqi 吳宏岐), "Qin Shihuang xunyou de shikong tezheng ji qi yuanyin fenxi" 秦始皇巡游的時空特徵及其原因分析, *Zhongguo lishi dili luncong* 中國歷史地理論叢 18 (2003): 130–38; and Lin Jianming 林劍鳴, *Qin Han shi* 秦漢史 (Shanghai renmin chubanshe, 1989), 164–75. The background, chronology, and interpretation of the steles are treated in Kern, *Stele Inscriptions*, and I draw from his work throughout. A modern, popular account of the progresses can be found in Meng Xianbin 孟憲斌, *Qin Shihuang chu xun ji* 秦始皇出巡記 (Xi'an: Sanqin chubanshe, 2006).

I follow the standard chronology of the steles. For an alternate chronology, see Tsuruma Kazuyuki 鶴間和幸, "Shi fuyuan Qin Shihuang dong xun ke shi wen" 試復原秦始皇東巡刻石文, in *Qinyong Qin wenhua yanjiu* 秦俑秦文化研究, ed. Qin Shihuang bingmayong bowuguan 秦始皇兵馬俑博物館 (Xi'an: Shaanxi renmin chubanshe, 2000), 686–96; see also the discussion in Kern, *Stele Inscriptions*, 4–5.

8. *Shiji*, 1.6.

9. For these events, see *Shiji*, 6.242–48, 28.1366–67.

10. Bujard, *Le sacrifice au Ciel dans la Chine ancienne: théorie et pratique sous les Han occidentaux* (Paris: École française d'Extrême-Orient, 2000), 137; *Shiji*, 28.1366, 28.1371. Mt. Zouyi is also known as Mt. Yi 嶧. According to a fragment of *Sandai dili shu* 三代地理書 preserved in *Taiping yulan*, 42.8a, the emperor ascended Mt. Zouyi in a *xiangche* 羊[:祥]車, which is explained either as a specially decorated cart or wagon, or as a palanquin; see Wei Zheng 魏徵 (580–643) et al., *Sui shu* 隋書 (Beijing: Zhonghua shuju, 1973), 10.192, 209; Tuotuo 脫脫 (1313–55), *Song shi* 宋史 (Beijing: Zhonghua shuju, 1977), 149.3491.

11. NB: I portray the following events by combining the descriptions in the "Feng shan shu," *Shiji*, 28.1366, and the "Qin Shihuang benji," *Shiji*, 6.242; there are some small differences. I also refer to the discussion in Bujard, *Le sacrifice au Ciel*, 135–39.

12. Bujard, *Le sacrifice au Ciel*, 135–38. Bujard, 135, says that description of the Yong rituals gives a general indication of what they might have been like; see *Shiji*, 28.1376–77.

13. *Shiji*, 6.244.

14. *Shiji*, 28.1367–68; Bujard, *Le sacrifice au Ciel*, 138.

15. *Shiji*, 28.1367.

16. *Shiji*, 28.1367.

17. James D. Sellmann, *Timing and Rulership in Master Lü's Spring and Autumn Annals (Lüshi chunqiu)* (Albany: State University of New York Press, 2002).

18. *Shiji*, 28.1356; *Liji zhushu*, 11.30b. It may be noted that the "Shun dian" 舜典 chapter of the received *Shangshu* says that while on his progress Shun visited the Southern Marchmount, which commentary identifies as Mt. Heng. However, "Shun dian" is known to be a later interpolation; see *Shangshu zhengyi*, 3.9b. Qian Mu 錢穆, *Shiji diming kao* 史記地名考 (Beijing: Shangwu yinshuguan, 2001), 104, identifies Mt. Heng as the Southern Marchmount, citing the "Feng shan shu"; see *Shiji*, 28.1356; see also *Han shu*, 25A.1191. There is considerable controversy among commentators about the identification of the Southern Marchmount, but Qian's view concords with that of Hao Yixing 郝懿行 (1757–1825), *Erya yishu* 爾雅義疏, in Hao Yixing et al., *Er ya, Guang ya, Fang yan, Shi ming: Qing shu sizhong hekan* 爾雅、廣雅、方言、釋名：清疏四種合刊 (Shanghai: Shanghai guji chubanshe, 1989), 224, where Hao also summarizes others' views on this topic. On the reverence accorded the marchmounts, see Terry Kleeman, "Mountain Deities in China: The Domestication of the Mountain God and the Subjugation of the Margins," *Journal of the American Oriental Society* 114.2 (1994): 228 and throughout.

19. Anlu was located in present-day Yunmeng 雲夢 country, Hubei. See *Shuihudi Qin mu zhujian*, 7; see also Huang Aimei 黃愛梅, "Shuihudi Qin jian yu Longgang Qin jian de bijiao" 睡虎地秦簡與龍崗秦簡的比較, *Huadong shifan daxue xuebao (Zhexue shehui kexue ban)* 華東師範大學學報 (哲學社會科學版) 4 (1997): 49, and Ma Feibai 馬非百, *Qin Shihuangdi zhuan* 秦始皇帝傳 (Nanjing: Jiangsu guji chubanshe, 1985), 399 and 429 n. 3.

20. In later periods, Mt. Xiang was (as it is today) an island in Dongting Lake 洞庭湖. At the time of the First Emperor's visit the lake was much smaller than it would become later and apparently did not encompass the mountain; see Zhang Xiugui 張修桂, "Dongtinghu yanbian de lishi guocheng" 洞庭湖演變的歷史過程, *Lishi dili* 歷史地理 1 (1981): 102–3 (particularly the map). Dongting might have been small, but it was recognized as an independent body of water and notable enough to be taken as the name for Dongting commandery 洞庭郡; Zhou Zhenhe 周鎮鶴, "Qindai Dongting, Cangwu liangjun xuanxiang" 秦代洞庭、蒼梧兩郡懸想, *Fudan xuebao (shehui kexue ban)* 復旦學報 (社會科學版) 5 (2005): 63–67, particularly 65.

21. Momiyama Akira 籾山明, *Shin no Shikōtei: tagen sekai no tōitsusha* 秦の始皇帝：多元世界の統一者 (Tokyo: Hakuteisha, 1994), 150–1.

22. *Shiji*, 6.249–50, 55.2034; *Han shu*, 40.2023; Kern, *Stele Inscriptions*, 3; Gu Zuyu 顧祖禹 (1624–1680), *Du shi fangyu jiyao* 讀史方輿紀要 (Taipei: Xinxing shuju, 1967), 36.23b.

23. The location of Jieshi has been a matter of contention, but it is now thought to have been located on the coast near Wanjiazhen 萬家鎮, Liaoning, at the Jiangnüshi 姜女石 site; see discussion in Hua Yubing 華玉冰, "Shilun Qin Shihuang dong xunde 'Jieshi' yu 'Jieshigong'" 試論秦始皇東巡的"碣石"與"碣石宮", *Kaogu* 考古 10 (1997): 81–86; and Liaoningsheng wenwu kaogu yanjiusuo 遼寧省文物考古研究所, "Liaoning Suizhongxian 'Jiangnüfen' Qin Han jianzhu yizhi fajue jianbao" 遼寧綏中縣"姜女墳"秦漢建築遺址發覺簡報, *Wenwu* 8 (1986): 25–40.

24. For descriptions of findings at this and associated sites, see Liaoningsheng wenwu kaogu yanjiusuo Jiangnüshi gongzuozhan, "Liaoning Suizhongxian Shibeidi yizhi 1996 niandu de fajue" 遼寧綏中縣石碑地遺址1996年度的發掘, *Kaogu* 8 (2001): 45–58; Liaoningsheng wenwu kaogu yanjiusuo Jiangnüshi gongzuozhan, "Liaoning Suizhongxian 'Jiangnüshi' Qin Han jianzhu qunzhi Shibeidi yizhi de kantan yu shijue" 遼寧綏中縣"姜女石"秦漢建築群址石碑地遺址的勘探與試掘, *Kaogu* 10 (1997): 36–46; Liaoningsheng wenwu kaogu yanjiusuo Jiangnüshi gongzuozhan, "Liaoning Suizhongxian Shibeidi Qin Han gongcheng yizhi 1993–1995 nian fajue jianbao" 遼寧綏中縣石碑地秦漢宮城遺址1993–1995年發掘簡報, *Kaogu* 10 (1997): 47–57; Liaoningsheng wenwu kaogu yanjiusuo Jiangnüshi gongzuozhan, "Liaoning Suizhongxian 'Jiangnüshi' Qin Han jianzhu qunzhi Wazidi yizhi yihao yaozhi" 遼寧綏中縣"姜女石"秦漢建築群址瓦子地遺址一號窯址, *Kaogu* 10 (1997): 58–60; Liaoningsheng wenwu kaogu yanjiusuo, "Liaoning Suizhongxian 'Jiangnüfen' Qin Han jianzhu yizhi fajue jianbao"; and Hua Yubing, "Shi lun Qin Shihuang dong xun de 'Jieshi' yu 'Jieshigong.'" For discussion of the end-tiles from the Shibeidi site, which form an important part of the dating, see Yang Rongchang 楊榮昌 and Wang Xiongfei 萬雄飛, "Suizhong Shibeidi yizhi Qin Han wadang yanjiu" 綏中石碑地遺址秦漢瓦當研究, in *Liaoning kaogu wenji* 遼寧考古文集, ed. Liaoningsheng wenwu kaogu yanjiusuo (Shenyang: Liaoning minzu chubanshe, 2003), 242–49; for a consideration of various tile fragments from the Shibeidi site, see Yang Rongchang, "Shibedi yizhi chutu Qin Han jianzhu

wajian bijiao yanjiu" 石碑地遺址出土秦漢建築瓦件比較研究, *Kaogu* 10 (1997): 87–93; see also *Shiji*, 6.251.

25. Liaoningsheng wenwu kaogu yanjiusuo Jiangnüshi gongzuozhan, "Liaoning Suizhongxian Shibeidi yizhi 1996 niandu de fajue," 57; see Edward H. Schafer, "The Development of Bathing Customs in Ancient and Medieval China and the History of the Floriate Clear Palace," *Journal of the American Oriental Society* 76.2 (1956): 59–60, on the necessity of bathing before various kinds of ceremonies, and Schafer, "Bathing," 71, on the lack of information about Qin practices. On purity and pollution, including discussion of the necessity of the former for various ritual, political, and other functions, see Robin D. S. Yates, "Purity and Pollution in Early China," in *Zhongguo kaoguxue yu lishixue zhi zhenghe yanjiu* 中國考古學與歷史學之整合研究, ed. Zang Zhenhua 臧振華 (Taipei: Zhongyang yanjiuyuan lishi yuyan yanjiusuo, 1997), 479–536.

26. Liaoningsheng wenwu kaogu yanjiusuo, "Liaoning Suizhongxian 'Jiangnüfen' Qin Han jianzhu yizhi fajue jianbao," 30–37, covers the Heishantou site, and 31 notes the presence of Shang and Zhou relics.

27. Hebeisheng wenwu yanjiusuo, Qinhuangdaoshi wenwu guanlichu, Beidaihequ wenwu baoguansuo, "Jinshanju Qindai jianzhu yizhi fajue baogao" 金山咀秦代建築遺址發掘報告, *Wenwu chunqiu* 文物春秋, supplement 1 (1992): 267–94.

28. *Shiji*, 2.52; *Shangshu zhengyi*, 6.5b; discussed in Kern, *Stele Inscriptions*, 116–17.

29. *Shiji*, 6.251.

30. Chen Shuguo, *Qin Han lizhi*, 58–60.

31. *Shiji*, 6.260, gives the date as the *guichou* 癸丑 day of the tenth month of the thirty-seventh year 三十七年十月癸丑; the conversion to Western reckoning follows Fang Shiming 方詩銘 and Fang Xiaofen 方小芬, *Zhongguo shi liri he Zhongxi liri duizhaobiao* 中國史曆日和中西曆日對照表 (Shanghai: Shanghai cishu, 1987); for principal accounts of this progress, see *Shiji*, 6.260–64, 28.1370.

32. This tradition is reported in various sources; see, e.g., *Taiping yulan*, 41.9a, which quotes the *Jun guo zhi* 郡國志, which is no longer extant.

33. Kern, *Stele Inscriptions*, 116–17.

34. *Shiji* refers only to a "great fish," *dayu* 大魚, and a "giant fish," *juyu* 巨魚. *Dayu* was common terminology for the whale. For example, Xu Shen defined "whale" as "The great fish of the sea" 海大魚也; see Duan Yucai 段玉裁 (1735–1815), *Shuowen jiezi zhu* 說文解字注 (Hangzhou: Zhejiang guji chubanshe, 1998), 11B.580. Other Han-time sources also mention "great fish," giving descriptions of size that can only refer to whales, e.g., *Han shu*, 27.1421. For a discussion of the weapon used, a ballista that shot multiple bolts, see Robin D. S. Yates, *Science and Civilisation in China*, vol. 5, part 6, Military Technology: Missiles and Sieges (Cambridge: Cambridge University Press, 1994), 187–203, especially 188.

35. This account combines what is found in the "Qin Shihuang benji," *Shiji*, 6.267, and "Feng shan shu," *Shiji*, 28.1370.

36. *Shiji*, 6.267.

37. He Pingli, *Xunshou*; and see, e.g., Michael G. Chang, *A Court on Horseback: Imperial Touring and the Construction of Qing Rule, 1680–1785* (Cambridge: Harvard University Asia Center, 2007).

38. *Shiji*, 6.267.

39. See discussion in Li Ling, *Zhongguo fangshu xukao* 中國方術續考 (Beijing: Dongfang chubanshe, 2000), 131–44; David Hawkes, "The Quest of the Goddess," *Asia Major* (new series) 13 (1967): 82; Lin Jianming, *Qin Han shi*, 166–67; He Pingli, *Xunshou yu fengshan*, 120–26; and He, "Xianqin xunshou shiji yu zhidu jilun," 79–87; Li Rui and Wu Hongqi, "Qin Shihuang xunyou de shikong tezheng ji qi yuanyin fenxi," 130–38; Wang Yongxia, "Qin Shihuang xunyou sixiang suyuan," 408–14; Yang Jianhong 楊建虹 and Yin Ying 殷英, "Qin Shihuang liuci xunyou chuyi" 秦始皇六次巡游芻議, *Yunnan shifan daxue xuebao* 雲南師範大學學報 30 (1998): 99–101.

40. See Kern, *Stele Inscriptions*, 116; Lao Gan, *Qin Han shi* 秦漢史 (Taipei: Wenhua daxue chubanbu, 1980), 8; and Lei Ge 雷戈, *Qin Han zhi ji de zhengzhi sixiang yu huangquan zhuyi* 秦漢之際的政治思想與皇權主義 (Shanghai: Shanghai guji chubanshe, 2006), 437–40, respectively. For other work that puts politics forth as the purpose of the steles, see, e.g., Zhang Huasong 張華松, "Shitan Qin Shihuang dongxun de yuanyin yu dongji" 試探秦始皇東巡的原因與動機, *Dongyue luncong* 東岳論叢 23 (2002): 104–7; Guo Jifen 郭繼汾 rejects the search for immortality drugs and points instead at political expansion as explanation for (at least part of) the supposed search after immortals; see Guo Jifen, "Qinhuang qiuxian bian" 秦皇求仙辨, *Hebei "Shehui kexue luntan"* 河北《社會科學論壇》4 (1994): 58–59, 63.

41. Han Fuzhi 韓復智, Ye Daxiong 葉達雄, Shao Taixin 邵台新, and Chen Wenhao 陳文豪, *Qin Han shi* 秦漢史 (Taipei: Guoli kongzhong daxue, 1996), 38; Victoria Tin-bor Hui, "The Emergence and Demise of Nascent Constitutional Rights: Comparing Ancient China and Early Modern Europe," *Journal of Political Philosophy* 9 (2001): 380.

42. *Shiji*, 6.252.

43. Kern, *Stele Inscriptions*, 106–7 and throughout.

44. Talal Asad, *Genealogies of Religion: Discipline and Reasons of Power in Christianity and Islam* (Baltimore: Johns Hopkins University Press, 1993); Keane, "The Evidence of the Senses and the Materiality of Religion"; Keane, "Market, Materiality and Moral Metalanguage"; Keane, "The Hazards of New Clothes"; Webb Keane, "Language and Religion," in *A Companion to Linguistic Anthropology*, ed. Alessandro Duranti (London: Blackwell Publishing, 2004), 431–448; Webb Keane, "Sincerity, 'Modernity,' and the Protestants," *Cultural Anthropology* 17 (2002): 65–92; Webb Keane, "Religious Language," *Annual Review of Anthropology* 26 (1997): 47–71; Rowe, "Receiver Psychology and the Evolution of Multicomponent Signals"; Brashier, *Ancestral Memory*.

45. Sosis, "Religious Behaviors, Badges, and Bans."

46. Pascal Boyer, "Functional Origins of Religious Concepts: Ontological and Strategic Selection in Evolved Minds," *Journal of the Royal Anthropological Institute*

(N.S.) 6 (2000): 195–214; Pascal Boyer and Charles Ramble, "Cognitive Templates for Religious Concepts: Cross-Cultural Evidence for Recall of Counter-Intuitive Representations," *Cognitive Science* 25 (2001): 538; Pascal Boyer, "Religious Thought and Behaviour as By-Products of Brain Function," *Trends in Cognitive Sciences* 7.3 (2003): 119–24.

47. Joseph Bulbulia, "The Cognitive and Evolutionary Psychology of Religion," *Biology and Philosophy* 19 (2004): 655–86; and, e.g., Scott Atran and Ara Norenzayan, "Religion's Evolutionary Landscape: Counterintuition, Commitment, Compassion, Communion," *Behavioral and Brain Sciences* 27 (2004): 713–770; Joseph Bulbulia, "Are There Any Religions? An Evolutionary Exploration," *Method & Theory in the Study of Religion* 17 (2005): 71–100.

48. See Chen Ning 陳寧, "Qin Shihuang 'shengwang' xinli tanxi" 秦始皇 "聖王" 心理探析, in *Qin wenhua luncong* 秦文化論叢, no. 12, ed. Qin Shihuang bingmayong bowuguan "luncong" bianweihui (Xi'an: Sanqin chubanshe, 2005), 584–93, who discusses how Qin Shihuang assumed the role of sage ruler, though crediting it to an actual change in attitude rather than a strategy. See also Robbins, "Ritual Communication and Linguistic Ideology," 595; and Morris Zelditch, "Processes of Legitimation: Recent Developments and New Directions," *Social Psychology Quarterly* 64 (2001): 4–17.

49. See Boyer, "Functional Origins of Religious Concepts," 195–214.

50. On this interpretation, see Amotz Zahavi's and related research, especially Zahavi and Zahavi, *The Handicap Principle*; see also, e.g., Jefferey M. Hurwit, "The Problem with Dexileos: Heroic and Other Nudities in Greek Art," *American Journal of Archaeology* 111 (2007): 45–47 and throughout.

51. Rappaport, *Ritual and Religion in the Making of Humanity*, 93.

52. Kern, *Stele Inscriptions*, 109, 112.

53. Zhang Zhongli, "Guanyu Qin shihuangdi quanli weishi de sikao" 關於秦始皇帝權力威勢的思考, in *Qin wenhua luncong* 秦文化論叢, no. 8, ed. Qin Shihuang bingmayong bowuguan "Luncong" bianweihui (Xi'an: Shaanxi renmin chubanshe, 2001), 52–54. NB: Zhang leaves out some things I include in my analysis and includes others.

54. Cf. Kern, *Stele Inscriptions*, and Tsuruma, "Shi fuyuan Qin Shihuang dong xun ke shi wen."

55. For this and the following see Kern, *Stele Inscriptions*, 50–58, 119–25, and 164.

56. Kern, *Stele Inscriptions*, 68–69; on the related theme of the stele in Han times as "outdoor bronze vessel," see K. E. Brashier, "Text and Ritual in Early Chinese Stelae," in *Text and Ritual in Early China*, ed. Martin Kern (Seattle: University of Washington Press, 2005), 269–74.

57. Wu Hung, *Monumentality in Early Chinese Art and Architecture* (Stanford: Stanford University Press, 1995); though, as Kern, *Stele Inscriptions*, 52, points out, Wu does not discuss the steles.

58. See Ma Feibai 馬非百, *Qin jishi* 秦集史 (Beijing: Zhonghua shuju, 1982), 769; Wang Liqi, *Wenxin diaolong jiaozheng* 文心雕龍校證 (Shanghai: Shanghai guji

chubanshe, 1980), 3.73; Chen Qiyou, *Han Feizi xin jiaozhu*, 11.689; see also the translation and discussion of two prayer tablets left on mountains in Yuri Pines, "The Question of Interpretation: Qin History in Light of New Epigraphic Sources," *Early China* 29 (2004): 4–23.

59. Cf. Kern, *Stele Inscriptions*, 148–54 and throughout; Lei Ge, *Qin Han zhi ji de zhengzhi sixiang yu huangquan zhuyi*, 437; and the related discussion in Pines, "The Question of Interpretation."

60. Yates, "Law and the Military in Early China," 40; Ye Shan 葉山 (Robin D. S. Yates), "Zu, shi yu nüxing: Zhanguo Qin Han shiqi xiaceng shehui de duxie nengli" 卒, 史與女性: 戰果秦漢時期下層社會的讀寫能力, in *Jian bo* 簡帛, no. 3, ed. Wuhan daxue jian bo yanjiu zhongxin (Shanghai: Shanghai guji chubanshe, 2008), 359–83; Anthony J. Barbieri-Low, *Artisans in Early Imperial China* (Seattle: University of Washington Press, 2007), 63–66. On officials whose tasks included reading texts aloud, see, e.g., Ma Yi 馬怡, "Bianshu shi tan" 扁書試探, in *Jian bo (di yi ji)* 簡帛 (第一輯), ed. Wuhan daxue jian bo yanjiu zhongxin 武漢大學簡帛研究中心 (Shanghai: Shanghai guji chubanshe, 2006), 415–28. See also chapter 7.

61. Edouard Chavannes, *Le T'ai Chan: Essai de monographie d'un culte chinois* (rpt. Farnborough: Gregg International Publishers Ltd., 1969 [1910]), 4.

62. The canonical source of this idea is "Wang zhi," *Liji zhushu*, 11.8b, 11a (including Zheng Xuan's commentary). It is also mentioned in *Bohu tong* and *Yantie lun*; see Chen Li 陳立 (1809–69), *Bohu tong shuzheng* 白虎通疏證 (Beijing: Zhonghua shuju, 1994), 4.140; and Wang Liqi, *Yantie lun jiaozhu*, 1.78.

63. See *Shuihudi Qin mu zhujian*, 20; see also Lei Ge, *Qin Han zhi ji de zhengzhi sixiang yu huangquan zhuyi*, 437–38, who argues the steles were aimed at the common population.

64. See Huang Hui 黃暉, *Lunheng jiaoshi* 論衡校釋 (Beijing: Zhonghua shuju, 1990), 20.855.

65. Yang and Yin, "Qin Shihuang liuci xunyou Chuyi," 100; see also the closing words of the stele inscription at Jieshi, *Shiji*, 1.252.

66. I discuss major examples in later chapters. Ma Feibai, *Qin Shihuangdi zhuan* 秦始皇帝傳 (Nanjing: Jiangsu guji chubanshe, 1985), 406–427, gives a long list of traces of the progresses, gathered from textual sources including local gazetteers, though a number of these are suspect. Ma includes quite a few bridges and other structures the First Emperor is said to have left behind.

67. See Boyer, "Functional Origins of Religious Concepts."

68. *Shiji*, 6.248, says that three thousand convicts took part in denuding Xiang Mountain.

69. Zhou Zhenhe, "Qindai Dongting, Cangwu liangjun xuanxiang," 65; Zhongguo kexueyuan "Zhongguo ziran dili" bianji weiyuanhui 中國科學院《中國自然地理》編輯委員會, *Zhongguo ziran dili: Lishi ziran dili* 中國自然地理: 歷史自然地理 (Beijing: Kexue chubanshe, 1982), 105.

70. Liu Xiang 劉向 (ca. 79–6 BC), *Zhanguo ce* 戰國策 (Shanghai: Shanghai guji chubanshe, 1998), 8.304–5 anthologizes an anecdote in which the "great fish of the sea" 海大魚—the whale—is described as something "nets cannot stop and

hooks cannot drag in" 網不能止, 鈎不能牽. A slightly different version of the same comes in the *Han Feizi*, confirming this was contemporary in the third century BC; see Chen Qiyou, *Han Feizi xin jiaozhu*, 8.517.

71. The carved whale is mentioned in the no-longer-extant *San Qin ji* 三秦記, quoted in commentaries and other works; see, e.g., commentary at Fan Ye 范曄 (398–445), *Hou Han shu* 後漢書 (Beijing: Zhonghua shuju, 1965), 3403; for a restored version of the *San Qin ji* with commentary, see *San Qin ji* in Liu Qingzhu 劉慶柱, ed., *San Qin ji jizhu, Guanzhong ji jizhu* 三秦記輯注, 關中記輯注 (Xi'an: Sanqin chubanshe, 2006), 8; the whale carving is also mentioned, e.g., in a fragment of Ruan Ji 阮籍 (210–63), *Qin ji* 秦記, quoted in *Shiji*, 6.251; see also Chen Xiaojie 陳曉捷, ed., *Guanzhong yizhi jizhu* 關中佚志輯注 (Xi'an: Sanqin chubanshe, 2006), 18.

72. Lin Jianming, *Qin Han shi*, 169–70.

73. *Shiji*, 6.251.

74. *Shiji*, 108.2859; *Han shu*, 52.2396.

75. See Gao Heng 高恒, "Qin Han difang zhian guanli de zhidu, zhiguan yu cuoshi" 秦漢地方管理的制度, 職官與措施, in *Qin Han fazhi lunkao* 秦漢法制論考 (Xiamen: Xiamen daxue chubanshe, 1994), 98–105, and Robin D. S. Yates, "Social Status in the Ch'in: Evidence from the Yün-meng Legal Documents. Part One: Commoners," *Harvard Journal of Asiatic Studies* 47.1 (1987): 219–31.

76. Gao Min 高敏, "Han chu falüxi quanbu jicheng Qin lü shuo: du Zhangjiashan Han jian 'Zouyanshu' zha ji" 漢初法律系全部繼承秦律說: 讀張家山漢簡 "奏讞書" 札記, in *Qin Han Wei Jin Nanbeichao shi lunkao* 秦漢魏晉南北朝史論考 (Beijing: Zhongguo shehui kexue chubanshe, 2004), 76–84.

77. Takigawa Kametarō 瀧川龜太郎 (b. 1865), *Shiki kaichū kōshō* 史記會注考證 (Taipei: Letian chubanshe, 1972), 6.122; and Chen Shuguo, *Qin Han lizhi*, 57–58; Lin Jianming, *Qin Han shi*, 170.

78. *Shiji*, 6.247.

79. *Shiji*, 6.248. *Shiji*, 4.169 refers to the capture of nine Zhou tripods by the state of Qin, and some scholars have argued that the First Emperor was trying to recover one of those. Contradictions between the accounts make this unlikely, and some scholars have asserted that those problems indicate the First Emperor's search for the Zhou tripod(s) in the River Si did not occur. However, since the *Shiji* account of this event does not refer to the nine tripods, simply to "Zhou tripod(s)," there is actually no necessary connection between the accounts. See Wang Yinglin 王應麟 (1223–1296), in Weng Yuanqi 翁元圻 (1750–1825), ed., *Weng zhu Kunxue jiwen* 翁注困學紀聞, *Sbby*, 11.32b–33a; William Hung 洪業 et al., *Chunqiu jingzhuan yinde* 春秋經傳引得 (Beiping: Yanjing daxue tushuguan, 1937), xci; Huang, *Lunheng*, 8.379. Furthermore, *Shiji*, 28.1383, and *Han shu*, 25A.1214, record that Emperor Wen also sought to recover Zhou tripods from the River Si, suggesting the idea persisted into Han times.

80. Cf. Kern, *Stele Inscriptions*, 157.

81. *Chunqiu Zuozhuan zhengyi*, 10.10a; see also Yang Bojun, *Chunqiu Zuozhuan zhu*, 235. Both Fan Ning 范甯 (339–401) and Yang Bojun's commentaries make it clear that spreading knowledge is the point here.

82. *Zhouyi zhengyi* 周易正義, 3.9a. Note that here and later I translate *jiao* as "influence." Although *jiao* often means "to teach; teaching," in a high-level political context like this one, it is better understood as a more general "influence" than as instruction. See also Duan Yucai, *Shuo wen jie zi zhu*, 127.

83. See Liu Wendian 劉文典, ed., *Huainan honglie jijie* 淮南鴻烈集解 (Beijing: Zhonghua shuju, 1989), 9.290.

84. Fan Ye, *Hou Han shu*, 3.154.

85. *Bohu tong shuzheng*, 6.289.

86. For example, *Shiji*, 7.296, records that as a youth Xiang Yu observed the First Emperor on a progress. Lei Ge, *Qin Han zhi ji de zhengzhi sixiang yu huangquan zhuyi*, 438, refers to records (*Shiji*, 8.344; *Han shu*, 1A.3) that Liu Bang also saw the first emperor on progress, but since the passage makes it clear that Liu Bang had been sent to the capital, it is not necessarily indicative of wider perceptions beyond that area.

87. See *Yantielun jiao zhu*, 29.355.

88. *Shuihudi Qin mu zhujian*, 7, and [[AU: provide x-ref at galleys]].

89. *Shiji*, 6.264.

Chapter 6. Roads to Rule: Construction as Communication

1. *Guoyu* 國語, *Sbby*, 5.11b; cf. Wang Su 王肅 (195–256), *Kongzi jiayu* 孔子家語, *Sbby*, 4.6a. On the technical aspects of early roads, see Joseph Needham, with Wang Ling and Lu Gwei-djen, *Science and Civilisation in China*, vol. 4, part 3: Civil Engineering and Nautics (Cambridge: Cambridge University Press, 1971), 1–38.

2. Ray Laurence, *The Roads of Roman Italy: Mobility and Cultural Change* (London: Routledge, 1999).

3. *Shiji*, 6.241; *Zizhi tongjian*, 7.238. Cf. "Liuguo nianbiao" 六國年表, which dates construction of both the temple and the highways to 219 BCE; *Shiji*, 15.757.

For a study of *yongdao*, see Wang Zijin, "Qin Han 'yongdao' kao" 秦漢"甬道"考, *Wenbo* 文博 2 (1993): 28–31.

4. *Shiji*, 6.256–57, 55.2042. They were also sometimes called "tower roads" (*gedao* 閣道). For a study of raised ways, see Wang Zijin and Ma Zhenzhi 馬振智, "Qin Han 'fudao' kao" 秦漢"復道"考, *Wenbo* 3 (1984): 20–24. David R. Knechtges, *Wen xuan or Selections of Refined Literature*, Volume 1: Rhapsodies on Metropolises and Capitals (Princeton: Princeton University Press, 1982), 128, which provides yet another term for these special imperial skyways, *niandao* 輦道 (also called *nianlu* 輦路), although I can locate no mention of this term in a Qin context.

5. *Shiji*, 6.241, 6.257; *Zizhi tongjian*, 7.238, 7.245–46.

6. *Shiji*, 55.2034, and *Han shu*, 40.2023; for a discussion of Jing Ke's famous attempt, with attention to later reception of the event, see Yuri Pines, "A Hero Terrorist: Adoration of Jing Ke Revisited," *Asia Major* (third series) 21.2 (2008): 1–34.

7. See commentary at *Shiji*, 7.304, and, e.g., *Shiji*, 7.325, 8.372.

8. Wang Zijin, "Qin Han 'yongdao' kao," 31.

9. *Shiji*, 7.325, 8.372–73, 56.2055, 89.2579; Wang Zijin, "Qin Han 'yongdao' kao," 29.

10. *Shiji*, 99.2725; *Han shu*, 43.2129–30; *Zizhi tongjian*, 12.415–16. The practice of clearing the roads was called *bi* 蹕; for discussion of it in the Qin context, see Ma Feibai, *Qin jishi*, 507; and Cui Bao 崔豹 (fl. 290–306), *Gu jin zhu* 古今注, *Sbby*, 1.3a. See also *Han shu*, 47.2208, 52.2394; *Zhouli zhushu*, 31.19a–b; Gao Cheng 高承 (11th c.), *Shiwu jiyuan* 事物紀原, *Skqs*, 3.2a. See also the incident in 177 BCE, in which a man from the country hid during Emperor Wen's passage; *Han shu*, 50.2310, discussed in chapter 7.

11. *Shiji*, 99.2725; *Han shu*, 43.2130. For recent discussion that includes these events, hypotheses about corresponding structures in the context of other emperors' tombs, and relevant archaeological results, see Jiao Nanfeng 焦南峰, "Zongmiao dao, you dao, yiguan dao—Xihan diling daolu zaitan" 宗廟道, 游道, 衣冠道—西漢帝陵道路再探, *Wen wu* 1 (2010): 73–77, 96.

12. Lewis, *Construction of Space*, 153–57 and throughout.

13. Wang and Ma, "Qin Han 'fudao' kao," 21; for the examples from *Mozi*, see Sun Yirang, *Mozi jiangu*, 15.607.

14. Among his many works, Shi Nianhai has articles about transportation in preunification China, including Shi Nianhai, "Chunqiu yiqian de jiaotong daolu" 春秋以前的交通道路, *Zhongguo lishi dili luncong* 中國歷史地理論叢 3 (1990): 5–37; and Shi Nianhai, "Zhanguo shiqi de jiaotong daolu" 戰國時期的交通道路, *Zhongguo lishi dili luncong* 1 (1991): 19–57; cf. *Liji zhushu*, 4.15b.

15. *Shiji*, 6.241, 87.2561.

16. Falkenhausen, *Chinese Society*, 328–38; Shi Nianhai, *Zhongguo gudu he wenhua*, 247–54; Jia's essay is found in *Han shu*, 51.2327–36; for discussion of the essay, see Reinhard Emmerich, "Präliminarien zu Jia Shan und dessen Werk," in *Über Himmel und Erde: Festschrift für Erling von Mende*, ed. Raimund Kolb and Martina Siebert (Wiesbaden: Harrassowitz, 2006), 55–83.

17. *Han shu*, 16.607, 45.2177, 45.2178, 51.2328, 72.3093–94; Cheng Shude 程樹德 (1877–1944), *Jiuchao lükao* 九朝律考, 2nd ed. (Beijing: Zhonghua shuju, 2006), 86, 90; Zhongguo wenwu yanjiusuo 中國文物研究所 and Hubeisheng wenwu kaogu yanjiusuo 湖北省文物考古研究所, *Longgang Qin jian* 龍崗秦簡 (Beijing: Zhonghua shuju, 2001), 95–96, 98; see also Knechtges, *Wen xuan*, 1: 104. There is some disagreement among the classical commentators about how to read Jia Shan's description of the highways; I follow Yan Shigu, at *Han shu*, 51.2329.

18. *Han shu*, 10.301.

19. *Shiji*, 126.3204; Ōba Osamu, "Bu-I shutsudo," 42–67; Guo Hao, "Handai wangzhang zhidu"; *Hou Han shu*, 3124; *Ernian lüling yu zou yan shu*, 231; Guo Hao, "Handai wangzhang zhidu"; cf. Zang Zhifei 臧知非, " 'Wangzhang zhaoshu' yu Handai yanglao zhidu" 王杖詔書與漢代養老制度, *Shi lin* 史林 2 (2002): 35–41, and Hong Huiyu 洪惠瑜, "Handai jinglao yu ci zhang zhidu zhi tantao"

漢代敬老與賜杖制度之探討, *Pingdong jiaoyu daxue xuebao—renwen shehui lei* 屏東教育大學學報—人文社會類 31 (2008): 65–86.

20. Wang Liqi, *Yantielun jiaozhu*, 10.566–67.

21. Li Zhongli 李仲立 and Liu Dezhen 劉得禎, "Qin Zhidao kaocha baogao: Gansu Qingyang diqu" 秦直道考察報告: 甘肅慶陽地區, *Shehui zongheng* 社會縱橫 2 (1991): 36; Li Zhongli, "Qin Zhidao xinlun" 秦直道新論, *Xibei shidi* 西北史地 4 (1997): 3; Bu Zhaowen 卜昭文, "Jin Zhilin tubu kaocha Qin zhidao ji" 靳之林徒步考察秦直道記, *Liaowang* 瞭望 43 (1984): 41, which says Jin gathered "firsthand information" that the Direct Road was not only militarily but also economically important.

22. See related discussion in Charles Sanft, "Rituals That Don't Reach, Punishments That Don't Impugn: Jia Yi on the Exclusions from Punishment and Ritual," *Journal of the American Oriental Society* 125 (2005): 31–44.

23. For a summary of Xiongnu history, including the dating of the rise of the Xiongnu proper, see Ma Liqing 馬利清, *Yuan Xiongnu, Xiongnu: lishi yu wenhua de kaoguxue tansuo* 原匈奴, 匈奴: 歷史與文化的考古學探索 (Hohot: Neimenggu daxue chubanshe, 2005).

24. *Shiji*, 88.2566; Lü Zhuomin 呂卓民, "Qin Zhidao qiyi bianxi" 秦直道歧義辨析, *Zhongguo lishi dili luncong* 中國歷史地理論叢 1 (1990): 98–99; Charles Sanft, "Debating the Route of the Qin Direct Road (Zhidao): Text and Excavation," *Frontiers of History in China* 6.3 (2011): 323–46.

25. See "Da dong" 大東 (Mao #203), *Maoshi zhengyi*, 13–1.7a; cf. translation in Arthur Waley, *The Book of Songs*, ed. Joseph R. Allen (New York: Grove Press, 1996), 186–88.

26. *Lunyu zhushu*, 15.7b, 18.1b; *Liji zhushu*, 42.7b.

27. *Shuihudi Qinmu zhujian*, 101–2, 115, 167; see also *Han shu*, 6.253, and discussion in Charles Sanft, "Notes on Penal Ritual and Subjective Truth under the Qin," *Asia Major* (third series) 22.1 (2008): 21–43.

28. *Shiji*, 6.256, 15.758, 88.2566–67, 110.2886; Sanft, "Debating the Route"; cf. Zhang Duoyong, "Qin Zhidao yanjiu zonglun," 193, who says that the reported length of 1,800 Qin *li* was equivalent to 750 km. Scholars previously assumed the Direct Road was a new construction; see, e.g., Lü Zhuomin, "Zailun Qin Zhidao" 再論秦直道, *Wenbo* 2 (1994): 87–93.

29. See Charles Sanft, "The Construction and Deconstruction of Epanggong: Notes from the Crossroads of History and Poetry," *Oriens Extremus* 47 (2008): 160–76.

30. *Shiji*, 6.265, 88.2570.

31. E.g., Yao Shengmin 姚生民, "Qin Zhidao yu Ganquangong" 秦直道與甘泉宮, *Wenbo* 5 (1997): 34–37; Bu Zhaowen, "Jin Zhilin tubu kaocha Qin Zhidao ji," 40–41.

32. Shi Nianhai 史念海, "Qin Shihuang Zhidao yiji de tansuo" 秦始皇直道遺跡的探索, *Shaanxi shifan daxue xuebao (zhexue shehui kexue ban)* 陝西師範大學學報 (哲學社會科學版) 3 (1975): 77–78 and throughout; Shi Nian-

hai, "Qin Shihuang Zhidao yiji de tansuo" 秦始皇直道遺跡的探索, *Wenwu* 10 (1975): 44–54, 67; Shi Nianhai, "Zhidao he Ganquangong yiji zhiyi" 直道和甘泉宮遺迹質疑, *Zhongguo lishi dili luncong* 中國歷史地理論叢 3 (1988): 75; Lü Zhuomin, "Zailun Qin Zhidao"; Yan'an diqu wenwu puchadui 延安地區文物普查隊), "Yan'an jingnei Qin Zhidao diaocha baogao zhi yi" 延安境內秦直道調查報告之一), *Kaogu yu wenwu* 考古與文物 1 (1989): 26–31; Wang Zijin, "Qin Zhidao de lishi wenhua guanzhao" 秦直道的歷史文化觀照, *Renwen zazhi* 人文雜誌 5 (2005): 107–12; Li Zhongli, "Gansu jingnei Qin Zhidao guanjian" 甘肅境內秦直道管見), *Renwen zazhi* 人文雜誌 3 (1993): 95; Li Zhongli and Liu Dezhen, "Qin Zhidao kaocha baogao: Gansu Qingyang diqu" 秦直道考察報告: 甘肅慶陽地區, *Shehui zongheng* 社會縱橫 2 (1991): 47–49, 36; Li Zhongli and Liu Dezhen, "Gansu Qingyang diqu Qin Zhidao diaocha ji" 甘肅慶陽地區秦直道調查記), *Kaogu yu wenwu* 考古與文物 5 (1991): 42–46, 112; Zhang Jiuhe 張久和, "Qinchao dui gudai Neimenggu bufen diqu de tongzhi he kaifa" 秦朝對古代內蒙古部分地區的統治和開發), *Neimenggu shehui kexue* 內蒙古社會) 23.3 (2002): 33–37; Xu Xing 徐行, "Shaanxi Qin Han shiqi daolu jiaotong fazhan yu wenhua chuanbo" 陝西秦漢, *Xi'an hangkong jishu gaodeng zhuanke xuexiao xuebao* 西安航空技術高等專科學校學報 22.2 (2004): 60–64.

33. Li Zhongli, "Qin Zhidao xinlun" 秦直道新論, *Xibei shidi* 西北史地 4 (1997): 1–6; Wang Zijin, "Qin Zhidao de lishi wenhua guanzhao."

34. E.g., Shi Nianhai, "Zhidao he Ganquangong yiji zhiyi," 49–59.

35. *Shiji*, 5.212, 6.252; *Zizhi tongjian*, 7.241; and see, e.g., *Shiji*, 69.2244, 70.2298, 43.1812–13; *Zhanguo ce*, 29.1039, 29.1052; *Zizhi tongjian*, 3.111; and see Shi Nianhai, "Zhidao he Ganquangong yiji zhiyi," 49–59; and Wang Beichen 王北辰, "Guqiaomen yu Qin Zhidao kao" 古橋門與秦直道考, *Beijing daxue xuebao (shehui kexue ban)* 北京大學學報(社會科學版) 1 (1988): 119–21.

36. Lü Zhuomin, "Zailun Qin Zhidao," 90–93. Shi Nianhai makes a similar point in passing; see Shi, *Zhongguo gudu he wenhua* 中國古都和文化 (Beijing: Zhonghua shuju, 1998), 248. On the document bureaucray of Qin and Han times, see Bu Xianqun 卜憲群, *Qin-Han guanliao zhidu* 秦漢官僚制度 (Beijing: Shehui kexue chubanshe, 2002); and see Tomiya, *Monjo gyōsei*, for the Han.

37. Li Zhongli and Liu Dezhen, "Gansu Qingyang diqu Qin Zhidao diaocha ji"; Li Zhongli and Liu Dezhen, "Qin Zhidao kaocha baogao"; Li Zhongli and Liu Dezhen, "Gansu Qingyang diqu Qin Zhidao kaocha baogao"; Li Zhongli, "Qin Zhidao xinlun."

38. Li Zhongli, "Qin Zhidao xinlun." On the existence of a "natural road" between north and south, see Wang Beichen, "Guqiaomen yu Qin Zhidao kao," 119

39. E.g., Shi Nianhai, "Qin Shihuang Zhidao yiji de tansuo."

40. See Jia Yi, "Guo Qin lun," in Qi Yuzhang, *Jiazi Xin shu jiao shi*, 1.1; *Shiji*, 79.2408, 86.2528; and He Jianzhang 何建章, *Zhanguo ce zhu shi* 戰國策注釋 (Beijing: Zhonghua shuju, 1990), 171. Shi Nianhai himself refers to the strategic duality of roads and the effects of the Direct Road's construction on the Qin capital's topographic defenses; see Shi, *Zhongguo gudu*, 248.

41. Wang Zijin, "Qin Zhidao de lishi wenhua guanzhao," 107–8.

42. Sun Xiangwu 孫相武, "Qin Zhidao diaocha ji" 秦直道調查記, *Wenbo* 4 (1988): 15–20; Xin Deyong, "Qin Han Zhidao yanjiu yu zhidao yiji de lishi jiazhi" 秦漢直道研究與直道遺跡的歷史價值, *Zhongguo lishi dili luncong* 中國歷史地理論叢 21.1 (2006): 95–107; Yao Shengmin, "Qin Zhidao yu Ganquangong" 秦直道與甘泉宮, *Wenbo* 5 (1997): 34–37.

43. See the review and evaluation of the debate on the route in Sanft, "Debating the Route of the Qin Direct Road."

44. *Han shu*, 28A.1545, and Yan Shigu's commentary at *Han shu*, 22.1065; *Shiji*, 10.425; see also David R. Knechtges, *Wen xuan, or Selections of Refined Literature*, volume 2: Rhapsodies on Sacrifices, Hunting, Travel, Sightseeing, Palaces and Halls, Rivers and Seas (Princeton: Princeton University Press, 1987), 164, 166.

45. *Shiji*, 6.232.

46. See Luo Mi 羅泌 (12th c.), *Lu shi* 路史, *Sbby*, 3.6a–b; also Chen Jing 陳桱 (fl. 1350–1369), *Tongjian xubian* 通鑑續編, *Skqs*, 1.11a–b; *Shiji*, 12.471, 12.482, 28.1402; *Han shu*, 6.193, 25B.1244; He Qinggu, *Sanfu huangtu jiao zhu*, 167; Gu Yanwu, *Lidai diwang zhaijing ji* 歷代帝王宅京記, *Skqs*, 5.19a; He Qinggu, *Sanfu huangtu jiao zhu*, 165.

47. Ma Liqing, *Yuanxiongnu, Ma Liqing*, 21–22; Li Ling, *Zhongguo fangshu xukao* 中國方術續考 (Beijing: Zhonghua shuju, 2006), 112; Yao Shengmin, *Ganquan gong zhi* 甘泉宮志 (Xi'an: Sanqin chubanshe, 2003). See Fang Xuanling 房玄齡 (578–648), *Jin shu* 晉書 (Beijing: Zhonghua shuju, 1974), 14.432; see also Du You, *Tong dian*, 174.4552; *Shiji*, 110.2909; *Han shu*, 94A.3769.

48. See similar arguments in Wang Xueyan 王雪岩, "Lüelun Qin-Han shiqi de Yunyang" 略論秦漢時期的雲陽, *Shaanxi jiaoyu xueyuan xuebao* 陝西教育學院學報 21.2 (2005): 81; and Li Ling, *Zhongguo fangshu xukao*, 118.

49. Watanabe Shin'ichirō, "Oto no teikoku: 'Kōshika' jūkyūshō no saishi kūkan to seiji kūkan" 音の帝国：「郊祀歌」十九章の祭祀空間と政治空間), in *Kokkyō o koeru "kōkyōsei" no hikakushiteki kenkyū* 国境をこえる "公共性" の比較史的研究, ed. Kawamura Sadae 河村貞枝 (Kyoto: Kyoto Prefectural University, 2006), 3–38, particularly 24–33; Li Ling, "An Archaeological Study of Taiyi 太一 (Grand One) Worship," trans. Donald Harper, *Early Medieval China* 2 (1995–96): 3–5; Li Ling, "An Archaeological Study," 16–17, also discusses the Ganquan Palace site, including mention of the Zhidao, which he calls just the "Qin roadway."

50. Shi Nianhai, "Lun Qin Jiuyuan shizhi de niandai" 論秦九原始置的年代, *Zhongguo lishi dili luncong* 中國歷史地理論叢 2 (1993): 57–64

51. Historians have disagreed about the dating of Jiuyuan; see discussion in Shi Nianhai, "Lun Qin Jiuyuan shizhi de niandai"; and Chen Cang 陳倉, "Zhanguo Zhao Jiuyuanjun bushuo" 戰國趙九原郡補說, *Zhongguo lishi dili luncong* 中國歷史地理論叢 2 (1994): 247–249; cf. *Zhanguo ce*, 1081, 1095; *Shiji*, 43.1811, 43.1812; and discussion in Xin Deyong, "Zhangjiashan Han jian suo shi Han chu xibeiyu bianjin jiexi: fulun Qin Zhaoxiangwang Changcheng beiduan zouxiang yu Jiuyuan Yunzhong liangjun zhanlüe diwei" 張家山漢簡所示漢初西北隅邊境解析—附論秦昭襄王長城北端走向與九原雲中兩郡戰略地位, *Lishi yanjiu* 歷史研究 1 (2006): 15–33.

52. Chen Cang, "Zhanguo Zhao Jiuyuanjun buzhuo," 249 and throughout; Shi Nianhai, "Lun Qin Jiuyuan shizhi de niandai," 57–64.

53. Nicola Di Cosmo, *Ancient China and Its Enemies: The Rise of Nomadic Power in East Asian History* (Cambridge: Cambridge University Press, 2002), 174–90 and throughout; Zhang Jiuhe 張久和, "Qinchao dui gudai Neimenggu bufen diqu de tongzhi he kaifa" 秦朝對古代內蒙古部分地區的統治和開發, *Neimenggu shehui kexue* 內蒙古社會 23.3 (2002): 33–37; Huang Wenbi, "Qianhan Xiongnu chanyu jian ting kao"; Gai Shanlin and Lu Sixian, "Yinshan nanlu de Zhao changcheng," 87–89.

54. My discussion of the stone carvings draws from Bayannaoershi wenwu gongzuozhan 巴彥淖爾市文物工作站 and Bayannaoershi bowuguan 巴彥淖爾市博物館, "Yinshan yanhua xin faxian" 陰山岩畫新發現, *Wenwu* 10 (2008): 70–79; Gai Shanlin, *Yinshan yanhua* 陰山巖畫 (Beijing: Wenwu chubanshe, 1986); Gai Shanlin, "Neimenggu Yinshan shanmai Langshan diqu yanhua" 內蒙古陰山山脈狼山地區岩畫, *Wenwu* 6 (1980): 1–11; Gai Shanlin, "Quan yanhua, quan, quan ji" 犬岩畫, 犬, 犬祭, *Beifang wenwu* 北方文物 3 (1989): 58–63, 90; Gai Shanlin and Lu Sixian 陸思賢, "Yinshan nanlu de Zhao changcheng" 陰山南麓的趙長城, in *Neimenggu wenwu ziliao xuji* 內蒙古文物資料續輯, ed. Neimenggu wenwu gongzuodui 內蒙古文物工作隊 (Hohot: n.p., 1984), 87–89; Gao Ping 高平, "Yinshan yanhua de xi yu you" 陰山岩畫的喜與憂, *Guangming ribao* 光明日報 (online at http://www.sach.gov.cn/tabid/299/InfoID/12274/default.aspx, posted 21 July 2008, accessed 31 March 2011); Shu Shunlin 舒順林, "Lun Xiongnuren de zhexue, zongjiao yu daode guannian" 論匈奴人的哲學, 宗教與道德觀念, *Neimenggu shida xuebao (zhexue shehui kexue ban)* 內蒙古師大學報 (哲學社會科學版) 2 (1992): 41–47; and Zhang Yan 張琰, Gao Yuan 高圓, and Li Xinya 李鑫雅, "Beifang mianju yanhua zhong yuanshi zongjiao hanyi de tixian" 北方面具岩畫中原始宗教含義的體現, *Neimenggu nongye daxue xuebao (shehui kexue ban)* 內蒙古農業大學學報(社會科學版) 4 (2007): 311–14; with additional references as necessary. Jin Zhilin 靳之林 mentions the existence of the petroglyphs in the Baotou area in context of discussing the Zhidao, though without drawing any conclusions about them; see Bu Zhaowen 卜昭文, "Jin Zhilin tubu kaocha Qin Zhidao ji" 靳之林徒步考察直道記, *Liaowang* 瞭望 43 (1984): 40–41.

55. Gai Shanlin, *Yinshan yanhua*.

56. Li Daoyuan, *Shui jing zhu* 水經注, ed. Wang Xianqian 王先謙 (1842–1918) (Chengdu: Ba-Shu shushe, 1985), 3.3b–4a.

57. Gai Shanlin, *Yinshan yanhua*; Gai Shanlin, "Neimenggu Yinshan shanmai Langshan diqu yanhua." On Xiongnu sun worship, see *Shiji*, 110.2892, and *Han shu*, 94A.3752. Shu Shunlin 舒順林, "Lun Xiongnuren de zhexue, zongjiao yu daode guannian" 論匈奴人的哲學, 宗教與道德觀念, *Neimenggu shida xuebao (zhexue shehui kexue ban)* 內蒙古師大學報 (哲學社會科學版) 2 (1992): 42, makes the link of Yinshan and the drawings there with worship, particularly those images of spirits. Baotoushi wenwu guanlisuo 包頭市文物管理所, "Neimenggu Daqingshan xiduan xinshiqi shidai yizhi" 內蒙古大青山西段新石器時代遺址, *Kaogu* 考古 6 (1986): 485–96, covers a number of sites located to the east of

Baotou: Xiyuan 西元, Shamujia 莎木佳, Heimaban 黑麻板, Natai 納太, Shabinya 莎濱崖, Xishata 西沙塔.

58. *Han shu*, 94B.3803; Huang Wenbi, "Qianhan Xiongnu chanyu jian ting kao" 前漢匈奴單于建庭考, *Zeshan banyue kan* 責善半月刊 2.5 (1941); reprinted in *Xiongnu shi lunwen xuanji* (1919–1979) 匈奴史論文選集 (1919–1979) (Beijing: Zhonghua shuju, 1983), 88–91; Di Cosmo, *Ancient China and Its Enemies*, 88.

59. Ma Liqing, "Cong kaoguxue wenhua de fenbu yu chuanbo kan Xiongnu jiangyu de bianqian" 從考古學文化的分布與傳播看匈奴疆域的變遷, *Neimenggu daxue xuebao (renwen shehui kexue ban)* 內蒙古大學學報(人文社會科學版) 1 (2005): 15–22; see also Ma Liqing, *Yuanxiongnu, Xiongnu*, 218–19 and throughout.

60. *Shiji*, 110.2892; *Han shu*, 94A.3752.

61. He Tianming 何天明, "Dui Xiongnu chuangjian zhengquan ruogan wenti de tantao—Xiongnu zhengquan shizi Maodun chanyu shuo zhiyi" 對匈奴創建政權若干問題的探討—匈奴政權始自冒頓單于說質疑, *Neimenggu shehui kexue (Hanwen ban)* 內蒙古社會科學(漢文版) 27.1 (2006): 40–45; He Tianming cites Tao Ketao 陶克濤, *Zhanxiang chunqiu* 氈鄉春秋 (Xiongnu pian 匈奴篇); Shu Shunlin 舒順林, "Lun Xiongnuren de zhexue, zongjiao yu daode guannian" 論匈奴人的哲學, 宗教與道德觀念, *Neimenggu shida xuebao (zhexue shehui kexue ban)* 內蒙古師大學報 (哲學社會科學版) 2 (1992): 41–47; Huang Wenbi, "Qianhan Xiongnu chanyu jian ting kao," 90–91; quote from *Han shu*, 94B.3803.

62. Ma Liqing, *Yuanxiongnu, Xiongnu*, 235; Di Cosmo, *Ancient China and Its Enemies*, 88.

63. Cai Yong, "Nan Xia Yu shang yan Xianbei ren fan zhu jun" 難夏育上言鮮卑仍犯諸郡, in *Cai Zhonglang ji* 蔡中郎集, *Sbby*, 7.8a.

64. As mentioned by Watanabe, "Oto no teikoku," 31; Bu Zhaowen, "Jin Zhilin tubu kaocha Qin Zhidao ji," 41; Wang Kai, "'Qin Zhidao' xintan" 秦直道新探, *Chengdu daxue xuebao (shekeban)* 成都大學學報 (社科版) 1 (1989): 38; and others. Given that a number of authors have mentioned these mounds, there seems little question that they are present, but the brief description of the Machi site given in Guojia wenwuju, ed., *Zhongguo wenwu dituji: Neimenggu zizhiqu fence*, 2:60, does not list them.

65. Brashier, "The Spirit Lord of Baishi Mountain: Feeding the Deities or Heeding the *yinyang*?" *Early China* 26–27 (2001–02): 163–64.

66. Egami Namio 江上波夫, "Kyōdo no saishi" 匈奴の祭祀, in *Yūrashia kodai hoppō bunka: Kyōdo bunka ronkō* ユウラシア古代北方文化: 匈奴文化論考 (rpt. Tokyo: Yamakawa Shuppansha, 1950 [1948]), 225–79; Xie Jian 謝劍, "Xiongnu zongjiao xinyang ji qi liubian" 匈奴宗教信仰及其流變, *Zhongyang yanjiuyuan lishi yuyan yanjiusuo jikan* 中央研究院歷史語言研究所集刊 42 (1971): 584–86.

67. Lewis, *Construction of Space*, 288–90.

Chapter 7. Law, Administration, and Communication

1. Pines, *Envisioning*, 182, 260 n. 65.

2. Ikeda On 池田溫, *Chūgoku kodai sekichō kenkyū: gaikan, rokubun* 中國古代籍帳研究—概觀, 錄文 (Tokyo: Tōkyō Daigaku Shuppansha, 1979), 14–15; Liu Shuying 劉淑英, "Xianqin de renkou tongji yu guanli" 先秦的人口統計與管理, *Renkou yu jingji* 人口與經濟 4 (1995): 50–51; Song Changbin 宋昌斌, *Zhongguo gudai huji zhidu shigao* 中國古代戶籍制度史稿 (Xi'an: Sanqin chubanshe, 1991), 23–24; Zhang Jinguang 張金光, *Qin zhi yanjiu* 秦制研究 (Shanghai: Shanghai guji chubanshe, 2004), 775; Wan Changhua and Zhao Xingbin, *Qin Han yilai jiceng xingzheng yanjiu*, 49; Song Changbin, *Zhongguo gudai huji zhidu shigao*, 30–31.

3. *Shiji*, 4.145; also recorded *Guoyu*, *Sbby*, 1.9b–10a.

4. *Chunqiu Zuozhuan zhengyi*, 19A.5b, 25.22a, 59.22b; cf. *Shiji*, 47.1932; see also Song Changbin, *Zhongguo gudai huji zhidu shigao*, 25–27, and, e.g., *Shangshu zhengyi*, 16.5a.

5. Song Changbin, *Zhongguo gudai huji zhidu shigao*, 19–20; Schaberg, "The *Zhouli* as Constitutional Text."

6. Song Changbin, *Zhongguo gudai huji zhidu shigao*, 37; *Zhouli zhushu*, 11.1a–13a, 14.13b–17b, 15.13b–19b, 35.24a–b.

7. Du Zhengsheng 杜正勝, *Bianhu qimin: chuantong zhengzhi shehui jiegou zhi xingcheng* 編戶齊民: 傳統政治社會結構之形成 (Taipei: Lianjing chuban shiye gongsi, 1990), 23–24; Xin Tian 辛田, "Mingji, huji, bianhu qimin" 名籍, 戶籍, 編戶齊民, *Renkou yu jingji* 人口與經濟 3 (2007): 55.

8. Chen Zhiguo 陳治國, "Cong Liye Qin jian kan Qin de gongwen zhidu" 從里耶秦簡看秦的公文制度, *Zhongguo lishi wenwu* 中國歷史文物 1 (2007): 61; Chen Zhi 陳直, "Shangji zhidu tongkao" 上計制度通考, in *Juyan Han jian yanjiu* 居延漢簡研究 (Tianjin: Tianjin guji chubanshe, 1986), 54–57; Ge Jianxiong 葛劍雄, *Zhongguo renkou shi* 中國人口史 (Shanghai: Fudan daxue chubanshe, 2002), 224–25; Han Lianqi 韓連琪, "Handai de huji he shangji zhidu" 漢代的戶籍和上計制度, in (idem.) *Xianqin Lianghan shi luncong* 先秦兩漢史論叢 (Ji'nan: Qi-Lu shushe, 1986), 378–96; Liu Shuying, "Xianqin de renkou tongji yu guanli"; Yan Gengwang 嚴耕望, *Zhongguo difang xingzheng zhidu shi* 中國地方行政制度史, part 1: Qin Han difang xingzheng zhidu 秦漢地方行政制度, 4th edition (Taipei: Zhongyang yanjiuyuan Lishi yuyan yanjiusuo, 1997), 257–68; Zhang Chunlong 張春龍 and Long Jingsha 龍京沙, "Liye Qin jian sanmei diming licheng mudu lüexi" 里耶秦簡三枚地名里程木牘略析, in *Jianbo* 簡帛, no. 1, ed. Wuhan daxue jianbo yanjiu zhongxin 武漢大學簡帛研究中心 (Shanghai: Shanghai guji chubanshe, 2006), 273.

9. Ikeda, *Chūgoku kodai sekichō kenkyū*, 17; see also Du Zhengsheng, *Bianhu qimin*, 24–25; Zhang Jinguang, *Qin zhi*, 774.

10. *Shiji*, 6.289; *Shiji*, 68.2230; Charles Sanft, "Shang Yang Was a Cooperator: Applying Axelrod's Analysis of Cooperation in Early China," *Philosophy East and West*, forthcoming.

11. Jiang Lihong, *Shangjun shu zhuizhi*, 5.114 and 1.34; Yu Zongfa 余宗發, *Xianqin zhuzi zai Qin di zhi fazhan* 先秦諸子學說在秦地之發展 (Taipei: Wenjin chubanshe, 1998), 145–46.

12. Chen Xie 陳絜, "Liye 'Huji jian' yu Zhanguo moqi de jiceng shehui" 里耶 "戶籍簡" 與戰國末期的基層社會, *Lishi yanjiu* 歷史研究 5 (2009): 37–38; Chen Wei, *Baoshan Chu jian chutan* 包山楚簡初探 (Wuhan: Wuhan daxue chubanshe, 1996), 124–31; for the original strips, see Hubeisheng Jingsha tielu kaogu dui, *Baoshan Chu jian*. Cf. Peng Hao 彭浩, "Baoshan Chu jian fanying de Chuguo falü yu sifa zhidu" 包山楚簡反映的楚國法律與司法制度, in *Baoshan Chu mu* 包山楚墓, ed. Hubeisheng Jingsha tielu kaogu dui 湖北省荊沙鐵路考古隊 (Beijing: Wenwu chubanshe, 1991), 548–49, which Chen Wei refutes; see also Susan Weld, "Chu Law in Action: Legal Documents from Tomb 2 at Baoshan," in *Defining Chu: Image and Reality in Ancient China* (Honolulu: University of Hawaii Press, 1999), 85–87, whose reading follows that of Peng Hao.

13. Hu'nansheng wenwu kaogu yanjiusuo 湖南省文物考古研究所, *Liye fajue baogao* 里耶發掘報告 (Changsha: Yuelu shushe, 2006), 203–8.

14. See Gao Min 高敏, "Qin Han de huji zhidu" 秦漢的戶籍制度, *Qiu suo* 求索 1 (1987): 72–77; Gao Min, "Cong 'Shuihudi Qin jian' kan Qin de ruogan zhidu" 從 "睡虎地秦簡"看秦的若干制度, in *Shuihudi Qin jian chu tan* 睡虎地秦簡初探 (Taipei: Wanjuanlou, 2000), 173–78; Ouyang Fenglian 歐陽鳳蓮, "'Shangjun shu' huji guanli sixiang yu Qin guo huji guanli zhidu" "商君書" 戶籍管理思想與秦國戶籍管理制度, *Gudai wenming* 古代文明 3.2 (2009): 57–63; Chen Xie, "Liye 'Huji jian' yu Zhanguo moqi de jiceng shehui," 35–37 and throughout.

15. *Shuihudi Qinmu zhujian*, 174; Gao Min, "Cong 'Shuihudi Qin jian' kan Qin de ruogan zhidu" 從 "睡虎地秦簡"看秦的若干制度, in *Shuihudi Qin jian chu tan* 睡虎地秦簡初探 (Taipei: Wanjuanlou, 2000), 178; Ouyang Fenglian, "'Shangjun shu' huji guanli sixiang yu Qin guo huji guanli zhidu," 61.

16. *Shiji*, 6.232.

17. *Shuihudi Qinmu zhujian*, 7; Gao Min, "Qin jian 'Biannian ji' yu 'Shiji'" 秦簡 "編年記"與"史記," in *Shuihudi Qin jian chu tan*, 89. Sixteen years old is seventeen *sui* in traditional reckoning. See Xu Fuchang, *Shuihudi Qin jian yanjiu*, 522–34; Du Zhengsheng, *Bianhu qimin*, 17–22; Zhu Jinshan 朱金嬋 and Yuan Yansheng 袁延勝, "Qin Han shiqi ren de shengao chutan" 秦漢時期人的身高初探, *Huabei shuilidian xueyuan xuebao (shekeban)* 華北水利電學院學報 (社科版) 23.3 (2007): 80–82; cf. Ding Guangxun 丁光勳, "Qin-Han shiqi de shifu, shiyi, zhongyi de nianling yanjiu" 秦漢時期的始傅, 始役, 終役的年齡研究, *Shanghai shifan daxue xuebao (zhexue shehui kexue ban)* 上海師範大學學報(哲學社會科學版) 32.4 (2003): 51–54.

18. *Shuihudi Qinmu zhujian*, 25, 148; Ikeda, *Chūgoku kodai sekichō kenkyū*, 19; and see, e.g., Chen Xie, "Liye 'Huji jian' yu Zhanguo moqi de jiceng shehui," 26–27; *Liye fajue baogao*, 194, 203–8; Zhang Rongqiang 張榮強, "Hu'nan Liye suochu 'Qindai Qianlingxian Nanyangli huban' yanjiu" 湖南里耶所出 "秦代遷陵縣南陽里戶版"研究, *Beijing shifan daxue xuebao (shehui kexue ban)* 北京師範大學學報(社會科學版) 4 (2008): 69, 72; *Ernian lüling yu Zouyanshu*, 222–23.

19. *Shiji*, 53.2014; *Han shu*, 1A.23, 39.2006; *Ernian lüling yu Zouyanshu*, 215, 222.

20. *Han shu*, 1B.54; translated with reference to Wang Xianqian, *Han shu bu zhu* 漢書補注 (1900 woodblock edition; rpt. Yangzhou: Guangling shushe, 2006), 1B.4b.
21. *Ernian lüling yu Zouyanshu*, 351.
22. See Sanft, "Rituals That Don't Reach."
23. *Ernian lüling yu Zouyanshu*, 337.
24. *Ernian lüling yu Zouyanshu*, 341.
25. *Ernian lüling yu Zouyanshu*, 343.
26. Ikeda, *Chūgoku kodai sekichō kenkyū*, 22; Nagata Hidemasa 永田英正, "Monjo gyōsei" 文書行政, in *In Shū Shin-Kan jidaishi no kihon mondai* 殷周秦漢時代史の基本問題, ed. In Shū Shin Kan jidaishi no kihon mondai henshūiinkai 殷周秦漢時代の基本問題編輯委員會 (Tokyo: Kyūko shoin, 2001), 281–82; *Ernian lüling yu Zouyanshu*, 222; Gao Min, "Qin Han de huji zhidu," 72–81; Han Lianqi, "Handai de huji he shangji zhidu," 382; Ouyang Fenglian "'Shangjun shu' huji guanli sixiang yu Qin guo huji guanli zhidu," 57–58; Zhang Jinguang, *Qin zhi*, 801–4.
27. Lianyungangshi bowuguan 連雲港市博物館 et al., *Yinwan Han mu jiandu* 尹灣漢墓簡牘 (Beijing: Zhonghua shuju, 1997), 77–81.
28. Ge Jianxiong, *Zhongguo renkou shi*, 232–34; Song Changbin, *Zhongguo gudai huji zhidu shigao*, 61; Gao Min, "Qin Han de huji zhidu," 79–81.
29. Yu Zhenbo 于振波, *Zoumalou Wu jian chutan* 走馬樓吳簡初探 (Taipei: Wenjin chubanshe 2004), 105.
30. Ikeda, *Chūgoku kodai sekichō kenkyū*, 20.
31. Gao Min, "Qin Han de huji zhidu," 72–81; Gao Min, in "Cong 'Shuihudi Qin jian' kan Qin de ruogan zhidu," 178; Zhang Junmin 張俊民, "Longshan Liye Qin jian erti" 龍山里耶秦簡二題, *Kaogu yu wenwu* 4 (2004): 44–45; Ouyang Fenglian, "'Shangjun shu' huji guanli sixiang yu Qin guo huji guanli zhidu," 57–63; see also Xu Fuchang, *Shuihudi Qin jian yanjiu*, 536.
32. Tu Mingfeng, "Qin Han huji zhidu de guanli jizhi yu gongneng" 秦漢戶籍制度的管理機制與功能, *Hubei jingguan xueyuan xuebao* 湖北警官學院學報 1 (2006): 83–85.
33. Han Lianqi, "Handai de huji he shangji zhidu," 379, 388–89.
34. On the change to the military system, see Mark Edward Lewis, "The Han Abolition of Universal Military Service," in *Warfare in Chinese History*, ed. Hans van de Ven (Leiden: Brill, 2000), 33–76.
35. Du Zhengsheng, *Bianhu qimin*, 28, 32–33, 34–48; Wan Changhua and Zhao Xingbin, *Qin Han yilai jiceng xingzheng yanjiu*, 46–52.
36. *Liye fajue baogao*, 194.
37. Du Zhengsheng, *Bianhu qimin*, 34–48; Wan Changhua and Zhao Xingbin, *Qin Han yilai jiceng xingzheng yanjiu*,46; *Huainanzi*, 11.832; see also *Han shu*, 24B.1183.
38. *Han shu*, 1A.23.
39. See Wang Liqi, *Yantielun jiaozhu*, 10.567; cf. Wang Xianqian, *Xunzi jijie*, 12.328; *Han shu*, 1A.23, 1B.80, 26.1302, see also, e.g., *Han shu*, 4.106. The Tang

emperor Gaozu 高祖 (Li Yuan 李淵, r. 618–626) did something very similar for like purposes at the outset of his reign; see Karl Bünger, *Quellen zur Rechtsgeschichte der T'ang-Zeit*, expanded edition, ed. Roman Malek (Sankt Augustin: Institut Monumenta Serica, 1996), 24–25.

40. *Han shu*, 34.1864.

41. *Han shu*, 1B.80–81; *Zizhi tongjian*, 12.407; Shiga Shūzō, *Chūgoku hōseishi ronshū*, 37.

42. See Charles Sanft, "Six of One, Two Dozen of the Other: The Abatement of Mutilating Punishments under Han Emperor Wen," *Asia Major* (third series) 18.1 (2005): 79–100.

43. *Han shu*, 56.2523.

44. *Han shu*, 69A.4077–78. See Sanft, "Edict of Monthly Ordinances"; and Gansusheng wenwu kaogu yanjiusuo 甘肅省文物考古研究所, eds., *Dunhuang Xuanquan yueling zhaotiao* 敦煌懸泉月令詔條 (Beijing: Zhonghua shuju, 2001).

45. Turner, "Law and Punishment," 63–4; *Shiji*, 102.2755; *Han shu*, 50.2310–11; *Zizhi tongjian*, 14.460–61.

46. *Han shu*, 48.3275–8.

47. *Han shu*, 45.2167–74; see also *Zizhi tongjian*, 19.623–24; Hsing I-T'ien, *Qin Han shi lungao*, 411–35; Tsuji Masahiro 辻正博, "Senkei, 'shisenkei,' ryūkei—'Tōdai ryūkei kō' horon" 遷刑・「徙遷刑」・流刑—「唐代流刑考」補論, in *Kōryo Chōkasan nihyakuyonjūnana gōbo shutsudo Kan ritsuryō no kenkyū* 江陵張家山二四七號墓出土漢律令の研究, ed. Tomiya Itaru (Kyoto: Hōyū Shoten, 2006), 305–39.

48. See, e.g., Chen Qiyou, *Han Feizi xin jiaozhu*, 386–87; Li Xiangfeng, *Guanzi jiaozhu*, 5.256; Jiang Lihong, *Shangjun shu zhuizhi*, 5.146; among others.

49. Wang Liqi, *Yantie lun jiaozhu*, 565–68. For additional examples, see, e.g. *Shiji*, 10.418; and *Han shu*, 89.3633.

50. Lewis, *The Construction of Space*, 161, 163; Lewis, 381–82 n. 117 gathers relevant examples from a number of sources; Liu Xi 劉熙 (ca. 2nd–3rd c.), *Shi ming* 釋名, *Skqs*, 8.4a; *Liji zhushu*, 11.26a; *Han shu*, 47.3253, 54.3436, 68.2946, 90.3668, 90.3671; see also *Han shu*, 38.1993 and commentary at *Han shu*, 5.146 n. 1; and *Han shu*, 36.1923–24, and Wang Xianqian, *Han shu bu zhu*, 36.3a–b.

51. *Han shu*, 92.3717, 92.3719, 77.3249, 99C.4192.

52. *Han shu*, 84.3439; *Zizhi tongjian*, 36.1164.

53. *Han shu*, 90.3673–74.

54. For classical expressions of this, see *Chunqiu Zuozhuan zhengyi*, 749–51; and Chen Qiyou, *Lüshi chunqiu xin jiaoshi*, 18.1187–88; see discussion in Hsing I-t'ien, *Qin Han shi lun gao*, 253–60; Ma Xiaohong 馬小紅, *Zhongguo gudai falü sixiang shi* 中國古代法律思想史 (Beijing: Falü chubanshe, 2003), 31–32; Chen Guyuan 陳顧遠, *Zhongguo fazhi shi* 中國法制史, 3rd edition (Changsha: Shangwu yinshuguan, 1940), 96–99; Shen Jiaben 沈家本 (1840–1913), *Lidai xingfa kao* 歷代刑法考 (Beijing: Zhonghua shuju, 1985), 838–40; Momiyama Akira 籾山明, "Hōka izen—Shunjūki ni okeru kei to chitsujo" 法家以前—春秋期における刑と秩序, *Tōyōshi kenkyū* 東洋史研究 39.2 (1980): 23–24; and Sanft, "Notes on Penal Ritual."

55. Ichisada Miyazaki, "The Administration of Justice during the Sung Dynasty," in *Essays on China's Legal Tradition*, ed. Jerome Alan Cohen, R. Randle Edwards, and Fu-mei Chang Chen (Princeton: Princeton University Press, 1980), 58–59; quote from 58.

56. As Shen Jiaben points out, the historical accounts about this suggestion's adoption are contradictory; Tuotuo 脫脫 (1313–1355), *Jin shi* 金史 (Beijing: Zhonghua shuju, 1975), 45.1021; Shen Jiaben, *Lidai xingfa kao*, 1057.

57. Paul Heng-chao Ch'en, *Chinese Legal Tradition under the Mongels: The Code of 1291 as Reconstructed* (Princeton: Princeton University Press, 1979), 88–98; Miyazaki, "The Administration of Justice," 59.

58. See, e.g., Jiang Lihong, *Shangjun shu zhuizhi*, 5.144–45; Falkenhausen, *Chinese Society*, 319–21; Ye Shan 葉山 (Robin D. S. Yates), "Qin de falü yu shehui—guanyu Zhangjiashan 'Ernian lüling' deng xin chutu wenxian de sikao" 秦的法律與社會—關於張家山"二年律令"等新出土文獻的思考, trans. Lin Fan 林凡, in *Rujia wenhua yanjiu* 儒家文化研究, no. 1, ed. Guo Qiyong 郭齊勇 (Beijing: Sanlian shudian, 2007), 305–6; and see *Shuihudi Qinmu zhujian*, 13–16; see also the introduction, annotated text, and discussion in Wu Fuzhu 吳福助, *Shuihudi Qin jian lunkao* 睡虎地秦簡論考 (Taipei: Wenjin chubanshe, 1994), 39–138; Chen Songchang 陳松長, "Yuelu shuyuan suocang Qin jian zongshu" 岳麓書院所藏秦簡綜述, *Wenwu* 文物 3 (2009): 87.

59. See Zhu Honglin 朱紅林, "Zhanguo shiqi guojia falü de chuanbo—zhujian Qin-Han lü yu 'Zhouli' bijiao yanjiu" 戰國時期國家法律的傳播—竹簡秦漢律與"周禮"比較研究, *Fazhi yu shehui fazhan* 法治與社會發展 3 (2009): 119–25.

60. Jiang Lihong, *Shangjun shu zhuizhi*, 2.57. On the Qin system, see *Shuihudi Qinmu zhujian*, 102–4; on the Han, see Peng, Chen, and Kudō, *Ernian lüling yu Zouyanshu*, 143–47; for records of Han law on this in received sources, see Cheng Shude, *Jiuchao lü kao*, 56.

61. *Han shu*, 83.3399; Jiang Lihong, *Shangjun shu zhuizhi*, 5.144; Bielenstein, *The Bureaucracy of Han Times*, 90–92; on appeals in Han times see also A.F. P. Hulsewé, *Remnants of Han Law*, Volume 1: Introductory Studies and an Annotated Translation of Chapters 22 and 23 of the *History of the Former Han Dynasty* (Leiden: E. J. Brill, 1955), 80–81, 90–92, and throughout.

62. *Han shu*, 65.2847.

63. *Han shu*, 90.3664–65, 37.1983.

64. Bu Xianqun, "Cong jianbo kan," 51. This edict and the "kingly staff" system have been the subject of numerous studies. For the edict and case summaries, see Ōba Osamu 大庭脩, "Bu-I shutsudo 'Ōjō shōsho, rei' satsu" 武威出土"王杖詔書,令"冊, in *Kankan kenkyū* 漢簡研究 (Kyoto: Hōyūsha, 1992), 42–67; Guo Hao 郭浩, "Handai wangzhang zhidu ruogan wenti kaobian" 漢代王杖制度若干問題考辨, *Shixue jikan* 史學集刊 3 (2008): 97–98; see further references in chapter 6.

65. Schaberg, "The *Zhouli* as Constitutional Text"; see also Xia Chuancai 夏傳才, *Shisanjing gailun* 十三經概論 (Tianjin: Tianjin renmin chubanshe, 1998), 201; Nivison, "*Chou li*."

66. *Zhouli zhushu*, 35. 7a, 12.6b, 12.8b; see also Sun Yirang, *Zhouli zhengyi*, 861–66; NB: *shishi* 士師 cannot be translated literally, see *Hanyu dacidian*,

Notes to Chapter 8   203

s.v. *shishi*; for additional examples, see *Zhouli zhushu*, 2.16a, 10.21b–22b, 29.5a, 34.17a–b. The "manager of grains" (*sijia* 司稼) posted agricultural information; see *Zhouli zhushu*, 16.22b, and Sun Yirang, *Zhouli zhengyi*, 1236–39.

67. The following discussion of *bianshu* draws from Tomiya Itaru, *Monjo gyōsei no Kan teikoku: mokkan, chikukan no jidai* 文書行政の漢帝國: 木簡, 竹簡の時代 (Nagoya: Nagoya Daigaku Shuppansha, 2010), 121–31; Ma Yi, "Bianshu shi tan"; Wu Wangzong, "Han jian suojian 'bianshu' tan xi"; Chen Pan 陳槃, *Han Jin yijian shixiao qizhong* 漢晉遺簡識小七種 (Shanghai: Shanghai guji chubanshe, 2009), 185–87; and Hu Pingsheng, "'Bianshu,' 'Da bianshu' kao" "扁書", "大扁書" 考, in *Dunhuang Xuanquan Yueling zhaotiao* 敦煌懸泉月令詔條 (Beijing: Zhonghua shuju, 2001), 48–54; additional references given as needed.

68. Xie Guihua 謝桂華, Li Junming 李均明, and Zhu Guozhao 朱國炤, *Juyan Han jian shiwen hejiao* 居延漢簡釋文合校 (Beijing: Wenwu chubanshe, 1987), 230 (no. 139.13).

69. Wu Rengxiang 吳礽驤, Li Yongliang 李永良, and Ma Jianhua 馬建華, *Dunhuang Han jian shiwen* 敦煌漢簡釋文 (Lanzhou: Gansu renmin chubanshe, 1991), 142; see also see Li Junming 李均明, "Eji'na Han jian fazhishi liaokao" 額濟納漢簡法制史料考, in *Ejina Han jian* 額濟納漢簡, ed. Wei Jian 魏堅 (Guilin: Guangxi shifan daxue chubanshe, 2005), 59.

70. Hu Pingsheng and Zhang Defang 張德芳, *Dunhuang Xuanquan Han jian shi cui* 敦煌懸泉漢簡釋粹 (Shanghai: Shanghai guji chubanshe, 2001), 115.

71. Wu Rengxiang, Li Yongliang, and Ma Jianhua, *Dunhuang Han jian shiwen*, 161, 218; Hu Pingsheng and Zhang Defang, *Dunhuang Xuanquan Han jian shicui*, 115; Li Junming 李均明 and He Shuangquan 何雙全, *Sanjian jiandu heji* 散見簡牘合輯 (Beijing: Wenwu chubanshe, 1990), 20.

72. Bu Xianqun, "Cong jianbo kan."

73. Tomiya, *Monjo gyōsei*, 126–27 and throughout.

74. See Yates, "Soldiers, Scribes, and Women," 339–69; Miyake, "Shin-Kan jidai no moji to shikiji," 215–17; Yates, "Law and the Military," 40.

75. Wei Jian 魏堅, *Eji'na Han jian* 額濟納漢簡 (Guilin: Guangxi shifan daxue chubanshe, 2005), 81; Gansusheng wenwu kaogu yanjiusuo 甘肅省文物考古研究所 et al., *Juyan xin jian* 居延新簡 (Beijing: Zhonghua shuju, 1994), 512.

Chapter 8. Conclusion

1. Jiayuguanshi wenwu baoguansuo 嘉峪關市文物保管所, "Yumenhuahai Handai fengsui yizhi chutu de jiandu" 玉門花海漢代烽燧遺址出土的簡牘, in *Hanjian yanjiu wenji* 漢簡研究文集, ed. Gansusheng wenwu gongzuodui 甘肅省文物工作隊 et al. (Lanzhou: Gansu renmin chubanshe, 1984), 16; see discussion in Zhang Xiaofeng 張小鋒, *Xihan zhonghouqi zhengju yanbian tanwei* 西漢中後期政局演變探微 (Tianjin: Tianjin guji chubanshe, 2007), 23–39.

2. Jiayuguanshi wenwu baoguansuo, "Yumenhuahai Handai fengsui yizhi chutu de jiandu," 16–21.

3. *Han shu*, 96B.3913; *Zizhi tongjian*, 22.738.

4. See Lydia H. Liu, *The Clash of Empires: The Invention of China in Modern World Making* (Cambridge: Harvard University Press, 2004), 77–79.

5. Benjamin A. Elman, *A Cultural History of Civil Examinations in Late Imperial China* (Berkeley: University of California Press, 2000), 83–84.

6. Gu Jiegang, "Qin-Han tongyi de youlai he Zhanguo ren duiyu shijie de xiangxiang" 秦漢統一的由來和戰國人對於世界的想像, in *Gushi bian* 古史辨, vol. 2 (rpt. Hong Kong: Taiping shuju, 1962 [1930]), 4–5, 9.

7. *Han shu*, 88.3612, see also Yan Shigu's commentary on the passage there.

8. *Han shu*, 40.2026–27; *Zizhi tongjian*, 9.298–99.

9. E.g., *Han shu*, 4.106, 51.2327–28, 70.3021, 85.3449–50,

10. See, e.g., Charles Sanft, "Dong Zhongshu's *Chunqiu jueyu* Reconsidered: On the Legal Interest in Subjective States and the Privilege of Hiding Family Members' Crimes as Developments from Earlier Practice," *Early China* 33–34 (2010–11): 141–69.

11. See, e.g., Mark Edward Lewis, *Sanctioned Violence in Early China*.

12. Qi Yuzhang, *Jiazi Xin shu jiao shi*, 1.15, 1.19.

13. See *Han shu*, 100A.4207, 100B.4244; *Hou Han shu*, 40A.1323; see also, e.g., Qi Yuzhang, *Jiazi Xin shu*, 3.303.

14. See Keane, "The Evidence of the Senses and the Materiality of Religion"; Keane, "Market, Materiality and Moral Metalanguage"; and Moore, "From Genericide to Viral Marketing."

15. See, e.g., Kern, *The Stele Inscriptions*, 17, 29, 48–49.

16. Cf. Sanft, "Six of One, Two Dozen of the Other: The Abatement of Mutilating Punishments under Han Emperor Wen."

17. Arthur F. Wright, *The Sui Dynasty* (New York: Alfred A. Knopf, 1978), 116.

18. Mark Edward Lewis, *China's Cosmopolitan Empire: The Tang Dynasty* (Cambridge: Belknap Press, 2009), 51.

19. Frank Münzel, "Some Remarks on Ming T'ai-tsu," *Archiv Orientální* 37.3 (1969): 385.

20. Lewis, *China's Cosmopolitan Empire*, 22–25, 114–20 (quote from 119).

21. Weikun Cheng, "Politics of the Queue: Agitation and Resistance in the Beginning and End of Qing China," in *Hair: Its Power and Meaning in Asian Cultures*, ed. Alf Hiltebeitel and Barbara D. Miller (Albany: State University of New York Press, 1998), 123–42.

22. Chwe, *Rational Ritual*, 90.

23. Cf. discussion in Edward Slingerland, *What Science Offers the Humanities: Integrating Body and Culture* (Cambridge: Cambridge University Press, 2008).

24. William A. Sewell Jr., *Logics of History: Social Theory and Social Transformation* (Chicago: University of Chicago Press, 2005).

25. Bliege Bird and Smith, "Signaling Theory," 221–23.

Bibliography

Abbreviations

Sbby *Sibu beiyao* 四部備要
Skqs *Siku quanshu* 四庫全書

Works Cited

Alcorta, Candace, and Richard Sosis. "Ritual, Emotion, and Sacred Symbols." *Human Nature* 16 (2005): 323–59.

———. "Rituals of Humans and Animals." In *Encyclopedia of Human-Animal Relationships*, volume 2, ed. Marc Bekoff, 599–605. Westport: Greenwood Publishers, 2007.

Alvard, Michael S. "The Adaptive Nature of Culture." *Evolutionary Anthropology* 12 (2003): 136–49.

Asad, Talal. *Genealogies of Religion: Discipline and Reasons of Power in Christianity and Islam*. Baltimore: Johns Hopkins University Press, 1993.

Atran, Scott, and Ara Norenzayan. "Religion's Evolutionary Landscape: Counterintuition, Commitment, Compassion, Communion." *Behavioral and Brain Sciences* 27 (2004): 713–70.

Avilés, Leticia. "Cooperation and Non-Linear Dynamics: An Ecological Perspective on the Evolution of Sociality." *Evolutionary Ecology Research* 1 (1999): 459–77.

Axelrod, Robert. *The Evolution of Cooperation*. Revised edition. New York: Basic Books, 2006.

———. "On Six Advances in Cooperation Theory." *Analyse & Kritik* 22 (2000): 130–51.

Bagley, Robert W. "Replication Techniques in Eastern Zhou Bronze Casting." In *History from Things: Essays on Material Culture*, ed. Steven Lubar and W. David Kingery, 231–41. Washington, DC: Smithsonian Institution, 1993.

Ban Gu 班固 (32–92). *Han shu* 漢書. Beijing: Zhonghua shuju, 1962.

In translating titles, I have referred to Hans Bielenstein, "The Bureaucracy of Han Times" (Cambridge: Cambridge University Press, 1980), and Charles O. Hucker, "A Dictionary of Official Titles in Imperial China" (Stanford: Stanford University Press, 1985), but not always followed them.

Baotoushi wenwu guanlisuo 包頭市文物管理所. "Neimenggu Daqingshan xiduan xinshiqi shidai yizhi" 內蒙古大青山西段新石器時代遺址. *Kaogu* 考古 6 (1986): 485–96.

Barbieri-Low, Anthony J. *Artisans in Early Imperial China*. Seattle: University of Washington Press, 2007.

———. "Craftsman's Literacy: Uses of Writing by Male and Female Artisans in Qin and Han China." In *Writing and Literacy in Early China: Studies from the Columbia Early China Seminar*, ed. Feng Li and David Prager Branner, 370–99. Seattle: University of Washington Press, 2011.

Bayannaoershi wenwu gongzuozhan 巴彥淖爾市文物工作站 and Bayannaoershi bowuguan 巴彥淖爾市博物館. "Yinshan yanhua xin faxian" 陰山岩畫新發現. *Wenwu* 文物 10 (2008): 70–79.

Bell, Catherine. *Ritual: Perspectives and Dimensions*. Oxford: Oxford University Press, 1997.

Bergstrom, Carl T., and Michael Lachmann. "Signaling Among Relatives. III. Talk Is Cheap." *Proceedings of the National Academy of Sciences of the United States of America* 95 (1998): 5100–5.

Bielenstein, Hans. *The Bureaucracy of Han Times*. Cambridge: Cambridge University Press, 1980.

Bliege Bird, Rebecca, and Eric Alden Smith. "Signaling Theory, Strategic Interaction, and Symbolic Capital." *Current Anthropology* 46.2 (2005): 221–48.

Boltz, William G. "Orthographic Variation in Early Chinese Manuscripts." *Acta Orientalia (Budapest)* 62 (2009): 89–113.

Boone, James L. "The Evolution of Magnanimity: When Is It Better to Give Than to Receive?" *Human Nature* 9 (1998): 1–21.

Boyd, Robert, Herbert Gintis, Samuel Bowles, and Peter J. Richerson. "The Evolution of Altruistic Punishment." *Proceedings of the National Academy of Science of the United States of America* 100 (2003): 3531–35.

Boyer, Pascal. "Functional Origins of Religious Concepts: Strategic and Ontological Selection in Evolved Minds." *Journal of the Royal Anthropological Institute* 6.2 (2000): 195–214.

———. "Religious Thought and Behaviour as By-Products of Brain Function." *Trends in Cognitive Sciences* 7.3 (2003): 119–24.

Boyer, Pascal, and Charles Ramble. "Cognitive Templates for Religious Concepts: Cross-Cultural Evidence for Recall of Counter-Intuitive Representations." *Cognitive Science* 25 (2001): 535–64.

Brashier, K. E. *Ancestral Memory in Early China*. Cambridge: Harvard University Asia Center, 2011.

———. "The Spirit Lord of Baishi Mountain: Feeding the Deities or Heeding the *yinyang*?" *Early China* 26–27 (2001–2002): 159–231.

———. "Text and Ritual in Early Chinese Stelae." In *Text and Ritual in Early China*, ed. Martin Kern, 249–84. Seattle: University of Washington Press, 2005.

Bu Xianqun 卜憲群. "Cong jianbo kan Qin Han xiangli de wenshu wenti" 從簡帛看秦漢鄉里的文書問題. *Wen shi zhe* 文史哲 6 (2007): 48–53.

———. *Qin Han guanliao zhidu* 秦漢官僚制度. Beijing: Shehui kexue chubanshe, 2002.
Bu Zhaowen 卜昭文. "Jin Zhilin tubu kaocha Qin Zhidao ji" 靳之林徒步考察直道記. *Liaowang* 瞭望 43 (1984): 40–41.
Bujard, Marianne. *Le sacrifice au Ciel dans la Chine ancienne: théorie et pratique sous les Han occidentaux*. Paris: École française d'Extrême-Orient, 2000.
Bulbulia, Joseph. "Are There Any Religions? An Evolutionary Exploration." *Method & Theory in the Study of Religion* 17 (2005): 71–100.
———. "The Cognitive and Evolutionary Psychology of Religion." *Biology and Philosophy* 19 (2004): 655–86.
Bünger, Karl. "Concluding Remarks on Two Aspects of the Chinese Unitary State as Compared with the European State System." In *Foundations and Limits of State Power in China*, ed. S. R. Schram, 313–23. London: School of Oriental and African Studies, 1987.
———. *Quellen zur Rechtsgeschichte der T'ang-Zeit*. Expanded edition. Edited by Roman Malek. Sankt Augustin: Institut Monumenta Serica, 1996.
Cai Yong 蔡邕. *Cai Zhonglang ji* 蔡中郎集. *Sbby*.
Chang, Michael G. *A Court on Horseback: Imperial Touring and the Construction of Qing Rule*. Cambridge: Harvard University Asia Center, 2007.
Chavannes, Edouard. *Le T'ai Chan: Essai de monographie d'un culte chinois*. Rpt. Farnborough: Gregg International Publishers Ltd., 1969 [1910].
Chen Cang 陳倉. "Zhanguo Zhao Jiuyuanjun bushuo" 戰國趙九原郡補說. *Zhongguo lishi dili luncong* 中國歷史地理論叢 2 (1994): 247–49.
Chen Guyuan 陳顧遠. *Zhongguo fazhi shi* 中國法制史. 3rd edition. Changsha: Shangwu yinshuguan, 1940.
Chen Jing 陳靜 and Wen Qi 文啟. "Qin Zhidao bujing Shangjun de zhengju" 秦直道不經上郡的證據. *Zhongguo lishi dili luncong* 1 (1998): 243–44.
Chen Jing 陳桱 (fl. 1350–1369). *Tongjian xubian* 通鑑續編. *Skqs*.
Chen Li 陳立 (1809–1869). *Bohu tong shu zheng* 白虎通疏證. Beijing: Zhonghua shuju, 1994.
Chen Ning 陳寧. "Qin Shihuang 'shengwang' xinli tanxi" 秦始皇"聖王"心理探析. In *Qin wenhua luncong* 秦文化論叢, no. 12, ed. Qin Shihuang bingmayong bowuguan "luncong" bianweihui 秦始皇兵馬俑博物館《論叢》編委会, 584–93. Xi'an: Sanqin chubanshe, 2005.
Chen Pan 陳槃. *Han Jin yijian shixiao qizhong* 漢晉遺簡識小七種. Shanghai: Shanghai guji chubanshe, 2009.
Chen Qiyou 陳奇猷. *Han Feizi xin jiaozhu* 韓非子新校注. Shanghai: Shanghai guji chubanshe, 2000
———. *Lüshi chunqiu xin jiaoshi* 呂氏春秋新校釋. Shanghai: Shanghai guji chubanshe, 2002.
Chen Shuguo 陳戍國. *Qin Han lizhi yanjiu* 秦漢禮制研究. Changsha: Hunan jiaoyu chubanshe, 1993.
———. *Xianqin lizhi yanjiu* 先秦禮制研究. Changsha: Hunan jiaoyu chubanshe, 1991.

Chen Songchang 陳松長. "Yuelu shuyuan suocang Qin jian zongshu" 岳麓書院所藏秦簡綜述. *Wenwu* 3 (2009): 75–88.

Chen Wei 陳偉. *Baoshan Chu jian chutan* 包山楚簡初探. Wuhan: Wuhan daxue chubanshe, 1996.

Chen Xiaojie 陳曉捷, ed. *Guanzhong yizhi ji zhu* 關中佚志輯注. Xi'an: Sanqin chubanshe, 2006.

Chen Xie 陳絜. "Liye 'Huji jian' yu Zhanguo moqi de jiceng shehui" 里耶"戶籍簡"與戰國末期的基層社會. *Lishi yanjiu* 歷史研究 5 (2009): 23–40.

Chen Yuan 陳垣. *Shihui juli* 史諱舉例. Shanghai: Shanghai shudian, 1997.

Chen Zhi 陳直(1901–1980). *Juyan Han jian yanjiu* 居延漢簡研究. Tianjin: Tianjin guji chubanshe, 1986.

———. "Kaogu luncong" 考古論叢. *Xibei daxue xuebao (zhexue shehui kexue ban)* 西北大學學報(哲學社會科學版) 1 (1957): 63–70.

———. "Qin Shihuang liu da tongyi zhengce de kaogu ziliao" 秦始皇六大統一政策的考古資料. *Lishi jiaoxue* 歷史教學 8 (1963): 26–30.

———. *Shiji xinzheng* 史記新證. Beijing: Zhonghua shuju, 2006.

Chen Zhiguo 陳治國. "Cong Liye Qin jian kan Qin de gongwen zhidu" 從里耶秦簡看秦的公文制度. *Zhongguo lishi wenwu* 中國歷史文物 1 (2007): 61–69.

Ch'en, Paul Heng-chao. *Chinese Legal Tradition under the Mongels: The Code of 1291 as Reconstructed*. Princeton: Princeton University Press, 1979.

Cheney, Dorothy L., and Robert M. Seyfarth. *Baboon Metaphysics: The Evolution of a Social Mind*. Chicago: University of Chicago Press, 2007.

Cheng Dachang 程大昌 (1123–95). *Yong lu* 雍錄. Beijing: Zhonghua shuju, 2002.

Cheng Shude 程樹德 (1877–1944). *Jiuchao lükao* 九朝律考. 2nd edition. Beijing: Zhonghua shuju, 2006.

Cheng, Weikun. "Politics of the Queue: Agitation and Resistance in the Beginning and End of Qing China." In *Hair: Its Power and Meaning in Asian Cultures*, ed. Alf Hiltebeitel and Barbara D. Miller, 123–42. Albany: State University of New York Press, 1998.

Cheng Ying 程穎. "'Chu heng' yu 'Qin heng'—Zhongguo zaoqi quanheng qiju sheji de liangzhong fanshi" 楚衡與"秦權"–中國早期權衡器具設計的兩種范式. *Suzhou gongyi meishu zhiye jishu xueyan xuebao* 蘇州工藝美術職業技術學院學報 3 (2007): 39–40.

Chevalier, Raymond. *Roman Roads*. Translated by N. H. Field. London: B. T. Batsford Ltd., 1976.

Chunqiu Zuozhuan zhengyi 春秋左傳正義. See *Shisanjing zhushu*.

Chwe, Michael Suk-Young. *Rational Ritual: Culture, Coordination, and Common Knowledge*. Princeton: Princeton University Press, 2001.

Clutton-Brock, Tim. "Breeding Together: Kin Selection and Mutualism in Cooperative Vertebrates." *Science* 296 (2002): 69–72.

Cook, Scott. "The Debate over Coercive Rulership and the 'Human Way' in Light of Recently Excavated Warring States Texts." *Harvard Journal of Asiatic Studies* 64.2 (2004): 399–440.

Courchamp, F., B. Grenfell, and T. Clutton-Brock. "Population Dynamics of Obligate Cooperators." *Proceedings of the Royal Society of London B* 266 (1999): 557–63.
Creel, Herrlee G. *The Origins of Statecraft in China*. Volume One: The Western Chou Empire. Chicago: University of Chicago Press, 1970.
Cronk, Lee. "The Application of Animal Signaling Theory to Human Phenomena: Some Thoughts and Clarifications." *Social Science Information* 44.4 (2005): 603–20.
——. "Is There a Role for Culture in Human Behavioral Ecology." *Ethology and Sociobiology* 16 (1995): 181–205.
——. *That Complex Whole: Culture and the Evolution of Human Behavior*. Boulder: Westview Press, 1999.
Cui Bao 崔豹 (fl. 290–306). *Gu jin zhu* 古今注. Sbby.
d'Errico, Francesco. "The Invisible Frontier: A Multiple Species Model for the Origin of Behavioral Modernity." *Evolutionary Anthropology* 12 (2003): 188–202.
Di Cosmo, Nicola. *Ancient China and Its Enemies: The Rise of Nomadic Power in East Asian History*. Cambridge: Cambridge University Press, 2002.
Ding Guangxun 丁光勳. "Qin-Han shiqi de shifu, shiyi, zhongyi de nianling yanjiu" 秦漢時期的始傅, 始役, 終役的年齡研究. *Shanghai shifan daxue xuebao (zhexue shehui kexue ban)* 上海師範大學學報(哲學社會科學版) 32.4 (2003): 51–54.
Du You 杜佑 (735–812). *Tong dian* 通典. Beijing: Zhonghua shuju, 1988.
Du Zhengsheng 杜正勝. *Bianhu qimin: chuantong zhengzhi shehui jiegou zhi xingcheng* 編戶齊民: 傳統政治社會結構之形成. Taipei: Lianjing chuban shiye gongsi, 1990.
Duan Yucai 段玉裁 (1735–1815). *Shuowen jiezi zhu* 說文解字注. Hangzhou: Zhejiang guji chubanshe, 1998.
Durrant, Stephen W. *The Cloudy Mirror: Tension and Conflict in the Writings of Sima Qian*. Albany: State University of New York Press, 1995.
Egami Namio 江上波夫. "Kyōdo no saishi" 匈奴の祭祀. In *Yūrashia kodai hoppō bunka: Kyōdo bunka ronkō* ユウアシア古代北方文化: 匈奴文化論考, 225–79. Rpt. Tokyo: Yamakawa Shuppansha, 1950 [1948].
Elman, Benjamin A. *A Cultural History of Civil Examinations in Late Imperial China*. Berkeley: University of California Press, 2000.
Emmerich, Reinhard. "Bemerkungen zu Huang und Lao in der frühen Han-Zeit: Erkentnisse aus *Shiji* und *Hanshu*." *Monumenta Serica* 43 (1995): 53–140.
——. "Präliminarien zu Jia Shan und dessen Werk." In *Über Himmel und Erde: Festschrift für Erling von Mende*, ed. Raimund Kolb and Martina Siebert, 55–83. Wiesbaden: Harrassowitz, 2006.
Ernian lüling yu Zouyanshu: Zhangjiashan ersiqihao Han mu chutu falü wenxian shidu 二年律令與奏讞書: 張家山二四七號漢墓出土法律文獻釋讀. Edited by Peng Hao, Chen Wei, and Kudō Mutoo 工藤元男. Shanghai: Shanghai guji, 2007.

Fairbank, John K. "A Preliminary Framework." In *The Chinese World Order: Traditional China's Foreign Relations*, ed. John K. Fairbank, 1–19. Cambridge: Harvard University Press, 1968.
Falkenhausen, Lothar von. *Chinese Society in the Age of Confucius (1000–250 BC): The Archaeological Evidence*. Los Angeles: Cotsen Institute of Archaeology, University of California, 2006.
———. "The Inscribed Bronzes from Yangjiacun: New Evidence on Social Structure and Historical Consciousness in Late Western Zhou China (c. 800 BC)." *Proceedings of the British Academy* 139 (2006): 239–96.
———. "Issues in Western Zhou Studies: A Review Article." *Early China* 18 (1993): 139–226.
———. *Suspended Music: Chime-Bells in the Culture of Bronze Age China*. Berkeley: University of California Press, 1993.
Fan Ye 范曄 (398–445). *Hou Han shu* 後漢書. Beijing: Zhonghua shuju, 1965.
Fan Zhiming 范致明 (*jinshi* 1100). *Yueyang fengtu ji* 岳陽風土記. Skqs.
Fang Shiming 方詩銘 and Fang Xiaofen 方小芬. *Zhongguo shi liri he Zhongxi liri duizhaobiao* 中國史曆日和中西曆日對照表. Shanghai: Shanghai cishu, 1987.
Fang Xuanling 房玄齡 (578–648). *Jin shu* 晉書. Beijing: Zhonghua shuju, 1974.
Fehr, Ernst, and Urs Fischbacher. "The Economics of Strong Reciprocity." In *Moral Sentiments and Material Interests: The Foundations of Cooperation in Economic Life*, ed. Herbert Gintis et al., 151–91. Cambridge: MIT Press, 2005.
Feuerwerker, Albert. *State and Society in Eighteenth-Century China: The Ch'ing Empire in Its Glory*. Ann Arbor: The University of Michigan Center for Chinese Studies, 1976.
Finsterbusch, Käte. *Verzeichnis und Motivindex der Han-Darstellungen*. Wiesbaden: Harrassowitz, 1971.
Fiskesjö, Magnus. "Rising from Blood-Stained Fields: Royal Hunting and State Formation in Shang China." *Bulletin of the Museum of Far Eastern Antiquities* 73 (2001): 49–191.
FitzGibbon, C. D., and J. H. Fanshawe. "Stotting in Thomson's Gazelles: An Honest Signal of Condition." *Behavioral Ecology and Sociobiology* 23 (1988): 69–74.
Foucault, Michel. *Discipline and Punish: The Birth of the Prison*. Translated by Alan Sheridan. New York: Vintage Books, 1979.
———. "Omnes et Singulatim: Towards a Critique of 'Political Reason.'" In *The Tanner Lectures on Human Values*, Volume 2, ed. S. McMurrin, 223–54. Cambridge: Cambridge University Press, 1981.
———. *Power*. Edited by James D. Faubion. New York: The New Press, 2000.
———. *Power/Knowledge: Selected Interviews and Other Writings 1972–1977*. Edited by Colin Gordon. New York: Pantheon Books, 1981 [1980].
———. *Security, Territory, Population: Lectures at the College de France, 1977–78*. Translated by Graham Burchell. New York: Palgrave Macmillan, 2007.
Fu Kaisen 福開森 (John Calvin Ferguson, 1866–1945). *Lidai zhulu jijin mu* 歷代著錄吉金目 (Catalog of the recorded bronzes of successive dynasties). Changsha: Shangwu yinshuguan, 1939.

Gai Shanlin 蓋山林. "Neimenggu Yinshan shanmai Langshan diqu yanhua" 內蒙古陰山山脈狼山地區岩畫. *Wenwu* 6 (1980): 1–11.

———. "Quan yanhua, quan, quan ji" 犬岩畫, 犬, 犬祭. *Beifang wenwu* 北方文物 3 (1989): 58–63, 90.

———. *Yinshan yanhua* 陰山巖畫. Beijing: Wenwu chubanshe, 1986.

Gai Shanlin and Lu Sixian 陸思賢. "Yinshan nanlu de Zhao changcheng" 陰山南麓的趙長城. In *Neimenggu wenwu ziliao xuji* 內蒙古文物資料續輯, ed. Neimenggu wenwu gongzuodui 內蒙古文物工作隊, 87–89. Hohot: N.p., 1984.

Galambos, Imre. "The Myth of the Qin Unification of Writing in Han Sources." *Acta Orientalia (Budapest)* 57.2 (2004): 181–203.

———. *Orthography of Early Chinese Writing: Evidence from Newly Excavated Manuscripts.* Budapest: Department of East Asian Studies, Eötvös Loránd University, 2006.

Galef, Bennett G., Jr., and Kevin M. Laland. "Social Learning in Animals: Empirical Studies and Theoretical Models." *Bioscience* 55 (2005): 489–99.

Gansusheng bowuguan 甘肅省博物館. "Gansu Wuwei Mojuzi Han mu fajue" 甘肅武威磨咀子漢墓發掘. *Kaogu* 9 (1960): 15–28.

Gansusheng wenwu kaogu yanjiusuo 甘肅省文物考古研究所, ed. *Dunhuang Xuanquan yueling zhaotiao* 敦煌懸泉月令詔條. Beijing: Zhonghua shuju, 2001.

Gansusheng wenwu kaogu yanjiusuo 甘肅省文物考古研究所, et al. *Juyan xin jian* 居延新簡. Beijing: Zhonghua shuju, 1994.

Gansusheng wenwuju 甘肅省文物局. *Qin Zhidao kaocha* 秦直道考察. Lanzhou: Lanzhou daxue chubanshe, 1996.

Gao Cheng 高承 (11th c.). *Shiwu jiyuan* 事物紀原. Skqs.

Gao Heng 高亨. *Guzi tongjia huidian* 古字通假彙典. Ji'nan: Qi Lu shushe, 1997.

Gao Heng 高恒. *Qin Han fazhi lunkao* 秦漢法制論考. Xiamen: Xiamen daxue chubanshe, 1994.

Gao Min 高敏. "Qin Han de huji zhidu" 秦漢的戶籍制度. *Qiu suo* 求索 1 (1987): 72–81.

———. *Qin Han Wei Jin Nanbeichao shi lunkao* 秦漢魏晉南北朝史論考. Beijing: Zhongguo shehui kexue chubanshe, 2004.

———. *Shuihudi Qin jian chu tan* 睡虎地秦簡初探. Taipei: Wanjuanlou, 2000.

Gao Ming 高明. *Boshu Laozi jiaozhu* 帛書老子校注. Beijing: Zhonghua shuju, 1996.

Gao Ping 高平. "Yinshan yanhua de xi yu you" 陰山岩畫的喜與憂. *Guangming ribao* 光明日報 (http://www.sach.gov.cn/tabid/299/InfoID/12274/default.aspx, posted 21 July 2008, accessed 1 April 2009).

Gardner, D. S. "Performativity in Ritual: The Mianmin Case." *Man* (N.S.) 18 (1983): 346–60.

Ge Jianxiong 葛劍雄. *Zhongguo renkou shi* 中國人口史. Shanghai: Fudan daxue chubanshe, 2002.

Gernet, Jacques. "Introduction." In *Foundations and Limits of State Power in China*, ed. S. R. Schram, xv–xxvii. London: School of Oriental and African Studies, 1987.

Getty, Thomas. "Handicap Signalling: When Fecundity and Viability Do Not Add Up." *Animal Behaviour* 56 (1998): 127–30.
Giele, Enno. *Imperial Decision-Making and Communication in Early China: A Study of Cai Yong's "Duduan."* Wiesbaden: Harrassowitz Verlag, 2006.
———. "Signatures of 'Scribes' in Early Imperial China." *Asiatische Studien* 1 (2005): 353–87.
Gintis, Herbert, et al. "Moral Sentiments and Material Interests: Origins, Evidence, and Consequences." In *Moral Sentiments and Material Interests: The Foundations of Cooperation in Economic Life*, ed. Herbert Gintis et al., 3–39. Cambridge: MIT Press, 2005.
Graham, A. C. *Disputers of the Tao: Philosophical Argument in Ancient China*. La Salle: Open Court, 1989.
Gu Jiegang 顧頡剛 (1893–1980). "Qin-Han tongyi de youlai he Zhanguo ren duiyu shijie de xiangxiang" 秦漢統一的由來和戰國人對於世界的想像. In *Gushi bian* 古史辨, volume 2, ed. Gu Jiegang, 1–10. Rpt. Hong Kong: Taiping shuju, 1962 [1930].
Gu Zuyu 顧祖禹 (1624–1680). *Du shi fangyu jiyao* 讀史方輿紀要. Taipei: Xinxing shuju, 1967.
*Guang yun*廣韻. *Sbby*.
Guo Dianchen 郭殿忱. "Qin mie Yiqu ji qi diwang kao" 秦滅義渠及其地望考. *Xibei shidi* 西北史地 1 (1996): 6–9, 58.
Guo Hao 郭浩. "Handai wangzhang zhidu ruogan wenti kaobian" 漢代王杖制度若干問題考辨. *Shixue jikan* 史學集刊 3 (2008): 94–99.
Guo Jifen 郭繼汾. "Qinhuang qiuxian bian" 秦皇求仙辨. *Hebei "Shehui kexue luntan"* 河北《社會科學論壇》 4 (1994): 58–59, 63.
Guo Moruo 郭沫若 (1892–1978). "Gudai wenzi zhi bianzheng de fazhan" 古代文字之辯證的發展. *Kaogu* 3 (1972): 2–13.
———. *Shi pipan shu* 十批判書. In *Guo Moruo quanji* 郭沫若全集. Beijing: Renmin chubanshe, 1982.
Guo Zizhi 郭子直. "Zhanguo Qin feng zongyi washu mingwen xinshi" 戰國秦封宗邑瓦書銘文新釋. *Guwenzi yanjiu* 古文字研究, no. 14, ed. Zhongguo guwenzi yanjiuhui 中國古文字研究會, 177–96. Beijing: Zhonghua shuju, 1986.
Guodian Chu mu zhujian 郭店楚墓竹簡. Edited by Jingmenshi bowuguan 荊門市博物館. Beijing: Wenwu chubanshe, 1998.
Guojia wenwuju 國家文物地圖集, ed. *Zhongguo wenwu dituji: Neimenggu zizhiqu fence* 中國文物地圖集：內蒙古自治區分冊. Xi'an: Xi'an ditu chubanshe, 2003.
Guojia wenwuju Qin zhidao yanjiu keti zu 國家文物局秦直道研究課題組, and Xunyixian bowuguan 旬邑縣博物館. "Xunyixian Qin zhidao yizhi kaocha baogao" 旬邑縣秦直道遺址考察報告. *Wenbo* 文博 3 (2006): 75–78.
Hagen, Edward H., and Gregory A. Bryant. "Music and Dance as a Coalition Signaling System." *Human Nature* 14 (2003): 21–51.

Han Baoquan 韓保全. "Qin Epanggong yizhi" 秦阿房宮遺址. *Wenbo* 2 (1996): 23–26.

Han Changsong 韓長松, Luo Huojin 羅火金, and Feng Chunyan 馮春艷. "Jiaozuo Lihe Han mu chutu qiceng liange caihuitao canglou shixi" 焦作李河漢墓出土七層連閣彩繪陶倉樓試析. *Zhongguo lishi wenwu* 中國歷史文物 1 (2010): 54–60.

Han Fuzhi 韓復智 et al. *Qin Han shi* 秦漢史. Taipei: Guoli kongzhong daxue, 1996.

Han Lianqi 韓連琪. "Handai de huji he shangji zhidu" 漢代的戶籍和上計制度. In *Xianqin Lianghan shi luncong* 先秦兩漢史論叢, 378–96. Ji'nan: Qi-Lu shushe, 1986.

Han shu 漢書. See Ban Gu.

Hao Yixing 郝懿行 (1757–1825). *Er ya yi shu* 爾雅義疏. In Hao Yixing et al., *Er ya, Guang ya, Fang yan, Shi ming: Qing shu sizhong hekan* 爾雅、廣雅、方言、釋名：清疏四種合刊. Shanghai: Shanghai guji chubanshe, 1989.

Hardy, Grant. *Worlds of Bronze and Bamboo: Sima Qian's Conquest of History*. New York: Columbia University Press, 1999.

Hawkes, David. "The Quest of the Goddess." *Asia Major* (new series) 13 (1967): 71–94.

Hayashi Minao 林巳奈夫. *Kandai no bunbutsu* 漢代の文物. 2nd edition. Kyoto: Hōyū shoten, 1996.

He Han 何漢. *Qin shi shuping* 秦史述評. Hefei: Huangshan shushe, 1986.

He Jianzhang 何建章. *Zhanguo ce zhu shi* 戰國策注釋. Beijing: Zhonghua shuju, 1990.

He Ning 何寧. *Huainanzi jishi* 淮南子集釋. Beijing: Zhonghua shuju, 1998.

He Pingli 何平立. "Xianqin xunshou shiji yu zhidu jilun" 先秦巡狩史迹與制度稽論. *Junshi lishi yanjiu* 軍事歷史研究 1 (2003): 79–87.

———. *Xunshou yu fengshan—Fengjian zhengzhi de wenhua guiji* 巡狩與封禪—封建政治的文化軌迹. Ji'nan: Qi Lu shushe, 2003.

He Tianming 何天明. "Dui Xiongnu chuangjian zhengquan ruogan wenti de tantao—Xiongnu zhengquan shizi Maodun chanyu shuo zhiyi" 對匈奴創建政權若干問題的探討—匈奴政權始自冒頓單于說質疑. *Neimenggu shehui kexue (Hanwen ban)* 內蒙古社會科學(漢文版) 27.1 (2006): 40–45.

He'nan bowuyuan 河南博物院. *He'nan chutu Handai jianzhu mingqi* 河南出土漢代建築明器. Zhengzhou: Daxiang chubanshe, 2002.

Heath, Joseph, and Andrew Potter. *Nation of Rebels: Why Counterculture Became Consumer Culture*. New York: Harper Paperbacks, 2004.

Hebeisheng wenwu guanlichu 河北省文物管理處. "Hebeisheng Pingshanxian Zhanguo shiqi Zhongshanguo muzang fajue jianbao" 河北省平山縣戰國時期中山國墓葬發掘簡報. *Wenwu* 1 (1979): 1–31.

Hebeisheng wenwu yanjiusuo 河北省文物研究所, Qinhuangdaoshi wenwu guanlichu 秦皇島市文物館里處, and Beidaihequ wenwu baoguansuo 北戴河區文物保管所. "Jinshanju Qindai jianzhu yizhi fajue baogao" 金山咀秦代建

築遺址發掘報告. *Wenwu chunqiu* 文物春秋 supplement 1 (1992): 267–94.

Henrich, Joseph, and Richard McElreath. "The Evolution of Cultural Evolution." *Evolutionary Anthropology* 12 (2003): 123–35.

Hogan, Robert, Gordon J. Curphy, and Joyce Hogan. "What We Know About Leadership." *American Psychologist* 49.6 (1994): 493–504.

Hogan, Robert, and Robert B. Kaiser. "What We Know About Leadership." *Review of General Psychology* 9.2 (2005): 169–80.

Hong Huiyu 洪惠瑜. "Handai jinglao yu ci zhang zhidu zhi tantao" 漢代敬老與賜杖制度之探討. *Pingdong jiaoyu daxue xuebao—renwen shehui lei* 屏東教育大學學報—人文社會類 31 (2008): 65–86.

Hou Xueshu 侯學書. "Qin zhao zhuke yu quanliang zhengzhi mudi kao" 秦詔鑄刻于權量政治目的考. *Jianghai xuekan* 江海學刊 6 (2004): 123–28.

Hsing I-t'ien 邢義田. *Qin Han shi lun gao* 秦漢史論稿. Taipei: Dongda tushu gongsi, 1987.

Hu Pingsheng 胡平生. "'Bianshu,' 'Da bianshu' kao" "扁書," "大扁書" 考. In *Dunhuang Xuanquan Yueling zhaotiao* 敦煌懸泉月令詔條, ed. Gansusheng wenwu kaogu yanjiusuo, 48–54. Beijing: Zhonghua shuju, 2001.

———. "Liye Qin jian 8–455 hao mufang xingzhi chuyi" 里耶秦簡8–455號木方性質芻議. In *Jianbo* 簡帛, no. 4, ed. Wuhan daxue jianbo yanjiu zhongxin 武漢大學簡帛研究中心, 17–25. Shanghai: Shanghai guji, 2009.

Hu Pingsheng and Zhang Defang 張德芳. *Dunhuang Xuanquan Han jian shi cui* 敦煌懸泉漢簡釋粹. Shanghai: Shanghai guji chubanshe, 2001.

Hua Yubing 華玉冰. "Shi lun Qin Shihuang dong xun de 'Jieshi' yu 'Jieshigong'" 試論秦始皇東巡的 "碣石" 與 "碣石宮." *Kaogu* 10 (1997): 81–86.

Hua Yubing and Yang Rongchang 楊榮昌. "Liaoning Suizhongxian Shibeidi Qin Han gongcheng yizhi 1993–1995 nian fajue jianbao" 遼寧綏中縣石碑地秦漢宮城遺址1993–1995年發掘簡報. *Kaogu* 10 (1997): 47–57.

Huang Aimei 黃愛梅. "Shuihudi Qin jian yu Longgang Qin jian de bijiao" 睡虎地秦簡與龍崗秦簡的比較. *Huadong shifan daxue xuebao (zhexue shehui kexue ban)* 華東師範大學學報 (哲學社會科學版) 4 (1997): 45–51.

Huang Hui 黃暉. *Lunheng jiaoshi* 論衡校釋. Beijing: Zhonghua shuju, 1990.

Huang, Ray. *China: A Macro History*. Armonk: M. E. Sharpe, 1997.

Huang Rucheng 黃汝成. *Ri zhi lu jishi* 日知錄集釋. Taibei: Guotai wenhua shiye gongsi, 1980.

Huang Wenbi 黃文弼. "Qianhan Xiongnu chanyu jian ting kao" 前漢匈奴單于建庭考. *Zeshan banyue kan* 責善半月刊 2.5 (1941). Reprinted in *Xiongnu shi lunwen xuanji (1919–1979)* 匈奴史論文選集 (1919–1979), ed. Lin Gan 林幹, 88–91. Beijing: Zhonghua shuju, 1983.

Hubeisheng Jingsha tielu kaogu dui 湖北省荊沙鐵路考古隊. *Baoshan Chu jian* 包山楚簡. Beijing: Wenwu chubanshe, 1991.

Hucker, Charles O. *A Dictionary of Official Titles in Imperial China*. Stanford: Stanford University Press, 1985.

Hui, Victoria Tin-bor. "The Emergence and Demise of Nascent Constitutional Rights: Comparing Ancient China and Early Modern Europe." *Journal of Political Philosophy* 9 (2001): 373–403.

———. *War and State Formation in Ancient China and Early Modern Europe*. Cambridge: Cambridge University Press, 2005.

Hulsewé, A. F. P. *Remnants of Ch'in Law: An Annotated Translation of the Ch'in Legal and Administrative Rules of the 3rd Century B.C. Discovered in Yün-meng Prefecture, Hu-pei Province, in 1975*. Leiden: E. J. Brill, 1985.

———. *Remnants of Han Law*. Volume 1: Introductory Studies and an Annotated Translation of Chapters 22 and 23 of the *History of the Former Han Dynasty*. Leiden: E. J. Brill, 1955.

———. "Weights and Measures in Ch'in Law." In *State and Law in East Asia: Festschrift Karl Bünger*, ed. Dieter Eikemeier and Herbert Franke, 25–39. Wiesbaden: Otto Harrassowitz, 1981.

Hu'nansheng wenwu kaogu yanjiusuo 湖南省文物考古研究所. *Liye fajue baogao* 里耶發掘報告. Changsha: Yuelu shushe, 2007.

Hurwit, Jefferey M. "The Problem with Dexileos: Heroic and Other Nudities in Greek Art." *American Journal of Archaeology* 111 (2007): 35–60.

Ikeda On 池田温. *Chūgoku kodai sekichō kenkyū: gaikan, rokubun* 中國古代籍帳研究—概觀, 錄文. Tokyo: Tōkyō Daigaku Shuppansha, 1979.

Irons, William. "An Evolutionary Critique of the Created Co-Creator Concept." *Zygon* 39 (2004): 773–90.

Ji Naijun 姬乃軍. "Shaanxi Zhidanxian Yongningxiang faxian Qin zhidao xinggong yizhi" 陝西志丹縣永寧鄉發現秦直道行宮遺址. *Kaogu* 10 (1992): 952–53.

Jian Bozan 剪伯贊 (1898–1968). *Qin Han shi* 秦漢史. Taipei: Yunlong chubanshe, 2003.

Jiang Lihong 蔣禮鴻. *Shangjun shu zhuizhi* 商君書錐指. Beijing: Zhonghua shuju, 1986.

Jiao Nanfeng 焦南峰. "Zongmiao dao, you dao, yiguan dao—Xihan diling daolu zaitan" 宗廟道, 游道, 衣冠道—西漢帝陵道路再探. *Wenwu* 1 (2010): 73–77, 96.

Jiayuguanshi wenwu baoguansuo 嘉峪關市文物保管所. "Yumenhuahai Handai feisui yizhi chutu de jiandu" 玉門花海漢代烽燧遺址出土的簡牘. In *Hanjian yanjiu wenji* 漢簡研究文集, ed. Gansusheng wenwu gongzuodui 甘肅省文物工作隊 et al., 15–33. Lanzhou: Gansu renmin chubanshe, 1984.

Johnstone, Rufus A., and Ken Norris. "Badges of Status and the Cost of Aggression." *Behavioral Ecology and Sociobiology* 32 (1993): 127–34.

Kaogu yanjiusuo bianjishi 考古研究所編輯室. "Wuwei Mojuzi Han mu chutu Wangzhang shijian shiwen" 武威磨咀子漢墓出土王杖十簡釋文. *Kaogu* 9 (1960): 29–30.

Keane, Webb. "The Evidence of the Senses and the Materiality of Religion." *Journal of the Royal Anthropological Institute* 14.1 (2008): 110–27.

———. "The Hazards of New Clothes: What Signs Make Possible." In *The Art of Clothing: A Pacific Experience*, ed. Susanne Küchler and Graeme Were, 1–16. London: UCL Press, 2005.

———. "Language and Religion." In *A Companion to Linguistic Anthropology*, ed. Alessandro Duranti, 431–48. London: Blackwell Publishing, 2004.

———. "Market, Materiality and Moral Metalanguage." *Anthropological Theory* 8.1 (2008): 27–42.

———. "Religious Language." *Annual Review of Anthropology* 26 (1997): 47–71.

———. "Sincerity, 'Modernity,' and the Protestants." *Cultural Anthropology* 17 (2002): 65–92.

Keesing, Roger M. "Anthropology as Interpretive Quest." *Current Anthropology* 28 (1987): 161–76.

Keightley, David N. "The Late Shang State: When, Where, and What?" In *The Origins of Chinese Civilization*, ed. David Keightley, 523–64. Berkeley: University of California Press, 1983.

Kenrick, Douglas T., et al. "Dynamical Evolutionary Psychology: Mapping the Domains of the New Interactionist Paradigm." *Personality and Social Psychology Review* 6 (2002): 347–56.

Kern, Martin. "Quotation and the Confucian Canon in Early Chinese Manuscripts: The Case of 'Zi yi' (Black Robes)." *Asiatische Studien* 59.1 (2005): 293–332.

———. "Ritual, Text, and the Formation of the Canon: Historical Transitions of Wen in Early China." *T'oung Pao* 87 (2001): 43–91.

———. *The Stele Inscriptions of Ch'in Shih-huang: Text and Ritual in Early Chinese Imperial Representation*. New Haven: American Oriental Society, 2000.

Kleeman, Terry. "Mountain Deities in China: The Domestication of the Mountain God and the Subjugation of the Margins." *Journal of the American Oriental Society* 114.2 (1994): 226–38.

Klein, Esther Sunkyung. "The History of a Historian: Perspectives on the Authorial Roles of Sima Qian." Ph.D. dissertation, Princeton University, 2010.

Knechtges, David R. *Wen xuan, or Selections of Refined Literature*. Volume 1: Rhapsodies on Metropolises and Capitals. Princeton: Princeton University Press, 1982.

———. *Wen xuan, or Selections of Refined Literature*. Volume 2: Rhapsodies on Sacrifices, Hunting, Travel, Sightseeing, Palaces and Halls, Rivers and Seas. Princeton: Princeton University Press, 1987.

Lachmann, Michael, Szalbolcs Számadó, and Carl T. Bergstrom. "Cost and Conflict in Animal Signals and Human Language." *Proceedings of the National Academy of Sciences of the United States of America* 98 (2001): 13189–94.

Laland, Kevin N., and William Hoppitt. "Do Animals Have Culture?" *Evolutionary Anthropology* 12 (2003): 150.

Lao Gan 勞榦 (b. 1907). *Qin Han shi* 秦漢史. Taipei: Wenhua daxue chubanbu, 1980.

Laurence, Ray. *The Roads of Roman Italy: Mobility and Cultural Change*. London: Routledge, 1999.

Le Blanc, Charles. "État et Société sous les premiers Han." In *La Société civile face à l'État: Dans les traditions chinoise, japonaise, coréenne et vietnamienne*, ed. Léon Vandermeersch, 29–46. Paris: École française d'Extrême-Orient, 1994.
Ledderose, Lothar. *Ten Thousand Things: Module and Mass Production in Chinese Art*. Princeton: Princeton University Press, 2000.
Leeson, Peter T. *The Invisible Hook: The Hidden Economics of Pirates*. Princeton: Princeton University Press, 2009.
———. "The Laws of Lawlessness." *Journal of Legal Studies* 38 (2009): 471–503.
Lei Ge 雷戈. *Qin Han zhi ji de zhengzhi sixiang yu huangquan zhuyi* 秦漢之際的政治思想與皇權主義. Shanghai: Shanghai guji chubanshe, 2006.
Lewis, Mark Edward. *China's Cosmopolitan Empire: The Tang Dynasty*. Cambridge: Belknap Press, 2009.
———. *The Construction of Space in Early China*. Albany: State University of New York Press, 2006.
———. *The Early Chinese Empires: Qin and Han*. Cambridge: Harvard University Press, 2007.
———. "The Han Abolition of Universal Military Service." In *Warfare in Chinese History*, ed. Hans van de Ven, 33–76. Leiden: Brill, 2000.
———. *Sanctioned Violence in Early China*. Albany: State University of New York Press, 1990.
———. "Warring States Political History." In *The Cambridge History of Ancient China: From the Origins of Civilization to 221 B.C.*, 587–650. Cambridge: Cambridge University Press, 1999.
———. *Writing and Authority in Early China*. Albany: State University of New York Press, 1999.
Li Daoyuan 酈道元 (d. 527). *Shui jing zhu* 水經注. *Skqs*.
———. *Shui jing zhu*. Edited by Wang Xianqian 王先謙 (1842–1918). Chengdu: Ba-Shu shushe, 1985.
Li Fang 李昉 (925–996) et al. *Taiping yulan* 太平御覽. Song woodblock edition; rpt. Taipei: Taiwan Shangwu yinshuguan, 1968.
Li Feng. "Ancient Reproductions and Calligraphic Variations: Studies of Western Zhou Bronzes with 'Identical' Inscriptions." *Early China* 22 (1997): 1–41.
———. *Bureaucracy and the State in Early China: Governing the Western Zhou*. Cambridge: Cambridge University Press, 2008.
———. "Feudalism and Western Zhou China: A Criticism." *Harvard Journal of Asiatic Studies* 63.1 (2003): 115–44.
———. *Landscape and Power in Early China: The Crisis and Fall of the Western Zhou, 1045–771 BC*. Cambridge: Cambridge University Press, 2006.
Liji zhushu 禮記注疏. See *Shisanjing zhushu*.
Li Jifu 李吉甫 (758–814). *Yuanhe jun xian zhi* 元和郡縣志. *Skqs*.
Li Junming 李均明. "Ejina Han jian fazhishi liaokao" 額濟納漢簡法制史料考. In *Ejina Han jian* 額濟納漢簡, ed. Wei Jian 魏堅, 54–70. Guilin: Guangxi shifan daxue chubanshe, 2005.

Li Junming and He Shuangquan 何雙全. *Sanjian jiandu heji* 散見簡牘合輯. Beijing: Wenwu chubanshe, 1990.

Li Ling 李零. *Zhongguo fangshu xukao* 中國方術續考. Beijing: Dongfang chubanshe, 2006.

———. "An Archaeological Study of Taiyi 太一 (Grand One) Worship." Translated by Donald Harper. *Early Medieval China* 2 (1995–1996): 1–39.

Li Rui 李瑞 and Wu Hongqi 吳宏岐. "Qin shihuang xunyou de shikong tezheng ji qi yuanyin fenxi" 秦始皇巡游的時空特徵及其原因分析. *Zhongguo lishi dili luncong* 18 (2003): 130–38.

Li Xiangfeng 黎翔鳳. *Guanzi jiaozhu* 管子校注. Beijing: Zhonghua shuju, 2004.

Li Xueqin 李學勤. *Eastern Zhou and Qin Civilizations*. Translated by K. C. Chang. New Haven: Yale University Press, 1985.

———. "Zhanguo Qin sinian washu kaoshi" 戰國秦四年瓦書考釋. In *Lianhe shuyuan sanshi zhounian jinian lunwenji* 聯合書院三十週年紀念論文集, ed. Lianhe shuyuan sanshi zhounian lunwenji bianji weiyuanhui 聯合書院三十周年紀念論文集編輯委員會, 71–77. Hong Kong: Lianhe shuyuan, 1986.

Li Zhongli 李仲立. "Gansu jingnei Qin Zhidao guanjian" 甘肅境內秦直道管見. *Renwen zazhi* 人文雜誌 3 (1993): 93–96.

———. "Qin Zhidao xinlun" 秦直道新論. *Xibei shidi* 西北史地 4 (1997): 1–6.

Li Zhongli, and Liu Dezhen 劉得禎. "Gansu Qingyang diqu Qin Zhidao diaocha ji" 甘肅慶陽地區秦直道調查記. *Kaogu yu wenwu* 考古與文物 5 (1991): 42–46, 112.

———. "Gansu Qingyang diqu Qin Zhidao kaocha baogao" 甘肅慶陽地區秦直道考察報告. *Gansu shehui kexue* 甘肅社會科學 3 (1991): 79–82.

———. "Qin Zhidao kaocha baogao: Gansu Qingyang diqu" 秦直道考察報告：甘肅慶陽地區. *Shehui zongheng* 社會縱橫 2 (1991): 47–49, 36.

Liang Yusheng 梁玉繩 (1744–1819). *Shiji zhiyi* 史記志疑. Beijing: Zhonghua shuju, 1981.

Lianyungangshi bowuguan 連雲港市博物館 et al. *Yinwan Han mu jiandu* 尹灣漢墓簡牘. Beijing: Zhonghua shuju, 1997.

Liaoningsheng wenwu kaogu yanjiusuo 遼寧省文物考古研究所. "Liaoning Suizhongxian 'Jiangnüfen' Qin Han jianzhu yizhi fajue jianbao" 遼寧綏中縣"姜女墳"秦漢建築遺址發覺簡報. *Wenwu* 8 (1986): 25–40.

Liaoningsheng wenwu kaogu yanjiusuo Jiangnüshi gongzuozhan 遼寧文物考古研究所姜女石工作站. "Liaoning Suizhongxian 'Jiangnüshi' Qin Han jianzhu qunzhi Shibeidi yizhi de kantan yu shijue" 遼寧綏中縣"姜女石"秦漢建築群址石碑地遺址的勘探與試掘. *Kaogu* 10 (1997): 36–46.

———. "Liaoning Suizhongxian Shibeidi yizhi 1996 niandu de fajue" 遼寧綏中縣石碑地遺址1996年度的發掘. *Kaogu* 8 (2001): 45–58.

Lin Jianming 林劍鳴. *Qin Han shi* 秦漢史. Shanghai renmin chubanshe, 1989.

Littrup, Leif. "The Un-Oppressive State and Comparative History: Some Observations on Ming-Qing Local Society." In *La société civile face à l'État dans les traditions chinoise, japonaise, coréenne et vietnamienne*, ed. Léon Vandermeersch, 157–72. Paris: École française d'Extrême-Orient, 1994.

Liu, Lydia H. *The Clash of Empires: The Invention of China in Modern World Making*. Cambridge: Harvard University Press, 2004.

Liu Qingzhu 劉慶柱, ed. *San Qin ji ji zhu, Guanzhong ji ji zhu* 三秦記輯注, 關中記輯注. Xi'an: Sanqin chubanshe, 2006.

Liu Shuying 劉淑英. "Xianqin de renkou tongji yu guanli" 先秦的人口統計與管理. *Renkou yu jingji* 人口與經濟 4 (1995): 50–55.

Liu Tizhi 劉體智 (1879–1963). *Shanzhai jijin lu* 善齋吉金錄. S.l.: N.p., ca. 1935.

Liu Wendian 劉文典, ed. *Huainan honglie jijie* 淮南鴻烈集解. Beijing: Zhonghua shuju, 1989.

Liu Xi 劉熙 (ca. 2nd–3rd c.). *Shi ming* 釋名. *Skqs*.

Liu Xiang 劉向 (ca. 77–ca. 6 BC). *Shuo yuan* 說苑.

———. *Zhanguo ce* 戰國策. Shanghai: Shanghai guji chubanshe, 1998.

Liu Zehua 劉澤華, Wang Maohe 汪茂和, and Wang Lanzhong 王蘭仲. *Zhuanzhi quanli yu Zhongguo shehui* 專制權力與中國社會. Tianjin: Tianjin guji chubanshe, 2005.

Loewe, Michael. "The Authority of the Emperors of Ch'in and Han." In *State and Law in East Asia: Festschrift Karl Bünger*, ed. Dieter Eikemeier and Herbert Franke, 80–111. Wiesbaden: Harrassowitz, 1981.

———. *The Government of the Qin and Han Empires, 221 B.C.E.–220 C.E.* Indianapolis: Hackett, 2006.

———. "Imperial Sovereignty: Dong Zhongshu's Contribution and His Predecessors." In *Foundations and Limits of State Power in China*, ed. S. R. Schram, 33–57. London: School of Oriental and African Studies, 1987.

———. "The Measurement of Grain During the Han Period." *T'oung Pao* 49 (1961): 64–95.

———. *The Men Who Governed Han China: Companion to "A Biographical Dictionary of the Qin, Former Han and Xin Periods."* Leiden: Brill, 2004.

———. "Yen t'ieh lun." In *Early Chinese Texts: A Bibliographical Guide*, ed. Michael Loewe, 477–82. Berkeley: Society for the Study of Early China, 1993.

Loewe, Michael, and Edward L. Shaughnessy, eds. *The Cambridge History of Ancient China: From the Origins of Civilization to 221 B.C.* Cambridge: Cambridge University Press, 1999.

Lü Dalin 呂大臨 (11th c.). *Kao gu tu* 考古圖. *Skqs*.

Lu Di 路笛. "Kongtongshan ming kao" 崆峒山名考. *Sichou zhi lu* 絲綢之路 4 (1998): 48.

Lü Simian 呂思勉. *Lü Simian dushi zhaji* 呂思勉讀史札記. Shanghai: Shanghai guji chubanshe, 1982.

———. *Zhongguo zhidu shi* 中國制度史. Shanghai: Shanghai jiaoyu chubanshe, 2002.

Lü Zhuomin 呂卓民. "Qin zhidao qiyi bianxi" 秦直道歧義辨析. *Zhongguo lishi dili luncong* 1 (1990): 89–105.

———. "Zailun Qin zhidao" 再論秦直道. *Wenbo* 2 (1994): 87–93.

Luo Fuyi 羅福頤, and Wang Rencong 王人聰. *Yinzhang gaishu* 印章概述. Beijing: Sanlian shudian, 1963.

Luo Mi 羅泌 (12th c.). *Lu shi* 路史. *Sbby*.
Ma Chengyuan 馬承源. "Shang Yang fangsheng he Zhanguo liangzhi" 商鞅方升和戰國量制. *Wenwu* 6 (1972): 17–24.
———, ed. *Shanghai bowuguan cang Zhanguo Chu zhushu* 上海博物館藏戰國楚竹書. Volume 1. Shanghai: Shanghai guji chubanshe, 2001.
———, ed. *Shanghai bowuguan cang Zhanguo Chu zhushu.* Volume 5. Shanghai: Shanghai guji chubanshe, 2005.
Ma Feibai 馬非百. *Qin jishi* 秦集史. Beijing: Zhonghua shuju, 1982.
———. *Qin Shihuangdi zhuan* 秦始皇帝傳. Nanjing: Jiangsu guji chubanshe, 1985.
Ma Liqing 馬利清. "Cong kaoguxue wenhua de fenbu yu chuanbo kan Xiongnu jiangyu de bianqian" 從考古學文化的分布與傳播看匈奴疆域的變遷. *Neimenggu daxue xuebao (renwen shehui kexue ban)* 內蒙古大學學報(人文社會科學版) 1 (2005): 15–22.
———. *Yuan Xiongnu, Xiongnu: lishi yu wenhua de kaoguxue tansuo* 原匈奴, 匈奴: 歷史與文化的考古學探索. Hohot: Neimenggu daxue chubanshe, 2005.
Ma Xiaohong 馬小紅. *Zhongguo gudai falü sixiang shi* 中國古代法律思想史. Beijing: Falü chubanshe, 2003.
Ma Yi 馬怡. "Bianshu shi tan" 扁書試探. In *Jian bo* 簡帛, no. 1., ed. Wuhan daxue jian bo yanjiu zhongxin, 415–28. Shanghai: Shanghai guji chubanshe, 2006.
Maoshi zhengyi 毛詩正義. See *Shisanjing zhushu*.
Mao Zedong 毛澤東 (1893–1976). *Mao Zedong xuanji* 毛澤東選集. 2nd edition. Beijing: Renmin chubanshe, 1953.
Maspero, Henri. "L'empire des Ts'in et des Han." In Henri Maspero and Étienne Balazs, *Histoire et institutions de la Chine ancienne des origines au XIIe siècle après J.-C.*, 41–79. Paris: Presses universitaires de France, 1967.
Maspero, Henri, and Jean Escarra. *Les institutions de la Chine*. Paris: Presses universitaires de France, 1952.
McNeal, Robin. "The Body as Metaphor for the Civil and Martial Components of Empire in Yi Zhou shu, Chapter 32: With an Excursion on the Composition and Structure of the *Yi Zhou shu*." *Journal of the American Oriental Society* 122.1 (2002): 46–60.
Meadows, Thomas Taylor. *The Chinese and Their Rebellions, Viewed in Connection with Their National Philosophy, Ethics, Legislation, and Administration. To Which Is Added, an Essay on Civilization and Its Present State in the East and West*. London: Smith, Elder & Co., 1856.
Meng Xianbin 孟憲斌. *Qin Shihuang chu xun ji* 秦始皇出巡記. Xi'an: Sanqin chubanshe, 2006.
Mengzi zhushu 孟子注疏. See *Shisanjing zhushu*.
Miyake Kiyoshi 宮宅潔. "Shin-Kan jidai no moji to shikiji—chikukan, mokkan kara mita" 秦漢時代の文字と識字—竹簡, 木簡からみた. In *Kanji no Chūgoku bunka* 漢字の中国文化, ed. Tomiya Itaru 冨谷至, 191–223. Kyoto: Showado, 2009.

Momiyama Akira 籾山明. "Hōka izen—Shunjūki ni okeru kei to chitsujo" 法家以前—春秋期における刑と秩序. *Tōyōshi kenkyū* 東洋史研究 39.2 (1980): 1–37.

———. *Shin no Shikōtei: tagen sekai no tōitsusha* 秦の始皇帝: 多元世界の統一者. Tokyo: Hakuteisha, 1994.

Moore, Robert E. "From Genericide to Viral Marketing: On 'Brand.'" *Language & Communication* 23 (2003): 331–57.

Münzel, Frank. "Some Remarks on Ming T'ai-tsu." *Archiv Orientální* 37.3 (1969): 377–403.

Nagata Hidemasa 永田英正. "Monjo gyōsei" 文書行政. In *In Shū Shin-Kan jidaishi no kihon mondai* 殷周秦漢時代史の基本問題, ed. In Shū Shin Kan jidaishi no kihon mondai henshūiinkai 殷周秦漢時代の基本問題編輯委員會, 281–304. Tokyo: Kyūko shoin, 2001.

Needham, Joseph, with Wang Ling and Lu Gwei-djen. *Science and Civilisation in China*. Volume 4, part 3: Civil Engineering and Nautics. Cambridge: Cambridge University Press, 1971.

Neiman, Fraser D. "Conspicuous Consumption as Wasteful Advertising: A Darwinian Perspective on Spatial Patterns in Classic Maya Terminal Monument Dates." In *Rediscovering Darwin: Evolutionary Theory and Archeological Explanation*, ed. C. M. Barton and G. A. Clark, 267–90. Washington, DC: American Anthropological Association, 1997.

Nickel, Lukas. "Tonkrieger auf der Seidenstrasse? Die Plastiken des Ersten Kaisers von China und die Hellenistische Skulptur Zentralasiens." *Zurich Studies in the History of Art* 13/14 (2006–2007): 125–50.

Nienhauser, William H., Jr., ed. *The Grand Scribe's Records*. Volume 1: The Memoirs of Pre-Han China. Bloomington: Indiana University Press, 1994.

Nishijima Sadao 西嶋定生 (1919–1998). *Chūgoku kodai teikoku no keisei to kōzō* 中國古代帝國の形成と構造. Tokyo: Tokyō Daigaku Shuppansha, 1961.

Nivison, David S. "*Chou li*." In *Early Chinese Texts: A Bibliographical Guide*, ed. Michael Loewe, 24–29. Berkeley: Society for the Study of Early China, 1993.

———. "The Paradox of 'Virtue.'" In *The Ways of Confucianism: Investigations in Chinese Philosophy*, ed. Bryan Van Norden, 31–43. Chicago: Open Court, 1996.

———. "Royal 'Virtue' in Shang Oracle Inscriptions." *Early China* 4 (1978–79): 52–55.

———. "'Virtue' in Bone and Bronze." In *The Ways of Confucianism: Investigations in Chinese Philosophy*, ed. Bryan Van Norden, 17–30. Chicago: Open Court, 1996.

Nowak, Martin A. "Five Rules for the Evolution of Cooperation." *Science* 314 (2006): 1560–63.

Nylan, Michael. "Sima Qian: A True Historian?" *Early China* 23–24 (1998–99): 203–46.

———. "Toward an Archaeology of Writing: Text, Ritual, and the Culture of Public Display in the Classical Period (475 B.C.E.–220 C.E.)." In *Text and Ritual in Early China*, ed. Martin Kern, 3–49. Seattle: University of Washington Press, 2005.

Ōba Osamu 大庭脩. *Kankan kenkyū* 漢簡研究. Kyoto: Hōyūsha, 1992.

Ouyang Fenglian 歐陽鳳蓮. "'Shangjun shu' huji guanli sixiang yu Qin guo huji guanli zhidu" "商君書" 戶籍管理思想與秦國戶籍管理制度. *Gudai wenming* 古代文明 3.2 (2009): 57–63.

Ouyang Xiu 歐陽修 (1007–1072). *Ji gu lu* 集古錄. Skqs.

Parish, William L., and Martin K. Whyte. *Village and Family in Contemporary China*. Chicago: University of Chicago Press, 1978.

Peirce, Charles. "Logic as Semiotic: The Theory of Signs." In *The Philosophical Writings of Peirce*, ed. Justus Buchler, 98–119. New York: Dover, 1955.

Peng Hao 彭浩. "Baoshan Chu jian fanying de Chuguo falü yu sifa zhidu" 包山楚簡反映的楚國法律與司法制度. In *Baoshan Chu mu* 包山楚墓, ed. Hubeisheng Jingsha tielu kaogu dui 湖北省荊沙鐵路考古隊, 548–54. Beijing: Wenwu chubanshe, 1991.

Pines, Yuri. "Biases and Their Sources: Qin History in the *Shiji*." *Oriens Extremus* 45 (2005–2006): 10–34.

———. *Envisioning Eternal Empire: Chinese Political Thought of the Warring States Era*. Honolulu: University of Hawaii Press, 2009.

———. "A Hero Terrorist: Adoration of Jing Ke Revisited." *Asia Major* (third series) 21.2 (2008): 1–34.

———. "'The One That Pervades the All' in Ancient Chinese Political Thought: The Origins of 'The Great Unity' Paradigm." *T'oung Pao* 86 (2000): 280–324.

———. "The Question of Interpretation: Qin History in Light of New Epigraphic Sources." *Early China* 29 (2004): 1–44.

———. "To Rebel Is Justified? The Image of Zhouxin and Legitimacy of Rebellion in Chinese Political Tradition." *Oriens Extremus* 47 (2008): 1–24.

Puett, Michael. *The Ambivalence of Creation: Debates Concerning Innovation and Artifice in Early China*. Stanford: Stanford University Press, 2001.

Pulleyblank, Edwin G. *Outline of Classical Chinese Grammar*. Vancouver: UBC Press, 1995.

Qi Yuzhang 祁玉章. *Jiazi Xin shu jiaoshi* 賈子新書校釋. Taipei: Zhongguo wenhua zazhi she, 1974.

Qian Mu 錢穆. *Gushi dili luncong* 古史地理論叢. Taipei: Dongda tushu gongsi, 1982.

———. *Shiji diming kao* 史記地名考. Beijing: Shangwu yinshuguan, 2001.

Qiu Guangming 丘光明. "Gaonu heshitongquan" 高奴禾石銅權. *Zhongguo zhiliang jishu jiandu* 中國質量技術監督 12 (2001): 62.

———. *Zhongguo lidai duliangheng kao* 中國歷代度量衡考. Beijing: Kexue chubanshe, 1992.

Quan Zuwang 全祖望 (1705–1755). *Hanshu dilizhi jiyi* 漢書地理志稽疑. In *Yueyatang congshu* 粵雅堂叢書. *Baibu congshu* 百部叢書 edition.

Rappaport, Roy A. *Ritual and Religion in the Making of Humanity*. Cambridge: Cambridge University Press, 1999.
Rawson, Jessica. "Ancient Chinese Bronzes." In *Ancient Chinese and Ordos Bronzes*, ed. Jessica Rawson and Emma Bunker, 13–61. Hong Kong: The Oriental Ceramic Society of Hong Kong, 1990.
Rickett, W. Allyn. "Kuan tzu." In *Early Chinese Texts: A Bibliographical Guide*, ed. Michael Loewe, 244–51. Berkeley: Society for the Study of Early China, 1993.
Robbins, Joel. "Ritual Communication and Linguistic Ideology." *Current Anthropology* 42 (2001): 591–614.
Rowe, Candy. "Receiver Psychology and the Evolution of Multicomponent Signals." *Animal Behaviour* 58 (1999): 921–31.
Rubin, Vitaly A. *Individual and State in Ancient China: Essays on Four Chinese Philosophers*. Translated by Steven I. Levine. New York: Columbia University Press, 1976.
Sanft, Charles. "The Construction and Deconstruction of Epanggong: Notes from the Crossroads of History and Poetry." *Oriens Extremus* 47 (2008): 160–76.
———. "Debating the Route of the Qin Direct Road (Zhidao): Text and Excavation." *Frontiers of History in China* 6.3 (2011): 323–46.
———. "Dong Zhongshu's *Chunqiu jueyu* Reconsidered: On the Legal Interest in Subjective States and the Privilege of Hiding Family Members' Crimes as Developments from Earlier Practice." *Early China* 33–34 (2010–2011): 141–69.
———. "Edict of Monthly Ordinances for the Four Seasons in Fifty Articles from 5 C.E.: Introduction to the Wall Inscription Discovered at Xuanquanzhi, with Annotated Translation." *Early China* 32 (2008–2009): 125–208.
———. "Law and Communication in Qin and Western Han China." *Journal of the Economic and Social History of the Orient* 53.5 (2010): 679–711.
———. "Notes on Penal Ritual and Subjective Truth under the Qin." *Asia Major* (third series) 22.1 (2008): 35–57.
———. "Progress and Publicity in Early China: Qin Shihuang, Ritual, and Common Knowledge." *Journal of Ritual Studies* 22.1 (2008): 21–43.
———. "Rituals That Don't Reach, Punishments That Don't Impugn: Jia Yi on the Exclusions from Punishment and Ritual." *Journal of the American Oriental Society* 125 (2005): 31–44.
———. "Rule: A Study of Jia Yi's Xin shu." Ph.D. dissertation, Westfälische Wilhelms-Universität Münster, 2005.
———. "Shang Yang Was a Cooperator: Applying Axelrod's Analysis of Cooperation in Early China." *Philosophy East and West*, forthcoming.
———. "Six of One, Two Dozen of the Other: The Abatement of Mutilating Punishments under Han Emperor Wen." *Asia Major* (third series) 18.1 (2005): 79–100.
Schaberg, David. "The *Zhouli* as Constitutional Text." In *Premodern East Asian Statecraft in Comparative Context: The Rituals of Zhou in Chinese and East Asian History*, ed. Benjamin A. Elman and Martin Kern, 33–63. Leiden: Brill, 2010.

Schafer, Edward H. "The Development of Bathing Customs in Ancient and Medieval China and the History of the Floriate Clear Palace." *Journal of the American Oriental Society* 76.2 (1956): 57–82.

Schaik, Carel P. van, et al. "Orangutan Cultures and the Evolution of Material Culture." *Science* 299 (2003): 102–5.

Schelling, Thomas C. *Micromotives and Macrobehavior*. New York: W. W. Norton, 2006 [1978].

———. *The Strategy of Conflict*. Cambridge: Harvard University Press, 1960; rpt. with a new preface, 1980.

Schwartz, Benjamin I. "The Primacy of the Political Order in East Asian Societies: Some Preliminary Generalizations." In *Foundations and Limits of State Power in China*, ed. S. R. Schram, 1–10. London: School of Oriental and African Studies, 1987.

Sellmann, James D. *Timing and Rulership in Master Lü's Spring and Autumn Annals (Lüshi chunqiu)*. Albany: State University of New York Press, 2002.

Sewell, William H., Jr. *Logics of History: Social Theory and Social Transformation*. Chicago: University of Chicago Press, 2005.

Shaanxisheng bowuguan 陝西省博物館. "Xi'anshi xijiao Gaoyaocun chutu Qin Gaonu tongshiquan" 西安市西郊高窰村出土秦高奴銅石權. *Wenwu* 9 (1964): 42–45.

Shang Zhiru 尚志儒, "Qin feng zongyi washu de jige wenti" 秦封宗邑瓦書的幾個問題. *Wenbo* 6 (1986): 43–49.

Shangshu zhengyi 尚書正義. See *Shisanjing zhushu*.

Shelach, Gideon. *Leadership Strategies, Economic Activity, and Interregional Interaction: Social Complexity in Northeast China*. New York: Kluwer Academic/Plenum, 1999.

———. *Prehistoric Societies on the Northern Frontiers of China: Archaeological perspectives on Identity Formation and Economic Change during the First Millennium BCE*. London: Equinox Publishing, 2009.

Shelach, Gideon, and Yuri Pines. "Secondary State Formation and the Development of Local Identity: Change and Continuity in the State of Qin (770–221 B.C.)." In *Archaeology of Asia*, ed. Miriam Stark, 202–30. Malden: Blackwell, 2006.

Shen Jiaben 沈家本 (1840–1913). *Lidai xingfa kao* 歷代刑法考. Beijing: Zhonghua shuju, 1985.

Shiji 史記. See Sima Qian.

Shi Nianhai 史念海. "Chunqiu yiqian de jiaotong daolu" 春秋以前的交通道路. *Zhongguo lishi dili luncong* 3 (1990): 5–37.

———. "Lun Qin Jiuyuan shizhi de niandai" 論秦九原始置的年代. *Zhongguo lishi dili luncong* 2 (1993): 57–64.

———. "Qin Shihuang Zhidao yiji de tansuo" 秦始皇直道遺跡的探索. *Shaanxi shifan daxue xuebao (zhexue shehui kexue ban)* 陝西師範大學學報 (哲學社會科學版) 3 (1975): 77–93.

———. "Qin Shihuang Zhidao yiji de tansuo" 秦始皇直道遺跡的探索. *Wenwu* 10 (1975): 44–54, 67.

———. "Zhanguo shiqi de jiaotong daolu" 戰國時期的交通道路. *Zhongguo lishi dili luncong* 1 (1991): 19–57.
———. "Zhidao he Ganquangong yiji zhiyi" 直道和甘泉宮遺迹質疑. *Zhongguo lishi dili luncong* 3 (1988): 45–84.
———. *Zhongguo gudu he wenhua* 中國古都和文化. Beijing: Zhonghua shuju, 1998.
Shi Shuqing 史樹青 and Xu Qingsong 許青松. "Qin Shihuang ershiliunian zhaoshu ji qi dazi zhaoban" 秦始皇二十六年詔書及其大字詔版. *Wenwu* 12 (1973): 14–17, 29.
Shiga Shūzō 滋賀秀三. *Chūgoku hōseishi ronshū: hōten to keibatsu* 中國法制史論集: 法典と刑罰. Tokyo: Sōbunsha, 2003.
Shisanjing zhushu 十三經注疏, ed. Ruan Yuan 阮元 (1764–1849). Taipei: Yiwen yinshuguan, 2001.
Shu Shunlin 舒順林. "Lun Xiongnuren de zhexue, zongjiao yu daode guannian" 論匈奴人的哲學, 宗教與道德觀念. *Neimenggu shida xuebao (zhexue shehui kexue ban)* 內蒙古師大學報 (哲學社會科學版) 2 (1992): 41–47.
Shue, Vivienne. *Peasant China in Transition*. Berkeley: University of California Press, 1980.
———. *The Reach of the State: Sketches of the Chinese Body Politic*. Stanford: Stanford University Press, 1988.
Shuihudi Qinmu zhujian 睡虎地秦墓竹簡. Edited by Shuihudi Qinmu zhujian zhengli xiaozu 睡虎地秦墓竹簡整理小組. Beijing: Wenwu chubanshe, 1990.
Silk, Joan B., Elizabeth Kaldor, and Robert Boyd. "Cheap Talk When Interests Conflict." *Animal Behaviour* 59 (2000): 423–32.
Silverstein, Michael. "The Uses and Utility of Ideology." In *Language Ideologies: Practice and Theory*, ed. Bambi B. Schieffelin, Kathryn A. Woolard, and Paul V. Kroskrity, 123–45. Oxford: Oxford University Press, 1998.
Sima Guang 司馬光 (1019–1086). *Zizhi tongjian* 資治通鑑. Beijing: Zhonghua shuju, 1956.
Sima Qian 司馬遷 (ca. 145–ca. 86 BCE). *Shiji* 史記. Beijing: Zhonghua shuju, 1959.
Slingerland, Edward. *What Science Offers the Humanities: Integrating Body and Culture*. Cambridge: Cambridge University Press, 2008.
Song Changbin 宋昌斌. *Zhongguo gudai huji zhidu shigao* 中國古代戶籍制度史稿. Xi'an: Sanqin chubanshe, 1991.
Song Wenhong 宋文紅. "Qin nongye falü zhidu tanwei" 秦農業法律制度探微. *Anhui nongye kexue* 安徽農業科學 34.4 (2006): 818–20.
Sosis, Richard. "The Adaptive Value of Religious Ritual." *American Scientist* 92 (2004): 166–72.
———. "Costly Signaling and Torch Fishing on Ifaluk Atoll." *Evolution and Human Behavior* 21 (2000): 223–44.
———. "Does Religion Promote Trust? The Role of Signaling, Reputation, and Punishment." *Interdisciplinary Journal of Research on Religion* 1 (2005): 1–30 [article no. 7].

———. "Religion and Intragroup Cooperation: Preliminary Results of a Comparative Analysis of Utopian Communities." *Cross-Cultural Research* 34 (2000): 70–87.

———. "Religious Behaviors, Badges, and Bans: Signaling Theory and the Evolution of Religion." In *Where God and Science Meet: How Brain and Evolutionary Studies Alter Our Understanding of Religion*, volume 1: Evolution, Genes, and the Religious Brain, ed. Patrick McNamara, 61–86. Westport: Praeger Publications, 2006.

———. "Why Aren't We All Hutterites? Costly Signaling Theory and Religious Behavior." *Human Nature* 14 (2003): 91–127.

Sosis, Richard, and Candace Alcorta. "Signaling, Solidarity, and the Sacred: The Evolution of Religious Behavior." *Evolutionary Anthropology* 12 (2003): 264–74.

Sosis, Richard, and Eric R. Bressler. "Cooperation and Commune Longevity: A Test of the Costly Signaling Theory of Religion." *Cross-Cultural Research* 278 (2003): 211–39.

Sosis, Richard, Howard C. Kress, and James S. Boster. "Scars for War: Evaluating Alternative Signaling Explanations for Cross-Cultural Variance in Ritual Costs." *Evolution and Human Behavior* 28 (2007): 234–47.

Sosis, Richard, and Bradley J. Ruffle. "Ideology, Religion, and the Evolution of Cooperation: Field Experiments on Israeli Kibbutzim." *Research in Economic Anthropology* 23 (2004): 89–117.

———. "Religious Ritual and Cooperation: Testing for a Relationship on Israeli Religious and Secular Kibbutzim." *Current Anthropology* 44 (2003): 713–22.

Stephens, P. A., W. J. Sutherland, and R. P. Freckleton. "What Is the Allee effect?" *Oikos* 87 (1999): 185–90.

Su Yucheng 宿玉成. "Zhidanxian faxian yichu Qindai jianzhu yizhi" 志丹縣發現一處秦代建築遺址. *Kaogu yu wenwu* 考古與文物 3 (1995): 77.

Sun Changxu 孫常敘. "Ze, fadu liangze, zeshi sanshi shijie" 則、灋度量則、則誓三事試解. In *Guwenzi yanjiu* 古文字研究, no. 7, ed. Zhongguo guwenzi yanjiuhui, 7–24. Beijing: Zhonghua shuju, 1982.

Sun Kai 孫楷 (1871–1907). *Qin hui yao* 秦會要. Edited by Yang Shanqun 楊善群. Shanghai: Shanghai guji chubanshe, 2004.

Sun Xiangwu 孫相武. "Qin zhidao diaocha ji" 秦直道調查記. *Wenbo* 4 (1988): 15–20.

Sun Xidan 孫希旦 (1736–1784). *Liji jijie* 禮記集解. Beijing: Zhonghua shuju, 1989.

Sun Xingyan et al., eds. *Han guan liuzhong* 漢官六種. Beijing: Zhonghua shuju, 1990.

Sun Yirang 孫詒讓 (1848–1908). *Mozi jiangu* 墨子閒詁. Beijing: Zhonghua shuju, 2001.

———. *Zhouli zhengyi* 周禮正義. Beijing: Zhonghua shuju, 1987.

Swidler, Ann. "Culture in Action: Symbols and Strategies." *American Sociological Review* 51 (1986): 273–86.

Takigawa Kametarō 瀧川亀太郎 (b. 1865). *Shiki kaichū kōshō* 史記會注考證. Taipei: Letian chubanshe, 1972.
Tao Yizeng 陶奕增 (Qing). *Heshuixian zhi* 合水縣志. S.l.: N.p., 1761.
Teng Ssu-yü, trans. *Family Instructions for the Yen Clan*. Leiden: E. J. Brill, 1968.
Tomasello, Michael. *The Cultural Origins of Human Cognition*. Cambridge: Harvard University Press, 1999.
———. *Why We Cooperate*. Cambridge: MIT Press, 2009.
Tomasello, Michael, Ann Cale Kruger, and Hilary Horn Ratner. "Cultural Learning." *Behavioral and Brain Sciences* 16 (1993): 495–552.
Tomiya Itaru 冨谷至. *Monjo gyōsei no Kan teikoku: mokkan, chikukan no jidai* 文書行政の漢帝國: 木簡, 竹簡の時代. Nagoya: Nagoya Daigaku Shuppansha, 2010.
Trigger, Bruce G. "Monumental Architecture: A Thermodynamic Explanation of Symbolic Behavior." *World Archaeology* 22.2 (1990): 119–32.
Tsuji Masahiro 辻正博. "Senkei, 'shisenkei,' ryūkei—'Tōdai ryūkei kō' horon" 遷刑・「徙遷刑」 ・流刑—「唐代流刑考」補論. In *Kōryo Chōkasan nihyakuyonjūnana gōbo shutsudo Kan ritsuryō no kenkyū* 江陵張家山二四七號墓出土漢律令の研究, ed. Tomiya Itaru, 305–39. Kyoto: Hōyū Shoten, 2006.
Tsuruma Kazuyuki 鶴間和幸. "Shi fuyuan Qin Shihuang dong xun ke shi wen" 試復原秦始皇東巡刻石文. In *Qinyong Qin wenhua yanjiu* 秦俑秦文化研究, ed. Qin Shihuang bingmayong bowuguan 秦始皇兵馬俑博物館, 686–96. Xian: Shaanxi renmin chubanshe, 2000.
Tu Mingfeng 涂明鳳. "Qin Han huji zhidu de guanli jizhi yu gongneng" 秦漢戶籍制度的管理機制與功能. *Hubei jingguan xueyuan xuebao* 湖北警官學院學報 1 (2006): 83–85.
Tuotuo 脫脫 (1313–1355). *Jin shi* 金史. Beijing: Zhonghua shuju, 1975.
———. *Song shi* 宋史. Beijing: Zhonghua shuju, 1977.
Tuomela, Raimo. *Cooperation: A Philosophical Study*. Dordrecht: Kluwer Academic Publishers, 2000.
Turner, Karen. "Law and Punishment in the Formation of Empire." In *Rome and China: Comparative Perspectives on Ancient World Empires*, ed. Walter Scheidel, 52–92. Oxford: Oxford University Press, 2009.
Twitchett, Denis, and Michael Loewe, eds. *The Cambridge History of China*. Volume 1: The Ch'in and Han Empires, 221 B.C.—A.D. 220. Cambridge: Cambridge University Press, 1986.
Unger, Ulrich (1930–2006). "Grammatik des Klassichen Chinesisch, II. Nominalsatz." Unpublished manuscript, version dated 1987.
Van Vugt, Mark. "Evolutionary Origins of Leadership and Followership." *Personality and Social Psychology Review* 10.4 (2006): 354–71.
Van Vugt, Mark, Robert Hogan, and Robert B. Kaiser. "Leadership, Followership, and Evolution: Some Lessons from the Past." *American Psychologist* 63.3 (2008): 182–96.

Waley, Arthur. *The Book of Songs*. Edited, with additional translations, Joseph R. Allen. New York: Grove Press, 1996.
Wan Changhua 萬昌華 and Zhao Xingbin 趙興彬. *Qin Han yilai jiceng xingzheng yanjiu* 秦漢以來基層行政研究. Ji'nan: Qi-Lu shushe, 2008.
Wang Beichen 王北辰. "Guqiaomen yu Qin zhidao kao" 古橋門與秦直道考. *Beijing daxue xuebao (shehui kexue ban)* 北京大學學報 (社會科學版) 1 (1988): 119–21.
Wang Bo 王博. *Jianbo sixiang wenxian lunji* 簡帛思想文獻論集. Taipei: Taiwan guji chubanshe, 2001.
Wang Daquan 汪大全 and Zhao Zongjun 趙宗軍. "Ashan jitan yu hulu chongbai kao" 阿善祭壇與葫蘆崇拜考. *Jiangxi jinrong zhigong daxue xuebao* 江西金融職工大學學報 21 (2008): 144–45.
Wang Fuchun 王富春. "Yulin jingnei Qin zhidao diaocha" 榆林境內秦知道調查. *Wenbo* 3 (2005): 64–67.
Wang Guowei 王國維. *Wang Guowei lunxueji* 王國維論學集. Edited by Fu Jie 傅杰. Beijing: Zhongguo shehui kexue chubanshe, 1997.
Wang Hui 王輝. "Qin qi mingwen congkao (xu)" 秦器銘文叢考(續). *Kaogu yu wenwu* 考古與文物 5 (1989): 117–24.
Wang Kai 王開. "'Qin Zhidao' xintan" 秦直道"新探. *Chengdu daxue xuebao (shekeban)* 成都大學學報 (社科版) 1 (1989): 36–50.
Wang Liqi 王利器. *Wenxin diaolong jiao zheng* 文心雕龍校證. Shanghai: Shanghai guji chubanshe, 1980.
———. *Xin yu jiaozhu* 新語校注. Beijing: Zhonghua shuju, 1986.
———. *Yanshi jiaxun jijie* 顏氏家訓集解. Revised and expanded edition. Beijing: Zhonghua shuju, 1993.
———. *Yantie lun jiaozhu* 鹽鐵論校注. Revised edition. Beijing: Zhonghua shuju, 1992.
Wang Ming 王酩. "Qindai 'Yishan keshi' kaoxi—jian lun gudai 'zou xia zhaoshu' zhidu" 秦代 "嶧山刻石" 考析—兼論古代 "奏下詔書"制度. *Shoudu shifan daxue xuebao (shehui kexue ban)* 首都師範大學學報 (社會科學版) 2 (2008): 36–38.
Wang Pinzhen 王聘珍 (18th c.). *Da Dai liji jie gu* 大戴禮記解詁. Beijing: Zhonghua shuju, 1983.
Wang Qi 王琦 and Du Jingwei 杜靜薇. "Qin quan" 秦權. *Dang'an* 檔案 1 (1999): 42–43.
Wang Sanxia 王三峽. "Qin jian 'jiu ke zhiwu' xiangguan wenzi de jiedu 秦簡 "久刻職物" 相關文字的解讀. *Changjiang daxue xuebao (shehui kexue ban)* 長江大學學報(社會科學版) 30.2 (2007): 82–85.
Wang Su 王肅 (195–256). *Kongzi jiayu* 孔子家語. *Sbby*.
Wang Wenjin 王文錦. *Liji yi jie* 禮記譯解. Beijing: Zhonghua shuju, 2001.
Wang Xianqian 王先謙 (1842–1918). *Han shu bu zhu* 漢書補注. 1900 woodblock edition; rpt. Yangzhou: Guangling shushe, 2006.
———. *Xunzi jijie* 荀子集解. Beijing: Zhonghua shuju, 1988.

Wang Xianshen 王先慎 (1859–1922). *Han Feizi jijie* 韓非子集解. Beijing: Zhonghua shuju, 1998.

Wang Xueyan 王雪巖. "Lüelun Qin-Han shiqi de Yunyang" 略論秦漢時期的雲陽. *Shaanxi jiaoyu xueyuan xuebao* 陝西教育學院學報 21.2 (2005): 79–82.

Wang Yinglin 王應麟 (1223–1296). *Yuhai* 玉海. Yuan woodblock; rpt. Taipei: Hualian chubanshe, 1974.

Wang Yinzhi 王引之 (1766–1834). *Jing yi shu wen* 經義述聞. Nanjing: Jiangsu guji chubanshe, 1985.

Wang Yonggang 王勇剛, Cui Fengguang 崔風光, and Li Yanli 李延麗. "Shaanxi Qin zhidao Ganquan duan faxian Qin Han jianzhu yizhi" 陝西秦直道甘泉段發現秦漢建築遺址. *Kaogu yu wenwu* 考古與文物 4 (2008): 14.

Wang Yongxia 王永霞. "Qin Shihuang xunyou sixiang suyuan" 秦始皇巡游思想溯源. In *Qin wenhua luncong*, no. 12, ed. Qin Shihuang bingmayong bowuguan "luncong" bianweihui 秦始皇兵馬俑博物館《論叢》編委會. Xi'an: Sanqin chubanshe, 2005.

Wang, Yü-ch'üan. "An Outline of the Central Government of the Former Han Dynasty." *Harvard Journal of Asiatic Studies* 12 (1949): 134–87.

Wang Zijin 王子今. "Qin guojun yuanxing shiji kaoshu" 秦國君遠行史迹考述. In *Qin wenhua luncong*, no. 8, ed. Qin Shihuang bingmayong bowuguan "luncong" bianweihui 秦始皇兵马俑博物馆《論叢》编委会. Xi'an: Shaanxi renmin chubanshe, 2001.

———. *Qin Han shiqi shengtai huanjing yanjiu* 秦漢時期生態環境研究. Beijing: Beijing daxue chubanshe, 2007.

———. "Qin Han 'yongdao' kao" 秦漢"甬道"考. *Wenbo* 2 (1993): 28–31.

———. "Qin Zhidao de lishi wenhua guanzhao" 秦直道的歷史文化觀照. *Renwen zazhi* 人文雜誌 5 (2005): 107–12.

Wang Zijin and Ma Zhenzhi 馬振智. "Qin Han 'fudao' kao" 秦漢"復道"考. *Wenbo* 3 (1984): 20–24.

Watanabe Shin'ichirō 渡邊信一郎. "Oto no teikoku: 'Kōshika' jūkyūshō no saishi kūkan to seiji kūkan" 音の帝國:「郊祀歌」十九章の祭祀空間と政治空間. In *Kokkyō o koeru "kōkyōsei" no hikakushiteki kenkyū* 國境をこえる"公共性"の比較史的研究, ed. Kawamura Sadae 河村貞枝, 3–38. Kyoto: Kyoto Prefectural University, 2006.

Weber, Max. *Die Wirtschaftsethik der Weltreligionen Konfuzianismus und Taoismus: Schriften 1915–1920*. Edited by Helwig Schmidt-Glinzer. Tübingen: J.C.B. Mohr, 1989.

Wei Jian 魏堅. *Eji'na Han jian* 額濟納漢簡. Guilin: Guangxi shifan daxue chubanshe, 2005.

Wei Zheng 魏徵 (580–643) et al. *Sui shu* 隋書. Beijing: Zhonghua shuju, 1973.

Weld, Susan Roosevelt. "Chu Law in Action: Legal Documents from Tomb 2 at Baoshan." In *Defining Chu: Image and Reality in Ancient China*, ed. Constance Cook and John S. Major, 77–97. Honolulu: University of Hawaii Press, 1999.

———. "Covenant in Jin's Walled Cities: The Discoveries at Houma and Wenxian." Ph.D. dissertation. Harvard University, 1990.

———. "The Covenant Texts from Houma and Wenxian." In *New Sources of Chinese History: An Introduction to the Reading of Inscriptions and Manuscripts*, ed. Edward L. Shaughnessy, 125–60. Berkeley: The Society for the Study of Early China, 1997.

Weng Yuanqi 翁元圻 (1750–1825), ed. *Weng zhu Kunxue jiwen* 翁注困學紀聞. *Sbby*.

Whyte, Martin K. *Small Groups and Political Rituals in China*. Berkeley: University of California Press, 1974.

Williams, Crispin. "A Methodological Procedure for the Analysis of the Wenxian Covenant Texts." *Asiatische Studien* 59.1 (2005): 61–114.

———. "Ten Thousand Names: Rank and Lineage Affiliation in the Wenxian Covenant Texts." *Asiatische Studien* 63.4 (2009): 959–89.

Wright, Arthur F. *The Sui Dynasty*. New York: Alfred A. Knopf, 1978.

Wu Fuzhu 吳福助. *Shuihudi Qin jian lunkao* 睡虎地秦簡論考. Taipei: Wenjin chubanshe, 1994.

Wu Hongqi 吳宏岐. "Qin Shihuang xunyou de shikong tezheng ji qi yuanyin fenxi" 秦始皇巡游的時空特徵及其原因分析. *Zhongguo lishi dili luncong* 18 (2003): 130–38.

Wu Hung 巫鴻. "Qin quan yanjiu" 秦權研究. *Gugong bowuyuan yuankan* 故宮博物院院刊 4 (1979): 33–47.

———. *Monumentality in Early Chinese Art and Architecture*. Stanford: Stanford University Press, 1995.

Wu Rengxiang 吳礽驤, Li Yongliang 李永良, and Ma Jianhua 馬建華. *Dunhuang Han jian shiwen* 敦煌漢簡釋文. Lanzhou: Gansu renmin chubanshe, 1991.

Wu Wangzong 吳旺宗. "Han jian suojian 'bianshu' tan xi" 漢簡所見"扁書"探析. *Lanzhou xuekan* 蘭州學刊 7 (2006): 27–8.

Wu Zeng 吳曾 (fl. 1127–1160). *Nenggaizhai manlu* 能改齋漫錄. *Skqs*.

Wuweixian bowuguan 武威縣博物館. "Wuwei xinchu Wangzhang zhaoling ce" 武威新出王杖詔令冊. In *Hanjian yanjiu wenji* 漢簡研究文集, ed. Gansusheng wenwu gongzuodui and Gansusheng bowuguan, 34–61. Lanzhou: Gansu renmin chubanshe, 1984.

Xia Chuancai 夏傳才. *Shisanjing gailun* 十三經概論. Tianjin: Tianjin renmin chubanshe, 1998.

Xiang Zonglu 向宗魯. *Shuo yuan jiao zheng* 說苑校證. Beijing: Zhonghua shuju, 1987.

Xie Guihua 謝桂華, Li Junming 李均明, and Zhu Guozhao 朱國炤. *Juyan Han jian shiwen hejiao* 居延漢簡釋文合校. Beijing: Wenwu chubanshe, 1987.

Xie Jian 謝劍. "Xiongnu zongjiao xinyang ji qi liubian" 匈奴宗教信仰及其流變. *Zhongyang yanjiuyuan lishi yuyan yanjiusuo jikan* 中央研究院歷史語言研究所集刊 42 (1971): 571–613.

Xin Deyong 辛德勇. "Qin Han Zhidao yanjiu yu zhidao yiji de lishi jiazhi" 秦漢直道研究與直道遺跡的歷史價值. *Zhongguo lishi dili luncong* 21.1 (2006): 95–107.

———. "Zhangjiashan Han jian suo shi Han chu xibeiyu bianjin jiexi: fulun Qin Zhaoxiangwang Changcheng beiduan zouxiang yu Jiuyuan Yunzhong liangjun zhanlüe diwei" 張家山漢簡所示漢初西北隅邊境解析——附論秦昭襄王長城北端走向與九原雲中兩郡戰略地位. *Lishi yanjiu* 歷史研究 1 (2006): 15–33.

Xin Tian 辛田. "Mingji, huji, bianhu qimin" 名籍, 戶籍, 編戶齊民. *Renkou yu jingji* 人口與經濟 3 (2007): 54–57, 77.

Xu Shihong 徐世虹. "Handai falü zaiti kaoshu" 漢代法律載體考述. In *Zhongguo fazhishi kaozheng* 中國法制史考證, ed. Yang Yifan 楊一凡. Part 1, volume 3: Lidai fazhi kao, Liang Han Wei Jin Nanbeichao fazhi kao 歷代法制考・兩漢魏晉南北朝法制考, ed. Gao Xuchen 高旭晨, 127–89. Beijing: Zhongguo shehui kexue chubanshe, 2003.

Xu Weiyu 許維遹. *Hanshi waizhuan jishi* 韓詩外傳集釋. Bejing: Zhonghua shuju, 1980.

Xu Xing 徐行. "Shaanxi Qin Han shiqi daolu jiaotong fazhan yu wenhua chuanbo" 陝西秦漢時期道路交通發展與文化傳撥. *Xi'an hangkong jishu gaodeng zhuanke xuexiao xuebao* 西安航空技術高等專科學校學報 22.2 (2004): 60–64.

Xu Yili 徐伊麗. "Qin zhidao huoxu bucunzai" 秦直道或許不存在. *Sichou zhi lu* 絲綢之路 4 (2006): 34–36.

Xu Yuangao 徐元誥. *Guo yu jijie* 國語集解. Beijing: Zhonghua shuju, 2002.

Xu Zongyan 許宗彥 (1768–1818). *Jianzhishuizhaiji* 鑑止水齋集. In *Huangqing jingjie* 皇清經解. Taipei: Yiwen yinshuguan, n.d. [ca. 1960].

Yan Gengwang 嚴耕望. *Zhongguo difang xingzheng zhidu shi* 中國地方行政制度史. Part 1: Qin Han difang xingzheng zhidu 秦漢地方行政制度. 4th edition. Taipei: Zhongyang yanjiuyuan Lishi yuyan yanjiusuo, 1997.

Yan Kejun 嚴可均 (1762–1843). *Quan Shanggu Sandai Qin Han Sanguo Liuchao wen* 全上古三代秦漢三國六朝文. Beijing: Zhonghua shuju, 1958.

Yan'an diqu wenwu puchadui 延安地區文物普查隊. "Yan'an jingnei Qin zhidao diaocha baogao zhi yi" 延安境內秦直道調查報告之一. *Kaogu yu wenwu* 考古與文物 1 (1989): 26–31.

Yan'an diqu wenwu puchadui. "Yan'an jingnei Qin zhidao diaocha baogao zhi er" 延安境內秦直道調查報告之二. *Kaogu yu wenwu* 5 (1991): 36–41.

Yang Bojun 楊伯峻. *Chunqiu Zuozhuan zhu* 春秋左傳注. Revised edition. Beijing: Zhonghua shuju, 1990.

Yang Jianhong 楊建虹 and Yin Ying 殷英. "Qin Shihuang liuci xunyou chuyi" 秦始皇六次巡游芻議. *Yunnan shifan daxue xuebao* 雲南師範大學學報 30 (1998): 99–101.

Yang Rongchang. "Shibedi yizhi chutu Qin Han jianzhu wajian bijiao yanjiu" 石碑地遺址出土秦漢建築瓦件比較研究. *Kaogu* 10 (1997): 87–93.

Yang Rongchang and Hua Yubing. "Liaoning Suizhongxian 'Jiangnüshi' Qin Han jianzhu qunzhi Wazidi yizhi yihao yaozhi" 遼寧綏中縣"姜女石"秦漢建築群址瓦子地遺址一號窯址. *Kaogu* 10 (1997): 58–60.

Yang Rongchang and Wang Xiongfei 萬雄飛. "Suizhong Shibeidi yizhi Qin Han wadang yanjiu" 綏中石碑地遺址秦漢瓦當研究. In *Liaoning kaogu wenji* 遼寧考古文集, ed. Liaoningsheng wenwu kaogu yanjiusuo, 242–49. Shenyang: Liaoning minzu chubanshe, 2003.

Yang Tianyu 楊天宇. *Liji yi zhu* 禮記譯注. Shanghai: Shanghai guji chubanshe, 2004.

Yang Yanqi 楊燕起. *Shiji quanyi* 史記全譯. Guiyang: Guizhou renmin chubanshe, 2001.

Yang Zhaoming 楊朝明. *Kongzi jiayu tongjie: Fu chutu ziliao yu xiangguan yanjiu* 孔子家語通解: 附出土資料與相關研究. Taipei: Wanguanlou, 2005.

Yao Shengmin 姚生民. "Qin Zhidao yu Ganquangong" 秦直道與甘泉宮. *Wenbo* 5 (1997): 34–37.

———. "Yunyanggong, Linguanggong, Ganquangong" 雲陽宮, 林光宮, 甘泉宮. *Wenbo* 4 (2002): 50–54.

———. *Ganquan gong zhi* 甘泉宮志. Xi'an: Sanqin chubanshe, 2003.

Yates, Robin D. S. "Cosmos, Central Authority, and Communities in the Early Chinese Empire." In *Empires: Perspectives from Archaeology and History*, ed. Susan Alcock et al., 351–68. Cambridge: Cambridge University Press, 2001.

———. "Law and the Military in Early China." In *Military Culture in Imperial China*, ed. Nicola Di Cosmo, 23–44. Cambridge: Harvard University Press, 2009.

———. "Purity and Pollution in Early China." In *Zhongguo kaoguxue yu lishixue zhi zhenghe yanjiu* 中國考古學與歷史學之整合研究, ed. Zang Zhenhua 臧振華, 479–536. Taipei: Zhongyang yanjiuyuan lishi yuyan yanjiusuo, 1997.

———. *Science and Civilisation in China*. Volume 5, part 6: Military Technology: Missiles and Sieges. Cambridge: Cambridge University Press, 1994.

———. "Social Status in the Ch'in: Evidence from the Yün-meng Legal Documents. Part One: Commoners." *Harvard Journal of Asiatic Studies* 47.1 (1987): 211–48.

———. "Soldiers, Scribes, and Women: Literacy among the Lower Orders in Early China." In *Writing and Literacy in Early China: Studies from the Columbia Early China Seminar*, ed. Feng Li and David Prager Branner, 339–69. Seattle: University of Washington Press, 2011.

Ye Shan 葉山 (Robin D. S. Yates). "Qin de falü yu shehui—guanyu Zhangjiashan 'Ernian lüling' deng xin chutu wenxian de sikao" 秦的法律與社會—關於張家山"二年律令"等新出土文獻的思考. Trans. Lin Fan 林凡. In *Rujia wenhua yanjiu* 儒家文化研究, no. 1, ed. Guo Qiyong 郭齊勇, 299–325. Beijing: Sanlian shudian, 2007.

———. "Zu, shi yu nüxing: Zhanguo Qin Han shiqi xiaceng shehui de duxie nengli" 卒, 史與女性: 戰果秦漢時期下層社會的讀寫能力. In *Jian bo*, no. 3, ed. Wuhan daxue jian bo yanjiu zhongxin, 359–83. Shanghai: Shanghai guji chubanshe, 2008.

Yoffee, Norman. *Myths of the Archaic State: Evolution of the Earliest Cities, States, and Civilizations*. Cambridge: Cambridge University Press, 2005.

Yu Weichao 俞偉超 and Gao Ming 高明. "Qin Shihuang tongyi duliangheng he wenzi de lishi gongji" 秦始皇統一度量衡和文字的歷史功績. *Wenwu* 12 (1973): 6–13.

Yu Zhenbo 于振波. *Zoumalou Wu jian chutan* 走馬樓吳簡初探. Taipei: Wenjin chubanshe, 2004.

Yu Zongfa 余宗發. *Xianqin zhuzi zai Qin di zhi fazhan* 先秦諸子學說在秦地之發展. Taipei: Wenjin chubanshe, 1998.

Yuan Zhongyi 袁仲一. *Qindai taowen* 秦代陶文. Xi'an: Sanqin chubanshe, 1987.

Zahavi, Amotz, and Avishag Zahavi. *The Handicap Principle: A Missing Piece of Darwin's Puzzle*. Translated by Naama Zahavi-Ely and Melvin Patrick Ely. Oxford: Oxford University Press, 1997.

Zang Zhifei 臧知非. "'Wangzhang zhaoshu' yu Handai yanglao zhidu" "王杖詔書"與漢代養老制度. *Shi lin* 史林 2 (2002): 35–41.

Zelditch, Morris. "Processes of Legitimation: Recent Developments and New Directions." *Social Psychology Quarterly* 64 (2001): 4–17.

Zeng Lei 曾磊. "Qin zhidao wei chongxiu shuo" 秦直道為重修說. *Hu'nan keji xueyuan xuebao* 湖南科技學院學報 7 (2008): 57–59.

Zhang Chunlong 張春龍 and Long Jingsha 龍京沙. "Liye Qin jian sanmei diming licheng mudu lüexi" 里耶秦簡三枚地名里程木牘略析. In *Jianbo* 簡帛, no. 1, ed. Wuhan daxue jianbo yanjiu zhongxin 武漢大學簡帛研究中心, 265–74. Shanghai: Shanghai guji chubanshe, 2006.

———. "Xiangxi Liye Qin jian 8–455 hao" 湘西里耶秦簡8–455號." In *Jianbo*, no. 4, ed. Wuhan daxue jianbo yanjiu zhongxin, 11–15. Shanghai: Shanghai guji, 2009.

Zhang Duoyong 張多勇. "Qin zhidao yanjiu zonglun" 秦直道研究綜論. *Gansu shehui kexue* 甘肅社會科學 5 (2005): 192–95.

Zhang Huasong 張華松. "Shitan Qin Shihuang dongxun de yuanyin yu dongji" 試探秦始皇東巡的原因與動機. *Dongyue luncong* 東岳論叢 23 (2002): 104–7.

Zhang Jinguang 張金光. *Qin zhi yanjiu* 秦制研究. Shanghai: Shanghai guji chubanshe, 2004.

Zhang Jiuhe 張久和. "Qinchao dui gudai Neimenggu bufen diqu de tongzhi he kaifa" 秦朝對古代內蒙古部分地區的統治和開發. *Neimenggu shehui kexue* 內蒙古社會 23.3 (2002): 33–37.

Zhang Junmin 張俊民, "Longshan Liye Qin jian erti" 龍山里耶秦簡二題. *Kaogu yu wenwu* 4 (2004): 43–47.

Zhang Rongming 張榮明. "Zhongguo shanggu guojia de chansheng ji tezheng" 中國上古國家的產生及特征. *Shixue yuekan* 史學月刊 2 (2001): 12–15.

Zhang Rongqiang 張榮強. "Hu'nan Liye suochu 'Qindai Qianlingxian Nanyangli huban' yanjiu" 湖南里耶所出 "秦代遷陵縣南陽里戶版"研究. *Beijing shifan daxue xuebao (shehui kexue ban)* 北京師範大學學報(社會科學版) 4 (2008): 68–80.

Zhang Wenzhi 張文質. "Qin zhaoban xundu yiyi" 秦詔版訓讀異議. *Hebei shifan daxue xuebao* 河北師範大學學報 3 (1982): 24–31.

Zhang Xiaofeng 張小鋒. *Xihan zhonghouqi zhengju yanbian tanwei* 西漢中後期政局演變探微. Tianjin: Tianjin guji chubanshe, 2007.

Zhang Xiugui 張修桂. "Dongtinghu yanbian de lishi guocheng" 洞庭湖演變的歷史過程. *Lishi dili* 歷史地理 1 (1981): 99–116.

Zhang Yachu 張亞初 and Liu Yu 劉雨. *Xizhou jinwen guanzhi yanjiu* 西周金文官制研究. Beijing: Zhonghua shuju, 1986.

Zhang Yan 張琰, Gao Yuan 高圓, and Li Xinya 李鑫雅. "Beifang mianju yanhua zhong yuanshi zongjiao hanyi de tixian" 北方面具岩畫中原始宗教含義的體現. *Neimenggu nongye daxue xuebao (shehui kexue ban)* 內蒙古農業大學學報(社會科學版) 4 (2007): 311–14.

Zhang Zhenze 張震澤, ed. *Sun Bin bingfa jiaoli* 孫臏兵法校理. Beijing: Zhonghua shuju, 1984.

Zhang Zhongli 張仲立. "Guanyu Qin shihuangdi quanli weishi de sikao" 關于秦始皇帝權力威勢的思考. In *Qin wenhua luncong*, no. 8, ed. Qin Shihuang bingmayong bowuguan "Luncong" bianweihui 秦始皇兵马俑博物馆《論叢》编委会. Xi'an: Shaanxi renmin chubanshe, 2001.

Zhao Ruiyun 趙瑞雲 and Zhao Xiaorong 趙曉榮. "Qin zhaoban yanjiu" 秦詔版研究. *Wenbo* 2 (2005): 78–83.

Zhao Ruiyun and Zhao Xiaorong. "Qin zhaoban yanjiu." *Wenbo* 3 (2005): 89–93.

Zheng Qiao 鄭樵 (1104–1162). *Er ya zhu* 爾雅註. *Skqs*.

Zhongguo kexueyuan "Zhongguo ziran dili" bianji weiyuanhui 中國科學院《中國自然地理》編輯委員會. *Zhongguo ziran dili: Lishi ziran dili* 中國自然地理: 歷史自然地理. Beijing: Kexue chubanshe, 1982.

Zhongguo shehui kexueyuan kaogu yanjiusuo Neimenggu gongzuodui 中國社會科學院考古研究所內蒙古工作隊. "Chifeng Zhizhushan yizhi de fajue" 赤峰蜘蛛山遺址的發掘. *Kaogu xuebao* 考古學報 2 (1979): 215–42.

Zhongguo shehui kexueyuan kaogu yanjiusuo 中國社會科學院考古研究所, ed. *Yin Zhou jinwen jicheng* 殷周金文集成. Revised and enlarged edition. Beijing: Zhonghua shuju, 2007.

Zhongguo wenwu yanjiusuo 中國文物研究所, and Hubeisheng wenwu kaogu yanjiusuo 湖北省文物考古研究所. *Longgang Qin jian* 龍崗秦簡. Beijing: Zhonghua shuju, 2001.

Zhou Zhenhe 周鎮鶴. "Qindai Dongting, Cangwu liangjun xuanxiang" 秦代洞庭、蒼梧兩郡懸想. *Fudan xuebao (shehui kexue ban)* 復旦學報 (社會科學版) 5 (2005): 63–67.

Zhouli zhushu 周禮注疏. See *Shisanjing zhushu*.

Zhouyi zhengyi 周易正義. See *Shisanjing zhushu*.

Zhu Honglin 朱紅林. "Zhanguo shiqi guojia falü de chuanbo—zhujian Qin-Han lü yu 'Zhouli' bjiao yanjiu" 戰國時期國家法律的傳播—竹簡秦漢律與"周禮"比較研究. *Fazhi yu shehui fazhan* 法治與社會發展 3 (2009): 119–25.

Zhu Jinshan 朱金嬋 and Yuan Yansheng 袁延勝. "Qin Han shiqi ren de shengao chutan" 秦漢時期人的身高初探. *Huabei shuilidian xueyuan xuebao (shekeban)* 華北水利電學院學報 (社科版) 23.3 (2007): 80–82.

Zhu Qianzhi 朱謙之. *Laozi jiaoshi* 老子校釋. Beijing: Zhonghua shuju, 1984.
Zhu Xi 朱熹 (1130–1200). *Chuci jizhu* 楚辭集注. *Skqs*.
Zhu Xiaoxin 朱筱新. "Dui Qin tongyi dulianghengzhi de zai renshi" 對秦統一度量衡制的再認識. *Beijing jiaoyu xueyuan xuebao* 北京教育學院學報 2 (2000): 6–10.

Index

Absolutism, 3, 4
Actions/activity: choosing alternatives for, 30; culture and, 20; dependence on expectation of what others will do, 21, 22; dynastic founders', 48, 49; group, 19, 20; political, 21; shared modes of, 19
Alvard, Michael, 19, 20
Anhui, 80
The Annals of Mr. Liu (*Lüshi chunqiu*), 35, 38, 39, 41, 45, 54, 55; "Delighting in Success," 54; "Employing the People," 45
"Annals of the First Emperor of Qin" ("Qin benji"), 79
Architecture, monumental, 154; as common knowledge, 28, 29, 95, 96; costs of, 28; as expression of control, 28, 95, 96; imperial projects, 82; as index of power, 28, 29; Jieshi Gate, 82; palace baths, 82; on progresses, 81, 82, 83, 95, 96, 149; as signal, 28
Austin, J.L., 28
Authority, 9; absolute, 151; central government, 123; checks on central, 5; coercion and, 45; of emperors, 3; indexes of, 88; as matter of persuasion, 21; metaknowledge of, 23; political, 22, 114; preceded by communication, 45; as "process of influence," 21; projecting, 44–46; publicity in form of declarations of, 6; reliance on, 45; social, 22; spiritual-ethical, 3
Axelrod, Robert, 21, 24

Ban Gu, 64, 71
Baotou, 115, 117
Beidi, 79
Bells, bronze, 70
Bielenstein, Hans, 4
"Black Robe" ("Zi yi"), 46, 47, 52, 54, 55
Bliege Bird, Rebecca, 26, 27
Book of Documents (*Shangshu*), 54, 55; "Jun Chen," 54; "Jun Ya," 54
The Book of Lord Shang (*Shangjun shu*), 44, 45, 49, 52, 53, 54, 55, 129; "Changing the Law," 49; household registration in, 128; propounds denunciation as part of legal practice, 141; on publicizing the law among common population, 141
Book of Odes (*Shijing*), 34, 35; "Numinous Tower," 34, 35, 36
Bourdieu, Pierre, 26
Brashier, K.E., 8, 120
Bright Hall (Mingtang), 114

Bronze: bells, 70; communicative purpose of, 70; "director of," 71; durability of, 71; mass communication and, 71–72; as medium for transmission of information, 71; plaques, 61, 62, 67, 68, 69, 70, 71, 72; references to groups on, 125; statues, 64; tablets, 68; texts on, 69–70; tripods, 96; underutilization of, 71; vessels, 71

Bünger, Karl, 4

Bureaucracy: document, 76; effect on emperors, 5; expansion of, 14; Han, 4; movement of information into, 6; power flowing downward in, 30; ritualized, 143; stratified, 3; universal registration of populace and, 14

Cai Yong, 119

Caring, universal, 39

Carvings, stone, 116, 117

Census. *See* Registration, household

Chang'an (Shaanxi), 60

Change: advisability of, 49; common knowledge and, 23, 48, 74–76; constancy and, 48–51; controlled, 50; dangers in, 49, 50; group-level, 23; in laws, 49, 50, 135, 136; opposition to, 48; by performative utterances, 28; risks of, 49; in ritual, 27; standardization of weights and measures and, 23; systemic, 48; vocabulary, 59

"Changing the Law" ("Bian fa"), 49

Cheng (Han emperor), 106

Chen Wei, 128

Chu, 79

Chwe, Michael Suk-Young, 12, 22, 23, 24, 42, 44, 45, 46, 89, 156, 157

Coercion, role in cooperation, 18

Commoners. *See* Population, common

Common knowledge: alteration of ways of doing and, 23; of authority instituting shared practice, 23; central position of for social function, 56; coordination problems and, 22–24; created through communication in multiple media, 1, 67; creation of, 12, 13, 22, 23, 42–48, 52, 72, 89–95; cultural practice and, 22, 23; differs from propaganda, 23; false, 25; of governing power, 13; importance of content in, 23; interpretation of garb and insignias and, 46; of the law, 141; made through use of existing precedents, 66–71; as means to broadcast power, 15; necessary part of ruling process, 1; political messages and, 152; by progresses, 77–99; of Qin dynasty, 13; role of change in creation of, 48; of the ruler, 42, 43, 44; shaping expectations of others' actions, 22; significant information in, 23; sovereign power and, 42–43; standardizations and, 57–63, 72–74; as state of shared knowledge in group, 22; through change and communication, 74–76

Communication: ability of ritual in, 27, 28; in absence of literacy, 145; bronze plaques and, 13; bureaucratic, 72, 123; clay vessels and, 13; clothing and ceremonial deportment as ways of, 46; common knowledge through, 1, 74–76; with common population, 53–55; components as medium and product of power, 30; comprehensible, 52; concerning the ruler/governance, 51–53; connected with standardizations, 57–63; construction as, 14, 101–121; coordination problems in, 22–24; costs, 26; at a distance, 71, 149; in early Chinese thought, 12, 33–56; as element of competition, 26; in establishment of social relations, 148; goals of, 23; imperial progresses as, 10, 87–89; importance of in governance, 12;

of intent, 21; interdisciplinary ideas on, 148; interpersonal, 20; law/administration and, 14, 15; mass, 13, 57–76, 71–72, 77; as means of resolving difficulties in cooperation, 12; media, 8, 149; necessity of for cooperation, 2; need for reliability in, 23; penal processes and, 138–140; perceptions of by population, 2; persuasion and, 28; by political authorities, 8; political potency of, 152; potential audiences for, 70–71; precedes authority, 45; of presence of single ruler, 12; by public ritual, 77; of punishments, 18; relationship to power, 30; reliability of, 24–26; religion and, 86–87; resolution of problems posed by cooperation and, 18–20; ritual, 46–48; of same message in different ways, 63; spreading means for cooperation by, 20; standardization and, 10, 13, 57–76; state centralization and, 5; symbolic, 26; system of avoidances in evoking and effacing emperor, 62–63; through changes in legal system, 134–138; through household registration, 123–134; untrue, 25; used to get support for ruler, 97; use of publicly posted documents for, 143–145; without words, 47
Competition: audience for, 26; communication as element of, 26; negative results of, 39
Conflict, cooperation and, 9
Confucius, 44, 46, 48, 65, 70, 101
Cook, Scott, 34
Cooperation: basis of human society, 2, 37; benefits of, 9, 11, 17, 18, 24, 31, 40; central position in human groups, 11, 17–18, 37; coercion and, 9; of common population in governance, 2; conflict and, 9; defining, 9; in early Chinese thought, 12, 33–36; by enemies, 11, 17; government's need for from populace, 7; group size and, 17, 18; human predilection for, 11, 17, 37; improvement in group function through, 19; interdisciplinary ideas on, 148; maintaining, 9; potency of willingness for, 36; power and, 9; predisposition to, 24, 37; problems of, 12, 18; requirements and limitations of, 17, 18; resolution of difficulties of, 12, 18; role in governance, 8–9, 34–36; role of coercion in, 18; sanctions and, 18; underestimation of importance of, 8
Coordination, greater achievement through, 20
Costs: communication, 26; endowment of signals with indexical characters guaranteeing reliability, 26, 27; turning ritual into indexes, 27
Covenants, 66, 67; state, 66
Creel, Herrlee, 6
Cronk, Lee, 19
Cultural: adaptation, 19, 37; conservatism, 20; interpretation of practices of, 22, 23; uniformity, 6
Culture: as body of information, 12; defining, 19; dependence on information sharing, 19; high, 75; as means of coordinating actions, 12, 18–20; popular, 45; received, 20; resolution of problems posed by group action and, 19; as socially transmitted information, 19; as "toolbox" for actions, 20; traditional, 127, 128; unified, 3

Decisions/decisionmaking: by common population, 30; dependence on perceptions of intent to cooperate, 24; exclusion of common population from, 53; made with finite information, 26; "why" of, 30, 31

240 Index

"Delighting in Success" ("Le cheng"), 54
Di Cosmo, Nicola, 116, 118
Director of bronze, 71
Discussions on Salt and Iron (Yantie lun), 36
"Document on Penal Law," 70
Documents: publicly posted, 143–145; read aloud, 144, 145
Du Mu, 109
Du Zhengsheng, 128, 133

Eight Spirits, 80
Elites. *See* Population, elite
Emperor(s). *See also* First Emperor of Qin: acting in the name of, 5; authority of, 3; at center of politics, 3; effect of bureaucracies on, 5; as foundation of all power, 3; as foundation of state, 4; political self of, 12; power of in allowing exceptions to rules and granting privileges, 107; presence hidden/advertised by walled roads, 14, 101–107; projecting political self of, 43–44; secrecy and, 42, 43; supreme political authority, 3; as ultimate power, 3
"Employing the People" ("Yong min"), 45
Epang Palace (Epanggong), 109
"Essay Criticizing the Qin," 153
"Essay on Ritual" ("Li lun"), 51

Fairbank, John, 5, 9
Fascism: as disease of power, 31; internal, 30, 31
Feng Quji, 59
First Emperor of Qin: actions providing pattern for imperial power, 1; assassination attempt on, 81, 94–95, 102; attempts mass communication, 71–72; attention to image management by, 74; brings back practice of progress, 78; builds legitimacy by linking self to previous rulers, 87, 88; builds on and adapts precedents, 66–71; campaigns to increase authority, 89–95; censure of, 1; creates common knowledge of himself, 57; death on Fifth Progress, 84, 85; desire to kill whale, 83, 84, 93–94; dissemination of commands of, 73; employment of mass communication by, 56; engaging in creation of common knowledge, 12; enlists support of populace before unification, 3; ensures that messages persisted beyond progresses, 13; explanations for presence on progresses, 84–86; imperial progresses of, 13, 77–99; imperial unification and, 40; indexing of new power of, 149; information conveyed in standardization edict by, 63–65; orders revisions to system of household registration, 129; peace during reign of, 153; punishment of mountain by, 14, 81, 92–93; roadway projects, 107–119; role of religion in communicative activities of, 86–87; standardization of weights and measures by, 40, 57–63; suppression of dissent by, 85; terminology for description of self, 59; unification of realm communicated by, 63, 64; use of progress for creating common knowledge, 86–99; vulnerability on progresses, 88
Five Emperors, 114
Focal points, 20–22; convergent expectations and, 21; coordination of activity around, 12, 20; function linked to culture, 21; as metaknowledge, 22; obvious nature of, 12, 20–22; past as source of, 21, 23; in planning Qin Direct Road, 110; potency of influence of, 21; resolution of coordination problems by, 56; ruler as, 12, 43–44; tradition as, 21

Foucault, Michel, 29–31

Gai Shanlin, 117
Ganquan, 113, 114, 115, 119–121. *See also* Qin Direct Road
Ganquan Mountains, 112, 113, 115
Gansu, 60, 114, 147
Gao Ming, 72
Gaonu (Shaanxi), 61
Gernet, Jacques, 5, 6
Giants, 64, 68, 178n39; statues of, 70
Giele, Enno, 4, 5, 6
Governance: authoritarian, 3; beginning with numerous changes, 48, 49; bureaucratic, 109, 111; communication of presence of single ruler, 42–48; contact with populace and, 123; cooperative, 148; as developed outgrowth of natural human tendencies, 6; display of laws relating to, 143; effective, 123; existence of choice as part of problems of, 30; fairness and uprightness in, 109; first task as achieving stability, 42; humane, 34; ideal, 39; interdisciplinary theory and, 8; limitations on, 5; lineage-centered, 37, 133; as matter of cooperation requiring communication/participation of common population, 2, 4, 33, 35, 36–38; as means by which the lord hides himself, 43; need for cooperation from populace for, 7, 36–38; non-active, 49; noncoercive, 8, 152; as projection of ruler's self, 44; proper methods metaphors of, 108, 109; required consultation in, 4; role of communication in function of, 12, 34–36, 36–38; seasonal, 66; social function of, 12; stability and, 47; standards of, 4; superficial, 5; systemic change in, 48; unified, 41; voluntary compliance and, 21
Grand Scribe, 66

"Great Learning" ("Da xue"), 35
"Great Tradition" ("Da zhuan"), 48, 50, 66
Great Walls, 118, 119
Group(s): coordination development, 41; damage to unity of the realm by, 39; differing levels of understanding in, 51–53; formation/existence, 38–41; formation through repetition of texts, 67; social nature of, 39
Guan Zhong, 34, 35, 65
Gu Jiegang, 148, 149
Guo Zizhi, 69

Han dynasty: archaeological finds from, 82; bureaucracy in, 4; common nature of raised ways during, 102; contact with populace, 123; criticism of Qin dynasty, 148; dealing with effects of Qin dynasty communication, 151; deterrence as goal of legal system during, 141; inheritance of Qin bureaucracy, 123, 124, 130; literacy in, 75; suspension of Qin legal system by, 153; system of weights and measures in, 59; systems of communication in, 75; unity as goal articulated by, 41; use of household registration for contact with populace, 127, 130–132
Han Feizi, 39, 40, 45, 49, 50, 52, 54, 97, 114
Han Lianqi, 133
Hebei, 60
Henan, 67
Historian's Records (*Shi ji*, Sima Qian), 11, 52, 60, 65, 68, 81, 83, 93, 96; account of First Emperor's progresses, 79, 81, 83; "Annals of the First Emperor of Qin," 79; corruptions and interpolations in, 10; description of unified system of highways and Qin Direct Road in,

Historian's Records (*Shi ji*, Sima Qian) *continued*
  105, 108, 109, 110, 113; on killing whales, 83, 84, 93–94; record of First Emperor's progresses, 80; search for assassin reported, 94–95; stele inscriptions in, 64–65; veracity of accounts of First Emperor's reign, 11; walled roads in, 102
History: as collective memory, 21; focal points and, 21, 22
History of the Han (*Han shu*), 118, 130, 139, 142
Houma, 67
Hou Xueshu, 73
Huang, Ray, 3
Huhai, 147
Hui, Victoria Tin-bor, 3, 6
Hui (Han emperor), 102–103
Huizhong, 79
Hunan, 132

Identity, political, 43
Ikeda On, 127, 133
Index(es): impracticbility of falsification of, 25; monumental architecture as, 25; of power, 25; ritual turned into, 27; transmission of information by means of, 25; use of signs of, 25
Information: about legal systems, 126; about populace, 126; achievement of goal of coordinated action, 12; acquisition of, 19–20; adaptation and change of, 19; collected through universal registration of populace, 14, 15; collection, 133; in common knowledge, 23; consolidation of, 130; control of access to, 140; conveyed by ritual, 27; culture as body of, 12; decisionmaking and, 26; dissemination of, 126, 144; distribution of, 9; gathered on populace, 124–127; movement of, 6; need for reliability in, 24, 25; placed in prominent places, 144; propagation concerning hierarchies of dress and insignia, 47; resolution of problems posed by cooperation and, 18–20; role in unification, 41–42; sent from center, 6; sharing, 19; socially transmitted, 12, 19, 20, 21; spread through publicly posted documents, 143–145; transfer between different systems, 28; transmission by means of indexes, 25; transmission of, 71; upward flow of, 133; use in decisionmaking, 24
Inner Mongolia, 60, 111, 145
Inscriptions: on bronze statues, 64; concerning standardization of weights and measures, 60–63; oracle bone, 124, 125; stele, 64–65, 90, 91; in texts, 60–63; on weapons, 65

Jiangsu, 60, 80, 132
Jia Shan, 105, 106
Jia Yi, 40, 46, 153
Jieshi, 81–83, 84
Jilin, 60
Jin dynasty, 67, 140
Jinshanju, 82
Jiuquan, 147
Jiuyuan, 115–116, 119–121. *See also* Qin Direct Road
"Jun Chen," 54
"Jun Ya," 54

Keane, Webb, 20, 24
Keightley, David, 78
Kern, Martin, 64, 85, 86, 89
"The King's System" ("Wang zhi"), 50, 80
Knowledge: common (*See* Common knowledge); generation of, 22; shared, 22
Kong Yingda, 46

Langshan Mountains, 115

Language: distrust of and ritual, 28; group-level changes and, 23; of "mandate of Heaven," 37
Langye, 80, 81, 83, 93, 95, 96
Laurance, Ray, 101
Law(s). *See also* Legal system: advertising existence of new rulers by, 154, 155; circumvention of, 140; common knowledge of, 141; comprehensible, 52; designed so that common population could understand, 51, 52; deterrence and, 139; dissemination of information about, 140, 143, 144; grasping subtleties of, 51; improving adherence to, 141; knowledge of by common population, 141; publicizing content of, 140, 141; public posting of, 144; of standardization, 58, 59; as subject of communication, 15; three sections of, 135, 136
Leadership: projection of, 44–46; reward and punishment used by, 45; stealth, 42, 43
Le Blanc, Charles, 4
Leeson, Peter T., 157
Legal system: changes to, 135, 136, 140, 150; common population and, 140–143; communication of law through, 52, 134–138; deterrence of malfeasance by officials, 141; formation of households and, 129; role in Han dynasty, 153
Lei Ge, 85
Lewis, Mark Edward, 1, 104, 139, 155
Liaodong, 84
Liaoning, 60, 81–83
Li Daoyuan, 117
Li Feng, 69
Lin Jianming, 94–95
Li Si, 57, 59, 71, 76
Literacy: in early dynasties, 75; limitations of, 144; military service and, 75, 76, 91, 145; steles and, 91; texts read aloud to bridge gap in, 144; underestimation of, 91
Littrup, Leif, 5
Liu An, 137, 138
Liu Bang, 102, 130, 132, 134, 135, 136, 149, 150, 153, 154
Liu Zehua, 3
Li Xueqin, 68
Liye, 128, 129
Li yun, 43
Li Zhongli, 111
Loewe, Michael, 3, 4
Longxi, 79
Lord of Earth, 80
Lord of the Four Seasons, 80, 93
Lord of the Sun, 80, 84
Lord of Yang, 80, 84, 93
Lord Xiang of Qin, 127
Lord Xiao, 53
The Lost Documents of Zhou (Yi Zhou shu), 66

Ma Chengyuan, 72
Ma Liqing, 118
Manager of contracts, 66
Manager of covenants, 66
Manager of the people, 126
Marchmounts, 80, 81
Maspero, Henri, 4
Master Guan (*Guanzi*), 34, 35, 39, 42, 45, 49, 50, 55, 126
Master Han Fei (*Han Feizi*), 39, 40, 45, 49, 50, 52, 54
Master Lao (*Laozi*), 44, 49, 50, 52
Master Mo (*Mozi*), 39
The Master of Huainan (*Huainanzi*), 47
Master of prohibitions, 144
Master Shen (*Shenzi*), 50
Master Xun (*Xunzi*), 38, 40, 41, 42, 43, 47, 48, 51, 53, 55, 65
Mauss, Marcel, 26
Ma Zhenzhi, 104
Meadows, Thomas Taylor, 4

Media: activities that serve other purposes and, 152; common knowledge in, 29; communications, 8, 149; creation of common knowledge through use of, 1; function of law as, 15; multiple, 29; varying prestige of, 13
Memory, collective, 21
Mencius, 34, 149
Meng Tian (General), 86, 109, 116
Ming dynasty, 155
Miyake Kiyoshi, 75
Mt. Cheng, 80, 84, 93
Mt. Heng, 80, 81
Mt. Hua, 90
Mt. Jitou, 79
Mt. Jiuyi, 83
Mt. Kuaiji, 83, 84
Mt. Liangfu, 80
Mt. Tai, 80, 91
Mt. Xiang, 81, 83, 92–93, 95
Mt. Zhifu, 80, 81, 93
Mt. Zouyi, 79
Mozi, 39, 104
Mt. Cheng, 80
Mt. Zhifu, 80, 84

"Numinous Tower" ("Ling tai," *Shijing*), 34, 35, 36

Obedience: creation of, 22; willing, 36, 47, 48
Organization: by lineage relationship, 67, 133; political form of, 67

Painted Rock Mountains, 117
Peirce, Charles, 25
Penal system: changes to, 39, 137; communication elements in, 149; decisionmaking for, 54; harshness of, 138; processes and communication, 138–140; publicizing, 140
Pengcheng, 80

Perceptions: importance of in determining obedience to government, 24
Petroglyphs, 117
Pines, Yuri, 10, 36, 37, 38, 41, 74, 75, 149
Plaques, bronze, 13, 61; durability of, 67; impressions from, 61, 62; inscribed with laws, 67; limited audience for, 70–71; mass production techniques, 69, 70; mechanical reproduction of, 62; oversized, 62; portable versions, 61; proclamation, 62, 68, 73, 74; signboard-style, 62; small rectangles, 61; square, rounded edge, 61
Political: authority, 3, 22, 114; discourse, 148; identity, 43; morality, 150; opinion, 37; power, 1, 22, 24, 26, 37, 42, 115, 152; signals, 28, 29; theories, 35; unification, 41
Population. *See* Registration, household
Population, common: awareness of higher-level governance by, 2; benefits commensurate to station, 41; complaints against government officials by, 141, 142; consulting with, 53–55; decisionmaking by, 30; degree of power for, 30; effects of alterations in laws on, 135; having ownership but no power, 4; importance of opinion of, 54; information given to on ruler/governance, 51–53; legal processes and, 140–143; limitations of records reflecting views of, 2; made aware of power of new ruler, 57; manipulation of through reward and punishment, 45; observation of imperial progresses by, 97, 98; passivity of in question, 2, 4, 7; permitted to express disatisfaction with ruler, 142, 143; in policy planning, 54; power of, 3, 7–8; recognition of power of, 56; role

in governance, 2, 4, 34–36; use of roads by, 105, 106

Population, elite: benefits commensurate to station, 40, 41; information given to on ruler/governance, 51–53; power of, 7; role in development of notion of ruler as unique, 36–37; status markers and, 46

Power: absolute, 3, 4; central, 5; as cluster of relations between individuals/groups, 29; common knowledge and, 42–43; of common population, 7–8; connection to secrecy, 104; cooperation and, 9; decision to submit to, 31; differentiated from force, 30; of establishing peace, 40; forms of, 29; Foucault's analysis of, 29–31; function in political systems, 29–31; function of, 4, 7; ideologies of, 5; imperial, 3, 4; institutional restrictions on, 4; legacy approaches to, 2–6; limitations on, 5; lying not in enforcement of rules but in allowing exceptions, 107; making claims to known, 44, 45; outward-downward flow of, 3; perception of, 46–48; political, 1, 15, 22, 24, 26, 37, 42, 115, 145, 152; publicity and, 44, 45; relationship to communication, 30; religious, 115; role of freedom in relationships of, 29; in social relationships, 29; sovereign, 42–43; symbols of, 145; top-down, 29

Progresses, imperial: acts to increase imperial authority, 89–95; ascension if mountains on, 79, 80; attempts to recover bronze tripods on, 96; change in character of, 78; changes in landscape in, 13; common knowledge generation and, 77–99; to communicate existence of new ruler, 87; communicative program to summarize emergence of Qin supremacy, 87–89; death of First Emperor on, 84, 85; as demonstration of sovereignty, 89; explanations for, 84–86; Fifth, 83–84; First, 79; of First Emperor of Qin, 77–84; Fourth, 81–83; imperial demands for destruction of fortifications on, 83, 95, 96; imperial vulnerability on, 88; indexes of authority on, 88; intervals, 78; as medium of communication, 10; memorials erected on, 80; for military inspections/expeditions, 78; monumental architecture and, 81, 82, 83, 149; movement through territory of former rivals, 88; as political ceremonies, 85; presence of remains at sites on, 82; prior to Qin dynasty, 77–79; as public communication, 96–98; as public notice of existence of emperor, 13; punishment of mountain in, 14, 81, 92–93; repeated performance of, 88, 89; ritual character of, 13, 78, 79, 83, 85; sacrifices on, 79, 80; Second, 79–81; of Second Emperor, 84; shifting power centers and, 78; showing that former lords were replaced, 89; as show of strength, 85; significance of sites visited on, 88; steles erected on, 79, 80, 90–92; suppression of dissent and, 85; Third, 81; through visits between equals, 78

Propaganda: defining, 24; differs from common knowledge, 23

Publicity: in form of declarations of authority, 6

Puett, Michael, 48, 50

Punishment: communication of, 18; as deterrence, 18; of mountain, 14, 81, 92–93

Qi, 79, 80, 81

Qin Direct Road (Zhidao), 14, 107–113; campaign against Xiongnu and, 109, 110, 111, 112; commemoration of Qin rule by, 111, 113; communication aspects of, 14, 110–113; communication of Upright Way of Qin, 109; construction of, 109–110; creation of common knowledge through, 105, 106, 107, 108, 120; endpoints of, 113–119; First Emperor's body returned to capital on, 110; meaning of name, 108–109; message of Qin supremacy in, 114, 120, 121; name references to fair taxation and legal system, 109; poetic reference as metaphor for proper governance, 108, 109; previous explanations for route of, 110–113; purpose of, 109; ritual and religious significance of termini, 14, 108, 110–121; route of, 108, 113–119; strengthening of ideology of unification by, 111; on top of Ziwuling Mountains, 110, 111, 112, 113, 114, 120; transmission and reception of imperial message and, 14

Qin dynasty: adaptation of previously used techniques for communication, 1, 37, 38, 71; attitude toward law, 74; brief reign of, 1; bureaucracy in, 123–134; change in common practice creating common knowledge in, 48; changes in legal system, 141; contact with populace, 123; cumulative cultural adaptation in, 37; deliberate nature of communication by, 10; deterrence as goal of legal system during, 141; development of common knowledge of, 13; development of unified state by, 37; effective penetration of Qin society, 124; establishment of central control in, 88; establishment of unified culture in, 3; literacy in, 75; monumental architecture in, 109; monumental public works during, 105, 106; obsession with "bigness," 1; persistent memory of, 148; pictured as cruel and abusive, 148, 151; possible root of word "China," 148; role of religion in communicative activities in, 86–87; seek to create myths of imperiality, 6; seen by some as self-aggrandizing, 11; standardization of weights and measures in, 57–63; state formation under, 3; success of communication activities in, 148; totalitarian nature of, 3; unified system of highways during, 14, 107–113; use of communication by, 7; use of household registration for contact with populace, 123, 127–130, 132–134; value on virtues of fairness and uprightness, 109

Qing dynasty, 5

Qin Shihuang. *See* First Emperor of Qin

Rappaport, Roy, 27, 28, 46, 87, 88, 90

Record of Ritual (*Liji*), 35, 43, 48, 50, 66; "Great Learning," 35; "Great Tradition," 48, 50, 66; "King's System," 50, 80; "Ritual's Changes," 43, 47

Registration, household, 124–127; benefits to populace from, 125; as communication to help create cooperation and integration at national level, 132–134; communicative intent of, 123–134; contact with government through, 123; determination of adulthood in, 129; division into groups of five, 127; early, 124–130; emergence of, 127–128; function of, 132–134; in Han dynasty, 128, 130–132; inclusion of age in, 129; inclusion of criminals in, 132; interrupted and restarted, 130, 132; labor service and, 128, 133; long-term developments in, 129; maintenance of security and, 133; by manager of the people, 126; as matter of common knowledge, 124, 131; as means to control populace, 133; for military purposes, 125, 127, 128; multigenerational, 129; mutual responsibility groups in, 127; for obedience and coordination, 131; origins of, 125, 126; as part of shift away from lineage-based social organization, 133; precursors of, 124–127; in Qin dynasty, 123, 127–130, 132–134; reporting crimes and, 127, 128; responsibility with males for, 129; surveillance purposes, 123; system changes, 129; taxation and, 133; used to communicate emperor's newly won position, 131

Religion: communicative activities and, 86–87; Qin Direct Road and, 14, 110–121; rituals of, 86, 87, 96, 97, 108, 110–119

Reward/punishment, 44–46, 52; capital, 139, 140; communicative value of, 138–140; as deterrent, 139; household registration and, 132; mutilating, 136; penal labor, 136; perceived fairness of, 137; for reporting crimes, 127, 128

Ritual(s). *See also* Progresses, imperial: ability as communication, 27, 28; adherence to, 140; bathing and, 82; behavior, 27; canonical form, 27, 88; communication, 46–48, 77; conveying information, 27; defining, 27; description of the past and, 47; distrust of language and, 28; extension of political self through, 47; generation of knowledge through, 22; as means to create common knowledge, 22; messages of, 27, 28; mutability and stability of, 27, 28; offerings as subset of, 51; persuasion of others through, 28; prognostication, 124; religious, 28, 86, 87, 96, 97, 108, 110–119; repeatability of, 27; significant costs of, 27; as visual medium, 47

"Ritual's Changes" ("Li yun"), 43, 47

Roads. *See also* Qin Direct Road: announcing importance of road by, 104; center lane use for emperor only, 106, 107; communication aspects of, 14, 106, 107; conspicuous nature of, 101; creation of common knowledge by, 102, 105, 106, 107, 120; economic effects of expansion of, 107; elevated, 101–107, 104; examples of emperor's power to make exceptions, 107; existence of prior to Qin Direct Road, 111, 112; expansion of political power and, 101; inconvenience to common population, 102, 104, 105; increased mobility and, 102; as indexical sign of imperial presence, 107; "king's staff" and, 106; military uses of, 102, 103, 110, 111, 112, 113; observed by common population, 104; politico-religious significance of end points, 14; presence of emperors hidden/advertised by, 101–107; projects by First Emperor of Qin, 101–119; punishment for illegal use of, 106; Qin imperial system, 105–113; raised, 101–107; regular exchange of governmental documents over, 111; transmission and reception of imperial messages and, 14; turning emperor's path into permanent signs, 150; walled, 14, 101–107; Xiao Pass Road, 112

Robbins, Joel, 28

Ru, 48, 65

Rubin, Vitaly, 3
Ruler. *See* Emperors

Sacrifices: to Eight Spirits, 80; to Lord of Earth, 80; to Lord of the Four Seasons, 80, 93; to Lord of the Sun, 80, 84; to Lord of Yang, 80, 84, 93; to mountains, 78, 80, 81, 83; during progresses, 79, 80; religious, 118; to rivers, 78, 80
Schaberg, David, 66, 143
Schelling, Thomas, 12, 20, 22, 23
Schwartz, Benjamin, 3
Seals, uses of, 62
Second Emperor of Qin, 52, 57, 71; addition to First Emperor's edict, 65; adds inscriptions to steles, 63, 64; attention to image management by, 74; dissemination of commands of, 73; imperial progress of, 84; political messages of, 74, 75; reputation as ruler, 147, 151; restarts construction of Qin Direct Road, 109, 110; says First Emperor responsible for unification, 74; supplementation of First Emperor's messages, 59
Secrecy, 42, 43, 44, 47
Sewell, William Jr., 158
Shaanxi, 60, 61, 68
Shandong, 60
Shangdang, 81
Shang dynasty, 35; progresses during, 78
Shangjun, 111
Shangshu, 54
Shang Yang, 53, 58, 60, 76, 97, 127, 128, 141
Shanxi, 60, 67, 81
Shenzi, 50
Shijing, 34, 35, 36
Shi Nianhai, 110, 111, 116
Shin'ichiro, Watanabe, 115
Shi Shuqing, 72
Shue, Vivienne, 2, 5
Shuihudi, 128, 129

Shun (sage ruler), 80, 83
Shusun Tong, 104, 105
Signs/signals: communication of unobservable things by, 26; instability of, 24; linguistic, 24; materiality of, 24; monumental architecture as, 27–29; political, 28; ritual, 27–29; sent simultaneously in multiple media, 29
Sima Qian, 10, 65, 84, 93, 102, 110. See also *Historian's Records* (*Shi ji*); describes First Emperor's rituals, 11
Smith, Eric Alden, 26, 27
Social: authority, 22; behavior, 31; breakdown, 39; classes, 51; function, 12; groups, 36, 51–53; identity, 5; intertexture, 2; life, 11; norms, 25; order, 28, 52, 140; organization, 6; relations, 29, 148; stability, 36, 47; theory, 26
Society: benefits of having rulers, 38; communication with all levels of, 8; creation of, 152; emperor as spiritual-ethical authority of, 3; existence of power at higher echelons of, 4; formation of, 17; functional, 152; function by means of cooperation, 34–36; government's need for cooperation from, 7; group formation/existence, 38–41; role of cooperation in, 8–9, 11; state of war with imperial dynasty, 3; subbureaucratic levels of, 5; understanding of workings of, 34–36
Song dynasty, 140
Standardization edict, 59; dissemination of, 60; formed by seal impressions, 62; information conveyed in, 63–65; inscribed on steles, 63–65; political motivation for, 73; relics bearing, 58, 60–63; seal impressions, 62
Standardization of weights and measures, 50, 57–63; artifacts with inscriptions concerning, 60–63;

bronze plaques and, 61; communication and, 10; consequences of, 10; enforcement of, 58; facilitation of taxation and, 72; by First Emperor of Qin, 40, 57–63; integration of new state and, 72; mass communication and, 13; as medium for political communication, 149; no "absolute" necessity for, 72, 73; origination of, 65, 66; pottery vessels and, 62, 69; previous explanations for, 72–74; promotion of trade and, 72; role in creation of common knowledge, 72–76; scoop measure and, 58, 60; single scale in, 58, 61; as task of "unifier of places," 66; trade/taxation and, 10; usefulness of, 23
State: centralization of, 5; classical, 5; emperor as foundation of, 4; formation, 3; local diversity in, 5; modern, 5; premodern, 5; "Un-Oppressive," 5
Statues, bronze: of "giants," 64.68, 70; inscriptions on, 64
Status: markers, 46; visual differentiation of, 46
Steles, 90–92, 154; erected on progresses, 80, 90–92; expansion of common knowledge and, 92; at First Emperor's progresses, 79; inscriptions on, 63–65, 90, 91; left in prominent locations, 91; literacy and, 91; locations of with religious significance, 91; rituals connected with, 85
Submanager of prisons, 143
Sui dynasty, 154
Sun Bin, 35
Surveillance, 123
Swidler, Ann, 20

Tablets: bronze, 68; buried, 71; clay, 68, 69, 71; inscribed, 68–69; mass production techniques, 69, 70

Taizu (Ming emperor), 141
Tang dynasty, 154, 155
Terra cotta army, 68, 70, 154
Texts: on bronze, 69–70; canonical, 65, 66; common knowledge of contents of, 66; covenant, 67, 70; early, 124, 125; with inscriptions concerning standardization, 60–63; mechanical reproduction of, 70; mention of earlier forms of related practice in, 65; officials connected with, 66, 67; premodern, 60; preservation of multiple copies of, 66, 67, 68, 69, 70; prognostication ritual, 124; read aloud in order to disseminate contents, 144; related to standardization edict, 64; reproduced, 67–70; ritual burial of, 67; role of repetition of in group formation, 67; timing of, 67; transmitted, 148
Theories: evolutionary, 26; interdisciplinary, 8, 31, 148; non-coercive political, 34; political, 35, 143; signaling, 26–29; social, 26; stealth leadership, 42, 43
"Three Virtues" ("San de"), 36
Through Discussions at White Tiger Pavilion (Bohu tong), 97
Tomasello, Michael, 19
Tombs: construction instructions, 68; plaques interred in, 68
Tomiya Itaru, 145
Trade: standardization of weights and measures and, 10, 72
Tradition, as focal point, 21
Transportation. *See also* Qin Direct Road; Roads: centralization of state and, 5; changes in modes of, 14; lack of, 5; raised ways/walled roads, 14, 101–107
Trigger, Bruce, 28
Tu Mingfeng, 133
Turner, Karen, 29, 136

Unifier of places, 66

Unity/unification: cultural, 3; damage to by groups, 39; different means of for different groups, 41; early existence of ideas of, 75, 148; ease of, 53, 54; failure of, 42; generating perception of among common population, 41; as goal and means, 41; goal of coordination and cooperation, 41–42; leaders as means of achieving, 41; political, 41; role of information in, 41–42; success of First Emperor of Qin, 59

Veblen, Thorstein, 26
Virtue, 47

Wan Changhua, 3, 133
Wang Chong, 91, 96
Wang Mang, 136, 139, 140, 145
Wang Wan, 59
Wang Yü-ch'üan, 3
Wang Zijin, 102, 104, 111, 113
Warring States period: archaeological finds from, 82; belief in common population as ultimate power in, 37; bronze tablets of, 68; differing systems of weights and measures, 58; non-coercive political theory and, 34; political involvement of common population in, 37; political organization in, 10, 126
Weapons: bronze, 65; inscriptions on, 65
Weber, Max, 5
Wei, 79, 81
Wei Zhuang, 59
Weld, Susan, 67
Wen (King of Zhou), 34, 35, 40, 68, 136, 150
Wenxian, 67
Western Zhou period, 37
Williams, Crispin, 67, 70
Wu (King of Zhou), 68, 69, 137, 142, 147

Wu Hung, 73, 90
Wu Pi, 137, 138
Wuwei, 143

Xianyang, 14, 81, 83, 106, 113, 134. *See also* Qin Direct Road
Xiao He, 130
Xiongnu, 109, 110, 111, 112, 114, 115, 116, 117, 118, 119, 148
Xi Qingsong, 72
Xuan (King of Zhou), 125
Xunzi (Xun Kuang), 38, 40, 41, 42, 43, 47, 48, 55, 65, 97, 149

Yan, 81
Yang Bojun, 69
Yao (sage ruler), 97
Yates, Robin D. S., 6, 75
Yellow Emperor, 79, 114
Ying Shao, 102
Yinshan mountain area, 115, 116–119, 119; as division between peoples, 118, 119; religious and ceremonial activity in, 116, 117, 118; stone carvings in, 116, 117
Yinwan, 132
Yiqu, 114, 115
Yoffee, Norman, 5, 9
Yuan dynasty, 141
Yungang, 114, 115
Yunmeng, 83
Yunyang, 113
Yu (sage ruler), 83
Yu Weichao, 72

Zahavi, Amotz, 25, 26
Zhangjiashan, 129, 131
Zhang Liang, 81, 94
Zhang Shizhi, 136, 137
Zhang Zhongli, 90
Zhao, 81
Zhao Ruiyun, 61
Zhao Xiaorong, 61
Zhao Xingbin, 3, 133

Zhidao. *See* Qin Direct Road
Zhongshan, 68
Zhou dynasty: descriptions of officials in, 126; lack of centralized administration in, 6; progresses during, 78
Zhou Rituals (*Zhouli*), 66, 70, 71, 124, 126, 127, 129, 141, 143, 144

Zhu Bo, 141, 142
Zhu Xiaoxin, 72, 73
Ziwuling Mountains, 110, 111, 112, 113, 114, 119
Zoumalou, 132
Zuo's Commentary (*Zuozhuan*), 47, 97, 125; "Document on Penal Law," 70

www.ingramcontent.com/pod-product-compliance
Ingram Content Group UK Ltd.
Pitfield, Milton Keynes, MK11 3LW, UK
UKHW041917140426
5217IPUK00013B/191